THE MAKING OF EARLY KASHMIR

This is the first full-length history of early Kashmir locating it beyond its regional context, from pre-history to the thirteenth century. Drawing on a variety of sources—including conventional archaeological and literary sources, as well as non-conventional sources like philology, toponym and surnames—it presents a connected history of early Kashmir over the *longue durée*. It challenges tendencies towards nationalist historiographies of the region by situating it in the context of the shared histories of humanity. The volume will be of great interest to scholars and researchers of history, archaeology, anthropology and South Asian studies.

Muhammad Ashraf Wani is former Professor and Head, Department of History, Dean, Social Sciences and Dean, Academic Affairs at the University of Kashmir. He has also served as Sectional President of the Indian History Congress and as a member of the Indian Council of Historical Research. He is the author of *Islam in Kashmir* and the co-author of *Prehistory of Kashmir*. For many years now, he has developed interest in early history of Kashmir and the present work is the outcome of this academic preoccupation of the author.

Aman Ashraf Wani is Senior lecturer in the School Education Department, Government of Jammu and Kashmir. He has done PhD in ancient history of Kashmir and is the co-author of *Prehistory of Kashmir*.

THE MAKING OF EARLY KASHMIR

Intercultural Networks and Identity Formation

Muhammad Ashraf Wani and Aman Ashraf Wani

Routledge
Taylor & Francis Group
LONDON AND NEW YORK

First published 2023
by Routledge
4 Park Square, Milton Park, Abingdon, Oxon OX14 4RN

and by Routledge
605 Third Avenue, New York, NY 10158

Routledge is an imprint of the Taylor & Francis Group, an informa business

British Library Cataloguing-in-Publication Data
A catalogue record for this book is available from the British Library

Library of Congress Cataloging-in-Publication Data
Names: Wani, Muhammad Ashraf, author. | Wani, Aman Ashraf, author.
Title: The making of early Kashmir : intercultural networks and the identity formation / Muhammad Ashraf Wani and Aman Ashraf Wani.
Description: Abingdon, Oxon ; New York, NY : Taylor & Francis Group, [2023] | Includes bibliographical references and index.
Summary: "This is the first full-length history of early Kashmir locating it beyond its regional context, from pre-history to the 13th century. Drawing on a variety of sources – including conventional archaeological and literary sources, as well as non-conventional sources like philology, toponym, surnames – it presents a connected history of early Kashmir over the longue duree. It also challenges tendencies towards nationalist historiographies of the region by situating it in the context of the shared histories of humanity. The volume will be of great interest to scholars and researchers of history, archaeology, and South Asian studies"— Provided by publisher.
Identifiers: LCCN 2022041100 | ISBN 9781032158303 (hardback) | ISBN 9781032435220 (paperback) | ISBN 9781003367697 (ebook)
Subjects: LCSH: Kashmir, Vale of (India)—Civilization.
Classification: LCC DS485.K25 W36 2023 | DDC 954.6—dc23/eng/20221007
LC record available at https://lccn.loc.gov/2022041100

ISBN: 978-1-032-15830-3 (hbk)
ISBN: 978-1-032-43522-0 (pbk)
ISBN: 978-1-003-36769-7 (ebk)

DOI: 10.4324/9781003367697

Typeset in Sabon
by Apex CoVantage, LLC

We dedicate this book to late Jana Akbar (the mother of the first author and the grandmother of the second author) who bore all conceivable hardships to shape the present and future of the family.

CONTENTS

List of figures *viii*
Preface *x*

1 Introduction 1

2 A Mosaic of Plural Sources: Immigrations, Interactions and the Cultural Foundations of Kashmir 27

3 A World Within a World: Encounters With Cosmopolitan Ecumenes and Transculturation (From Greeks to Huns) 89

4 Empire at the Frontier: The Kashmir Empire and Cross-Cultural Networks (Karkotas to Loharas) 185

5 Shared History: Kashmir and the Immediate Borderlands 269

6 Conclusion 281

Bibliography *289*
Index *311*

FIGURES

1.1	Tile with composite mythical animals.	23
1.2	Intertwined Lions, Stone.	23
2.1	Rectangular and round shaped punch-marked coins.	79
2.2	Rectangular copper punch-marked coins.	79
3.1	Terracotta fragmentary draped Hellenistic female figurine (left). Terracotta figurine in Hellenistic style (middle). Terracotta semi-draped Hellenistic female figurine (right), Semthan.	161
3.2	Silver coin of Diodotus.	161
3.3	Silver coin of Euthydemus.	161
3.4	Copper coin of Eucratides.	161
3.5	Silver square coin of Appollodotus.	161
3.6	Copper coin of Appollodotus.	162
3.7	Silver coin of Menander.	162
3.8	Silver coin of Menander.	162
3.9	Square copper coin of Menander.	162
3.10	Silver coin of Hippostratos.	162
3.11	Cocks fighting over what appears to be a lily bud.	163
3.12	In central circle, a cock, with foliate tail; surrounded by circle of roundels; the whole within rectangular frame of pearls.	163
3.13	Greek art Cock and band-cup.	163
3.14	Greek Attic vase-painting with cock-fighting.	163
3.15	Durga or Maheshvari. Bejbehara.	163
3.16	Motif of a dancing girl with scarf in her two hands.	163
3.17	Woman wearing big ear rings and locket, Harwan (left); (b) Terracotta pendant from necklace of colossal figure of a Bodhisattva. Harwan (right).	164
3.18	Silver coin of Azes.	164
3.19	Copper coin of Abdagases.	164
3.20	Copper coins of Zeinoses.	164
3.21	Copper coins of Zeinoses.	164

3.22 Fully accoutred horseman in armour riding at full gallop and drawing his bow. 165
3.23 Wall of Apsidal Temple in Diaper-Pebble Style. 165
3.24 Triple base of Stupa in Diaper-Rubble Style, Harwan. 165
3.25 Upper part of an archer wearing a conical cap, Harwan. 166
3.26 A dancer wearing large ear rings and dressed in loose robe and trousers, with a long scarf held in both hands, which she waves over her head, Harwan. 166
3.27 A huntsman with bow and arrow riding at full gallop, wearing a *pattikam*. Harwan. 166
3.28 Terracotta heads, Ushkar. 166
3.29 Left: Female figure wearing *kancuka*; Right: Standing soldier. 167
3.30 Copper coin (local series) of Kujula Kadphises. 167
3.31 Copper coin of Vima Kadphises. 167
3.32 Copper coin (local series) of Vima Kadphises. 167
3.33 Gold dinar of Kaniṣka. 168
3.34 Gold dinar of Kaniṣka. 168
3.35 Copper coin of Kaniṣka. 168
3.36 Copper coin of Kaniṣka (local series). 168
3.37 Copper coin (local series) of Kaniṣka. 168
3.38 Copper coin (local series) of Kaniṣka. 168
3.39 Copper coin (local series) of Huvishka. 169
3.40 Copper coin (local series) of Vasudeva. 169
3.41 Terracotta plaques showing miniature stupas. 169
3.42 Tile with man and deer, Hoinar. 169
3.43 Tile with man carrying pots and a women carrying a bowl, Harwan. 170
3.44 Female musician Harwan. 170
3.45 Tile with conversing couple sitting in the balcony. Harwan. 170
3.46 Two pairs of men and women facing each other in a balcony. 171
3.47 Women with net-like hair style, wearing big ear rings and locket like ornament. 171
3.48 Upper register: three musicians. The one to left plays flute; the centre one, cymbals; and the third, a pair of drums. 171
3.49 Humans with animal face and tail, and in dancing posture, Hutmur. 172
3.50 Base gold coin of Kidara Kuṣāṇas. 172
3.51 Toramana copper coins. 172

PREFACE

This book tries to enter again into the realm opened up by us some two decades ago to join the scholarship that celebrates shared history of humankind by citing profuse evidence with bold strokes. Although a small place, the cultural history of Kashmir manifests an astonishing capacity of integrating a wide spectrum of cultures and an aptitude for articulating its own vision of the world. At a time when the forces having stakes in divisive politics are out to project the strains of the present on the past, the subjects like connected histories have a strong innate force to disarticulate the proponents of counter view without 'dethroning the past.' It is with this avowed belief and agenda that we chose this topic which looks at the history of early Kashmir beyond region/nation-centric bunkers.

If this book adds to the existing body of knowledge on the subject, even modestly, we would feel to have been rewarded at our puny efforts. Our purpose will be served if it makes the present and the future generations to think to attain a new unity by extending our horizons and approaches to the study of cultures beyond borders. And should it elicit sympathy with the people who suffered following the subversion of geographical centrality and regional exchange for which Kashmir was known since times immemorial, we would find this small contribution much more fulfilling.

It goes without saying that knowledge creation is an exercise which is partly borrowed and partly new; even the new owes its emergence to the existing. Therefore, all those authors who either supplied us with primary information or provided us insights to organise and interpret the material deserve our special thanks and deep sense of gratitude.

In 2017, we published our textbook, *Prehistory of Kashmir*. Prof. Irfan Habib, Professor Emeritus AMU, Aligarh, Prof. K Paddayya Professor Emeritus, Deccan College, Pune, and Prof. Alison Betts, of the University of Sydney expressed generous words on the book which encouraged us to expedite the process of completing this work. We once again thank them all for their encouragement. Dr. GR Mir went through the first draft of this project and made valuable suggestions. We are grateful to him beyond words.

The publication of this book would have been considerably delayed without the untiring efforts of Dr. Feroz Ahmad Wani who burnt midnight oil in typing and retyping; arranging the figures, footnotes and bibliography; and setting of the book with all his masterful skill he has learnt over a long period. We have no words to express our indebtedness to him for the exemplary patience and perseverance he showed in doing this exacting work.

We are grateful to a number of our well-wishers for their guidance and support. Special mention may be made of Prof. AQ Rafiqi whom we and our progeny would always remain indebted for the encouragement and recognition at a critical moment of our careers.

We are indebted to Mr. Rizwan-ur Rehman and Aadil Jan for spending their valuable time with us in giving final touches to this book. Rabia Qureshi, the curator of SPS Museum, was so courteous in her treatment that she did not even allow us to thank her for her exemplary helping attitude. Stay blessed, the worthy officer. Her other colleagues were also equally helpful. Words fail to thank them all.

We were benefitted by the discussions we had with Prof. Gulshan Majeed, Prof. MA Kaw, Prof. Aijaz Bandey, Prof. Naseem Ahmad, Prof. Shad Ramzan, Prof. GN Khaki, Dr. Mumtaz Yatoo, Dr. Javid ul Aziz, Dr. Fayaz Ahmad, Dr. Shajer us Shafiq Jan, Dr. Idrees Kant, Dr. Ajmal Shah, Dr. Younis Rashid, Dr. Abdul Rashid Lone, Mr. Haroon Rashid and Dr. Shahnawaz Shah. We express our heartfelt thanks to them. We have no words to express our deep sense of gratitude to Dr. Javaid, Dr. Fahmida Wani, Dr. Javid Ahmad Bhat, Mr. Ali Mohammad Shah, Abdul Rehaman Bhat, Mohammad Jabar Shah, Syed Āmir Geelani and my very dear sisters—Sarah and Sayeeda and their families for their love and encouragement. Ms. Sameena, librarian, Department of History, University of Kashmir, and Mr. Younis Ahmad of the same department have always been forthcoming in helping us. We are deeply beholden to them.

Dr. Aijaz Ashraf Wani deserves our special thanks for his keen interest to see this book being published by some reputed publishing house. The writing of this project would have been impossible without the cooperation of every member of our family, especially the head of the family, Ms. Raja and her two pillars, Dr. Shazia and Dr. Shaheena. Words fail to express our gratitude to them. We would be eternally rewarded if this book inspires our new generation to carry forward the tradition of adding to the existing body of knowledge and develop a constructive outlook on life that unites the people rather than dividing them.

Muhammad Ashraf Wani
Aman Ashraf Wani
Srinagar
(October 2021)

1

INTRODUCTION

> Specificity, priority, nationality: words to be crossed off from the vocabulary of History.[1]
>
> (Febvre)

> Historians, however microcosmic, must be for universalism, not out of loyalty to an ideal to which many of us remain attached but because it is the necessary condition for understanding the history of humanity, including that of any special section of humanity. For all human collectivities necessarily are and have been part of a larger and more complex world.[2]
>
> (Hobsbawm)

> the "world" in world history is not necessarily a Hegelian nexus requiring totalistic narratives but rather a research space that encourages scholars to critically reconsider categories such as "nation" or "civilization" in the light of translocal perspectives.[3]
>
> (Sachsenmaier)

History Beyond Enclosures

Situating regional, supra-regional and even continental histories in the context of the greater world around them is nowadays a reputable academic engagement among a section of professional historians.[4] It offers an alternative to the dominance of a historiography structured around the two western categories, "nation" and "civilization," which "are often presented as the subjects and not the products of history,"[5] and thus pregnant with, even deliberately constructed for, taking "the path to xenophobia and cultural paranoia."[6] Hence, the preoccupation of the contemporary historiography to look at history from the perspective of intercultural networks has been informed by a strong human interest: it aims at pooling its share to the struggle that the productive scholarship is fighting to respond to the

DOI: 10.4324/9781003367697-1

challenges history and humanity face by isolating the history of one part of humanity from its wider context to *make* a "civilization," "nation" or an identity.[7]

This kind of "civilizationalism"/"nationalism"/"regionalism" is "the idolization of a ghost. It is a cause of war."[8] It "radically distorts the social and cultural space" making it "closed and sedentary when it is open and mobile"; it "divides the world into eternal divisions"; drawing "far-reaching boundaries around national cultures"; it "divides insiders and outsiders, natives and foreigners"; it "fractures and immobilises history"; it is "a project of intellectual and political elite who have stakes in boundaries, separations, distances and oppositions" among communities and nations.[9] This is besides the fact that with these invented and imagined categories as "civilization"/"nation" as one's frame of reference, it creates bias and impairs the possibility of writing a relatively objective history. The serious limitations of identity history informed by "nationalism" have been vociferously highlighted by Eric Hobsbawm:

> The standard example of an identity culture which anchors itself to the past by means of myths dressed up as history is nationalism. Of this Ernest Renan observed more than a century ago, 'Forgetting, even getting history wrong, is an essential factor in the formation of a nation, which is why the progress of historical studies is often a danger to nationality.' For nations are historically novel entities pretending to have existed for a very long time. Inevitably the nationalist version of their history consists of anachronism, omission, decontextualization and, in extreme cases, lies. To a lesser extent this is true of all forms of identity history, old or new.[10]

Indeed, looking at history beyond borders is one of the basic conditions for writing a realistic history, and the realistic approach to the study of a region, continent, country, empire or any other politically defined territory. After all, the history of mankind is the history of flows, movements and circulations. In his influential article, "Regions Unbound: Towards a New Politics of Place," Ash Amin rightly disputes with the mainstream view of regions which conceptualises them as territorial entities constitutively separate and different from other regions. This imaginary, says Amin, is odd because "these are sites routinely implicated in distant connections and influences, disallowing a conceptualization of a place culture in terms of spatial formations."[11] Doubtlessly, at no period were these spaces nested territorial formations composed of "discernible inside and outside." Making the same point in the context of "cultures" and "civilizations" in a rather combative tone and tenor, Sheldon Pollock, the literary historian of South Asia, wrote:

> From whatever vantage point we look, if we are prepared to look historically, civilizations reveal themselves to be processes and not things. And as processes they ultimately have no boundaries; people are constantly receiving and passing on cultural goods. No form of culture can therefore ever be 'indigenous'; that term, it bears repeating, is only the name we give to what exhausts our capacity for historicization. When taken as anything more than this, the idea inhibits our perceiving that all cultures participate in what are ultimately global networks of begging, borrowing, and stealing, imitating and emulating – all the while constructing themselves precisely by subletting this history and affirming a specious autogenesis. From the processual perspective, "culture" or "civilization" (as in "Indian Civilization 101") becomes nothing but an arbitrary moment illegitimately generalized, a freeze frame in a film taken for the whole story. Each of these moments is in fact only an instance of exchange, an entrepot, a site for reprocessing cultural goods that are always already someone else's.
>
> This circulatory character of culture is never countenanced in indigenist thought (or never at least by recipient, only by donors). In civilizationalism it is simply lost in a haze of general historical amnesia. In the vernacular variety of civilizationalism, namely nationalism, it is actively buried in a surfeit of history.[12]

Taking issue with the idea of "civilization" that underlies most of the work of the contemporary historians despite generally eschewing from using the term, David Ludden, an authority on South Asian history, pointed out:

> [T]he idea of civilisation necessarily (if not intentionally) induces a reading back of "present-national sentiments" into a timeless past; it thereby prevents history from working against cultural hegemonies in the present by stultifying our analysis of mobility, context, agency, contingency, and change. It makes it difficult for any analyst to separate immediately present conditions from those of the past, by embedding today in the timeless repetitions of cultures.[13]

The idea of "a world of bounded spaces and identities" that ignores agency and circulation encourages the "vertical fallacy," according to the art historian Finbarr Flood. Because according to this idea the human agents who create cultural forms and practices "can be adequately represented by oppositional tabulations." Explaining this "fallacy" in the context of his field of interest, Flood maintains:

> The objects with which the identities and identifications of premodern subjects were imbricated and by which they were implicated have . . . been imbued with an identity that inheres in essence, form and structure rather than agency, circulation and use. With both subjects and objects subordinated to a "spatial incarceration" (to borrow Arjun Appadurai's term), the transcultural artifacts, individuals, spaces, and practices . . . are necessarily marginal phenomena.[14]

While relational reading of any research space that works with the ontology of flow and connectivity is important regardless of time and space, it is perhaps more needed for the study of premodern history which is underlined by mass migrations in search of relieved conditions and greener pastures in an environment of borderless world and historical displacements and cultural shifts. To be sure, almost all the passes and bypasses, which connect the world today, were discovered by the mobile people of the mobile world called prehistoric or preliterate world. It is these people who were the first to knit the world together by their remarkable mobility, global distribution and circulation. Hence, it would not be an exaggeration to say that there is prehistory to global history. The millennia between the post preliterate world and modern world were the millennia of proliferation of political regions, state-building, building of empires, global trade networks, contingent cosmopolitanisms and considerable economic development, ramifying networks and generating mass diasporas, both subaltern and elites.[15] The millennia are also underlined by the rise of plethora of religious beliefs and sects with missionary zeal to expand their geographical reach, producing "preconditions for established patterns of circulation to undergo radical transformations of intensity or scale," to borrow the words of Flood.[16] Together with this, we should also recognise that the inventions, discoveries, path-breaking ideas, institutions and practices were the handiwork of different places, sites and regions from where they circulated to different parts of globe through different patterns of encounter and process of transculturation. Therefore, no cultural space can claim to be autonomous and local *per se*. The affinities in cultural productions (notwithstanding the continuous process of "cultural translation," mediation and negotiation) as well as the similarities in physiognomy (despite the transhistorical prevalence of *métissages*) that we find among different regional spaces spanning a large landmass are a clear testimony to a common past shared by humanity.

The idea of borderless history does not entail deterritorialised concept of identity. The history of an empire, country, continent, region or a locality cannot be discarded. What is, however, necessary is to situate these histories in the context of global history. The perspective of negotiating between the local and the translocal is not only in line with the demands of the world in which we live, but it is also closer to objectivity than the traditional history we inherited from the nineteenth century. No locality, region or continent has been an island, entire of itself. Instead, they evolved and grew only through the medium of contact—the local with the region, the region with supra-region, supra-region with the continent, and continent with the world, thus connecting the part with the whole. The archaeological discoveries, which broadened our perspectives in time and space and added centuries to our historical vision, destroyed the parochial, regional and even continental conceptions, making it possible to escape the fetters of imprisoning the study of history in the pigeon holes of region- or nation-centric bunkers.

At any rate, like other branches of history, translocal history is a separate branch of historical study with its own ambitions and methods. While its purpose is to make sense of history and to unify mankind, the method is to study the local in the context of globe and the globe in relation to the local. We may picture the family, the local community, the region, the supra-region, the continent and the world as a series of concentric circles, each requiring to be studied with constant reference to the one outside it.[17] Local or regional history is a method of ascertaining facts about the universal history by a minute examination of those areas that combine to make the world. It is like a scientist studying natural phenomena through a microscope, by making use of rich archaeological and written materials available at local level, and more so by studying non-conventional sources, namely, physiognomy, surnames, place names, languages, traditions, customs, beliefs, science, technology, art and architecture—in fact the total history in the framework of entangled histories to obtain refreshingly a rich material to construct the shared history of mankind. The study of links and flows, movement of people, ideas, products, processes and patterns, networks, diasporas, circulation, mediation, reception and transformation of cultural goods and practices, alterity, forms of exclusion or othering as well as resistance, fragmentation and conflict, hybridisation, appropriation, looking for sources and affinities beyond borders and the like would always be preferred themes of this special branch of history called shared history, ecumenical history, universal history, global history, international history and its neologisms ranging from "connected histories,"[18] "entangled histories,"[19] transcultural history, translocal history to *histoire croisée*;[20] and their lesser ambitious variant, namely, borderlands history—all aiming at developing more plural vision of the past, in terms of both encounters and perspectives. However, for vindicating the claim for writing this history every single locality, region, continent, country and empire needs to be studied, of course, with outward rather than the traditional inward-looking approach to history.

In returning to transcultural history today we, in fact, revive an old tradition going back to the origins of history writing. Polybius (208–162 BCE), the greatest of the Hellenistic historians, persuasively argued in favour of connected histories.[21] Ibn Khaldun (1332–1406 CE), while giving a theory of cultural change in history, emphasised on encounter, circulation, displacement and negotiation. He, like the postcolonial historians, insisted more on conquest, occupation, subversion, resistance and accommodation in creating cultural mixing[22] rather than "mixing simply happens."[23] He maintains that what follows after conquest is neither old nor new. While the conqueror changes the conquered society, the later also changes the former, and the story goes on unendingly. Voltaire's great contribution to history and humanity was to bring extra-European world in the field of enquiry and thus acknowledged the plural sources of human civilisation.[24] Ranke, the celebrated nineteenth-century historian, was also of the view that no history can be written but universal history.[25] Among the twentieth-century historians who launched a crusade against Euro-centric and nationalist historiography, the name of Arnold Toynbee is worth mentioning.[26] Yet, Marc Bloch's *Histoire comparée* and the speech he delivered in Oslo in 1928 *Congrès international des sciences historiques*, in which he called for a comparative historical approach, mark a watershed in the history of connected histories. The Annales school's insistence on comparative method involving comparisons between the countries to know whether a given problem could be located elsewhere, concurrently or otherwise, ultimately transcended the frontiers of European states and even the boundaries of continent itself. Bloch articulated this proclaimed transborder ambition of history when he wrote, "There is no history of France, but a history of Europe," an assertion picked up later by Fernand Braudel to which he immediately added, "There is no history of Europe, but a history of the world," even as he was seeking to establish the "identity of France.".[27] Adherence to "civilizational," "national" and "regional" paradigms faced a continuous challenge then onwards from many groups, organisations, institutions, movements and individuals[28] which for the paucity of space we are unfortunately unable to discuss here. Suffice it to say that for the last three decades the "transcultural turn" in history assumed a global trend following public debates about the waning importance of the nation state and the concomitant growth of globalisation studies in the social sciences,[29] and also because "cultural chauvinists mobilize their troops again."[30]

Situating Early Kashmir

Though in size and population a small place and even as surrounded by high mountain ramparts, the Kashmir Valley had been till recent past a space of the flows, a key site of intercultural contact, a zone of cultural hybridity[31] and, thus, an excellent example of mini global culture. After all, far from being an isolated periphery—the notion held by some scholars[32]—Kashmir was politically integrated with its neighbouring world—sometimes as a part of the great empires that emerged on its borders, and sometimes having others as its vassals, the details of which have been given in the following chapters. Besides, it was a place located in an orbit of international networks of travel, trade, migration and knowledge exchanges.

No wonder then, since the time of its very occupation by the humans up to the recent past, Kashmir had been virtually a *cul-de-sac* into which peoples infiltrated from different parts of the world giving birth to a complex ethnic mosaic of the population, changing cultural identities over time and a dynamic process of hybridisation. Indeed, if we keenly observe a sizeable gathering drawn from different parts of the valley, we will straightaway get many faces representing various ethnic and sub-ethnic groups spanning a host of countries from China to Europe and from Eurasia to India, and in the process, it will break down the walls between the territorial divisions of the world. The same result we may get if we analyse the different aspects of Kashmir society and trace their roots. Certainly, the early Kashmir emerged out of constant operation of circulation, reception and transformation of a whole variety of inflows it received from different immediate and distant neighbours in the wake of conquests, immigrations, settlements and the constant movement of people flowing back and forth generated by power, patronage, trade, knowledge, religion, search for greener pastures and favourable conditions. Given the relationally constituted culture of Kashmir, it is understandable that the orientation of writing this work is informed by its proclaimed ambition of situating early Kashmir history in the context of neighbouring world. This intercultural dimension of early Kashmir history allows us to agree with James Clifford that "Cultural centres, discrete regions and territories, do not exist prior to contacts."[33]

The mountain ring around the valley no doubt made the passage to and from Kashmir hazardous, but it is difficult to agree with Walter Slaje, who says that "Kashmir was hermetically sealed off" and "secluded from the plains of India" from the beginning of the eleventh century until the end of the nineteenth century.[34] Slaje substantiates his view by quoting Al-Biruni who found Kashmir virtually shut for the foreigners towards the beginning of the eleventh century.[35] The closure of "entrances and roads leading to Kashmir" during that critical moment has to be understood in the context of inevitable danger of the Ghaznavid invasion that loomed large over Kashmir during the period when not only the neighbourhood of Kashmir had fallen before its armies, but Kashmir too was subjected to many abortive Turkish incursions.[36] That the policy of closing Kashmir to foreigners was only a temporary affair is sufficiently borne out by the presence of "hundreds of [*Turuśka*] captains" in the armies of eleventh- and twelfth-century Kashmiri rajas.[37] In the same period, we also find the influx of people from erstwhile Śhahi kingdom, "foreign horse dealers," dealers in "*Turuśka* girls, born in various distant regions," artists from "*Turuśka* country," employment of singers and dancers of "other lands," induction of brahmanas from Karnataka in the nobility of Kalasa, liberal patronage to talent "who had arrived from various countries" by Harśa and the existence of a colony of *saracens* (Muslims) in the thirteenth century,[38] to cite only a few examples, making it abundantly clear that Kashmir was not under any geographical siege; instead, the commercial, cultural and diplomatic relations with the neighbouring world continued unabated except for a brief disruption during Mahmud's invasion of north India. Even, according to Al-Biruni himself, during the period of Mahmud's invasion, a large number of Hindus fled from the north-west and western borderlands of Kashmir and sought shelter in the valley.[39]

It was not a one-way traffic however. The Kashmiris also travelled to different parts of the neighbouring world for educational, religious and commercial purposes, besides going in search of greener pastures and relieved conditions. Evidence on emigrations and travel of Kashmiris is not only supplied by *Rājataraṅgiṇī* and other local sources,[40] it is also provided by non-local sources. For example, the inscriptions at the Tiruvalleswarar temple in the South Madurai (Tamil Nadu) constructed under the Pallavas clearly state the settlement of Kashmiri brahmanas there.[41] This diaspora of Kashmiri brahmanas was connected with the spread of Śaivism and Vaiṣṇavism in different parts of the subcontinent. The relations with South India were so deep-rooted that the political vicissitudes had hardly any impact on the continuity of these relations as we find one of the generals of Vijayanagara emperors settling about 60 Kashmiri brahmanas in his territory.[42] There is also a mention of the presence of Kashmiri brahmanas in Nepal about CE 1200.[43] Al-Biruni also mentions the presence of Kashmiri brahmanas in north-west and the Punjab.[44] This is besides the impressive presence of Kashmiri Buddhist scholars cum missionaries in Tibet, Central Asia and China.[45] Slaje also quotes the system of watch stations at the passes to support his narrative of secluded position of Kashmir. No doubt there was a well-established system of watch stations (*dranga*) at the passes of Kashmir but their purpose was to collect customs dues and to check invasions[46] rather than defending the country's policy of splendid isolation.

Certainly, the geographical centrality of Kashmir relegated the mountain ramparts around it to a mere geographical expression situated as it was amidst the great imitable models of the then world—China in the east, Central Asia in the north, Iran in the north-west and India in the west—generating considerable movement of people and goods thanks to a large number of passes which gave a passage to and from the valley. According to Abul Fazl, 26 routes connected Kashmir with India alone, though Bhimber-Hirpur and Baramulla-Pakhli routes were mainly adopted.[47] While the Hirpur route connected Kashmir with the Punjab, the Baramulla route was the shortest line of communication to the Indus Valley and Hazara and thence to North West frontier provinces, Afghanistan, Iran and Central Asia. It is significant to note that the Chinese pilgrims Hiuen-Tsang and Ou-k'ong also followed this route on their way to Kashmir.[48] Evidently, they adopted the Peshwar-Pamir route via Hunza and Gilgit. Beyond the Pamirs were the two major Central Asian marts—Kashgar and Yarkand. Two other routes that connected Kashmir with Central Asia and China were the Karnah-Chilas route and the Gurez-Baltistan route. The Karna-Chilas route connected Kashmir with Afghanistan and then with Central Asia and Iran through Hazara and Swat. It also led to Gilgit and Baltistan through Chitral and then to Kashgar and Khotan. The Gurez-Baltistan route connected Kashmir with Kashgar through Pamir. With Yarkand as the objective, one had a choice of three passes after Hunza: Shimshal, Khunjerab and Mintaka. Indeed, Gurez-Baltistan route was the main route that connected Kashmir with modern Chinese Turkistan (Yarkand, Khotan, Kashgar, Kucha etc.) and then ultimately with China. Ou-k'ong also mentions this route as the main communication line connecting Kashmir with the neighbouring world towards its north.[49] Another route that connected Kashmir with Tibet and China passed over Zojila.[50] Its significance is also acknowledged by Ou-k'ong.[51] It is in place to mention that all these routes were the feeders of the famous Silk Route, which went all the way from China to Rome in the early Christian era.

Considering the importance of studying regions in the perspective of their relationally constituted nature, it was towards the turn of the last century that we, in the department of history, and the Centre of Central Asian Studies, University of Kashmir, chose to situate the history of Kashmir beyond region-centric bunkers and made the subject as one of the priority areas of research. With the result, we produced a few articles and MPhil and PhD theses on the subject.[52] Recently, Shonaleeka Kaul published a scholarly work, *The Making of Early Kashmir: Landscape and Identity in the Rājataraṅgiṇī*. One of its objectives was to study the early history of Kashmir through the paradigm of "connected history":

> I believe the choices early Kashmir made that shaped the cultural identity and location were based on a very open and active, if uneven, historical interface with surrounding cultures.[53]

However, unable to look at Kashmir history beyond nation-centric bunkers, she circumscribes this network of shaping interactions within the national boundaries ignoring the geographical centrality of Kashmir that privileged it to become an important network node of regional and global exchange sitting as it is in the nexus of South, East and Central Asia besides having remained a part of great empires including the Indian empires that emerged on its borders; or ruled over others including the parts of India and Central Asia. Thus, while glossing over Kashmir's interface with a multitude of surrounding empires and cultural zones, she emphasises only on Kashmir's connectivity with and cultural flows from the "Indic mainland." '

> Without questioning the well-established incursion of Indo-Greek, Śaka, Pehlava, Kuṣāṇa and Huna political elements into the region in the early historical period, and notwithstanding Kashmir's contiguity or proximity to different culture zones, the range of evidence on hand leads one to question the assumption that early Kashmir somehow constituted a cultural hybrid, falling between a variety of hyphenated cultural regimes. Reinstating into view the western Himalayas, it then considers the entire regional spread—from Gandhara and Ladakh to Jammu, the Punjab and Kashmir up to Himachal Pradesh—in terms of its connected histories and that of the Indic mainland.[54]

Kaul omits admitting that the entire region of western Himalayas from Gandhara to Gilgit had a dense network of connections with proximate and distant neighbours influencing its every sphere of life. In the whole area extending from Indus Kohistan to the districts of Gilgit and Baltistan, numerous inscriptions written in Kharoshthi, Brahmi, Sogdian, Bactrian, Chinese and Hebrew covering the time between the second century BCE and ninth century CE have been found and studied by scholars.[55] The uninterrupted transregional contacts of the region regardless of the political and cultural changes in the world around it is attested by a series of Arabic inscriptions from Tangtse in Ladakh datable from ninth century onwards.[56] There are also series of royal scenes painted in a Buddhist temple at Alchi in Ladakh (believed to have been executed between 1150 and 1220), especially the one showing "the robe worn by the ruler, for it corresponds to the *qabā*, a type of dress well known in the Islamic world."[57]

Clearly, the sub-regional cultures of western Himalayas cannot be understood without situating them in the context of Chinese, Central Asian, West Asian, Greek and Indian cosmopolitanisms which thrived on its borders and penetrated in the region through multiple channels. Going against the established view of Kashmir's intimate relations with the north-west, Kaul is not inclined to accept that Kashmir was culturally a part of the subcontinental north-west, which, during the early period, emerged as a great cosmopolitan ecumene owing to cultural flows from many directions. The reason for this denial lies in Kaul's disdain for seeing the historical significance of early Kashmir in its access and exposure to non-Indic realms and affairs through north-western part of the Indian subcontinent "characterized in history as gateway or outward-looking highways to Central Asia and western Asia."[58] Indeed, Kaul's main preoccupation is to establish the cultural location and identity of western Himalayan region including early Kashmir in relation to the "Indic mainland" alone on the altar of other equally powerful influences.

True, from the sixth century CE, Kashmir gravitated more towards the Sanskritic world. But prior to that whole of the subcontinent including Kashmir was immensely influenced by many important cosmopolitan ecumenes which penetrated through conquests, migrations and a variety of contacts, mainly through the north-western parts of the subcontinent. To be sure, the 'Indic mainland,' which came to exercise a sovereign influence on Kashmir from the sixth century and onwards, was itself shaped in the cosmopolitan crucible in the wake of "continuous circulation of cultural goods that we know marks all of cultural history."[59]

Kaul cites *Rājataraṅgiṇī's* "choice of frame" to support her thesis of "Indic predisposition of early Kashmir" disregarding the fact that this picture of "Indic Kashmir" is from a Sanskrit literary work written by a "pure" brahmana in his anxiety to claim a space for Kashmir within a Sanskritic and brahmanical tradition.[60] Though she tries to seek corroboration from the 'alternative imaginaries and landscapes' from material evidence, she conveniently suppresses the "total" alternative imaginary which, instead of pointing out the sources of early Kashmir within the Indian subcontinent alone, brings out the global ingredients in its making. In his review of Kaul's book, Luther Obrock also expresses serious reservations about her predetermined agenda of showing Kashmir "a particular regional instantiation of the Indic," and a "stable Sanskritic identity,"[61] ignoring Kashmir's multidimensional contacts with its whole neighbourhood and the resultant dynamic identity formations at different stages of its dynamic history. This book, therefore, argues that the cultural elements of early Kashmir including its people were sourced from different geographies—proximate and distant—including the Indian subcontinent. Importantly, of the plethora of subcontinental regions with which Kashmir had close relations, those situated in its immediate west and north-west were so closer to it that they were considered culturally one single complex.[62]

To substantiate our assertion of the plural sources of Kashmir culture, we have chosen a long period beginning from prehistoric times and brought it down to the thirteenth century CE. The choice of time line is deliberate because, unlike the subsequent phases, the linkages of the early phase of Kashmir with the outside world are little known. Secondly, it was during this longest period of Kashmir history that the foundations of Kashmir culture underlined by exchanges, give and take, accommodation, dynamism and fluidity were laid out to which the subsequent changes had to fit in to meet the demands of congruence and compatibility.

Although many scholarly works have been written on the early history of Kashmir, the longest phase (from the beginnings up to the sixth century CE) has been dismissed by all of them just in a few lines except for prehistory which has received considerable attention from the archaeologists. This is also the case even with such outstanding works as SC Ray's *Early History and Culture of Kashmir*. The doyen of ancient Kashmir history, MA Stein also did not discuss the early history of Kashmir upto the beginning of sixth century CE except for a brief mention of Mauryas and Kuṣāṇas. The reason for almost leaving out this period by the historians is not difficult to seek should we consider that at the time when they wrote archaeology was still in its infancy. Burzahom had not yet revealed itself fully and the spade had not even touched Gufkral and Semthan. As archaeological sources constitute the basic building blocks for reconstructing the history of the period, it is no wonder that these works could not give even an outline history of the period.

Some signal discoveries made by archaeology during the second half of the twentieth century and after brought with them the message that a historiographical revolution would occur in Kashmir following the new finds. However, so far the historians failed to respond to this announcement: the new evidence that was thrown up by archaeology has not been utilised by them. Quoting BA Chattopadhyaya that culture in a "regional context assumes a recognisable distinct shape only through history and only through different scales of interaction and integration," Kaul rightly argues that "regions are therefore best studied in *longue duree*."[63] However, except for a brief and selective reference to the longest phase of early Kashmir, she mainly draws on the information relevant for the postfifth-century Kashmir. This book therefore fulfils the condition of studying history in *longue durée* by tracing the relationally constituted cultural realm of Kashmir from the time the early man appeared there. The present work tries to tap all the available information to give not only a connected history of early Kashmir over the *longue durée*, but it also suggests that there is a need to make a conceptual breakthrough in the history of Kashmir by situating it in the context of shared histories of humanity, requiring "reconfiguration of premodern cultural geography, moving beyond the linear borders of the modern nation-state and the static taxonomies of modern scholarships."[64]

Sources

Considering the scope and subject matter of our study, its treatment is predicated on tapping all those sources which, on the one hand, provide us information about the cultural history of early Kashmir, and, on the other, help us in situating it in a wider context by identifying those sites and interaction zones which acted as its fountainheads and cultural entrepots; and in whose making Kashmir also participated subsequently. Therefore, for us both the local sources and those which shed light on the then world and the borderlands of Kashmir are equally important. While for the information on trans-border histories we drew on modern scholarly works, for capturing the past of Kashmir, we consulted different categories of sources without giving precedence to one over the other.

Before making a mention of the different types of sources, it needs to be emphasised that we treat all of them—written texts, visual texts, buildings and other discrete material objects—as cultural artefacts,[65] produced by human beings and for some purpose. Thus, before considering them as transparent windows onto an aspect of the past, they require the historian first to reconstruct them as an object of knowledge.[66] The cultural historians propose examining the cultural artefacts within the systems of *production*, *signification*, and *reception* "that give rise to an artefact and from which it derives its meanings."[67] No longer now, the text—written or visual—is like a stable vessel containing a fixed meaning. It is rather a dynamic entity producing and sustaining a range of meanings.[68] We are sensitive to the fact that the cultural artefacts do not necessarily mirror their times; instead, they are predetermined and selective, and they seek rhetorically to construct and guide their readers. What is handed down to us is only a tip of an iceberg. The voices of powerless are silenced in both material and textual sources. We have also learnt from symbolic anthropologists to read and examine public behaviour, social actions and events for what they *say* rather than what they do.[69] With these preliminary remarks, we will briefly mention the different kinds of sources with special reference to their relative significance in the context of the subject matter of this book.

Material Culture

While taking issue with the historians of medieval South Asia for privileging texts over objects as sources of information, Finbarr Flood rightly argues that artefacts are potentially complementary rather than supplementary source of information for writing medieval South Asian histories.[70] This is not only truer in case of the space and chronological scope of this book, but material culture constitutes our main source, to say the least. For constructing the history of Kashmir up to the beginning of the sixth century CE, it is virtually the only source, and for the period from the sixth century on, it provides fresh insights and novel perspectives. Even though the archaeologist's spade has shown only a peripheral presence in Kashmir, a few sites excavated so far provide valuable evidence on Kashmir's contacts with the neighbouring world and the role of "cultural circulation" in the emergence and growth of Kashmir as a cultural realm. The exogenous roots of the Neolithism of Kashmir are revealed by the finds of many Neolithic sites of Kashmir, especially Burzahom and Gufkral, which have been studied in conjunction with the prehistoric sites of China, Russia, Mediterranean World, West Asia, Central Asia, Afghanistan and the borderlands spanning from Swat to the Punjab and from Swat Kohistan to Gilgit and Baltistan. The comparative study of the finds shows that culturally Kashmir was a part of greater Asia and Eastern Europe during the longest period of its history, so akin are their Neolithic finds, the details of which have been given in the second chapter of this book. The Semthan archaeological site provides a connected information hub on the successive occupation of Kashmir by the Mauryas, Bactrian-Greeks, Śakas, Parthians, Kuṣāṇas and Huns. Of the important finds, mention may be made of NBPW and punch-marked coins, Indo-Greek coins, many terracotta figurines showing Hellenistic and Gandhara influences, coins of Śakas and Parthians, pottery, terracotta and copper coins of Kuṣāṇas, clay seal with Brahmi and Kharoshthi scripts, mud bricks, rubble and diaper pebble walls besides brick tiles with faint motifs. The overall culture is in conformity with what one finds in Gandhara.

The most fascinating and invaluable evidence on the subject of our study is provided by the Harwan site, which we prefer to call a global site for its remarkable cosmopolitan character typifying Kashmir a place of cross-cultural convergence. Although the question of the identity of Harwan has evoked much controversy, some arguing that it is pre-Kuṣāṇa site and some that it is a Kuṣāṇa site,[71] nevertheless there is much weight in the argument which articulates that this place was originally a Saka-Parthian site, and it was during the Kuṣāṇa period that the material of this structure was used for constructing Buddhist structures at lower terraces. The overall plan of Harwan is identical with the fire temple at Surkh Kotal (Bactria). Like Surkh Kotal, Harwan is a terraced structure with a courtyard surrounding the main temple located on the highest level. Both Harwan and Surkh Kotal originally had a stairway leading through the centre of each terrace. The apsidal temple, preceded by an oblong hall, has resemblance to the temple of Artemis-Nanaia at Dura-Europos (a famous Parthian site) and also with the apsidal structure of Sirkap, the Graeco-Parthian city (see Chapter 3). The facial characteristics of the human figures stamped on the tiles bear close resemblance to those of the inhabitants of the regions roundabout Yarkand and Kashgar whose heavy features, prominent cheek bones, narrow, sunk and slanting eyes and receding foreheads are faithfully represented on the tiles.[72] The masonry style adopted at Harwan underwent a systematic evolution. The rubble style started the fashion followed by pebble, diaper pebble and diaper rubble style. The same was obtained successively at Taxila under the influence of Greeks and Parthians (see Chapter 3). The rich galore of ornamentation of Harwan tiles presents a vivid evidence of the impact of many great cultural centres of the ancient world on Kashmir. According to Percy Brown, Harwan tiles "represent motifs suggestive of more than half a dozen alien civilizations of the ancient world besides others which are indigenous and local."[73] Such are the Bharhut railings, the Greek Swan, the Sassanian foliated fret, the Indian elephant, the Assyrian lion and "Parthian shot." The details about costumes, coiffures, cosmetics and amusements as reflected from the motifs stamped on Harwan tiles showing the impact of Greek, Scytho-Parthian and Kuṣāṇa influences, have been given in Chapter 3. No less significant evidence depicted by Harwan tiles is the synthesis of Graeco-Parthian art. While Harwan artists followed the Greek art in that the figures are shown in every attitude and the head is shown in profile and the body facing front, they also imitated some salient features of Parthian art, namely, linearity of contour, painstaking depiction of details of dress, ethnic characteristics, scenes of combat, chase and portrayal of scenes of hunt in flying gallop. However, the Parthian frontality and the neglect of body are missing (see Chapter 3).

Besides Harwan, a number of Kuṣāṇa sites have been identified though the work of most of these sites did not progress beyond trial excavations. Of these sites, mention may be made of Doen Pather, Hoinar, Hutmur, Ahan, Kotbal, Ushkur and Kanispur. The finds present close affinity with Gandhara culture. Apart from the invariable presence of Kuṣāṇa tiles with motifs of Buddhist emblems and the Kuṣāṇa dress, we come across a significant motif on some Hoinar tiles representing two winged lions locked in a fierce combat (Fig. 1.1). This motif has a parallel in Iran at Qateh-Yazgrad, a Parthian site (Fig. 1.2). It is also reminiscent of ancient Mesopotamian tradition. Such motifs are often encountered in Scythian burials and are also reported from Nuristan in Afghanistan.[74] The stucco figures found at Ushkur present a striking affinity with the sites of Akhnoor, Hadda, Fondukistan, Begram, Andnatapa, Airtam, Kizil and Dandan-Uiliq Khotan pointing to a common artistic tradition.[75]

The stone temples of Kashmir also provide living evidence about Kashmir's contacts with the neighbouring world and the influences they exercised in Kashmir. Coomaraswamy sums up the forging of "syncretic culture" in Kashmir with special reference to successful blending of Indigenous and trans-regional elements in the construction of stone temples:

> The typical Brahmanical temple of Kashmir from about 750–1250 A.D. has a special character of its own, and in some uses a curiously European aspect, due in part to the Gandharan inheritance of certain elements, though all the details are Indian.[76]

Sir Alexander Cunningham, who made a special study of the temples of Kashmir, concluded that many features of Kashmiri temples were borrowed from Greek art, such as columns of Doric order, pediments and trefoil arch.[77] The other elements that have been associated with Gandhara style are chequered pattern, stirring course of lion and Atlantes and the zigzag pattern on the pilasters. The Indian influences can be found in such motifs as water pot, lotus flower and lotus petals on cornices of capitals, geese, parrots and Yakshas, Garudas and Gandharvas. The variety of motifs on the pilasters of Avantiswami Temple also tells us the same story—that the cultural landscape of Kashmir was inspired by the influences radiating from different cultural centres.[78] However, the monuments simultaneously reveal another fact – that they were not simply constituted by an admixture of different structures and notions, instead by a dynamic condition in which transformations were wrought through negotiation. This is why that the art historians call it Kashmir style.[79]

"As in architecture," says Pratapaditya Pal,

> so also in Kashmir style sculpture, the roots lay in the Gandharan sculptural tradition. The influence of Gandhara is prominently perceptible in pre-Karkota Kashmir sculpture, but by the seventh century Kashmiri artists seem to have become more aware of the fifth-century Gupta style of the Gangetic plains. Because of the strong presence of Tocharians and other Central Asian peoples, particularly in Karkota Kashmir, one occasionally comes across elements that may have been borrowed from those regions as well as from China.[80]

The creation of a separate identity in the multicultural frontier setting is not only visible in working out a "hybrid solution," but the Kashmir sculpture is also distinctive in plastic qualities, facial features and the mode of attire.[81]

Many designs on the pottery, namely, wavy lines, wedge pattern and opposite triangles discovered by Mumtaz Yatoo at different sites in north Kashmir,[82] have their proto types in the Fergana Valley and Khorezm.[83]

A number of coins belonging to the Mauryas, Indo-Greeks, Śakas, Parthians, Kuṣāṇas, Huns and the subsequent rulers of Kashmir, found in different parts of the valley and preserved mostly in the SPS Museum, Srinagar, provide us significant information on contacts, cultural flows and receptions. Coinage is the only category of source, which furnishes tangible evidence about the successive encounters of Kashmir with Muryan, Indo-Greek, Śaka-Parthian and Kuṣāṇa cosmopolitanisms. It is also the single source to enlighten us about the monetary systems of early Kashmir and their transcultural context. It also provides unique information about the scripts of the period. The iconography of the coins is one of the principal sources about art and belief system, which in turn shed an important light on networks, translation, transculturation, accommodation, change and continuity.

In effect, material culture as a whole depicts "networks of affinity not bounded by religions, ethnic or linguistic identity but by possession, consumption and display." It provides a rewarding information about "constitutive relationships between subjects, objects and political formations and the ways in which these relationships were implicated in processes of transculturation." It also allows us to be live to continuities and discontinuities and shifts in the nature of cross-cultural interaction through time.[84] Material culture shows "how in different times and places the same object could be seen differently, and to realize the extent to which the issue of cultural differentiation and variation of the 'gaze' mattered to artists, their patrons, and the audiences."[85] Thus, Flood rightly calls material culture as "objects of translation," the title of his seminal book. However, it is not only the material culture of South Asia that shows practices of translation, its texts too "demonstrate a sustained and largely successful effort at intercultural translation."[86]

Textual Sources

Of the written sources, mention may be made of the *Nīlamata Purāna* (NP), *Viṣṇudharmottara Purāna* (VDhP), travel accounts of Hiuen Tsang and Ou-k'ong, Al-Biruni's *Kitāb fi tahqiq-i-mali 'l-Hind*, popularly known as *Kitāb-ul-Hind*, *Rājataraṅgiṇī* of Kalhana and a mass of literatures written in different genres by Sanskrit philosophers, litterateurs, linguists, grammarians and poets. Written between the seventh and eighth centuries, the NP brings out Kashmir as a place of immigrants and settlers leading to encounters and ultimately compromises among different ethnic and cultural groups. Conscious of the contributions made by diaspora to the evolution and growth of Kashmir as an important cultural centre, the NP makes it obligatory upon the king and the people of Kashmir that "All the people immigrating (to Kashmir) from the other directions, should be honoured.'"[87] It acknowledges that before the coming of Aryans, whom it calls human beings, Kashmir was inhabited by 'other' groups whom it, like a typical brahmanical work, calls by derogative names—Nāgas and Piśācas. What is, however, significant is that the NP recognises the importance of these early inhabitants of Kashmir forcing the Aryans to accommodate them in the brahmanic pantheon and assimilate their beliefs so much so that the spring divinities (Nāgas) occupy the position next to none in the sacred landscape of Kashmir constructed by the NP. And the 'twice born' had to necessarily observe the rites and ceremonies associated with Nāga divinities as well as with Nikumbha, the leader of the Piśācas.[88] The reverence for Buddha and the respect for Buddhists also figure among the instructions to be followed by the 'twice born' for their entitlement to live in Kashmir. The NP describes Buddha as incarnation of Viṣṇu and prescribes the celebration of his birthday.[89]

The NP also shows that by the time it was written Kashmir had become a part of the Indic *Weltanschauung*, the development which picked up forcefully from 530 CE following the preferential patronage of the rulers to *Śaivism* and *Vaiṣṇavism* which *inter alia* encouraged large-scale immigrations of brahmanas from different parts of the subcontinent.[90] However, as borne out by the NP, the domination of Brahmanism was also the result of vital compromises made by it by giving concessions to the circumstances. No wonder then, the NP is called an "assimilative text,"[91] though we would prefer to call it a cultural artefact emblematic of 'cultural translation.' Besides accommodating local beliefs, practices and power holders in its sacred space, it gives equal position to *Śaiva* and *Vaiṣṇava* divinities so much so that according to Ronald Inden, "it is difficult to tell which is superior."[92] The translated nature of the NP becomes understandable when it is considered that it is a self-conscious textual practice, a strategy to construct hegemony and dominance, not only by remaining sensitive to local mores and sensibilities and giving them a due position in the brahmanical sacral space, but also by co-opting and altering the geography of Kashmir. The NP makes all the Vedic-Purānic gods and goddesses to occupy the mountains, rivers and lakes of Kashmir turning the valley into a self-contained cosmos quite identical to the Indic cosmos. Thus, by elevating the landscape of Kashmir to the subcontinental Sanskritic tradition, the NP constructed a sacred geography of Kashmir, which runs parallel to the subcontinental sacral sites.[93] With its own Ganga, Yamuna, Prayaga, Varanasi, Kashi, Mathura etc., a Kashmiri follower had not to make subcontinental pilgrimages to perform the basic rituals. According to Ronald Inden, the NP is "about the theistic and royal wish to make Kashmir into an imperial kingdom by proudly displaying its regional markings and using them to position itself in relation to India as a whole."[94]

That the hegemony of religion/sect was the function of power is clear from the NP. As long as Vaiṣṇavism was the worldview of the ruling class, Viṣṇu was the leading deity of the NP, and a large number of festivals were celebrated in his honour and only one in honour of Śiva.[95] This hierarchical order changes in the later one-third of the *Nīlamata* as Śiva takes the place of Viṣṇu. Clearly, the later portion of the NP was written during the tenth and eleventh centuries when Śaivism was the dominant tradition.

The VDhP was written in the eighth century presumably under the patronage of Chandrapida Vajraditya and Muktapida Lalitaditya.[96] Like the NP, the VDhP is, according to Ronald Inden, both articulative and articulated text. Embodying a self-conscious narrative, VDhP is about working out of a Vaiṣṇava world vision that is also a Kashmiri imperial wish.[97]

> The conquest of the quarters that Muktapida undertook was informed by the narrative and discursive contents of VDhP, whereas the vision of the text [the institution of a kingdom embracing the entire earth in which the Viṣṇu of the Pancarartrins received recognition as overlord of the cosmos] was itself tailored to the situation.[98]

Inden is also of the opinion that VDhP was 'one of the major texts involved in the rise to hegemony of "temple Hinduism" at the expense of both the Vedic sacrificial liturgy and Buddhist monasticism.'[99] A king successful in battle was supposed to build temples. And this is what Lalitaditya did after conquering most of the neighbouring territories. Part 3 of the VDhP focuses on the construction of temples and images. That is why it is an important source for the art historians. And for us, it is useful to appreciate the forging of hybrid tradition through appropriation of forms of other traditions.[100] It is believed that the Pancharatra order that emerged in Kashmir under the Karkotas was the "ancestor of most of the orders of Vaişṇavas that arose later throughout the subcontinent."[101]

Hiuen Tsang's *Si-Yu-Ki* provides us important information on different subjects. It furnishes corroborative evidence that Kashmir was a part of the Mauryan empire as he saw many Aśokan stupas in Kashmir. He also gives a detailed account about the Fourth Buddhist Council held in Kashmir under the patronage of Kaniṣka. Hiuen Tsang's information on the political geography of Kashmir is also valuable. He clearly mentions that the Kashmir empire included all the neighbouring hill states around 627 CE when he visited Kashmir. Equally important is the mention of Kashmir as a great centre of learning. Hiuen Tsang's own travel to Kashmir is no less significant in that it shows that one of the routes adopted between China and Kashmir was through Swat as the Chinese traveller followed this route for his visit to Kashmir. Secondly, Hiuen Tsang's coming to Kashmir all the way from China to learn at the feet of Kashmiri Buddhist scholars shows that education was one of the important modes of contact between Kashmir and the neighbouring world. Ou-k'ong's travel account has also the same significance as he also visited Kashmir for the same purpose and left behind a record about the flourishing condition of Buddhism in Kashmir during the period of his visit.

Al-Biruni did not visit Kashmir. He collected information about it from the Kashmiris whom he met between 1017 and 1030 CE while making sojourn to Peshawar, Multan and the Punjab to collect material for his *Kitāb fi tahqiq-i-mali 'l-Hind*. He mentions that the Kashmiri rajas had sealed their borders following the threat of Ghaznavid invasion. Also, according to him, Kashmir was subjected to plundering raids from the people of hill states surrounding it. His information that the Kashmiris celebrated a political festival to commemorate the victory Lalitaditya had won over the Turks partly substantiates the 'digvijaya' image portrayed by Kalhana about Lalitaditya. Al-Biruni's account that the brahmanas of Gandhara and the Punjab fled to Kashmir and other places after the Ghaznavid invasion, and that the Kashmiri rulers treated with special favour the Jews, who probably visited Kashmir in connection with trade, is quite informative. No less important is to learn from him that Kashmir exported flowers to India. Al-Biruni also substantiates the evidence that Kashmir had become one among the highest seats of Sanskrit learning of the subcontinent by the beginning of the eleventh century.

Rājataraṅgiṇī of Kalhana written in 1149–1150 CE is the only historical work which has come down to us. Claiming, though, to have written the history of Kashmir from the "birth of Kashmir," the chronicle is both parsimonious and legendry up to the beginning of the sixth century CE. The history of more than 3,500 years of Kashmir, if we count only from the time when permanent settlements began in Kashmir, is dismissed in a few pages, obviously because Kalhana faced the paucity of sources. Within this short and fabled account contained in the first two tarangas, there is mention of Kashmir being a part of the Mauryan and Kuṣāṇa empires, which supports the available archaeological evidence in this regard. From the sixth century onwards Kalhana gives comparatively a detailed account, and within the ruler-centred history, Kalhana supplies some important information which helps us, though dimly, to construct the relationally constituted history of Kashmir.

Explaining the legendry nature of Kalhana's early account, Kumkum Roy says, "This is a time-frame within which literal truth is somewhat irrelevant: what seems to be central is the creation of a mythical past, a space within which an ideal socio-political order could be projected."[102] Indeed, the myth woven by the NP and reproduced by Kalhana was a well-thought-out strategy to appropriate the past to serve the power-backed "present." Both wrote when Brahmanism was the dominant tradition of Kashmir; being brahmanas both wrote within the Sanskritic and brahmanical tradition, and both belonged to the reformulated Brahmanism forged in the Kashmir milieu over centuries of Brahmanism's struggle to establish hegemony by giving concessions to local circumstances underlined by fusion and fission. Thus, both the authors credited Kashmir having been created, inhabited and sustained by brahmanical and non-brahmanical but brahmanised deities (such as Nāga divinities) and both treat with respect the Buddha, Śiva and Viṣṇu. However, the reference to other groups/cultures, which ran counter to brahmanical ideas and could not be fused with them, is either made casually and with the treatment of "othering" or they were rejected by silence and exclusion.

Although for Kalhana Aryavarta/Madhyadeśa/Ganga Valley—the centre of brahmanical world view—is the imitable model, he, like the author of the NP, projects Kashmir more than the Middle Region of India. Because it is a country with "not a space as large as a grain of sesamum without a Tirtha"; it "may be conquered by the forces of spiritual merits but not by forces of soldiers. Learning, lofty houses, saffron, icy water and grapes – things that even in heaven are difficult to find are common there."[103] The uniqueness of Kashmir is also exhibited in its salubrious climate and harmless flora, fauna and water bodies. What is more, Kalhana "reinforces the notion of the centrality of the Mandala by locating it at the epicentre of a series of concentric circles."[104] Also, Kalhana is at pains to portray Kashmir as an empire and its rulers as king of kings, vanquishing the great rulers of even distant lands and bringing the whole immediate and distant territories under their control. It is in light of this universal wish of Kalhana with Kashmiri kings in control of the entire world that the poet-chronicler puts the following words in the mouth of the people who had assembled to greet Matrgupta—sent by Vikramaditya to rule Kashmir on his behalf—at the time of his inauguration.

> May you rule over this our land, since King Vikramaditya whom we had ourselves asked to protect it, has designated you as one equal to himself. Do not believe, O king, that this country by which at all times [other] countries have been granted, was granted [in your case] by others. As parents are only the [immediate] cause for the production

> of a birth which one obtains by one's own [previous] deeds, thus too are other [kings] for that of a throne in the case of kings. Since [matters] stand thus, you ought, O king, not to lower our and your own dignity by acknowledging someone else as your master.[105]

To be sure, Kalhana's indulgence in myth-making and fantasies is as important for us as his matter-of-fact detail from the beginning of eleventh century. The myths reflect upon the mentality of the time and the existing values and aspirations, which constitute one of the most driving forces that shape history. Myths, exaggerations, judgements, general observations and maxims are an important part of the poet-chronicler's history in poetry. Nevertheless, there is a good deal of information on contacts, inflows and transformations, which is evident from the details given in this book while discussing the post-fifth-century Kashmir.

Being a great centre of learning, Kashmir produced a mass of literature on religion, philosophy, logic, literary theory, grammar, poetry and "translational story literature" (*ślokakathā*), which is of immense importance for locating the position of Kashmir within the "Sanskritic cosmopolis," to borrow the term of Pollock. It shows that Kashmir was not merely an extension of the great cultural centres that sprang up around it; but it also made a significant contribution to their making. For example, the new philosophical-literary aesthetic elaborated by the eleventh-century Kashmiri scholars transformed "Sanskrit literary theory fundamentally and permanently."[106] Similarly, according to Whitney Cox, the 'fervid literary activity' in South India from late eleventh century was largely because of the impact of the learned culture of the Kashmir Valley.[107] Kashmir is also known for making innovations in religious philosophy. This is borne out by the extant religious literature, especially the literature on Buddhism, Śaivism and Vaiṣṇavism produced by Kashmiri scholars generating a fervid flow of literati and religious missionaries back and forth between Kashmir and the neighbouring world. Obrock is more attracted by Sanskrit Kavyas' "daring and audacious experiment in self assertion." So, he suggests: "This is the Kashmir cultural historians should be after, recovering traces of real people, debates and arguments, expressed in polished Sanskrit, yet bound to the lived world of saffron, snow and the mountains beyond."[108]

Language, the Real Mirror

Our discussion on sources would be incomplete if we do not underline the importance of the Kashmiri language (*Koshur*) in constructing the role of circulation and translation in making the history of early Kashmir. The Kashmiri language is largely a loan-oriented language, that is, its word fund is sourced from different languages. It has Dardic basis, showing that the earliest settlers of Kashmir had branched off from the Dardic spoken people who occupied a large mountainous area towards the north and north-western borders of Kashmir. Every second word of the Kashmiri language is of Sanskritic origin, pointing to Kashmir's long encounter with Sanskritic tradition (before it was replaced by Persianate-Islamic tradition) displacing most of the existing vocabulary. Like any other patronage language, Sanskrit (the language of the Gods, to quote the metaphor of Pollock) was not only the language of literature and administration but also the language of two other important beliefs of the time—Buddhism and Jainism. Ultimately it became "an instrument of polity" and "a source of personal charisma" making the power seekers "to participate in the prestige economy of Sanskrit."[109] With all these assets, Sanskrit (like Persian, Urdu and English subsequently) influenced the Kashmiri language through the process of displacement—replacement—enrichment. Yet despite the predominance of Sanskrit vocabulary, the Kashmiri language contains a large number of words derived from many other different linguistic-cultural regions. That is why different scholars have propounded different theories about the origin of Kashmiri language.[110] We believe that if the comparison is extended to cover other languages spoken in the neighbouring regions, it may throw fresh information in this regard.

Being a repository of multicultural word fund, the Kashmiri language not only confirms the archaeological and textual evidence of Kashmir's encounter with different cultural centres of the world, but it also provides novel information on influences not found in any other category of source—written or visual. The Kashmiri language is also emblematic of dynamism of Kashmiri society: it changed with the change of times, especially when the change was backed by power or had utilitarian value. However, the change was neither total nor complete as is shown by the retention of an equally good number of oldest vocabulary as well as the nativisation of Sanskrit and other non-Kashmiri words. In spite of never enjoying political patronage instead being constantly discouraged by denigrating it as the language of uncouth,[111] the Kashmiri language continued to be the language of the masses, the mother tongue of Kashmir, showing the resilience of Kashmiri society as well as allowing us to agree with Jonathan Hay that "imperially marginal can be locally dominant."[112] It is, therefore, not surprising that the most distinctive feature of the Kashmiri language, like any other mother tongue, is that while all other categories of sources are translational, predetermined and necessarily selective, the lexicon of the Kashmiri language—vocabulary, metaphors, sayings, place names, surnames and personal names—captures the whole gamut of the society and that too in its fullness and in true colours, recording the facts as they are leaving nothing out, not even what the historians of the twenty-first century naively consider unworthy for attention though they are no less important than the "capital" facts. Indeed, the only source that cannot disappoint any historian of Kashmir, belonging to any sub-specialisation, or looking for answers to complex issues, is the lexicon of the Kashmiri language.

All said and done, large and sometimes crippling gaps in our information made a detailed, coherent and well-ordered narrative of events extremely difficult. Clearly, alongside the aforementioned sources, no satisfactory history on the subject under study is possible without more archaeological discoveries, and drawing on philology, toponym (place names), surnames, physiognomy and the cultural remains of the past. We have made a modest beginning in this direction. But much needs to be done, which is possible only through a collaborative effort by the scholars belonging to different related disciplines and geographies. Therefore, what follows is only a skeleton, a silhouette of an apparently eventful history, perhaps never to be fully brought to light except entering into a continuous dialogue with the past "preserved in half-effaced outlines of history"[113] handed down to us and that too selectively.

Figure 1.1 Tile with composite mythical animals.

Hoinar (Lidder Valley)
(SPS Museum, Srinagar)

Figure 1.2 Intertwined Lions, Stone.

Qateh-Yazgrad, Iran
(After Bhan, 1987)

Notes

1 Febvre (1929), 73; quoted by Kaufmann *et al.* (2015), 6–7.
2 Hobsbawm (2008), 365.
3 Sachsenmaier (2007), 469.
4 For a useful recent survey of the field, see Osterhammel (2011), 93–112; Bentley (2011); also see Sachsenmaier, 465–489; Bayly *et al.* (2006), 1441–1464; Werner and Zimmermann (2006), 30–50; Gould (2007), 764–786; Seigel (2004), 431–446; Subrahmanyam (1997), 735–762; Tignor *et al.* (2011).
5 See Dirlik (2003), 91–133; Sachsenmaier, 469. On the basis of his in-depth study of premodern South Asia, Sheldon Pollock also questions the already-perfected

formations ascribed to "civilizations" and "nations" observing that "Both theories of civilizations and theories of nations typically ignore complexity, heterogeneity, and historical process – precisely what the materials from premodern South Asia compel us to acknowledge." Pollock (2006), 34–35.

6 Subrahmanyam (2001).

7 Hobsbawm, 365; Ludden (1994), 1–23.

8 Winetrout (1975), 21.

9 The observations written within quotes are those of David Ludden. For details, see Ludden (1994), 1–23.

10 Hobsbawm, 357.

11 Amin (2004), 33–44.

12 Pollock (2006), 538–39.

13 Ludden, 1–23.

14 Flood (2009), 265.

15 In proposing a periodisation of world history, Jerry Bentley identifies three main kinds of processes, namely, mass migration, empire building and long-distance trade as having had "significant repercussions across the boundary lines of societies and cultural regions" Bentley (1996), 752, 756. For an excellent summation of these developments in South Asia, see Ludden.

16 Flood, 5.

17 In this way there is much substance in the opinion of the most of the practitioners of international history who do not see it a new master narrative; instead they regard it an "additional stratum in the 'onion model' between local, regional and national history on the one hand and global on the other: transnational history defies this logic of layers and can directly connect the local to the supranational or transcontinental" Patel (2010), 2.

18 Subrahmanyam (1997).

19 Lepenies (2003).

20 Werner and Zimmermann (2003), 7–36.

21 Polybius remarked,

> He who believes that by studying isolated histories he can acquire a just view of history as a whole is, as it seems to me, much in the case of one who, after having looked at the dissevered limbs of an animal once alive and beautiful, fancies he has been as good as an eyewitness of the creature itself in all its action and grace.
>
> Durrant, 615

22 Ibn Khaldun (1978), 24–25.

23 Dean and Leibsohn (2003), 8.

24 Durrant and Durrant (1965).

25 Stern (1972), 61.

26 Winetrout, 20.

27 Braudel (1983), 14; quoted by Aymard and Mukhia (1988), 2.

28 For details, see Sachsenmaier; Osterhammel; Bentley (2011); Kaufmann *et al.*

29 Sachsenmaier, 470–72.

30 Ludden, 1.

31 We don't use "hybridity" in the colonialist context of nineteenth century, but from the perspective of postcolonial studies where hybridity refers less to biology and organic processes than to political and cultural events in which conquests and colonisation, and resistance and subversion play significant roles. Young (1995); Papastergiadis (1997), 257–81; Werner and Zimmermann (2003).

32 See Stein (1979), I: 30, 132; Slaje (2012), 10–11; Thaper (1968), 60–61; Basham (1961), 57; Huntington (1985), 353.
33 Clifford (1997), 3.
34 Slaje (2012), 10–11.
35 Al-Biruni (1993), I: 206.
36 Between 1014 and 1021, Mahmud of Ghazni made two attempts to conquer Kashmir, but he failed both the times owing to the strong fortress of Loharkot and bad weather. Gardizi (1928), 73–79.
37 Kalhana, VII: 188, 1149; VIII: 885–87, 919–23, 2264.
38 See Chapter IV.
39 Al-Biruni, I: I, 22.
40 Kalhana, IV: 631–32; VIII: 2227 sqq; Witzel (2008), 68–70.
41 Witzel (2008), 68.
42 Witzel (2008), 69.
43 Witzel (2008), 69.
44 Al-Biruni, II: 181. Also, see Stein (1979), II: 359–60 n. 46.
45 See Chapters 3 and 4 of this book.
46 See Stein (1979), II: 291–292.
47 Abul Fazl (1869), 350.
48 Stein (1979), II: 401.
49 Stein (1979), II: 358.
50 For details, see Dowson (1850), 372–385.
51 *Ou-k'ong*, 356; quoted by Stein (1979), II: 357–58.
52 Wani (2002); idem (2013); Jan (2006); Wani (2015).
53 Kaul (2018), 106–7.
54 Kaul (2018), 106.
55 Ghosh (2011), 6–7.
56 Vohra (1995), 419–29.
57 For details, see Luczanits (2005), 74; Goepper (1990); Flood, 65–66.
58 Kaul (2018), 105.
59 Pollock (2006), 265.
60 Roy (2003), 56.
61 Obrock (2020), 161, 164.
62 Allchin and Allchin (1981), 116; also, see Pal (1989). For details, see the following chapters of this book.
63 Kaul (2018), 126.
64 Flood, 2.
65 Ashplant and Smyth (2001), 5.
66 Spiegel (1997), 196.
67 The *production* includes its authorship (individual or collective), its mode of publication (i.e., of bringing before people), and its contemporary historical and cultural context. The systems of *signification* include the formal conventions within which the artefact was produced (such as literary and linguistic structuring, conventions and tropes of the texts, style of the painting and the like). The *reception* of the artefact involves studying how it was received and 'read' by contemporaries and of the various meanings attached to it later in changing historical times by creative adaptation and cultural translation. LaCapra (1985), 127–29; Berk (1997), 195–97; Bennett (1983), 214–27; Ashplant and Smyth, 5–6.
68 Greenblatt (1990), 151.
69 Biersack (1989), 74–75; Geertz (1975), 412–53; Ashplant and Smyth, 33.
70 Flood, 11–12.

71 For different views, see Fisher (1989b), 1–16; Bhan (1986); Bandey (1992); Wani (2002), 167–75.
72 Kak (1933), 110.
73 Brown (1959), 151.
74 Bhan (1987), 77; also, see idem, (2010), 13.
75 Bhan (2010), 23.
76 Coomaraswamy (1965), 143.
77 Cunningham (1848), 241–327.
78 Fisher (1989a), 40.
79 For details, see Pal (1989).
80 Pal (1989a), vi.
81 Pal (1989). The long tunic or coat and trousers are common for both men and women; and when the woman is shown wearing a sari, she is still provided with a tailored blouse.
82 Yatoo (2011), 153.
83 Sharma (1970), 115.
84 Flood, 11–12.
85 Kaufmann *et al.*, 18.
86 Pollock (1993), 285.
87 *Nīlamata Purāna*, 872–73.
88 Ibid, 223–224, 231, 388–421, 575–581, 683–692, 870–871.
89 Ibid, 709–13.
90 Kalhana, I: 312–316, 339–345
91 See Sharma (2008), 123–45.
92 Inden (2000), 78.
93 Slaje (2012); Sharma (2008), 123–45.
94 Inden (2000), 54.
95 *Nīlamata Purāna*, 523 sqq.
96 Inden (2000), Introduction, 26.
97 Ibid.
98 Ibid.
99 Ibid, 27.
100 Ibid, 54.
101 Ibid, 54; idem (2008), 546.
102 Roy (2003), 53.
103 Kalhana, I: 38–42.
104 Roy (2003), 55.
105 Kalhana, III: 242–245.
106 Pollock (2006), 105–06.
107 Cox (2016), 177.
108 Obrock (2020), 164.
109 Pollock (2006), 56–59, 72–73.
110 See Chapter III of this book.
111 Kalhana, V: 397, 398.
112 Hay (1999), 7.
113 This term was used by Helmuth von Moltke (1800–1891), a Danish-Prussian military strategist, traveller and historian, and approvingly quoted by Stein in the Introduction of his *Illustrated Rājataraṅgiṇī*. Obrock (2013), 21.

2

A MOSAIC OF PLURAL SOURCES

Immigrations, Interactions and the Cultural Foundations of Kashmir

> Interest in human origins so transcended nationalistic attitudes that these (interdisciplinary) teams (working on prehistory) are also now international in outlook and composition and work in closest collaboration.[1]
>
> —(JS Desmond Clark)

Inflows, Contacts and the Making of Palaeolithic and Neolithic Cultures

The common ancestry thesis of mankind constitutes the first significant evidence towards formulating a unitary view of history. It is almost unanimously agreed by the scientists that the Anatomically Modern Man (AMM) evolved out of a series of early human species; and except for the *neanderthalensis*, the early "true" human species as well as the AMM (Homo sapiens) first emerged in Africa and then spread to different parts of the world.[2]

Homo habilis is probably the first "true" human species. He is dated to 2.5 million years BP. After Africa the fossils of *Homo habilis* have been found in China, Spain, Georgia (Caucasus) and Java (Indonesia). All are of almost similar date, 1.8 million or 1.9 million years old. In the immediate neighbourhood of Kashmir, Pakistan too bears traces of the presence of *Homo habilis* as his tools have been found at Riwat[3] in the Soan Valley of the Potwar plateau (western Punjab, Pakistan). These Soan tools go back to over two million years.[4] Similar tools located in Himachal Pradesh have been assigned to almost similar date.[5]

Given the fact that *Homo habilis* was very much present in the immediate west and south-east borderlands of Kashmir, with which Kashmir always maintained intimate relations because of geographical proximity, the presence of this human species in Kashmir too could be a reasonable inference even if one may not have found any evidence in this regard. But fortunately, thanks to the untiring efforts of the archaeologists, the presence of *Homo habilis* in Kashmir as early as two million years BP has been reasonably

DOI: 10.4324/9781003367697-2

established. As is also true of its immediate neighbourhoods, the hominid remains of *Homo habilis* have not been found in Kashmir. What has, however, been certainly discovered is his stone artefacts, which he made by using block-on-block and stone hammer methods. The eminent archaeologist of India, HD Sankalia and his team discovered for the first time in 1969 two lower Palaeolithic tools in the Liddar Valley (Pahalgam). One was a massive flake measuring 25.7 × 16.5 × 6 cm and the other, a roughly pear-shaped crude hand axe measuring 14.5 × 9.6 × 6.5 cm. Technologically, it is Abbevillian. According to Sankalia, these tools are the earliest palaeoliths in Asia; and he attributed them to the first interglacial period when environmentally this period of glaciation was the best suitable period for man's habitation.[6] The Palaeolithic tools of *Homo habilis* have also been found by another archaeologist, Prof. RV Joshi and his team in the river valleys of the Lidder, Sind and the Rembiara.[7]

Homo erectus is about two million years old. The presence of *Homo erectus* is fairly widespread. The fossils of *Homo erectus* have been found in China and Java. They are datable to 700,000 years BP. The chopper-type tools of *Homo erectus* have also been found in the neighbourhood of Kashmir, namely, in the Soan Valley across the Jhelum in Pakistan[8] and Beas, Banganga and other valleys of Himachal Pradesh.[9] These tools have been dated to over one million years BP,[10] that is, older than their presence in China and Java. Besides the chopping tools, an Acheulean hand axe has been found in the Soan Valley, which appeared around 700,000 to 500,000 years BP.[11] In recent years Acheulean sites have also been discovered in the sub-Himalayan tract in the Punjab.[12]

At different places of Kashmir, namely, Pahalgam (Liddar Valley), Prang and Wazwan (Sindh Valley), Balapur (Shopian) and from the high reaches of Sukhnag (to the east of the Pir Panjal range), many early Palaeolithic tool types have been found. They are an Abbevillian hand axe and a few choppers.[13] Aijaz Bandey and his team from Kashmir University also found some early Palaeolithic tools at Manasbal. More importantly, they found some caves which formed the habitation places of Palaeolithic man.[14]

Neanderthal man evolved in Europe out of *Homo erectus* and flourished within the period 230,000 to 30,000 years BP. Neanderthal man has also been located in West Asia and further eastward at a date of 50,000 years BP and in Central Asia and Northern China with unassigned dates. In the neighbourhood of Kashmir, the Levallois–Mousterian tools have been found at Darra-e-Kur (50,000 years BP) and Kara Kamar (30,000 years BP) in Afghanistan, and at Sanghao Cave in Pakistan.[15]

Aijaz Bandey found many bifacial cleavers, hand axes, pointed tools and scrapers of Middle Acheulean technique on the gentle mountain slope overlooking the Manasbal lake. He also discovered an evolved Acheulean hand axe belonging to the Middle Palaeolithic period at Bomai near the Wular Lake.[16] Although Bandey did not find any Mousterian cores at Manasbal,

Paterson and others collected 'thin flakes' fabricated in Levallois technique from Somber and alluvial terraces on the bank of the Jhelum.[17] It is, therefore, reasonable to conclude that in Kashmir, as elsewhere, it was Neanderthal man who was the maker of this culture.

The AMM originated in Africa about 115,000 years BP and from there spread throughout the globe. The skeletal remains of modern human have been found in various parts of the world besides Africa. He appeared in West Asia around 100,000 years BP; in Australia about 60,000 years BP and in Sri Lanka around 34,000 years BP. In the immediate neighbourhood of Kashmir, Middle Palaeolithic tools (including flake blades) have been found in the Soan Valley and Rohri Hills in Pakistan. These tools are datable to 60,000 to 20,000 years BP.[18] As the Middle Palaeolithic tools were made by modern humans, it is easy to infer that he was present in the immediate neighbourhood of Kashmir not later than 20,000 years BP.

The existence of modern humans in Kashmir around 18,000 years BP is fairly attested to by the Upper Palaeolithic tools found at various places in the valley. The most prominent of these places is Sombur (near Pampore) where more than a hundred artefacts have been found testifying to the existence of distinct blade and burin industry.[19]

The principal tool types found there are burins, points and borers. These tools are datable to 18000 BP. Upper Palaeolithic tools have also been found at many other places, namely, Kulladur, Bhatta Chak, Tapriballa and Huin in Baramulla district, and at Khan Sahib and Habah Shah Sahib in Budgam district.[20] The tools discovered at these places are represented by backed knives, elongated parallel-sided double scrapers, waisted tools, grinders and pounders.

A no less significant finding of the period is the rock engraving, the first and the last of this kind so far found in Kashmir. Discovered at Bomai in north Kashmir by Aijaz Bandey, the rock engraving depicts a sketchy scene of chase and game.[21] It is most probable that the rock art people of Kashmir were immigrants from Chilas, which, because of the presence of huge number of rock carvings, is called the place of "Rock Art people."[22] Swat, with which Kashmir too had very close relations throughout the history, was also famous for rock art.[23]

To sum up, right from the early Palaeolithic times, Kashmir was intimately connected with its immediate borderlands and through them with the distant world. Certainly, the early man came to Kashmir from its immediate neighbourhoods, though these neighbours were not more than entrepots receiving and passing on people and cultural goods.

Neolithic Revolution

Notwithstanding the presence of widespread upper Palaeolithic in Kashmir, the Mesolithic industry is intriguingly missing there. However around 3149

BC, we come across the beginning of Neolithic culture which went on growing with the passage of time. To be sure, the Neolithic culture is the first fully known culture of Kashmir. Having begun around 3149 BCE, it continued for about 1,500 years. It is, therefore, not surprising that so far four dozen Neolithic sites spreading over different nooks of Kashmir have been found,[24] albeit research in archaeological field in general and exploration of archaeological sites in particular have been by any standard abysmally nominal in Jammu and Kashmir. Out of these four dozen Neolithic sites, systematic excavations on a large scale have, however, been conducted only at two sites, namely, Burzahom and Gufkral followed by a limited excavation of Kanispur and Qasim Bagh.

Burzahom

Situated on a flat-topped plateau,[25] the world famous Burzahom site revealed the changing character of the Neolithic culture due to immigrations and contacts with the neighbouring cultures. It is precisely for this reason that the archaeologists have divided the Burzahom Neolithic culture into different phases such as Aceramic Neolithic, Ceramic Neolithic-A and Ceramic Neolithic-B.

Aceramic Neolithic

Aceramic Burzahom is represented by dwelling pits and bone and stone tools. The dwelling pits dug out in the loess deposits were both circular and rectangular. The diameter and depth of the dwellings were not uniform. The largest circular and rectangular pits and pit chambers measured 2.74 m (top) × 4.57 m (base) × 3.95 m (depth) and 6.40 m (top) × 7.0 m (base) × 1.50 (depth), respectively.[26] The other related finds are post holes, hearths, storage pits and animal bones. The stone implements are represented by axes, drills, picks, points, pestles, pounders, querns and mace heads. Of the bone tools, mention may be made of points, needles, harpoons and scrapers.[27]

Ceramic Neolithic-A

Besides the continuities of Aceramic Neolithic, namely, dwelling pits, stone and bone implements and animal bones, the Ceramic Neolithic-A is marked by the presence of domestication of agriculture and making of handmade pottery. The remains of wheat, barley, lentil, peach, walnut and apricot are important discoveries of the period. Pea was introduced by the end of this period.[28]

The handmade ware types are coarse grey ware, coarse dull red ware, black burnished ware and fine grey ware. The pottery shapes encountered are jar, bowl, vase and dish-on-stand with mat impressions on base and irregular brush marks.[29]

Ceramic Neolithic-B

The Ceramic Neolithic-B is characterised by many far-reaching developments. These include the construction of aboveground structures survived by a good number of plastered mud floors with post holes for erecting a wooden superstructure.[30] Besides the continuity of the earlier pottery types, the distinctive pottery of this phase is wheel-made red ware and gritty red ware with shades of bright red and light grey. The pottery shapes include long-necked jar, round cup, deep bowl, dish-on-stand, bowl with or without stand, bowl hemispherical or deep, with and without a ring base, dish-on-stand with triangular perforation and parallel grooves on the body, funnel mouth vessel and globular pot. A more distinctive pottery type of the phase is a vase with flaring rim and base.[31] Mat impression in the base is the chief characteristic.[32] An important discovery at Burzahom belonging either to the end of this phase or to the beginning of the Megalithic Period is one large globular pot carrying on its surface, the painting in black of a long and curved horned head of an animal.[33] Another significant find of the same period at Burzahom is a wheel-thrown red ware pot containing 950 beads fashioned out of agate and carnelian with excellent workmanship.

About the tools three developments are noticeable. Their number has increased, they are better finished and some new tools, especially rectangular harvesters, have been added to the existing kit of stone and bone implements.[34] With regard to crops, alongside the continuity of earlier crops such as wheat, barley, lentil, pea, peach, walnut and apricot, three important additions are rice, grapes and almond, which were introduced by the end of the period.[35]

A significant find of the period is two stone slabs with engravings. One slab depicts a hunting scene.[36] The upper portion of the slab has the engraving of two suns and a dog. The lower register portrays a stag (*hangul*) being attacked from rear as well as front. One person attacks him from behind with a spear, and the other (his counterpart) from the front with an arrow. The engraving on the other slab, though incomplete, depicts a hut and the hind portion of an animal.

The excavations have also revealed human and animal burials for the first time in our history.[37] The distinctive features of human burials are as follows: The graves were circular shaped pits measuring 1.17 m at the top and 2.03 m at the base. They were found within the habitation area, mostly underlying the floors of the houses at a depth of 1.20 to 2.90 m. Burials were both primary and secondary. Yet primary burials were more common.

Out of seven burials, only two were secondary. The burials had generally a north-east to south-west or south-east to north-west orientation. The bodies were kept in different positions: flexed/foetal/crouching/reclining. The most intriguing is the posture of a lady who, in a crouching position, has her arms raised up to the head and the palms covering the face.[38] She is wearing a neck ornament of fine carnelian barrel-shaped beads. The bones were painted with red ochre. The graves contained grave goods, which included animal bones, pots and ornaments.[39]

Not only humans but animals were also ceremonially buried.[40] Eleven animal burials have been found in the habitation area. However only two belong to this phase and nine belong to the subsequent period, showing that the practice assumed more currency with the passage of time. Like humans, both flexed and fractional burials were performed in regard to animals too. Flexed burial is of a dog and parts of a stag and dogs together. During the subsequent period (megalithic phase), the burial of fragmentary bones of dogs, sheep, goats and antler has been found. Besides independent animal burials, animal bones were also buried with human beings pointing to the rite of food offerings to the dead.

Animals were generally buried in regularly dug-out grave pits within the habitation area as was done in the case of human burials. The animals found buried are dog, sheep, goat, ibex and wolf.

Another significant find of the time is a skull showing 11 trepanning marks on the parietal bone between bregma and lambada.[41] The finds of many copper objects belonging to the last phase of the Neolithic period unmistakably indicate Kashmir's Chalcolithic contacts with Harappan civilisation. This contact is further substantiated by the depiction of a horned animal on a painted pot and carnelian beads at Burzahom, and the emmer wheat mingled with millet at Kanispur.

Gufkral

Like Burzahom, the Gufkral site is also situated on a *karewa*. The excavators have also sub-divided the cultural deposits of the Neolithic period into three phases classified as Aceramic Neolithic, Ceramic Neolithic-A and Ceramic Neolithic-B.[42]

Aceramic Neolithic

On the structural side, the aceramic Gufkral presents similarity as well as dissimilarity with aceramic Burzahom. While at Burzahom we find only dwelling pits and pit chambers at this stage, Gufkral revealed both subterranean houses and aboveground houses. So far as earth houses are concerned, initially only circular dwelling pits were constructed. It was in the subsequent occupation that rectangular pits were made. However, alongside the subterranean houses, a number of mud platforms with post holes have been encountered. These mud platforms had a coat of red ochre and hard kankar lime. Over the floor were found pebble hearths and pit hearths. The post-holes suggest thatched wooden roofing arrangements over platforms. Significantly, these mud platforms were under constant occupation generation after generation as at least 15 layers of repairs and re-plastering were noticed.[43]

Like Burzahom, both stone and bone tools have been found, though there were more of the latter. Of stone tools, mention is made of celts, ring stones, adzes, slicers, scrappers, points, pestles and pounders. The 42 bone tools found at the site comprise needles, harpoons, awls, points, scrapers, arrow heads and barrel-shaped beads.[44]

A no less significant finding of this period is the discovery of animal bones and plant remains. The animal bones retrieved from the site are of wild goat, wild cattle, red deer, wolf, Himalayan ibex and bear. The grains identified were wheat, barley and lentil.[45]

Ceramic Neolithic-A

Alongside the continuities of the aceramic period, namely, dwelling pits, dwelling platforms with postholes, stone and bone tools and grains of wheat, barley and lentils, the Ceramic Neolithic-A period is characterised by the appearance of handmade pottery, potter's kiln, circular mud structure, semi-precious stones and bones of domesticated sheep, cattle and dog.[46] The pottery found is mostly grey with a small quantity of dull rough red ware; and the main shapes were big jars, bowls, basins and dish-on-stand with mat impression on the bases, pinched designs and reed impressions on both exterior and interior of the pots.[47]

Ceramic Neolithic-B

The major developments of the period are a great spurt in structural activity represented by the earlier circular pit dwellings and storage pits with post holes; circular mud walls, which appeared in the Early Neolithic period, and the newly emerged mud and rubble walls.[48] In addition to the continuity of the earlier grey ware and dull rough red ware, the new introductions to pottery are burnished grey ware, burnished black ware, wheel made black burnished ware and red gritty ware.[49] In pottery shapes the additions are long-necked jars, channel spouted vessel and dish-on-stand with triangular perforated designs. In the tool kit of the time, the new entries comprise double-holed harvesters and spindle whorls, terracotta bangles, carnelian beads, cowrie shells, pot shards with graffiti marks, copper objects and a hairpin with a flattened coiled head.[50] As far as the animal remains are concerned, the new appearances are pig, fish, hedgehog, rodents and beaver. Evidently pig was among the domestic animals of the period. An important development in cereal cultivation was the introduction of millet and rice. At the end of this period, millet was seen mingled with rice. At the same time Chalcolithic contacts developed between Kashmir and the Harappan civilisation as is indicated by the finds of many metal objects made of copper.

Kanispur

Like Burzahom and Gufkral, Kanispur represents an evolutionary Neolithic culture from aceramic to ceramic cultures.[51] Though its lowest stratum is bereft of any ceramic industry, it is, nevertheless, marked by a ground stone industry represented by a polished stone celt. The aceramic phase was followed by successive ceramic phases. According to Mani, the Neolithic people of Kanispur initially inhabited the flat top of the *karewa/wuder*, but subsequently, with demographic growth, the people also occupied the slopes especially during the late ceramic Neolithic phase.

In the style of other early Neolithians of Kashmir, the early Neolithic people of Kanispur lived in subterranean houses as is evidenced by a circular pit cut through the earlier levels of the ceramic Neolithic. It was narrower at the top opening and broader at the base with a diameter of 2.43 m. Subsequently, the people began to build aboveground houses as, like Gufkral, successive floor levels with post holes were noticed including a rectangular hearth and Neolithic pottery. The people made use of bone and stone tools. Five bone points and six polished stone celts were found during the ceramic phase.

The ceramic industry consisted of both hand-made and wheel-thrown pottery. Fine grey ware of medium or thick fabric, coarse grey ware, red ware, dull red ware and black wares of both plain and burnished varieties characterised the pottery of the period along with mat impressions on the bases of pots, reed impressions on their surfaces, pinched designs, oblique decorations, deep incised lines, notchings and semi-perforated decorations. The significant pottery shapes included jars, vases, long-necked vases, bowls and dishes-on-stand.[52]

There is also evidence of a mix of hunting-gathering and domesticated economy as besides the bones of animals and birds as well as an antler, Kanispur has also revealed the cultivation of emmer wheat (*Triticum dicoccum)* and barley during the first ceramic levels. According to Mani, the technology of emmer wheat cultivation seems to have been transferred to Kashmir from Middle East through Central Asia via Iran. Interestingly, emmer wheat has been found at Kunal in district Hissar (Haryana) mingled with barley in the same manner as it is found in Kashmir.[53]

The most important evidence thrown up by Kanispur, however, is that it has pushed back the beginnings of the Neolithic period in Kashmir by more than 200 years from what is popularly believed by archaeologists on the evidence of Burzahom and Gufkral. A calibrated C-14 date on one charcoal sample from Kanispur is 3361 BCE to 2937 BCE (average being 3149 BCE).[54]

The descending order of radiocarbon evidence from Kanispur to Gufkral through Burzahom coupled with the direction of the source of the Kashmir Neolithic culture suggests that the earliest Neolithic settlers from Central

Asia or north-west India occupied the western lands of Kashmir Valley like Kanispur, and then they gradually moved to central Kashmir represented by Burzahom followed by their further movement towards the south-eastern part of Kashmir around Gufkral. Thus, while the evidence of their presence at Kanispur dates back no later than 3149 BCE, the age of the earliest levels of Burzahom and Gufkral is around 3000 BCE and 2990 BCE, respectively.[55]

Qasim Bagh

Qasim Bagh Neolithic site is situated on a flat *wuder* (*karewa*) near Hygam village in district Baramulla. The site was first identified during transect-based survey by Mumtaz Yatoo in 2012 during his PhD programme at the University of Leicester, UK. The site is being further probed by Mumtaz Yatoo under the project 'Neolithic Kashmir' with the assistance of Prof. Alison Betts, University of Sydney, Australia. It has revealed a number of large conical pits, coarse grey ware, fine grey and black ware and fine buff ware. Among the stone tools celts, sling balls, pounders and stone bowls were found. Furthermore, a spindle whorl and a few terracotta figurines were also collected from the surface of the site.[56]

Locating the Neolithic Culture of Kashmir: The Parallel Universes of Kashmir Neolithic and the Neolithic Cultures of the Neighbouring World

Views of Modern Scholars

How did the Neolithic culture come into existence in Kashmir? Was it the result of the endogenous evolutionary developments, or did it come into existence mainly because of exogenous influences? Prof. HD Sankalia believes that the people of Neolithic Kashmir were not natives; they had come from outside. He reasons out his argument saying that the "gradual local development is not hitherto known nor are their antecedents known."[57] TN Khazanchi also supports the contention of Sankalia. According to him, the Neolithic people of Kashmir came from Central Asia, particularly from north and central China. His theory is based on some affinities between the Neolithic culture of Kashmir and the Neolithic cultures of north and central China, Shilka Valley and some Neolithic sites in the eastern Siberia.[58] WA Fairservis and KN Dikshit opine that the Neolithic culture of Kashmir is either a part or an extension of East Asian culture.[59] Fairservis finds direct analogies of textured (combed) pottery, rectangular knives, polished stone celts of ovid or quadrangular type and mace heads in southern Siberia, Mongolia, Manchuria and northern China. He also finds parallels of dog-eating, flexed burials and pole houses in eastern and northern China.[60] Stacul is struck by the affinities of Neolithic Kashmir with aspects of the Neolithic of Inner Asia, especially with some finds encountered in Chinese Neolithic sites. No wonder, in 1993, he wrote an article under the rubric "Neolithic Inner Asian Traditions in Northern Indo-Pakistani Valleys."[61] Fuller in his later synthesis calls the Neolithic cultural complex of northern valleys of the subcontinent as "East Asian Horizon" in South Asia. His thesis is based on the mid-fourth millennium BP introduction of Chinese sickle blades, East Asian stone fruits and rice grains morphologically similar to *japonica* types in the Kashmir and Swat Valleys.[62] Basing his argument on these strong archaeological linkages, Parpola even suggested that the inhabitants of Kashmir and Swat Neolithic may have been speakers of a Sino-Tibetan language.[63]

Plural Sources

While agreeing with the view that the Neolithic culture of Kashmir evolved largely because of exogenous influences, we believe that its sources were more plural than adumbrated by the aforementioned scholars. Certainly, the Neolithic culture of Kashmir was not only an extension of east Asian and Central Asian cultures but it was, as we shall see in following pages, drawn from a multitude of cultural centres. It is, therefore, no exaggeration to say that the Neolithic culture of Kashmir is a mini-global cultural site. The ingredients of this cultural formation, however, did not transmit to Kashmir directly from its original sources; instead, they passed on to Kashmir through its immediate borderlands extending from Gilgit-Baltistan through Chilas and Swat Kohistan to the Punjab plains. Situated as these secondary sources were on the borders of East Asia, Central Asia, West Asia and India, they transmitted to Kashmir a cosmopolitan culture drawn from great centres of the time. It is, therefore, not surprising that while, on the one hand, the scholars refer to the Neolithic cultural complex of the northern valleys of the Subcontinent as an extension of Neolithic of Inner Asia or they prefer to call it "East Asian Horizon in South Asia," this culture is also commonly called as the Northern Neolithic[64] or the Kashmir-Swat Neolithic.[65]

Immigrations, Connections and the Making of Early Neolithic

To substantiate the argument that the Neolithic culture of Kashmir is largely a consequence of cultural flows from a variety of proximate and distant neighbourhoods through immigrations and contacts, it is necessary to answer the following questions:

1) What is the antiquity of the pre-Neolithic cultures in Kashmir?
2) Do these cultures follow a continuous sequence?

3) How far do the aspects of the Neolithic culture of Kashmir resemble with the Neolithic cultures of its immediate and distant neighbourhoods?

Archaeology has no doubt shown a remote antiquity of the appearance of humans in Kashmir. It is also true that there was a widespread Upper Palaeolithic culture in Kashmir around 16000 BCE. But what is problematic is that between 16000 BCE and 3149 BCE (when beginnings of Neolithism appeared in Kashmir), there is an archaeological vacuum in Kashmir. Continuity breaks after the Upper Palaeolithic period. There are no finds of Mesolithic or proto-Neolithic period. The Neolithic sites do not show evolutionary changes through time before the Neolithisation of the culture. None of the sites has yielded microliths. The absence of a stone blade industry is significant: there is something abrupt and intrusive at the sites. Although the presence of aceramic phase at Kanispur, Burzahom and Gufkral points to autochthonous character of the Neolithic culture, one is immediately forced to withdraw from making this assumption as the antiquity of this phase is too late to be imagined from a culture which had such a well-developed Upper Palaeolithic around 16000 BCE, and in whose neighbourhood Neolithism had begun not later than seventh millennium BCE—the neighbourhood whose Upper Palaeolithic culture was contemporaneous with the Upper Palaeolithic of Kashmir.[66]

How to explain the archaeological vacuum of Kashmir between 16000 BCE and 3149 BCE or what accounted for the abrupt beginning of Neolithism in the valley? Why despite the presence of sequential Palaeolithic cultures, Mesolithic culture is missing and the roots of the Neolithic culture of Kashmir have to be searched elsewhere? For an answer to these mutually interrelated questions, we have to turn to the palaeoclimatologists and pay attention to what they say about climatic changes in Kashmir around 9000 BP. According to the recently conducted palaeoclimatic researches, around 9000 BP, the climate of Kashmir underwent a significant change underlined by severe cold and heavy rains.[67] These climatic severities seem to have caused a heavy toll of life forcing the people to leave the land and seek refuge in neighbouring regions. Such cold conditions were also perhaps responsible for the extinction of such animals like elephants or horses whose fossil remains have been obtained from the *karewa* beds. The weather conditions, however, improved around 5200 BP as is shown by the replacement of conifers by the broad leaved elements showing warm climatic conditions.[68] With the improvement of weather, the history of human settlements started afresh in Kashmir. And this time it was the settlement of Neolithic people who immigrated to Kashmir from the neighbouring lands situated immediately on its northern and western borders—the areas with which Kashmir had had long intimate relations, and which were comparatively better placed to interact with bigger civilisations, namely, Chinese, Central Asian, Mesopotamian, Iranian and early Harappan.

Affinities Between the Early Neolithic of Kashmir and the Neolithic Cultures of Neighbouring World

It can genuinely be asked: on what basis do we say that culturally Kashmir is a mini globe; and how to justify that the global cultures transmitted to Kashmir through its immediate borderlands via immigrations, settlements and contacts? Our assertion is based on two fundamental factors: first, there is a close affinity between the Neolithic culture of Kashmir and the Neolithic cultures of distant and immediate neighbourhoods of Kashmir; second, the antiquity of these cultures is much older than that of Kashmir, the details of which are given as under.

Aceramic Neolithic

The earliest phase of the Kashmir Neolithic was aceramic, which began around ca. 3149 BCE. In this respect Kashmir is not an exception. The valley was surrounded by a number of sites which had passed through the aceramic Neolithic phase long before Kashmir started with it. The important sites of this category are Kile Gul Muhammad I, Mehargarh I, Gumla I and Baleli mound.[69] The pre-ceramic phases of Mehargarh, Kile Gul Muhammad and Gumla are dated seventh millennium BCE, 4980–3760 BCE and pre-2940 BCE, respectively.[70] It seems that aceramic Neolithic people of Kashmir came from some nearby aceramic Neolithic sites like Gumla which continued to be aceramic till late times.[71] Certainly, the aceramic Neolithic antiquity of Kashmir may go slightly beyond 3149 BCE if a site with aceramic Neolithic assemblage is discovered in the immediate north or west of Kashmir. After all, the immigrants from the borderlands, situated on the north and west of Kashmir, would have preferred nearer *Karewas* rather than the ones like Kanispur, which was not so close to the borders. Burzahom and Gufkral settlers were among the relatively later immigrants drawn from aceramic Neolithic sites situated in the valleys of the Himalayas or located on the Potwar Plateau.

Dwelling Pits

Another important feature of the aceramic and ceramic I of Neolithism of Kashmir is dwelling pits. Dwelling pits have been found in Russia, Ukraine, China, Japan and West Asia much before we encounter them in Kashmir and its borderlands. In Russia, pit dwellings occur from the Palaeolithic times. At least about a dozen sites have been discovered there with a characteristic trait of pit dwelling.[72] In China dwelling pits with storage pits have been found at Lung-ma around the lake Changerh, Ching-ping, Yang-shao-T'sun in Honan, His and Yin-T'sun in Shansi, Pan-po-T'sun in Shenis and Ma-chia Yao in Kansu province, Pai-Shah-Cheng and Huangho.[73] Dwelling pits are also found in the Lung Shan culture extending from Hopeito

Cheki-ang to Honan.[74] In Japan many dwelling pits have been found at various prehistoric sites from the early Jomon period to the final Jomon period.[75] Pit dwellings have also been found at many Neolithic sites in West Asia, namely, Beidha (Levant),[76] Ramad (Levant),[77] M'Lefaat (Iraq),[78] Tape Asiab (Iran)[79] and Tape Sarab (Iran).[80]

Archaeology has discovered many sites close to the borders of Kashmir with dwelling pits also called 'earth houses' or subterranean houses. The nearest parallel of Kashmir Neolithic dwelling pits is at Sarai Khola, the settlement situated about three kilometre south-west of the early historic city of Taxila. The site is located on the Potwar plateau, which is situated close to the western borders of Kashmir. The excavations have revealed the presence of several pit dwellings during Neolithic occupation of the site.[81] Evidence of dwelling and storage pits has also come from Swat Valley where the site called Loebanr has revealed dwelling pits contemporaneous with pit-dwelling phase of Neolithic Kashmir.[82] Like Kashmir, these pits were cut in the natural soil and were circular or circular-oval in plan.[83] Another important site close to the north-western borders of Kashmir to yield dwelling pits is Lewan situated 23 km south of Bannu city. The dwelling pits discovered from the site are, like the Kashmir pit dwellings, round, rectangular and irregular in shapes.[84]

Red-ochreous Painted Floors

The presence of red-ochreous painted floors is conspicuously noticed in the aceramic phase and ceramic phase I of Kashmir. This practice is also found at many Neolithic sites of West Asia,[85] Central Asia[86] and in the Indian sub-continent at Mehargarh.[87] Floors decorated with red ochre have been encountered at Hacilar (Anatolia), Can Hassan (Anatolia 7000 BCE),[88] at Djeitun Depe and Chakmakli Depe (South Turkmenia) in 5000 BCE and 3600–3000 BCE, respectively,[89] Deh Luran plain (Iran)[90] and at Mehargarh (Baluchistan).[91] However, the Gufkral and Burzahom cultures cannot be linked with any of these cultures, because chronologically they are widely separated from each other. The nearby contemporary sites having this cultural trait still await the archaeologist's spade. Yet, considering the strong linkage of Kashmir Neolithic with the Neolithic of its neighbourhood and the fact that by all means Kashmir is a secondary rather than primary Neolithic zone, the presence of such cultures using red-ochreous painted floors near its borders seems a reasonable inference.

Bone and Stone Tools

A significant finding of the Neolithic Kashmir, which maintained its presence throughout the period, is that of bone and stone tools. During the aceramic phase the bone tools were made in the form of needles, points, harpoons, awls, piercers, scrapers and arrow heads. Bone tools have been rampantly found in Russia,[92] Central Asia,[93] China,[94] Japan,[95] Iraq,[96] Iran[97] and Turkey.[98] The transmission of technology and culture from one place to another is typically evidenced by the dispersal of bone harpoons which spread through Russia to Siberia in 3000 BCE[99] and from there to China and Japan[100] and to Kashmir through Central Asia. This tradition is still alive in Central Asia[101] as well as in Kashmir where it is called *narus* although bone is now replaced by iron.

Long before Kashmir, we come across a wide-spread bone industry in its neighbourhood, especially at Mehargarh, Rana Ghundai, Anjira, Jalilpur, Gumla, Sarai Khola, Loebanr and Aligrama (in Swat Valley).[102] While the manufacture of bone awls, points and needles was a commonplace phenomenon, Sarai Khola bone tool included chisels, perforators, buttons, combs, hair dividers and pressure flakes.[103] The only form of the bone tools not found so far in the immediate neighbourhood of Kashmir is harpoon. However, it was a common tool used by the fishermen of Central Asia, Russia, Siberia, Japan and China.[104] The latter obviously passed it to Kashmir through many routes via Central Asia and Tibet.

The stone tools found in Kashmir included adzes, celts, chisels, wedges, points, sewing knives, scrapers, picks, hoes, mace heads, sling balls, grinders and harvesters. These tools have been yielded by almost all sites located on the border lands of Kashmir, especially the ones situated in the Swat Valley.[105] Polished stone axes similar to those from Burzahom are also reported from West Asia[106] and southern India.[107] Asthana regards the polished stone tools to have come from West Asia, particularly Iran, where they are found in earlier contexts.[108]

Agriculture

WHEAT

The oldest known Neolithic site of Kashmir, namely, Kanispur, has thrown up the evidence of the cultivation of emmer wheat (*Triticum dicoccum*).[109] This highly arid zone crop originated in the Middle East and was transmitted to Central Asia via Iran and Afghanistan.[110] Closer to Kashmir, Baluchistan presents the earliest evidence of this variety. Significantly, both barley and emmer wheat of Kanispur share affinities with botanical assemblage from Mehargarh[111] and the other sites in Baluchistan datable to 6000–5000 BCE.[112] That Baluchistan acted as the immediate source of emmer wheat cultivation in Kashmir and its immediate neighbourhood is also substantiated by the finds of emmer wheat from early Harappan deposits at Kunal in district Hissar (Haryana) where evidence of pit dwelling has also been noticed.[113] Importantly, emmer wheat has been found at Kunal "mingled with barley and in the same manner it is found in mingled condition at Kaniṣkapura."[114] Emmer wheat has also been reported from the early and mature phases of Harappan settlement at Rohira in the Punjab.[115]

Two more varieties of wheat species have been recovered from Burzahom, Gufkral and Qasim Bagh. They are *Triticum aestivum* and *Triticum sphaerococcum*,[116] and both are the cultivated forms of wheat. *Triticum aestivum* was grown in West Asia around 5500 BCE.[117] As the domestication of *Triticum aestivum* in Kashmir dates from 3000 BCE, and this species was found in the Harappan sites after 2500 BCE, it is believed that Kashmir received this breed from some other source.[118] However, *Triticum sphaerococcum* was grown neither in West Asia nor in the Indian sub-continent at the time it was reported from Kashmir.[119] Until its cultivation is reported from any pre-Harappan site, Kashmir can stake claim for being the innovator of this variety of wheat.

BARLEY

Burzahom and Gufkral finds have revealed that the cultivated species of barley, *Hordeum vulgare* and its sub-species *Hordeum vulgare Linn Varhexastrichum* were grown in Kashmir from the aceramic Neolithic period.[120] It was also around the same time that barley was noticed at Kanispur.[121] Like wheat, barley was also first grown in West Asia around 7000 BCE and the cultivation of *Hordeum vulgare* is datable to 6000 BCE.[122] In the neighbourhood of Kashmir, *Hordeum vulgare* cultivation was found at Mehargarh between 6000 and 5000 BCE.[123]

LENTIL

Lentils recovered from Burzahom and Gufkral are *Lens culinaris* and *Lens esculenta*, respectively.[124] Both these varieties were found in West Asia around 5000 BCE.[125] However, no evidence about lentil cultivation is known from the Harappan sites, which shows that Kashmir received the crop from West Asia through some other source.[126]

Stock Raising

With regard to animal husbandry, the Neolithic man carried with him a strong tradition of domesticating sheep and goat, which had a long tradition in West Asia and other neighbouring regions[127] though at Mehrgarh 'domesticated cattle predominated in comparison to sheep and goat.'[128]

Inflows, Contacts and the Making of Middle Neolithic

After about 400 years since the Neolithic people occupied Kanispur *karewa*, we find either some new people coming and settling in the valley or the early inhabitants further extending their contacts. This is evident from some new introductions around 2520 BCE, inaugurating a new phase of Neolithic culture. The new introductions were handmade pottery, pea cultivation and domestication of some new animals. Whether some new people came or contacts were extended, one thing is clear: the direction of immigrations and contacts remained the same. In case the change occurred because of the fresh immigrations, the immigrants certainly belonged to the same ethnic, culture and language group to which the early settlers belonged. That is why they settled with the early inhabitants without any conflict as is shown by the Neolithic cultural sequence. Moreover, the early culture was religiously maintained. For example, *inter alia*, they too were pit dwellers as is shown not only by Gufkral but also by Burzahom, which was occupied afresh during this period. In the event the new introductions were made by establishing fresh contacts; still the direction of the contacts remained focused towards the traditional lands bordering the north and west of Kashmir. This is substantiated by a strong affinity between this cultural phase of Kashmir and the contemporary cultures of Potwar region and Swat Valley represented by Loebanr, Aligrama and the other sites.

Handmade Pottery and Pottery Types

The handmade pottery of this phase comprised three principal fabrics—thick coarse grey ware, fine grey ware and gritty dull ware. The shapes represented are globular jars, bowls, basins and dish-on-stand with mat impressions on the bases. Referring to the close affinity between the potteries of Kashmir and those found at different sites of Swat Valley and Sarai Khola I, Allchins observes, "The coarse and burnished grey and brown wares of the early Swat sites recall in general terms those of Burzahom and Saria Khola, and lead us to believe that they all belonged to a single complex."[129] In the Swat Valley, Loebanr III has black grey burnished pottery. The pottery is coarse and gritty and has basket impressions at the base.[130] The same type of pottery is reported from Period III at Ghaligai (in Swat Valley). Stacul writes that at Ghaligai (strata 17 and 16), the vases recovered are handmade, of a very textured paste. The colour of the paste is greyish and the bottom bears mat impressions.[131] A grey vase with an ovoid body and mat impressions on the base has been reported from Buktara I.[132] Stacul says that "similar vases, mat impressed on the base, handmade, with rudimental grey paste, have been found in Burzahom."[133] Mughal has compared the pottery of period I at Sarai Khola with Burzahom pottery. According to him, the main similarity between the potteries of Sarai Khola and Burzahom is that they are handmade and have basket impressions at the base.[134] Coiled mat impressions on the base of some pots also occur in the early pottery at Gumla, Lewan and Mehrgarh.[135] The pottery of Kashmir has some similarity with the pottery of China. In China too, pot was made by coiling method and had grey and black burnished texture. The mat or basket impressions are also ubiquitous in Chinese pottery.[136]

Other New Introductions

Other notable introductions of the Neolithic phase II of Kashmir are cultivation of pea and domestication of cattle, fowl and dog. Also noteworthy is the presence of two beads of precious stones out of which one was carnelian.

Pea

Two varieties of pea, namely, *Pisum arvense Linn* and *Pisum sativum*, were grown during the period.[137] Both these varieties are believed to have emerged from their wild ancestor *Pisum elatius* and the intermediary form *Pea arvense*. Both these varieties have been found in West Asia around 7000–5000 BCE.[138] Loebanr III also revealed the evidence of rice, lentils and the field pea (*Pisum arvense*) besides wheat and barley.[139] *Pisum arvense* has also been found at Harappa (2250 BCE).[140]

Cattle

The domestication of cattle began in West Asia and Mehargarh as far back as 7000–6000 BCE.[141] And with the beginning of Neolithism in Kashmir, cattle husbandry had played an important role in the subsistence pattern of the neighbouring cultures of Kashmir.[142]

FOWL AND DOG

The taming of fowl and dog also seems to have been learnt either through contacts or through the medium of immigrations from Swat Valley, which had intimate contacts with China where dog was treated as good as a family member.[143] However, it may be noted that in the immediate neighbourhood of Kashmir, Afghanistan was also perhaps the first to exploit horse and dog. Mundigak I has yielded the remains of horse and dog.[144]

PRECIOUS STONES

Beads of semi-precious stones like lapis lazuli, carnelian, agate, steatite, turquoise and Jasper were very popular in the neighbouring Neolithic cultures of Kashmir.[145]

Mobility, Circulation and the Making of Mature Neolithic Between 2000 and 1500 BCE, Kashmir Neolithic culture entered into a new phase marked by some far-reaching developments. The finds which represent these developments are dwelling structures made of mud or brick or both, wattle and daub houses, cultivation of millet, rice, grapes (*vitis vinifera*), almonds, walnuts and peach, domestication of pig, rectangular perforated stone harvesters and spindle whorls, better finished bone tools, crucible, a few copper arrow heads, a ring, bangles and a hair pin with flattened coiled head, a comma-shaped pendent of light green jade, 950 beads fashioned out of agate and carnelian, terracotta bangles, cowry shells, black burnished ware, painted pots, red ware pots, red ware painted with a horned deity, channel spouted vessels, a shard bearing graffiti, long-necked jars, dish-on-stand with triangular perforated designs on the stem region; burials within the settlements and under the house floor or in compounds, flexed and crouched burials, primary and secondary burials, corpses daubed with red ochre, grave goods, animal burials, trepanning and an engraved hunting scene on a stone slab.

These finds indicate two developments: (1) immigration of new people with new cultural items that were common in the culture zones they came from and (2) considerable growth in interaction between Kashmir and the neighbouring regions actuated by economic, climatic and cultural factors. In order to form an idea about the cultural zone from where these new people came and with which Kashmir developed intimate contacts resulting in the introduction of new technology and culture, it is necessary to search parallels of these cultural items in the immediate and extended neighbourhoods of Kashmir.

Parallels Between the Mature Neolithic of Kashmir and the Neolithic Cultures of the Neighbouring World

Aboveground Houses

Dwelling structures made of mud and brick have been quite often reported from different neighbouring sites, namely, Rehman Dheri, Tarakai Qila, Gumla II and Sarai Khola II.[146] Wattle and daub houses were also found at Aligrama and Loebanr.[147] An aboveground structure of the Neolithic period, which can be retrieved by following regressive method, is *du'ong*. *Du'ong* is a square or rectangular two-storey pole house. While the ground floor was used for cooking purposes, the first story formed the bed room. *Du'ong* invariably had a roof raised on vertical poles. This pole house has survived to us in its actual shape albeit today it is seen only in maize fields to provide safe shelter to watchers of these fields. Is *du'ong* a derivative of Chinese *dougong* which means a network of wooden frames? It seems probably so because pole houses are also found in eastern (Lung Shan) and northern (Yang Shao) China.[148]

Introduction of New Crops

Millet

The earliest evidence of millet cultivation has come from Gufkral[149] and Qasim Bagh.[150] At Gufkral, it has been found mingled with rice; and the variety was in all probability either *Panicum* or *setaria*, for they were also identified in the early historical botanical assemblages of Semthan in South Kashmir, and were grown in Kashmir till recently.[151] Alongside these varieties, we see the introduction of broomcorn millet, the earliest evidence of which is presented by Qasim Bagh (ca. 2000 BCE). To quote its excavators, "The most statistically and economically significant of the identified species are the two cereal crops – free thrashing wheat (*Triticumaestivum*) and broomcorn millet (*Panicummillaceum*)."[152] The earliest cultivated millet discovered in the world has been unearthed in North China at a number of sites classified as Cishan or Peiligang culture.[153] The earliest site of this culture found so far was excavated in 1986 near Nanzhuangtou village in Xushui county in southern Hebei.[154] Several radiocarbon dates from charcoal samples place the site very close to 10,000 years BP.[155] Although the wild species of both genera—*Setaria italica* and *Panicum miliaceum*, the two pillars of Old World millet culture—are found through Eurasia, and palaeobotanical research of the initial cultivation of millets has not yet been started, we can say that in view of the great antiquity of known millet remains in north China, there is a strong presumption that both may have been first cultivated in the Yellow River Valley.[156] This is also supported by more recent research. "The recent gene sequencing of modern landraces indicates a higher genetic diversity among East Asian broomcorn millets, supporting the notion of a single domestication event somewhere in China."[157] It was from China that the technology of millet cultivation spread first in the neighbourhood of Kashmir and then in the valley. The evidence of millet at Tasbas and Begash in Kazakhstan and Shortughai in northern Afghanistan and Ojakly in southern Turkmenistan in fourth millennium BP[158] suggests that the technology of millet cultivation transmitted to Kashmir through Central Asia via Swat. It is of special interest to note that after the Chinese word *peilgang*, millet is called *penge* in Kashmiri. This is unambiguously a derivative of *peilgang* (millet). As is true of many other crops, it was again Swat, which transmitted the millet cultivation to Kashmir.

Rice

The botanical assemblage from Gufkral and Burzahom *inter alia* contains the cultivated rice, *oryza sativa*.[159] It was introduced in Kashmir around

1700 BCE. Clearly, of all the cereals, it was a late comer. Until recently, it was believed that it was from India that rice culture spread to different parts of South East Asia, Thailand, Vietnam and West and South China. But this thesis does not hold good today as the carbon dates of Koldihwa (UP) and Mahagara, which were supposed to indicate the wild and cultivated rice around sixth millennium BCE, have been called into question.[160] Indeed, the cultivation of rice in India does not go beyond 2000 BCE about which exact evidence pertains to Gangetic basin.[161] It was only towards the end of Harappan period that evidence of rice has been found at Rangpur and Lothal.[162] The most recent investigations jointly undertaken by Sino-American team headed by Yan Wenming and Richard S Mac Neish have established a far earlier date of rice cultivation in China. Examining the two caves in Wannian country, northern Jiangxi, downstream along the Yangzi River from Hunan, they have brought to light rice pollen and phytoliths of *Oryza sativa*, both domesticated and wild, from layers of both caves tentatively dated by radiocarbon to just under 10,000 years BP.[163] The nearest source which transferred rice culture to Kashmir is Swat where rice was cultivated not later than the mid-third millennium BCE.[164] Referring to the multi-cropping agriculture system of Swat Costantini writes, "Wheat, barley, and rice formed part of the diet in Swat by the mid-third millennium."[165] Swat itself borrowed the rice culture from China with which it had trade and other contacts. To quote Allchins, "The presence of rice in Swat is particularly interesting. So too is the evidence of trade and other more profound contacts with the Chinese world."[166] It may be mentioned that the rice grains found in Kashmir and Swat are morphologically similar to *japonica* type.[167]

Horticulture

Kashmir also borrowed the technology of grape cultivation from Swat. An exciting find at Loebanr III is a grape seed (*Vitis Vinifera*).[168] The radiocarbon evidence from Loebanr suggests that this cultural tradition continued until the opening centuries of the second millennium BCE.[169]

Almond originated in the area between Central and West Asia[170], and peach and apricot originated in western China.[171] The technology of domestication of these plants was obviously brought to Kashmir by the immigrants from Dardistan, Little and Great Tibet and Swat, which bordered China and Central Asia.

Pig

Pig (*Sus cristatus*) is found at more than one Harappan site.[172]

New Stone Tools

Stone Harvesters

Rectangular or semi-lunar polished stone knives—a significant find from Burzahom—is a distinctive feature of Far-Eastern Neolithic cultures. It is found chiefly in northern China where about a dozen sites have yielded similar objects.[173] The rectangular perforated stone knives are a characteristic of Neolithic cultures of north China. In the neighbourhood, the perforated stone knives have been found at Kalako-deray, Swat.[174] Like Swat,[175] Yatoo *et al.* also found single holed harvester, schist disks and terracotta bobbin during their survey of north-west Kashmir.[176]

Shouldered Celt

Shouldered celt has been found for the first time by Yatoo at the Neolithic sites of Baramulla.[177] It has affinity with shouldered celts reported earlier from China.

Spindle Whorls and Crucibles

Spindle whorls have been recovered from Mundigak (southern Afghanistan) and Swat.[178] Fragments of several crucibles have been found in Mehrgarh III.[179]

Copper Objects

While almost each site situated in the west of Kashmir yielded the evidence of the presence of copper objects, we may specially refer to the ones which are nearest to the valley. Mention may be made of Gumla II-III, and Sarai Khola II. Sarai Khola has given a wide range of objects: antimony rods, pins, nail parers, spearheads, bangles, rings and needles.[180] The copper hair pins discovered from Gufkral have parallels in Mediterranean regions, Hissar III (Iran), Anau (Turkistan), Mohenjo-daro, Chanhu-daro, Jhukar (Pakistan) and Manda (Jammu).[181] Stuart Piggott carried out a study of such sites where double-spiral-headed pins have been found. Besides Mohenjo-daro and Chanhu-daro in the Indus, he has located 17 other sites, spreading from Greece to the Persian Gulf and Caucasus to the Indus, where such pins are available. While certifying their wide-spread distribution, Stuart Piggott opines that double-spiral-headed pins actually originated in the Aegean-Anatolian region from where they spread to north Persia and onwards to the Indus around 2500 BCE.[182]

Beads of Precious Stones, Terracotta Bangles and Shells

Agate and carnelian beads were a characteristic trait of the north-western borderland cultures of Kashmir.[183] Yet, the immediate source of carnelian and agate beads of Kashmir was Sarai Khola, which has shown a considerable presence of them.[184] Terracotta bangles in abundance are reported from Baluchistan and the Indus Valley.[185] The nearest parallels of Kashmir bangles are the ones found in Sarai Khola, Gumla II and Munda IA.[186] Shell was widely distributed and attested to at Damb Sadaat II-III, Mundigak, Gumla III, Sarai Khola II, Kot Diji, Jalilpur etc.[187]

Pottery Types

The use of potter's wheel was made in Sumer and Iran simultaneously around 5000 BCE.[188] Wheel made pottery begins to appear at Mehrgarh ca. 4300 BCE.[189] To be sure, at the time we find the presence of potter's wheel in Kashmir, it was already in vogue for quite some time in India and China.[190] Potter's wheel, kiln and painted pottery had a long history by then in the regions around Kashmir. This is shown by different varieties of wheel-thrown painted pots known by different culture labels.[191] Notwithstanding the different origins of these potteries, Sarai Khola, Lewan, Gumla and Rehman Dheri acted, as usual, the basic intermediary channels of their transmission to Kashmir. This is substantiated by the materials and shapes of some pots which strikingly take after the pottery found at these sites. The best example is the wheel-made fine globular red-ware pot, carrying a painting in black of a wild goat with long curved horns and hanging ears. The same representations have been found at Hissar (Iran), Kot Diji, Gumla, Rahman Dheri, Sarai Khola and Lewan.[192] It is significant to mention that, according to Sankalia, the motif of an animal head with long curved horns, which the Burzahom wheel-made red ware pot carries, has greater resemblance to the one from Hissar (Iran) than to the other from Sind.[193]

Other pottery shapes which confirm Kashmir's contacts with these regions and their impact on pottery tradition of the valley are the channel spouted vessels (found at Gufkral) and dish-on-stand. The channel spouted vessel found from Gufkral has a long history in West Asia and Iran.[194] It has been traced back to Crete. It reached central India around 1500 BCE.[195] It is almost of the same date in Kashmir. Dish on stand was a very popular Kot Dijian ware.[196] Its extension to the north is attested at Sarai Khola[197] in the Taxila Valley and to the north-west in the Gomal Valley where Gumla, Hathala, Rehman Dheri, Karam Shah and Lewan have yielded this ware.[198] Graffiti marks have been found on the pottery of Rehman Dheri, Sarai Khola, Kot Diji etc.[199]

Human Burials

The painting of skeleton with red ochre is an old tradition. The practice prevailed in Palaeolithic Russia and continued up to Neolithic times.[200] Many red painted burials have also been reported from China, Japan, Levant and Anatolia.[201] However, after Russia, a large number of painted burials have been reported from Iran.[202] As in Kashmir, we find in Khuzestan (Iran) dead being buried under the house floor; and the burials were both of primary and secondary types.[203] Trepanning also existed in other Neolithic cultures in Asia and Europe.[204]

Animal Burials

Animal burials are reported from many sites in Europe and Central Asia. However, contemporaneous with Kashmir Neolithic are the animal burials found at Darra-e-Kūr in Badakhshan, Afghanistan.[205] From the Neolithic levels, the excavator found three burials of domestic goats. They tally them with animal burials of Burzahom as they too are both complete and fractional, situated within the habitation and independent as well as along with human burials.[206] While the goat burial of Kashmir has affinity with the neighbouring Afghanistan, dog and horse burial was a widespread cultural trait of China.[207] The dog was apparently almost a cult animal in the Shilka cave culture of the Upper Amur;[208] and dogs were until recently sacrificed and buried with their owners among such people as the Gilyaks, Ulchis and Goldis of this region.[209] The dog burials are also reported in the Ang-Ang-His culture of Manchuria.[210] In the Xiajiadian culture (eleventh to fourth century BCE), a special place was reserved for dogs whose remains have been found in both dwelling sites and sacrificial pits.[211]

Rock Art

The rock art of Kashmir can be placed in the context of its immediate surrounding areas, particularly in Chilas and Swat. Writing about the distinctive position of Chilas as an unparalleled area in having a large number of rock carvings, Dani writes, "The largest concentration of such ruins – the greatest number of rock carvings at any place in the world – is at Chilas proper or either side of the river Indus."[212] The art prevailed in the region continuously from prehistoric times to historical period. No wonder, then, that the early people of this area are called "People of the Rock Art." The antiquity of the Chilas rock art goes back to the sixth or fifth millennium BCE. About the stone engravings of Kashmir, which may be placed in the middle of the third millennium BCE, Dani opines that "the technique of stone engraving has a general resemblance to the engravings from Chilas area." There is some uniqueness in some scenes engraved on the stone slabs of Kashmir, but some scenes present a close affinity with those of Chilas rock carvings. There too we find hunting scenes a common occurrence: hunters hunting with bows and arrows; hunters accompanied by dogs, and the male genital organs clearly indicated. Rock engravings have also been found in Swat at Gogdara and Haithiano Kandao. They bear similarity with some of the carvings from Chilas and its surrounding areas and can be dated to the middle of the third millennium BCE. From Gagdara a wheeled chariot has been found. This is placed in the second millennium BCE. The rock art of Chilas and Swat, which formed the source of Kashmir rock art, is itself an extension of the rock art of trans-Pamir, Siberian and Xinjiang regions, where it goes back to Palaeolithic time.

Naga Cult

The Naga worship, the most primitive but popular cult of Kashmir throughout its history, despite the subsequent religious changes, was most probably introduced in Kashmir during the Neolithic period by the early settlers who, as we have seen, migrated to Kashmir from the territories situated on its northern and western borders. The evidence regarding the prevalence of this cult in the north of Kashmir comes from the prehistoric rock carvings of Chilas;[213] and about the popularity of this cult in the immediate west of Kashmir archaeology has provided us sufficient information.[214] Nāgas (serpents), according to the popular belief in Kashmir, are tutelary deities living in the springs and lakes of the valley. They can also appear in human shape.[215] The same belief was perhaps held by the prehistoric people of neighbouring Chilas. Dani has reported a prehistoric anthropomorphic figure from Chilas which is probably a snake god having association with water:

> Of far greater importance is another anthropomorphic figure at Ziarat I site on a double-triangle, meeting at the faced boulder. This figure is of a unique formation. The main body is formed by a double apex and enclosed within a square. At the meeting of the triangles there are four dots. The standing hair are shown by vertical lines on the top of the body. The face is not shown at all. Both the hands, which are pecked solid, and have five fingers each, are at an incline. From the left arm a snake emerges upward. Below the body two legs taper down in outline and drawn in a fashion that shows joint legs of a type known in the terracotta of the Bronze Age. The feet, which are joined, are shown sideways in a way that they give the appearance of a boat. *The twin aspect of the deity is quite clear. He has association with snake and hence could be snake-god. At the same time the boat-like feet formation suggests river connection*

> *and hence he could be a river god. However, technical relationship with other anthropomorphic figures of the area shows the continuity of a concept that appears to be prehistoric in origin.* The only other new feature is the standing hair over the body representing head portion.[216] (Emphasis added)

The existence of the Naga cult in the immediate north-west of Kashmir is testified by the presence of terracotta figurines in the form of serpent-legged deities and representation of serpent deities on shards and pots discovered from Gumla, Kot Diji, Anjira, Rehman Dheri, Jhang Batar etc. belonging to about fourth-fifth millennium BCE.[217] "Taxila," says Saifur Rahman Dar, "has always been regarded as a strong centre of Naga Worship."[218]

It may, however, be mentioned that though the Naga cult transmitted to Kashmir from its immediate northern and western bordering territories, the original sources of this belief have, however, to be searched elsewhere. Scholars have traced deep-rooted similarities of serpent symbology between pre-Aryan people living in the west of Kashmir[219] and the people of Middle East—Turanians, Kurds, Akkadians, Chaldeans and Persians.[220] This suggests that "they belonged to a common social and cultural stock."[221] The Naga cult also prevailed in Khotan. The Naga worshippers of the valley, it appears, had some connection with such of the tribes in the Khotan Oasis. This is corroborated by some identical myths. For example, Hiuen Tsang narrates a legend as to how the widow of a Naga—a Nagin—stopped the water of a stream east of Khotan's capital, and let the water flow when a minister of noble birth sacrificed himself by entering the stream and married her.[222] More or less on the same pattern, Aṡoka's son, Jaluka, is supposed to have entered the lake of Nāgas by stopping the waters and had intercourse with Naga maidens so as to give charm to his body.[223] It is interesting to note that the worship of Nagin as snake goddess was prevalent in the West as well. An excellent and charming statue of the snake goddess in ivory and gold dated the sixteenth century BCE comes from Minoan—the Island of Crete in eastern Mediterranean.[224]

True, there is no evidence of the prevalence of Naga or any other cult in Kashmir during the Neolithic period. Yet, the fact that the Naga cult was a popular belief in the neighbourhood of Kashmir, which formed the fountainhead of the Neolithic culture of Kashmir, and that the Aryans had to confront with the Nāgas in Kashmir and had to accommodate them in their pantheon,[225] tempts one to conclude that Naga worship in Kashmir is as old as the antiquity of its contacts with its neighbourhood where it was as old as the fourth-fifth millennium BCE. As late as in the twilight of sixteenth century, the famous Mughal historian Abul Fazl noted that in Kashmir:

> There are 45 places dedicated to the worship of *Ṡiva*, 64 to *Viṣṇu*, 3 to Brahma and 22 to Durga, but in the seven hundred places

> there are graven images of snakes which they worship and regarding which wonderful legends are told.[226]

This is also supported by the local sources. In an appendix to the later *Rājataraṅgiṇīs* occurs the passage:

> And now, there are forty five Śiva (*girīśa*), sixty Viṣṇu (*cakrāyudha*), three Brahmā (statues), one says, and twenty-two Śakti (images) having residences with no beginnings; seven hundred serpents, with Nīla at their head, who have their home in the Tīrthas, and there are more than fourteen well-known (ones) in the country of Kashmir.[227]

The unparalleled importance of the Naga belief in Kashmir can also be ascertained from the fact that unlike the Indian rajas who prided themselves on being descendants of the Sun (suryavanśi) and the Moon (chandravanśi), the seventh-century powerful kings of Kashmir claimed their descent from the Karkota Naga.[228]

The deeply embedded faith which the Naga cult enjoyed in Kashmir even after it became a predominantly Muslim society[229] testifies to the fact that it was not only the oldest faith of Kashmir but also the one which ruled the worldview of Kashmiris for the longest period of time.

Language and the Identity of Early Settlers

The archaeological evidence with regard to the identity of the early settlers of Kashmir is also substantiated by the linguistic analysis of the Kashmiri language. According to the famous linguist, George Grierson, the Kashmiri language belongs to the Dardic group of languages. To quote him verbatim:

> That Kashmiri language has a Dardic basis is a matter of which no philologist can have any doubt . . . its basis–in other words, its phonetic system, its accidence, its syntax, its prosody– is Dardic. It must be classified as such.[230]

The Dardic group of languages is contemptuously called by a generic term *Paisaci* in ancient Sanskrit literature. According to Grierson, "It denoted those languages which were spoken in the area between the Hindukush and the Indian frontier in which the *kafir* speeches, Khowar, Shina, Kohistani and Kashmiri are now the vernaculars."[231] The area comprised the present Gilgit, Chilas, Astor, Gurez, Kashmir, Indus and Swat Kohistan.[232] The fact that the Kashmiri language belongs to the family of Dardic languages is also attested to by a large number of common words we find in Shina, Kohistani, Bashgali, Burushaski, Kashmiri and other Dardic languages in spite of revolutionary cultural changes, substituting old words by new ones.

Who were these Dards? To which race did they belong? Were they a branch of Aryans or did they belong to some non-Aryan group living in the area (like Dravidians) prior to the coming of the Aryans? If we believe Grierson, then the Dards belonged to the Aryan race though not the scions of Indo-Aryans as, according to him, the Kashmiri language is an independent branch of the Aryan language like Sanskrit and Iranian languages.[233]

However, it is difficult to agree with Grierson because the Aryans had all contempt for these early settlers. They not only called them by derogatory names such as *Pisaćas* (flesh devourers) but they also did not regard them even as humans.[234] In fact, there is no cultural compatibility between the Aryans and these early settlers. Neither, according to the Aryan sources, was there any affinity between the languages of the two, nor was their life style in accord with one another.[235] The Sanskrit sources portray them strikingly two opposite groups having no compatibility with each another. Akhtar Mohiuddin rightly argues:

> Would any nation, people or race, give itself such a humiliating name? Is it not invariably others who give such derogatory names to rival nations, people or race? The word 'piśāca,' being a derogatory name, could not have been given by any people to themselves.[236]

As a matter of fact, before the coming of the Aryans, Dardistan was inhabited by a local population who spoke a non-Aryan language, perhaps Burushaski. This is also the view of Grierson:

> Over the whole of Dardistan, there is an underlayer of Burushaski words . . . These words are found in localities far from the present habitat of Burushaski, and the inference is that, before the arrival of the Pisachas, the whole of Dardistan was once inhabited by the ancestors of the present owners of Hunza and Nagar. It is not impossible that they were identical with the Nagas who according to Kashmir mythology, were the original inhabitants of the happy Valley before the arrival of the Pisachas, and after whom every mountain and spring in Kashmir is named. Be that as it may, at the bottom of the Dardic languages, there is a small, and quite unimportant, element of Burushaski.[237]

SC Ray while giving meaning to the underlayer of Burushaski words in Dardistan including Kashmir says:

> It is the view of the linguists that when small tribes are found clinging to a dying form of speech, surrounded by powerful languages which have superseded the neighbouring speeches, and which have started to supersede this form of speech also, it may be concluded that the dying language is the language of the land and it gives clue to the

> racial affinities of its speakers. This is exactly the case with the Dardic group of languages. Over the whole of Dardistan including Kashmir there is an underlayer of Burushaski words and phrases.[238]

It is also in place to mention that a late grammar composed about 1550 CE in Andhra Pradesh, the *Ṣaḍbhāṣācandrikā* (Moonlight of the six language), describes the "regions" of the *Paiśācas,* which include Kashmir too. The other regions are "Pāṇḍya country [in the heart of Tamilnadu], Bāhlīka [in northern Afghanistan], Siṃha [Sindh], Nepāla, Kundala (north Karnataka), Sugheṣṇa [?], Bhoja [?, V.I. Bhoṭa, Tibet] and Gāndhāra [the region of Peshawar in today's Pakistan], and Haivakannojana [?]."[239]

In her recent paper, "Ancestral Dravidian languages in Indus civilization: Ultraconserved Dravidian Tooth-word Reveals Deep Linguistic Ancestry and Supports Genetics" Bahata Ansumali Mukhopadhyay has shown that ancestral Dravidian was one of the most popular tongues spoken across the greater Indus Valley. However, she put an important disclaimer saying that it would be wrong to assume that only a single language or language group was spoken across the huge area of Indus Valley civilisation as " 'Even today, people across the greater Indus valley speak' several tongues including Indo-Aryan, Dardic, Iranian, along with the isolated Dravidian language Brahui and the language isolate Burushaski."[240]

There is a possibility for linguists working on the origin of Kashmiri language to benefit from the insights of Johannes Fabian who challenges the notion that Swahili "diffused" to Shaba from some point in East or central Africa, asserting that the language "emerged" as a range of speech patterns rather than descending from a single ancestor language.[241]

Surnames on the Identity of Early Settlers

Kram (surname) composition of Kashmir society and the relative numerical strength of each *kram* group are yet another clue of knowing the geocultural region of the origin of different *kram* groups and their comparative antiquity of immigration and settlement in the valley. The more a *kram* group is numerically greater, the more is the ancientness of its immigration and settlement in the valley. However, one may caveat that the *kram* is to be linguistically compatible with the time. Like any other place, Kashmiri society is divided into many groups, each having a distinctive surname (*kram).* In terms of numbers, these *kram* groups can be put in a hierarchical order as the size of different *kram* groups varies from one another. And if we read this differential numerical strength of *krams* together with the knowledge of Kashmir history, the logic behind this variation would unfold before us as the history of Kashmir is the history of immigrations and settlements, which continued till the beginning of the twentieth century. Thus the demographic position of a *kram* group is proportionate to the antiquity of its settlement in the valley. Those *kram* groups who settled in the Valley during the early and the longest phase of its history namely Neolithic period, their number could be logically greater than the number of other groups.

The main earliest *krams* of Kashmir are Bhat, Dar, Magrey, Loan, Tantray, Rather, Pal, Tak, Lavai, Chak, Dangar, Thakur etc. And among these *kram* groups, Bhats constitute the largest number albeit like many other people belonging to different ethnic groups/tribes, some Bhats also either changed their *kram* with changing *reference cultures*, or some came to be known at different periods of time after their professions, nicknames or places of their origin. From where did these Bhats come? Al-Biruni helps us to identify the geographical area where Bhat was the prestigious title. To quote him:

> In the mountains of Bolar and Shamilan there live Turkish tribes called Bhattavaryan. Their king has the title Bhatta-Shah. Their towns are Gilgit, Aswira (Astor) and Shiltan (Chilas).[242]

Thus "Bhatta" was a coveted title/surname in Dardistan. And when these people migrated to Kashmir, they quite expectedly called themselves and were called by others by their own surname, Bhat. Shah seems the much later addition to their original title (Bhat), made under the Sassanian influence. Kashmir continued to be the destination of the people of Dardistan in view of its comparative geographical advantage. This is evidenced by constant migrations from the area till late times as well as by their continuous inroads to which Kashmir was subjected, attracting the attention of Al-Biruni.[243] It may also be mentioned that the *kram* Bhat was not carried by all tribes and groups that migrated to Kashmir from different areas of Dardistan. For example, the predecessor of the famous *kram* group Chak (Langar Chak) also came from Dardistan in the early twenties of the fourteenth century CE.[244]

While the predominant Bhat population of Kashmir indicates that the majority of early settlers in Kashmir came from Dardistan, the Palaeolithic tools and Neolithic assemblages make it abundantly clear that immigrations from the Punjab plains, Potwar plateau and Indus Valley were not less impressive. It is significant to note that the anthropological study of human skeletal remains from Burzahom has revealed that the crania, which are basically long headed, resemble more closely with Harappan cemetery R 37.[245]

Place Names as a Source

Michael Witzel finds the study of non-Sanskritised place names of Kashmir rewarding in identifying the ethnicity and language of the earliest inhabitants of Kashmir:

> Such place names [which are not Sanskritized] deserve a detailed study, especially those that cannot be traced back to royal

foundations. They may indicate an earlier level of settlement, and some of them seem to reflect the language of the original inhabitants of the Valley whom *Nilamata Purana*, in typical fashion, calls 'Nagas' and 'Piśācas'.[246]

Ethnographic Evidence

The ethnographic study of the Kashmiri people would prove of immense help in establishing on scientific grounds the ethnic relationship of the Kashmiri people with the people of the neighbouring world. Unfortunately no such study has been made yet. The majority of the Kashmiri people, however, possess a light transparent brown skin and are usually of medium to tall stature. "They are much dolichocephalic, have a well-developed forehead, a long narrow face, regular features and a prominent, straight and fairly cut laptorrhine nose." The same type is found among the people of Afghanistan, North West Frontier Provinces, northern Punjab, Hazara, Chitral, Chilas, Astor, Gilgit and other areas of Dardistan.[247] "The probable area of characterization of this race, therefore, seems to have been between the Hindukush and the Sulaiman mountain," from where it spread to its neighbouring areas. This race is called Indo-Afghan by Haddon,[248] Nordic by Guha[249] and Indid by Von Eickstedt.[250]

Summing Up

The details documented earlier make it abundantly clear that the Neolithic culture of Kashmir is the product of circulatory process. It evolved, changed and developed basically because of transmission of cultures consequent upon immigrations, settlements and contacts. However, none of the immediate neighbourhoods of Kashmir—wherefrom the earliest settlers came—was inhabited by one single race. Instead, like their cultures, the people of these borderlands were also drawn from different neighbouring cultural realms in an aura characterised by frequent diasporas and settlements in new areas. This is clear from the diverse physiognomy of the people inhabiting these regions, sub-regions and localities, and consequentially by the variegated physiognomy of the people of Kashmir. Further, although the adjoining borderlands of Kashmir acted as the immediate source of its Neolithic culture, the fact, however, remains that in regard to cultural transmission, their position was not more than a transit depot that deals with the goods that are actually the products of other lands. To be sure, some areas stole a march over others in making a specific invention or discovery and it was from these centres that new technological and cultural goods spread to different parts of the globe, leading either to the emergence of a large cultural zone or a "global culture" after some important characteristics came to be shared by all cultures.

In the case of Kashmir, the primary sources of its culture were Mesopotamia, Iran, China, Russia, Mediterranean world, Central Asia and India. However, the cultural goods of these sites did not migrate to Kashmir directly. Instead, they slowly transmitted to its neighbourhood stage by stage through migrations and trade from where Kashmir imported them consequent upon the arrival of new people from these areas. The neighbourhood, which acted as the immediate source of Kashmir culture, comprised Gilgit, Baltistan, Hunza, Nagar, Astor, Chilas, Hazara, Potwar region (present, Islamabad, Rawalpindi, Peshawar and Taxila), Swat, Baluchistan, Sind and the Punjab. The main evidence of Kashmir being a part of the cultural complex of Shina speaking neighbourhood (Gilgit, Astor, Chilas etc.) is the Kashmiri language, ethnoarchaeology and the rock art. The intimate affinity between Kashmir and its western and north-western borderlands is supported not only by philology but also by archaeology. The finds of various early sites of Swat, Potwar region and Kashmir leave no room to doubt that they belong, in the words of Allchins, "to a single complex."[251] However, this cultural complex was itself the product of a plethora of cultural products borrowed from many sites situated in the proximate and distant neighbourhoods. Thus, like any other region, the early history of Kashmir cannot be understood unless we situate it in the context of "global" history.

Advent of Aryans and Cultural Comingling

Michael Witzel believes that "the history of the Kashmiri Brahmans may even go back all the way to the Vedic period as the Valley and its surroundings were already known in Vedic times."[252] Unfortunately the evidence on Aryan immigration into Kashmir is extremely slender when compared with Swat, the well-known intermediary of cultural transmission to Kashmir. There are just a few shreds of evidence obtained from the late Neolithic and Megalithic level of Burzahom and Gufkral, as well as from the Pre-Northern Black Polished Ware (NBPW) level of another important archaeological site—Semthan, which perhaps point to the Aryan migration to Kashmir from ca. 1700 to 1500 BCE. As discussed earlier, during the late Neolithic period, we saw the introduction of rice, millet, rectangular stone sickles, grey burnished ware and the occurrence of different articles of copper, jade, agate and carnelian. Subsequently, during the Megalithic period, we also encounter stone-walled houses. Such developments along with the introduction of horses in Swat around 1700 BCE have been explained in the context of wide-ranging cultural exchanges including immigrations particularly of Indo-Aryans.[253]

The same may hold true of Kashmir as well. Certainly, the presence of horse in Kashmir at this stage is yet to be established. But the occurrence of associated developments—multi-cropping system, stone-walled houses, rectangular holed stone sickles, grey burnished ware, copper objects and many precious stones—coupled with the intimate relations between Swat and Kashmir since hoary past, to the extent of making Kashmir and Swat a single complex, tend one to presume that the lack of evidence regarding horse is perhaps only because of inadequate presence of archaeologist's spade in Kashmir.

The period I of Semthan (700–500 BCE) has revealed grey ware along with sturdy red, fine red and ochrous red wares.[254] Archaeologists call it pre-NBPW, that is, the ware which was encountered in India during the Aryan phase. The pottery forms found at this level also bear generic relationship with the late phase of the post Harappan pottery of Banawali and Bara phase of the plains of the Punjab and Haryana.[255] Recently a site has been spotted on the highest terrace of village Hutmur overlooking the river Liddar. An exciting discovery was of plain grey ware under the remains of a later structure.[256] The plain grey, as we know, is anterior to painted grey ware. It is, therefore, quite probable that the Aryans entered into Kashmir via Swat.[257]

A later canonical work of Kashmiri brahmanas, *Nīlamata Purāna*, which, according to Ronald Inden, is a reworking of earlier discursive material which may or may not have constituted a formal written material,[258] also records the arrival of Aryans, though it is clothed in folklore and informed by the dominant tradition—Brahmanism. According to *Nīlamata Purāna*, before the coming of Aryans, whom it calls human beings, there lived two main culture groups in Kashmir whom the Sanskrit writer of the *Purāna* pejoratively called *Nāgas*[259] and *Paiśācas*.[260] Since in the Sanskrit language *naga* means serpent, the Aryans contemptuously called those tribes of Kashmir as *nāgas* whose totem was snake. The *Pisaca* means flesh eaters—the derogatory name given by the Aryans to that culture group of Kashmir which put a stiff resistance against Aryan domination of Kashmir. The *Nīlamata* makes it abundantly clear that the Aryans had to face a great deal of hostility from both the *Nāgas* and the *Paiśācas* so much so that they had ultimately to make vital compromises with their adversaries even to the extent of incorporating their leaders in their pantheon and assimilating their beliefs. The *Nīlamata Purāna* contains the instructions supposed to have been related by Nīla, the king of Nāgas, to the brahmana Chandra Deva with the direction that for living in Kashmir the Aryans and all others, who would like to live in Kashmir, shall have to act upon them.[261] According to the *Purāna*, it was obligatory for the Aryans to worship the king of Nāgas, Nīla Naga. And for brahmanising the practices contained in the *Purāna*, it was asserted that Viṣṇu declared the Nīla as a part of his own self, and "He who disobeys his order meets destruction at my hand."[262] Also, the *Purāna* claimed that the Nīla received the instructions from *Keśava*.[263] Besides worshipping Nīla, it was obligatory for the brahmanas to worship around 603 Nāgas contained in the *Purāna*.[264] Considering the significance bestowed upon the Naga worship, it is not surprising that Abul Fazl found 700 places with graven images of snakes which the Kashmiri brahmanas worshipped.[265] That in comparison to the Puranic trinity of Brahma, *Viṣṇu* and *Śiva*, there were many-fold places in Kashmir with graven images of snakes worshipped by the Kashmiri brahmanas even in the sixteenth century points to the resilience of the local traditions. It is also interesting that the Buddhist tradition mentions only Nāgas whom the Buddhist missionaries had to contest in Kashmir.[266]

The policy of assimilation and the consequential reformulation of their religion by the Aryans were also followed in case of the *Paiśācas*. Significantly, the first "holy practice," which the Vedic people had to observe for living in Kashmir, was that they had to celebrate with elaborate rituals the full moon night of 15th of Asvayuj for the worship of Nikumbha, the chief of the Paiśācas.[267] The elaborate rituals are discussed in 33 verses of the *Nīlamata Purāna*[268] showing that this was the most important religious ritual which the Vedic people had to observe. And alongside the goddess Uma being the river Vitasta, Lakshmi the river Visoka, Aditi the river Trikoti and Sachi the river Harsapatha, Deti the mother of Detiyas (demons) became the river Chandravati.[269]

The identity markers of the Aryan culture were domestication of horses for riding and driving carts, use of bows and arrows placed in quivers, male-dominated society, cremation of the dead, the cult of fire and, above all, the Indo-Aryan language.[270] However, as in many matters of religion, so in language too, the local culture triumphed over the intruding tongue. As the overwhelming local population spoke a different tongue, *koshur*, it forced the new comers to learn it to claim a membership of the host society, even though the conquerors downgraded the local language, imposed their own mother tongue as official language and considered it sacred for being the language of their scriptures.[271]

Coming of the New People and the Second Technological and Cultural Revolution (1000–600 BCE)

In this sub-theme we argue that from around 1000 BCE Kashmir witnessed another major technological and cultural revolution following the fresh waves of immigrations from the technologically advanced neighbourhood. They did not only introduce new technology and culture but it was with their coming that the technologies introduced during the late Neolithic period began to make real impact. The reasons were both cultural and environmental. The new immigrants belonged to the cultural zone/s where rice, millet, copper, crucible, hand spindle, potter's wheel, new pottery types and stone harvesters—the introductions of late Neolithic in Kashmir—were established attributes of their culture for quite a long period. Thus, with their arrivals, the rice and the associated culture assumed popularity, which hitherto had been delayed as the adoption of new changes demanded the change of habit of mind which, needless to emphasise, changes very slowly. Also, the adoption of rice cultivation on a mass scale presupposed the desiccation of valley floor. The use of some other products, namely, wheel thrown pottery and copper goods, introduced during the late Neolithic period, depended on "obtaining power"[272] of the people. The main medium of obtaining goods produced by others was exchange of goods by goods. Clearly, barter is the child of surplus production; and the surplus production in climatic conditions of Kashmir could be expected only in the popular practice of rice culture. The adoption of rice culture at mass level depended on the cultivatability of the appreciable part of the Valley floor and the massive immigrations of the people from the rice grown areas of the neighbourhood. Both took centuries, indeed.

The ethnobotanical researches show that until 1000 BCE, neither rice nor millet made any worthwhile inroads into the traditional cropping pattern of Kashmir. It was during the pre-NBPW period (1000–600 BCE) that we find a dramatic increase in rice cultivation at Semthan as its share among the cereal crops rose spectacularly to 55.8% (see Table 2.1). True, the statistical

Table 2.1 Percentage of cereals in Agriculture on the basis of crop remains recovered from Burzahom and Semthan

Site	*Period*	*Wheat*	*Barley*	*Rice*	*Oats*	*Total percentage of cereals*
Burzahom	Phase I Aceramic Neolithic (2520–2000 BCE)	78.5%	21.5%	x	x	73.68%
Burzahom	Phase II Mature Neolithic (2000–1500 BCE)	73.68%	26.32	x	x	67.5%
Burzahom	Phase III Megalithic (1000–700 BCE)	65.9%	25%	9.1%	x	62.8%
Semthan	Phase I Pre–NBP (700–500 BCE)	30.8%	14.4%	55.8%	x	85%
Burzahom	Post Megalithic Phase IV (600–200 BCE)	60%	25%	14.50%	x	54.4%
Semthan	Period II NBP Phase (600–200 BCE)	25%	56.25%	17.5%	1.1%	78.8%
Semthan	Period III (200 BCE–001 CE)	4.4%	67.6%	23.5%	4.4%	80%
Semthan	Period IV (001 CE–500 CE)	39.3%	27.8%	28%	4.5%	72.3%

(*Source:* Farooq A Lone, 1993)

information for the subsequent period does not bear out the continuity of this impressive statistics of rice presence; nonetheless, the rice cultivation showed a constant upward trend from 1000 BCE; and around 600–200 BCE, its share among the cereal crops was 17.58%, very close to wheat whose share shows dramatic fall from 65.9% at Burzahom in 1000–700 BCE to 25% at Semthan in ca. 600–200 BCE.

From a comparative study of the percentage of three major cereals: wheat, barley and rice, retrieved from the prehistoric site of Burzahom and the proto historical site, Semthan, it seems that the rice cultivation became pronounced only with the arrival of new people who settled at Semthan. This is evident from the fact that while the percentage of wheat, barley and rice at Burzahom ranged between 65% and 60%, 25% and 25%, and 9% and 14% from 1000 BCE and 200 BCE, respectively, the relative presence of wheat, barley and rice at Semthan during the same period ranges between 30 and 25%, 56 and 14%, and 55 and 17%, respectively. Thus, while there is considerable fall in the traditional staple crop and food, namely, wheat at Semthan, there is consistent rise of rice cultivation. Even if we ignore the presence of 56% of barley and 55% of rice during the first phase by considering them aberrations in consistency, rice was fast competing with the two heritage crops (wheat and barley—the former staple and the later subsidiary) between 1000 BCE and 600 BCE in contrast to its superficial presence during the later Neolithic period when it found its way into Kashmir from the nearby Swat. Initially slow and subsequently fast raising of rice had its own logic. Being the only cereals cultivated in Kashmir for a long period of one and a half million years, wheat as a staple crop and staple food shaped a deep-seated mentality refusing to change easily till rice cultivation unfolded its advantages fully and a sizeable area of the valley floor became cultivable after the slow process of its desiccation.

Evidently, the Semthan settlers seem to be a new cultural group who immigrated freshly from some neighbouring rice zone where rice had become the favourite food and consequently the favoured crop. And the area from where they seem to have come is most probably from Swat to the Punjab where rice had become a widespread crop. That Semthan settlers belonged to a different culture is evidenced not only by an appreciable presence of rice culture among them as compared to age-old sites of Burzahom and Gufkral but also by the presence of other cultural artefacts, namely, iron and pottery.[273]

It goes without saying that the introduction of rice cultivation was a revolutionary development. The per unit productivity of rice is far greater than the traditionally cultivated rain-fed crops—wheat and barley. Rice being a *kharif* crop and wheat and barley being *rabi* crops, paddy cultivation also graduated Kashmir from one-crop-a year economy to two-crop-a year economy though not raised from the same piece of land, but one crop from dry land (*wuder/karewa* land) and the other from low-lying areas, traditionally now under rice cultivation for its easy access to irrigation. Millet, which was introduced along with rice, could supplement food deficiency as unlike wheat and barley it was an autumn crop and was raised like wheat and barley in dry lands. Besides bringing economic and demographic changes as well as change in food habits, rice cultivation had inherent pressure to change the settlement pattern of Kashmir from predominantly *wuder* settlements to predominantly valley floor settlements.

That the real shift from hunting to agriculture economy took place around 1000 BC is also borne out by the presence of a far-reaching number of stone harvesters during the period vis-à-vis the later Neolithic phase. While the assemblage of late Neolithic phase threw up only two harvesters, their number grew as much as 54 during what is called Megalithic phase datable ca. 1000 BCE.[274] With the popularisation of rice and millet as well as horse, a new socio-economic pattern emerged in Kashmir. This observation agrees with Meadow's view about western Baluchistan: "The second agricultural revolution in this part . . . comes with the introduction of rice, millet, sorghum, camel and horse."[275]

Beginning of Chalcolithic Period

The presence of a few copper objects—arrow heads, hair pins, rings, bangles and antimony rods—in the late Neolithic assemblages of Burzahom and Gufkral has evinced a debate about their origin. Khazanchi and Dikshit believe that these copper objects are intrusions from pre-Harappan/Harappan cultures.[276] Conversely Bandey asserts that these were not imports, but were manufactured locally under Harappan influences. However, he hastens to add that these manufactures did not change the "prehistoric character of this [Neolithic] culture."[277]

When did the Neolithic culture graduate into Chalcolithic culture? It is difficult to say in the absence of concrete evidence. However, it can be perhaps said with a fair amount of certainty that around 1000 BCE, Kashmir had already entered into Chalcolithic phase. This assertion is based on two facts. First, in ca. 1000 BCE, the number of stone and bone tools is seen considerably low in comparison to the preceding periods; and their quality is also much inferior vis-à-vis the Neolithic tools as they bear polish of a low order.[278] Needless to say, Chalcolithic phase of human history is characterised by the simultaneous use of bronze and stone tools. It is possible that the divided attention and preference for bronze tools for utilitarian reasons lessened the number and quality of bone and stone tools. Yet we come across an important development in bone tool making: they are provided with handles made mostly from the tibia of a goat and sheep.[279] The second evidence for Kashmir having made a transition to Chalcolithic culture before 1000 BCE is the presence of more utilitarian copper objects like knife and double-edged points from the Megalithic period.[280] Also, along with Burzahom and Gufkral, the copper objects were encountered in the cist graves found in Kashmir recently.[281] The presence of cist graves also points to the influence of "Gandhara Grave Culture," which is marked by cist graves and bronze.[282]

By the time copper was found in Kashmir (2000–1500 BCE), copper and bronze had already assumed an important position in its neighbourhood as raw material for military hardware, agricultural tools and utensils. It is quite probable that the metal was introduced to Kashmir from Swat and Gilgit with which Kashmir was intimately connected. It may be mentioned that "comparatively high number of copper weapons" were found in proto-historic Swat[283] and a large horde of bronze objects including specimens of trunnion axes were discovered at a spot in the Gilgit Karakoram.[284]

Beginning of Iron working

From Gufkral three unidentified iron artefacts plus two needles and one nail were reported from the Megalithic phase with a date range of ca. 1550–1300 uncial. BCE.[285] After critically examining all the modern researches on early iron finds in India, Irfan Habib maintains that "all 14 C dates for the earliest iron levels in India appear to cluster around 1000 BCE or a little earlier."[286] Iron objects assignable to the opening of first millennium BCE have been found in Gandhara graves.[287] Recently the excavations at Charsadda by the Bredford–Peshawar team discovered 25 iron artefacts with archaeometallurgical evidence—a few iron slag pieces. These were assigned to ca. 1200–900 BCE.[288] For Kashmir the iron working in Gandhara is very crucial should we bear in mind that Kashmir was geographically and culturally a part of Gandhara. It is, therefore, no wonder that around the same period we find iron in Kashmir.

Megaliths

Megaliths[289] were a specific type of prehistoric monuments built of big stones. They have almost a worldwide distribution. They have been found in Europe, Africa, South America, Melanesia, Arabian Peninsula, Madagascar, Western Asia, Caucasus, India and Indonesia.[290] With such a vast presence, their types, forms and ages varied among different geographies. Broadly speaking there were two categories of Megalithic monuments: the stone chambers (so-called tombs) and the free-standing monuments called menhir alignments. Menhirs are of varied types—circles or single standing stone.

In Kashmir only two types of free-standing monuments have survived to us. These are either semi-circle or single standing stones. While mostly they are found in semi-circles, in exceptional cases, they are located alone. The stone slabs are natural stones, roughly shaped and tapering towards the top. This is in contrast to Europe where they are placed upright on their narrow ends. In Europe these monuments were constructed between the seventh and fourth millennium BP.[291] In Kashmir they seem to have been built during the Bronze Age and early Iron Age. The size of these stones varies between 6.55 m and 2.96 m. Because of the massive dimensions of the stones, their acquisition and handling puzzle even a modern mind about the achievement of these prehistoric people otherwise regarded as primitive. It is for the same reason that in the folklore, these constructions have been ascribed not to humans but to giants or creation of supernatural forces.[292]

The megaliths have been found at Burzahom, Gufkral, Brah, Waztal, Tarakpur, Sombur, Pampur, Dadasara and Hariparigam. However, with the extant evidence, it is not possible to draw a conclusion about the spatial distribution of these megalithic monuments and their approximate number. As elsewhere, the megaliths have disappeared as a result of their reuse for construction purposes because of agrarian expansion and new settlements. Therefore, the present evidence does not help us in drawing reliable conclusions about the numerical distribution of megalithic monuments. Similarly the existing menhirs probably constitute only the remains of a full-fledged monument.

The menhirs are of local stone, transported over a distance of three to four kilometres. The efforts needed for quarrying, transporting and erecting the blocks show the extraordinary importance attached to these megaliths. The experimental archaeology would show that it would take scores of people and many days to transport a stone from its source. The techniques employed to move them must have been the same we find elsewhere: inclined planes, levers, split tree trunks, ropes of hide and perhaps draught animals.[293]

Notwithstanding the fact that the menhirs have been found world over, there is scarcely any knowledge of their functioning except for those places, like Peninsular India, where they are sepulchral. As in Europe, the purpose of menhirs in Kashmir can only be conjectured. They are non-sepulchral because they are not associated with any skeletal remains. Are these menhirs the precursors of the latter tombs aimed at commemorating the memory of the tribes—the tribes which lived separately at separate places? Were they installed to symbolise the greatness of tribes in both the eyes of the contemporaries and their succeeding generations? Or were these ceremonial stones to represent the movement of the sun and the moon in relation to the sky? Or are they religious structures, regarded as symbols of extraordinary power of the forces of nature? It is still a riddle.

Whatever the purpose might have been behind installing these big stones upright, the demanding labour, which these menhirs entailed, alludes to the fact that some powerful force—either mundane or religious—was at the root of this memorable activity of the prehistoric man. This building activity implied some kind of central command for coordinating labour for large-scale undertakings. "It must have been some sort of hierarchical society in which the menhirs had a consensus creating function, perhaps some kind of religious chiefdom." Perhaps these monumental stone circles/isolated stones also showed where important power centres were situated.

> They also marked festival places where people gathered for ceremonies. Power, religion and pleasure seem to have lived in symbiosis. Chiefdom, priesthood and the people merged into each other. Hierarchy was related to the control of ritual and control of masses.[294]

As already mentioned, megaliths have been found in the lands bordering on the Mediterranean and the Atlante, in the Caucasus and in Iran.[295] In the Indian subcontinent, peninsular India was the stronghold of the Megalithic culture.[296] There the *menhirs* were regarded as memorial stones.[297] Megaliths have also been found at some places of north and north-eastern India.[298] However, in the context of Kashmir, the nearest places where megaliths have been found are Baluchistan and Dardistan, particularly Yasin and Chitral. Biddulph was the first to describe the megaliths of Ghizer and Yasin valleys.

> In the Woorshigoom and Kho valleys, a number of remarkable stone tables of great antiquity are found. They are about 3feet in diameter, and are formed of huge boulders, arranged with great precision with a flat side outwards, so placed as to form a perfect circle about 3½feet high. On these are placed a number of flattish boulders of nearly equal size, projecting a few inches beyond the edge of the circle all round. The centre is filled with small stones and rubbish, which may or may not have been as originally intended. The labour of transporting and placing in position such huge blocks must have been immense. The local tradition is that they were the work of giants in old days. At Chashi and Yassin there are collections of several of these tables. Between these points and the upper part of the Woorshigoom Valley there are single tables scattered about. . . . The circle in most perfect preservation is situated on the tongue of land formed by the junction of the river near Goopis. Vigne mentions having been told about these circles when at Astor. They are in all probability funeral mounds.[299]

About the widespread megalithic culture in Yasin, Dani writes

> In Yasin the scattered boulders, cut into rectangular shape, are still seen standing in the fields. However, in the *bagh* (garden) of a local

> villager, by name Ishaq, there is one big circle of stones having a diameter of 33 feet with upright stones numbering forty . . . the big megalithic circle tomb appears to be monumental in origin . . . only future excavations can determine the exact nature of these tombs.[300]

Surely, the building of megaliths points to the domination of Kashmir by a new group that in all probability came from Chitral and Yasin, where megalithic culture was a widespread phenomenon. These borderlands of Kashmir had themselves borrowed this culture from others. It had perhaps its source in the Mediterranean region. It travelled all the way from its place of origin undergoing long journeys till it reached the Hindu Kush and the Karakoram as, for example, is the case of the trunnion axes found in Darel Valley datable to second millennium BCE.[301] Significantly enough, the megalithic pattern of Kashmir points to western affiliation. For example, like European menhirs, they form a semicircle and fall under the alignment type of megaliths. Also, as observed in Kashmir, some of the menhirs in plains of Salisbury, South England, also bear cup marks.[302] It is also significant to mention here that the menhirs of the Peninsular India also point to the influence of the west and chronologically they are younger to the Megaliths of Chitral and Yasin.[303]

Cist Graves

Alongside Megaliths, a different type of archaeological data represented by cist graves has been reported from the valley that speaks of the penetration of an entirely different people, belonging to the so-called Gandhara Grave Culture. The cist graves have been reported from a high plateau on the left bank of river Lidder near Pahalgam. These graves are like box chambers with orthostats on the four sides surmounted by cap stones. The grave goods included pottery (some pots besmeared with red ochre internally), copper rings and wire, shell and some such objects. In one of the smaller pots with flaring rim, smoothened neck and sides, a tooth and some isolated bones probably of a human being were also reported.[304]

The nearest parallels of the cist graves of Kashmir are found in the Nuristan Province in Afghanistan, Swat and in many neighbouring valleys—Dir, Chitral etc. collectively called 'Gandhara Grave Culture.'[305] The archaeological record of the principal sites of this culture is summarised by Allchins,[306] and they reached to the conclusion that "The obvious comparisons for these objects and for the graves themselves are not to be in India or Pakistan, but in Iran and the Caucasus."[307]

The presence of menhirs and cist graves shows that two cultural groups came to Kashmir during the period: one belonging to menhir culture and the other to the cist grave culture. The menhir culture group had connections with Chitral and Yasin, and the cist grave culture had links with Swat and further down with Indus Kohistan. It may, however, be mentioned that "Gandhara Grave culture" had made rapid strides in menhir culture zone as well. Hence both the cultures obtained simultaneously in some areas, namely, Chitral.[308] In some zones as Chilas and Darel, only pit graves have been reported so far.[309] Since the megaliths of Kashmir are not associated with any skeletal remains and the cist graves do not possess menhirs except slab, it seems that the immigrants came in different tribal groups and each of them occupied different *karewas*. As somewhere the menhirs overlap the Neolithic settlements, it seems that those sections of fresh immigrants, who preferred to settle along with the earlier settlers, most probably belonged to the ethnic stock of their host group. This seems most probable not only because the Neolithic people of Kashmir, as we have seen, mostly came from the north and north-west of Kashmir but also because the Megalithic period is characterised by many continuities especially in ritual and habit,[310] which change very slowly.

Iranian and Indian Contacts

ACHAEMENIAN INFLUENCES

In 516 BCE, Darius the Achaemenian ruler of Iran extended his empire up to India by annexing Sindh, North-west Frontier and the parts of the Punjab. These territories continued to be a part of Iranian empire till Alexander invaded India in 326 BCE. We learn from the Greek sources that at the time of Iranian invasion Kashmir was a part of Gandhara. Hecataeus of Miletus, who was a contemporary of Cyrus and Darius, refers to Kaspapyros, that is, Kashmir as a Gandharic city.[311] *Milindapanha* compounded the two territories as Kashmira-Gandhara.[312] Patanjali, who lived about 150 BCE, also combines Madra (the Punjab) and Kashmir recalling the compound of the *Milindapanha*, Kashmira-Gandhara.[313] At the time of Alexander's invasion, Kashmir seems to have been under the rule of king Abhisara (Hazara). It is said that when Alexander was returning from India, he tasked the king of Abhisara to rule over Kashmir.[314] Thus all the available evidence points to Kashmir having remained a part of Gandhara and the Punjab, both politically and culturally. It is therefore quite probable that Kashmir too would have remained under the Achaemenians during their long rule of about 200 years over Gandhara and the parts of the Punjab, paving the way for Iranian influences. This is besides the fact that even without being a part of Persian empire, Achaemenid occupation of the immediate north-west and south-west borderlands of Kashmir for a long period of about two centuries was bound to influence Kashmir given its intimate relations with these neighbourhoods. The Persian influences also penetrated indirectly through the agency of Mauryas, who were influenced by Persian culture and who, as we shall see in the following pages, ruled Kashmir for a long time.

As the Achaemenids were the first to construct a real empire in the world,[315] it may be perhaps reasonable to infer that it was during their occupation that Kashmir emerged a single political entity through the intervention of Achaemenid governors, who integrated the self-ruled tribes occupying different parts of the valley. The Achaemenids also introduced writing in India.[316] There is no archaeological evidence about the presence of writing in India after the disappearance of Indus civilisation in 1900 BCE. The Achaemenids were the first Iranian speakers to introduce writing well before the sixth century BCE.[317] It is, therefore, plausible to suggest that Kashmir too learnt writing under the Achaemenid influence. The script introduced by the Achaemenids in their Indian possessions was Aramaic. The Kharoshthi script, which became common in Gandhara as well as in Kashmir, was also carved out of Aramaic. In Chapter 3, we will see the deep imprints of Zoroastrianism on the culture of ancient Kashmir. It is quite possible that, as in Taxila,[318] the process started with considerable vigour during the long Achaemenian rule over Kashmir and its neighbourhood. The Persian influences through the medium of Achaemenid occupation as well as owing to the contiguity of Mauryan empire with Iran are also seen in various aspects of Mauryan culture. The Mauryan kings, like the Persian monarchs, lived in seclusion (only appearing for solemn occasions);[319] the pillared hall at Patliputra, the Mauryan capital, is of Achaemenid type with some 80 monolithic columns having "high the polish characteristic Persepolitan masonry."[320] The Buddhist architecture of Aśoka, with its bell capitals and winged lions, shows many traces of Persian or Assyrian influences received through Persia;[321] Aśoka's policy of propagating Dhamma through rock inscriptions is reminiscent of similar practice among the Persian as we find at Behistun, Persepolis and Naqsh-e-Rustam;[322] the royal road running through the Mauryan empire finds a parallel in the royal road of the Achaemenids;[323] the idea of using stone by Mauryan artists in place of wood, brick and stucco was also borrowed from the Persians.[324] Indeed, the Mauryan culture was a hybridisation of Indian and West Asian cultural elements, and it is this syncretic culture which transmitted to Kashmir after it became a part of the Mauryan empire, the details of which are given in the following sub-heading.

MAURYAN INFLUENCES

In the beginning of the third century BCE, there emerged a vast empire on the borders of Kashmir, which included a major part of the Indian subcontinent and extended up to eastern Afghanistan. It was the Mauryan empire founded by Chandragupta Maurya (321 BCE). Given the past as well as future history of Kashmir and considering the might of Chandragupta, it is most probable that Kashmir too would have fallen into the hands of Mauryas after they conquered its neighbourhood—Gandhara. It is quite likely especially when we consider that Kashmir and Gandhara formed one political unit in the pre-Aśokan days, according to the Buddhist texts.[325] This is also corroborated by Greek records as mentioned in the preceding pages. There is also a track record that whenever Gandhara fell into the hands of any power, it had its immediate impact upon the political fate of Kashmir too. The excavator of the Semthan site also believes that the beginning of Semthan NBPW could be traced much before the time of Aśoka.[326]

Although there is dearth of direct evidence of the fall out of the Mauryan occupation of the neighbourhood of Kashmir on the latter during the time of Chandragupta Maurya, we have clear evidence in the *Rājataraṅgiṇī* that Kashmir was a part of the Mauryan empire during the reign of Aśoka (269–232 BCE), though we have to give allowance for the error Kalhana makes in representing Aśoka as a local ruler.[327] After all, Kalhana had to depend upon the folklore for the early history of Kashmir. Minus this error, Aśoka is the first ruler among the early rulers recorded by Kalhana about whom we have a genuine tradition. Kalhana's brief but significant information about the king marks him out as the Mauryan emperor. He refers to him as a follower of Jina, that is, Buddha and the builder of numerous *stupas*.[328] Kalhana's representation of the king as a pious follower of the teachings of Buddha is in full agreement with historical fact as vouched for by Aśoka's own famous inscriptions. The reminiscences which Kashmir tradition has retained of this great ruler, though scanty as they are, claim special interest as they point to the exemplary role played by the King in shaping the culture of Kashmir—too exemplary to be forgotten even after the lapse of centuries together. That the famous Mauryan ruler ruled Kashmir is also corroborated by Hiuen Tsang (631 CE), who saw Aśokan *stupas* in the valley.[329] Also, in the *Mahāvamsa*, Kashmir is grouped with other outlying territories of the empire of Aśoka.[330]

The Semthan (Bijbehara, Kashmir) excavations leave no room to doubt about Kashmir being a part of the Mauryan empire.[331] It has yielded two significant characteristics of the Mauryan culture, namely, NBPW and punch-marked coins.[332] What is more, along with NBPW, Semthan also yielded its associated types, such as black-slipped ware, plain red ware and grey ware.[333] Having a broad uniformity with the ceramic industry of India, this early historic pottery indicates an obvious contact with the plains of India. The NBPW culture has also been found at other sites, such as Buna Gantamulla and Kanispur in Baramulla.[334]

Jalauka, whom the tradition preserved by Kalhana represents as the son and successor of Aśoka, appears before us as the popular hero. He is described as a great warrior who cleared the land of the oppressing *Mlecchas*

(Indo-Greeks) and effected extensive conquests.[335] From the subdued land, he, according to Kalhana, brought settlers to Kashmir,[336] and established for the first time a complete system of administration.[337] Tradition portrays him a pre-eminent pious Śaiva.[338] It is, however, impossible for us to verify the authenticity of this Kashmiri tradition regarding Jalauka. According to Romila Thapar, as Jaluka is "foreign to any of the king lists of the Mauryas," he "may possibly be a confused rendering of the name Kunala, the son of Asoka whom the later placed in charge of the region from the Indus as far as the Chinese frontier which included Khotan, Kashmir and Gandhara."[339]

The Mauryan rule, which lasted for not less than 80 years (even if we presume that Kashmir came under the control of Mauryas only during the reign of Aśoka), forms a significant phase in the history of Kashmir as it brought Kashmir and the Indian subcontinent closer to each other beyond precedent. Until then, Kashmir was intimately related only to a very limited area of the Indian subcontinent, namely, the Punjab and North-West Frontier, especially Hazara, Swat and Potwar region. Now Kashmir got connected with the heart of India—middle Gangetic plains, which set a stage for extending and deepening Kashmir's relations with distant parts of India as we see in the subsequent centuries.

MECHANISMS OF CIRCULATION

Perhaps the most significant contribution of the Mauryas as great empire builders is that besides having integrated India politically, they showed equal interest in achieving cultural unification of the country. The existence of inscriptions, occasional NBPW potsherds and punch-marked coins in Bengal, Orissa, Andhra, Karnataka as well as in Kashmir (in Kashmir, however, no inscriptions have been found so far) from about 300 BCE shows that attempts were made to spread elements of the middle Gangetic basin culture in distant areas.[340]

As elsewhere, the Mauryan culture spread in the valley through different channels. The occupation of distant lands like Kashmir necessitated not only deputing trusted governors, top officials and army contingents from the centre to rule on behalf of the central authority, but it entailed more than that—creating a local support structure by encouraging migrations to Kashmir from the heart lands of the empire and establishing new settlements under the patronage of the state. The process seems to be in accord with the instructions of Kautilya, who advised that new settlements should be founded with the help of cultivators, who were apparently Vaiśyas, and with that of Shudra labourers who should be drafted from overpopulated areas.[341] That new cultural groups having Gangetic association were settled in different parts of the valley is evidenced by Semthan finds and many more NBPW sites, namely, Buna Gantamulla and Kanispura in Baramulla.[342] Since the Mauryan culture was the culture of the ruling class, it became a *reference culture*. In other words, for all those who aspired a membership of a high culture, it became necessary to see their faces through the mirror of Mauryan culture.

Another and the most effective channel through which Mauryan culture spread in Kashmir was the missionaries who, as we shall see, were sent to Kashmir for winning conversions to Buddhism. These missionaries established *sangramas* (monasteries) in different nooks of the valley under the patronage of the state. It may be in place to mention here that there are many villages in Kashmir named as *sangram*, obviously because these settlements came into existence around the *sangramas* established there.[343] With the establishment of *sangramas* in different parts of Kashmir, the Indian culture got disseminated in the whole valley.

For a proper understanding and appreciation of the impact of Mauryan culture upon Kashmir, it is pertinent to know the salient features of this culture. It is now well established that the material culture in the Gangetic basin during the Mauryas was based on an intensive use of iron, wet rice cultivation, prevalence of writing, plenty of punch-marked coins, abundance of beautiful pottery (NBPW), introduction of burnt bricks, ring wells, wooden architecture, high technical skill in stone masonry and, above all, the rise of towns.[344] So far as administrative and ideological apparatus of the Mauryas is concerned, they developed an elaborate administrative mechanism and had a vast bureaucracy working under royal absolutism. During the period of Aśoka *Dhamma* was the governing ideology of the state.[345]

Intensive Use of Iron While there are few references to iron artefacts in Kashmir before the penetration of Mauryan culture, the only similarity with Iron Age material culture appears to be associated with NBPW found at Semthan along with an arrow head and a few slag pieces.[346] Clearly, on account of the contacts with the Mauryas, Kashmir entered into a full-fledged Iron Age era, though except for a few iron objects, iron tools of the period have not survived to us.[347] Having easy access to the rich iron ores of South Bihar, the people of the Gangetic plains had made an intensive use of iron by the time Kashmir was conquered by the Mauryas. They used iron implements such as socketed axes, sickles and ploughshare, which spread to the outlying areas, particularly those which formed a part of the Mauryan empire.[348] It is important to mention that the ploughshare of Kashmiri plough takes after typologically the Mauryan ploughshare; and some Kashmiri ploughs closely resemble with the ploughs operating in India.[349]

Promotion of Rice Culture Alongside popularising plough agriculture, especially the use of iron plough share, the Mauryan impact led to the second major revolution in promoting rice culture in Kashmir.[350] Undoubtedly, as we saw, rice cultivation made rapid strides in Kashmir from ca. 1000

BCE, but wheat and barley were still preferred crops because of the habit of mind. During the Mauryas, rice was the staple cereal in eastern Utter Pradesh and Bihar. What is more, we find the practice of transplantation of paddy obtaining in the middle Gangetic plains since about 500 BCE.[351] It is most probable that the practice spread to Kashmir as well. It may be mentioned that the wet rice cultivation is the only kind of rice cultivation known in the history of Kashmir; and transplantation is one of the popular traditional practices, the other being broadcasting (*wootur*). Significantly, Patanjali's *Mahābhāsya* (ca. 150 BCE) makes a solitary mention of Kashmir, and that too only to reveal that rice was already being cultivated in the valley at that time,[352] testifying the marked presence of rice among the crops raised then in Kashmir.

The introduction of iron ploughshare and gradual shift from rain fed crops to wet rice cultivation ushered in an agricultural revolution in Kashmir. Not only that now it became easier to bring new lands under cultivation, but what is more, the per unit production of rice was many times more than the traditionally grown rain fed cereals.[353] This is the reason that with the popularity of rice cultivation—the process which started with Semthan settlers and received great fillip with the coming of the Mauryas—the traditional pattern of the rural settlements also changed drastically. Since paddy could be grown in the valley floor only, the people moved to the habitable low-lying areas in preference to the table lands (*wadurs*) as was customary prior to the popularisation of rice culture.[354] Not surprisingly, therefore, the land-man ratio in the valley floor presents a contrast to the land-man ratio obtained in the *karewas*: in the valley floor population is far greater than the availability of land. Reverse is the case in the *karewa* ecotypes. This is the legacy of the times when rice cultivation assumed currency in Kashmir.

Northern Black Polished Ware As is true of other places which came into contact with the Mauryas, the period witnessed the introduction of the finest pottery type ever to be developed in India—the NBPW. It developed around 500 BCE and is associated with the life of Gautama Buddha, his contemporary personalities and the Mauryas.[355] From its homeland in the central Gangetic plain, it travelled through administrators, traders and missionaries to Taxila and Charsadda—two famous cities of Gandhara in the north, to distant places in the south like Amravati on the Krishna, to west as far as Somnath and in the east to Gaur and Pandua in east Bengal.[356] With its discovery in the valley, the evidence of the extent of Mauryan sway and its cultural impact up to Kashmir has been established beyond doubt. In the valley, the NBPW was first found at Semthan.[357] It was associated with red and grey wares (600–200 BCE). Subsequently in course of exploration many more NBPW sites like Buna-Gautamulla and Kansipur were spotted.[358] A few shards were also encountered at the later phase of Burzahom and Gufkral settlements.[359] The wide distribution of the NBPW not only indicates the wide-spread impact of NBPW culture on Kashmir but it also shows that the period witnessed the introduction of the technology of this deluxe pottery. This technology was apparently introduced in Kashmir by the Indian potters who accompanied Mauryan administrators and Buddhist missionaries. The NBPW was extremely glossy and shinning type of pottery serving as the tableware of richer people. It represents the technical skill of the early Indian potter at its best. So is true of the Kashmiri potter, who showed remarkable imitative power in producing this what is also called "prince among the Indian potteries."

Stone Architecture The main activity which Kalhana attributes to Aśoka as a ruler of Kashmir is the construction of stupas, vihāras, chaityas and temples.[360] Four of his stupas even existed at the time of Hiuen Tsang's visit to the valley in the middle of the seventh century CE.[361] The archaeological spade has yet to uncover any trace of these earlier structures. We also do not know anything of their architectural details except what Kalhana says about a chaitya built by Aśoka that its "height could not be reached by the eye."[362] Equally important is the mention that the king removed "the old stuccoed enclosure of the shrine of Vijayesvara, built [in its stead] a new one of stone."[363] That the stuccoed constructions were replaced by stone is further authenticated by the exposure of rubble wall in the excavations at Semthan in Period II.[364] Such specimens, though isolated at the moment, are of great significance as they indicate the beginning of stone architecture in Kashmir which, in course of time, developed into a glorious architecture as is shown by the stone temple ruins of the early medieval Kashmir.

In this regard we have to remember that the Mauryas made a remarkable contribution to Indian art and architecture. While Chandragupta Maurya patronised wooden architecture,[365] Aśoka introduced stone masonry on a wide scale.[366] Given the advances made by the Mauryas in masonry work, it may be reasonable to conclude that the stone art and architecture began in Kashmir on account of the spread of Mauryan culture. The solitary fragment of a lion capital still lying on the left bank of the Vitasta at present-day Vejibror may not actually belong to an Aśokan pillar, but it certainly belongs to the Aśokan tradition.

Kharoshthi Script In the interest of unifying the country, Aśoka respected such scripts as Brahmi, Kharoshthi, Aramaic and Greek. He also accommodated such languages as Greek, Prakrit and Sanskrit. The epigraphical records reveal that prior to the Mauryas Kharoshthi was the common script of Gandhara,[367] and quite possibly of Kashmir too. It was so common that Aśoka had to write some inscriptions in the north-west in this script. For example, we find close to the border of Kashmir at Mansehra near Abbottabad and at Shahbazgarhi near Peshawar Aśokan edicts written in Kharoshthi,[368] showing that the Kharoshthi script continued to be the main script of the region during the Mauryas. Indeed, as is true of north-west India, the Kharoshthi was the main script of Kashmir till fifth century CE as is shown by the Harwan tiles. Kharoshthi script had evolved from Aramaic; and like Aramaic, it was written from right to left. It was used for almost 700 years from 300 BCE to the middle of the fifth century CE. Gandhara was its place of birth but specimens of this script have been found over a vast territory extending from Gandhara in the west to Mathura and Patna in the east and Central Asia in the north to Mohenjo-daro in the South. It was a fully developed phonetic script and was well-adapted to the sounds of *prakrit*, then spoken in the Indus-land, now Pakistan. In its developed form, Kharoshthi appears to have been first used by Aśoka for his Rock Edicts for the propagation of Buddhism. The Greeks, Scythians and Parthians used this script to their best advantage as a medium of communication between the local people and their foreign overlords. Its use reached its maximum during Kuṣāṇa rule in the second-third century CE.[369]

Punch-marked Coins Although certain terms in later Vedic literature are interpreted to suggest the use of coins, actual coins have not been found in India before the age of the Buddha. These were made largely of silver though a few coppers also appear. These coins bear the stamps of one to five punches. By reason that these were punched with certain marks, these coins are known amongst numismatists and historians as "punch-marked coins." The punching device of these coins bears no inscriptions. Instead, they have devices such as hills, trees, birds, animals, religious symbols and the like. Each of the symbols is found confined to the coins of a particular area or on those of a particular variety or type. More than 300 hoards of punch-marked coins are known. These were found in almost every part of the Mauryan empire. However, the coins of different regions differ from one another in their execution, fabric, weight, quality of metal and symbology.[370]

In Kashmir the punch-marked silver coins and cast copper coins have been found with NBPW at Semthan.[371] Earlier to this, two punch-marked coins were discovered by GB Bleazby somewhere in Kashmir.[372] They are recorded in numismatic collection of SPS Museum, Srinagar. Iqbal Ahmad also claims to have "come across several four and five symboled punch-marked coins in private collections maintained in Srinagar city."[373] The punch-marked coins found in Kashmir are mostly of Magadhan type. They bear four to five symbols stamped over the face of the coin, reverse being almost blank. Only in rare cases they bear some minute impressions (Figs. 2.1 and 2.2). These coins, however, still await a study by an expert. It is intriguing that despite being closely related with Gandhara, no bent bar coin has so far been found in Kashmir.

Along with the political integration of Kashmir with a vast empire, coinage might have promoted considerably the internal as well as external trade of Kashmir improving the economic condition of the state and some sections of the society. The new imports like NBPW, copper and silver accounted for the introduction of new technology, cultural growth and a further fillip to investments on luxuries by upper classes. The latter phenomenon has always been accompanied by two contradictory developments—exploitation of the working classes and increase in production.

Beginning of Urbanism One significant contribution of the Mauryas to Kashmir is the introduction of urban culture. Whether there was any city in Kashmir prior to the Mauryas, it is not known. What is, however, clearly known is that, according to Kalhana, Aśoka built a great city and named it Śrinagari. To quote him, "The illustrious King [Aśoka] built the town of Śrinagari, which was most important on account of its ninety-six lakhs of houses resplendent with wealth."[374] Śrinagari has been identified at the site of the present town of Pandrethan (Kalhana's *Puranadhisthana*) including the area called Badami Bagh, presently under the possession of the army. Pandrethan is a corrupt form of *Puranadhisthana,* meaning old capital, which the place came to be called when the capital was shifted to the site of present Srinagar (around Hari Parbat) by Pravarasena II at the end of the sixth century CE.[375] Although the new capital was named as Pravarapura, it too became popular by the name of Śrinagari. Being the capital of Kashmir for more than 800 years, the name Śrinagari had become synonymous with the capital to the popular mind and imagination. Moreover, Pravarasena's city was practically contiguous to the older Śrinagari and existed for centuries side by side with it. We can hence easily understand why popular usage retained the old familiar designation for the new capital too. This is exactly what we see with regard to the cities founded in the vicinity of Delhi by successive kings. All of them continued to be known simply by the name of Delhi, though each of them was originally intended to bear the distinctive name of its founder.

Though the city founded by Aśoka had sunk to small importance already by the twelfth century, extensive remains of ancient buildings can still be traced on the terraced slopes rising immediately to the north and north-east of modern Pandrethan.[376]

The foundation of the city Śrinagri in Kashmir by Aśoka has to be understood in the backdrop of the NBPW culture. Besides other things, this culture is marked by the emergence of a large number of towns. That is why this phase of Indian history is called the period of Second Urbanisation in India.[377] Many important towns had already come into existence in the middle Gangetic basin and other parts of India. Mention may be made of Kausambi, Sravasti, Ayodhya, Kapilavastu, Varanasi, Vaishali, Rajgir, Patliputra, Champa, Mathura, Ujjain, Taxila etc.[378] It was this city culture which the Mauryans introduced in Kashmir resulting in the foundation of the first known city in Kashmir.

However, for the foundation of a city, it was a pre-requisite to achieve a required economic growth. Unless the villages would grow surplus food to feed city population and provide raw material for its crafts, and unless there was sufficient scope for internal and external trade which is the life blood for the survival of cities, it was neither possible to build a city like Śrinagari nor could it be maintained. The Mauryan period, as we saw, witnessed a remarkable economic development owing to intensive use of iron, popularity of wet rice cultivation, availability of a wide market to Kashmiri merchants following the political integration of Kashmir with a big empire, and the introduction of punch-marked coins. All these factors provided necessary ingredients for the emergence of a major city in Kashmir. It may be in place to mention here that the selection of site for Śrinagari reflects Seleucid tradition especially for its location on the river bank and the backing of hills.[379]

Imperial Organisation It is well known that in no other period of ancient history we hear of so many officers as in Mauryan times. If we believe Kautilya, there were 27 superintendents (*adhyakśas)* only to regulate economic activities of the state.[380] The central government maintained about two dozen departments. The administration of the capital city, Patliputra, was carried on by six committees, each consisting of five members.[381] The elaborate system of administration organised by the Mauryas had a direct impact on the administrative system of the provinces under their control. Not surprisingly, therefore, we find Kalhana crediting Jaluka, the supposed successor of Aśoka, for having established 18 offices (*karmasthana*) in Kashmir against the seven which existed until then. For the establishment of these offices, the ruler brought experts from outside. Giving allowance for his "political fiction," Kalhana's information is worth quoting:

> Having conquered the earth, including Kanyakubja and other [countries], he [Jaluka] settled from that region people of four castes in his own land, and [particularly] righteous men acquainted with legal procedure. Upto that time there existed in this land, which had not yet reached its proper development in legal administration, wealth and other [respects], a government like in most countries.

> There were [only] seven main state officials: the judge, the revenue superintendent, the treasurer, the commander of the army, the envoy, the *purohita*, and the astrologer. By establishing eighteen offices (*karamasthana*) in accordance with traditional usage, the king created from that time onwards a condition of things as under Yudhisthira.[382]

This statement sheds light on some important developments which took place in Kashmir during the Mauryas. First, Kashmir achieved an unprecedented economic development which necessitated as well as made possible to establish an elaborate administrative organisation. Second, during the period, a large number of experts in statecraft were brought from outside and settled in Kashmir. And last but not least, Kashmir entered into an era of full-fledged political organisation with a well-knit administrative system backed by a vast bureaucracy.

Religious Developments

Religious Scenario at the Advent of Buddhism About the religious conditions of Kashmir on the eve of the Mauryan occupation of Kashmir, we have no direct and concrete contemporary evidence except what one can gather from latter sources and indirectly from comparative history. Being a part of the geographical and cultural complex of the borderlands situated on its immediate west and north-west, the world-view of Kashmiris was always shaped by the religious developments occurring in these neighbourhoods. It is, therefore, understandable to see almost identical sequence of religious developments between them and Kashmir throughout its history. In the borderlands of Kashmir we find Naga cult, perhaps the earliest and the most popular belief.[383] The available evidence of Śaiva rites and symbols is no later than Harappan culture.[384] The worship of Viṣṇu was popular in Gandhara as early as the fifth century BCE.[385] The Aryans introduced Vedic religion around 1700–500 BCE. The Persian occupation of Gandhara led to the spread of Zoroastrianism in the region.[386] Notwithstanding the presence of the same beliefs and cults in Kashmir at the advent of Buddhism, Naga cult was still a dominant tradition. This is the reason why the Buddhist tradition mentions only Nāgas whom the Buddhist missionaries had to contest in Kashmir.[387]

Introduction of Buddhism The antiquity of Buddhism in Kashmir is shrouded in controversy as some Buddhist texts attribute it to the time of Aśoka; and some trace its history to much earlier times.[388] The majority of the Buddhist sources, however, favour the first view and give credit to Majjhantika, a monk of Varanasi and a disciple of Ananda, sent to Kashmir during the time of Aśoka. *Mahavamsa*, the Ceylonese chronicle, says that after the Third Buddhist Council Moggaliputta Tissa, the spiritual guide of King Aśoka sent missionaries to different countries to propagate Buddhism. And one of them was Majjhantika who was deputed to Kashmir and Gandhara.[389] The story of the introduction of Buddhism in Kashmir by Majjhantika is told in several other Buddhist texts, namely, the Tibetan *Dulva*, *Aśokavadana*, *Avadanakalpalata*[390] and the travel accounts left by Hiuen Tsang.[391]

Having made his newly founded city—Śrinagari—as the centre of Buddhism, which it continued to enjoy for centuries together, as is revealed by archaeological evidence,[392] Aśoka also built *sangramas, vihāras, chaityas* and *stupas* in different parts of the valley. For instance, Kashmiri tradition, as preserved by Kalhana, credits Aśoka for having built numerous stupas at Śuskaletra (Hukhalitar) and Vitastara (?):

> This king who had freed himself from sins and had embraced the doctrine of Jina, covered Śuskaletra and Vitastātra with numerous stupas. At the town of Vitastātra there stood within the precincts of the Dharmāranya Vihara a Caitya built by him, the height of which could not be reached by the eye.[393]

Five centuries before Kalhana, Hiuen Tsang also recorded his personal testimony to the existence of four stupas built by Aśoka in the valley, one of which was as high as 50 feet.[394] Aśoka not only built monasteries and stupas but, according to the Tibetan accounts, he also gifted the Kashmir kingdom to the *sangha* itself.[395]

It may be significant to mention that there are many villages in Kashmir known by the name of *sangrama*, obviously for having emerged around the Buddhist monasteries. We also find many identical place names in Kashmir and the Indian plains. For example, Muqam, Poshkar and Vagad, which were famous centres of meditation of the Buddhist monks as is also evident by their geographical location situated as these places are on the lush green hillocks of Kashmir. It was owing to their identical importance with such centres elsewhere in India, that the immigrant Buddhist missionaries called them by the names already famous in the Buddhist creed. The special importance of these places as suitable spots for meditation continued despite religious changes. After the spread of Islam in Kashmir, they became the abodes of Muslim Rishis who had inherited the deeply embedded local traditions.

The preceding details make it abundantly clear that the history of Kashmir is the history of change mainly caused by empire builders, immigrations, flows, subversion, resistance and accommodation. The following chapter will carry forward this story by embracing a vast period when Kashmir remained a part of great cosmopolitan ecumenes originating from Central Asia and extending up to India.

Figure 2.1 Rectangular and round shaped punch-marked coins.

Obverse: punched with sun and six armed symbols. Tree in reeling and arched hill symbols
Reverse: blank or sometimes bear minute impressions
(SPS Museum, Srinagar)

Figure 2.2 Rectangular copper punch-marked coins.

Obverse: Punched with sun, six armed and bull symbols
Reverse: Blank (Semthan, Bijbehara Kashmir)

Notes

1 Sankalia (1977), 2.
2 For up-to-date and comprehensive account of the theories of human evolution since Darwin presented his theory of evolution by natural selection in 1859, and the diffusion of humankind, see Jones, Martin and Pilbean (1992), 86–107; De Laet (1994); Cavalli-Saforza, Menozzi and Piazza (1994); Larick and Ciochon (1996); Gabunia and Vekua (1995), 375: 509–12; Wanpo *et al.* (1995), 378–87; Swisher III *et al.* (1994), 263: 1118–21.
3 Rendell (1981), 3–9; Allchin (1986), 2: 69–83; Rendell and Dennell (1985), 26(5): 393; Dennell (1995), 20(1): 21–28; Salim (1997), 20(2).
4 Rendell (1981); Allchin (1986), 2: 69–83; Rendell and Dennell, 393; Dennell, 21–28; Salim, 20(2).

5 Paterson and Drummond (1962), 95.
6 Sankalia (1974a); Bandey (2009), 45–46.
7 Joshi *et al.* (1976), 5(3): 369–79.
8 Allchin (1986), 2: 69–83.
9 Lal (1956), 12: 58–92.
10 Paterson and Drummond, 95.
11 Ibid.
12 Mohapatra (1982), 28–37.
13 Joshi *et al.*, 369–79.
14 Bandey (2009), 53–57.
15 Cf. Habib and Habib (2012), 5.
16 Bandey (2009), 53–55.
17 de Terra and Paterson (1939), 233.
18 Rendell, 3–9; Allchin (1986), 2: 69–83; Rendell and Dennell, 393; Dennell, 21–28.
19 de Terra and Paterson, 233.
20 Shali (1993), 55.
21 Bandey (2009), 106–07.
22 Dani (1989), 110.
23 Ibid, 91.
24 See Wani and Wani (2018), 29–30.
25 The flat-topped plateaus, which occupy about half of the space of the valley, are lacustrine deposits (lake deposits). In the geological literature they are famous by their Persian name *karewas* though in the local parlance they are called *wuder*.
26 *Indian Archaeology – A Review,* 1961–62; Khazanchi (1976), 25–27.
27 *Indian Archaeology – A Review* (1960–61 to 1973–74).
28 Buth and Kaw (1985), 109–13.
29 Pant (1981); also see Bandey (2009).
30 *Indian Archaeology – A Review* (1961–62).
31 Pant; also see Bandey (2009).
32 Ibid.
33 Khazanchi and Dikshit (1979–80), 9: 49; Saar (1992), 13–14.
34 *Indian Archaeology – A Review,* (1961–62).
35 Lone *et al.* (1993), 144.
36 The slab, measuring 70×45 cm is flat on both sides, irregularly cut and smoother on the engraved face. The hunting scene on the slab covers an area of 48×27 cm. Pande (1971), XIV: 194–98.
37 For details, see Sharma (1967), 16(3).
38 Sharma (1967), 16(3).
39 Ibid.
40 Sharma (1968a), 1/2: 40–44; *Indian Archaeology – A Review* (1962–63).
41 Basu and Pal (1980), 17; Sankhyan and Weber (2001), II (5): 375–80.
42 Sharma (1981); idem (1982a); idem (1982b); idem (1986).
43 Ibid.
44 Ibid.
45 Ibid.
46 Ibid.
47 Ibid.
48 Ibid.
49 Ibid.
50 Ibid.
51 Mani (2000), 10: 1–28. Also see Mani (2008), 18: 229–247.

52 Ibid.
53 Ibid.
54 Mani (2004), 1(1): 137–143.
55 See Wani and Wani, op. cit., 43–44.
56 For details, see Yatoo (2012); also, Spate *et al.* (2017), 11: 568–77.
57 Sankalia (1974b), 303.
58 Khazanchi (1977), 24.
59 Fairservis (1971), 312–13; Diksht (1982), VI: 53.
60 Fairservis (1971), 312–13.
61 Stacul, G. 1994, 707–714.
62 Fuller (2006), 20(1): 1–86.
63 Parpola (1994), 142.
64 Aggarwal (1982); Allchin and Allchin (1981), 116; Pande (1971), XIV: 134.
65 Parpola, 142.
66 For example, Mehargarh. For details, see Jarrige and Lechevallier (1979), 463–535.
67 Rekha Dodia *et al.* (1984), 105.
68 Dodia *et al.*, 105.
69 Jarrige and Lechevallier; Fairservis (1956), 45(2): 349; Dani (1970–71).
70 Fairservis (1956), 45(2): 349; Jarrige and Lechevallier; Dani (1970–71).
71 Dani (1970–71); Jarrige and Lechevallier; Fairservis (1956), 45(2): 349.
72 Mongait (1961), 91, 92, 109 & 122; Bryusov (1952), 21: 78–79.
73 Cheng (1959), I: 54, 59, 76, 107 & 133.
74 Watson (1961), 50.
75 Groote (1951), 37, 44–45, 51, 59, 61 & 69.
76 Singh (1974), 42, 48 & 49.
77 Singh, (1974), op cit.
78 Mellaart (1975), 74.
79 Singh (1974), 166.
80 Ibid, 167.
81 Allchin and Allchin, 110.
82 Stacul (1977), 27: 227–253.
83 Ibid.
84 Durrani (1981), 134–35; Allchin and Knox (1979), 241–44.
85 Mellaart (1975), 191; Shashi Asthana, *Pre-Harappan Cultures of India and the Borderlands*, (1985), 25; Singh (1974), 100, 150, 167, 190
86 Gupta, *Archaeology of Soviet Central Asia and Indian Borderlands*. Asthana, *Pre-Harappan Cultures of India and the Borderlands*, (DATE), 35; Masson and Sarianidi (1972), 36.
87 Jarrige and Lechevallier (1979).
88 Ibid, 68, 105.
89 Masson and Sarianidi (1972), 36 & 48.
90 Singh (1974), 186.
91 Jarrige and Lechevallier, 10.
92 Mongait (1961), 100, 110.
93 Masson and Sarianidi (1972), 36, 48.
94 Cheng (1959), 90, 131; Chang (1963), 66, 94.
95 Groote (1951), 37, 38, 61, 62, 65 & 68.
96 Solecki and Rose (1961), 58–60; Braidwood and Howe (1960), 248; Braidwood and Braidwood (1950), 24: 189–95.
97 Hole and Flannery (1962), 24: 97–148; Meldagard, Morten and Thrane, "Excavations at Tepe Guran Luristan." In: *Acta Archaeology*, (DATE), 34: 97–133.

98 Todd (1966), 16: 139–63.
99 Lommel (1966), 45.
100 Ibid.
101 Ibid.
102 Lommel (1966), 45; Ross (1946), 5(4): 296; Fairservis (1956), 45(2): 233; De Cardi (1965), 2: 101; Mughal (1972), 8:117–24; Dani (1970–71), 84–85; Halim (1970–72), 7/8: 20–22.
103 Halim (1970–72), 7/8: 20–22.
104 Lommel (1966), 65.
105 For details, see Asthana (1985), 200–204.
106 Asthana (1976), 80.
107 Ibid, 77.
108 Ibid, 77, 80.
109 Mani (2004), 1(1):137–43. Also, see idem (2008), 18: 229–247; Saraswat and Pokharia (2004).
110 Saraswat and Pokharia (2004).
111 Costantini (1981), 29–33.
112 Renfrew (1973).
113 Mani, (2004 and 2008).
114 Ibid.
115 Ibid.
116 For Burzahom and Gufkral, see Lone *et al.* (1993), 204–207; *Indian Archaeology: A Review* (IAR), 1981–82, 19–25. And for Qasim Bagh, see Spate *et al.* (2017), 11:568–77; Yatoo (2012).
117 Renfrew (1973).
118 Lone *et al.* (1993), 204–207.
119 Ibid.
120 Ibid, 125.
121 Mani (2004)
122 Harlon and Zohary (1966), 153(3740):1074–80; Hellback (1966), 20: 350.
123 Jarrige and Meadow (1980), 243(2): 122–32.
124 Lone *et al.* (1993), 137.
125 Renfrew (1973).
126 Lone *et al.* (1993), 138.
127 Asthana (1975), 191.
128 Ibid.
129 Allchin and Allchin, 116.
130 Stacul (1977), 27: 235.
131 Stacul (1967), 17(3/4): 209.
132 Ibid.
133 Ibid, 210. For similar views, see Lahiri (1992), 150.
134 Mughal (1972), 8:36.
135 Allchin and Allchin, 111.
136 Cheng (1959), 57, 61, 80, 92, 100, 125, 139, 143, 149.
137 Lone *et al.* (1993), 13.
138 Renfrew (1973).
139 Allchin and Allchin, 115.
140 Vats (1940); quoted by Bandey (2009), 204.
141 Asthana (1975), 191.
142 Ibid, 191–194.
143 Allchin and Allchin, 116.
144 Shaffer (1978), 149.
145 For details, see Asthana (1975), 204.

146 Durrani (1981), 135; Dani (1970–71), 44; *Pakistan Archaeology* (1968), 35–36.
147 G Stacul (1987), 1992–3.
148 Fairservis (1971), 312–13.
149 Lone *et al.* (1993), 13.
150 Spate *et al.* (2017), 11:568–77; Yatoo (2012).
151 Lone *et al.* (1993), 13.
152 Spate *et al* (2017), 11:568–77.
153 Chang, *The Archaeology of Ancient China*, 87–95.
154 MacNeish and Libby (1995), 13. Vide, Loewe and Shaughnessy (1999), 46.
155 Ibid.
156 Ibid, 45–46.
157 Hunt *et al.* (2012), 20(22).
158 Miller *et al.* (2016), 26(10): 1566–75.
159 Lone *et al.* (1993), 13.
160 Ghosh and Chakrabarti (1980), IV: 60.
161 Ibid, 60–61.
162 Mittre and Savithri (1982), 205–21.
163 MacNeish and Libby (1995), 13.
164 Costantini (1987), 155–165.
165 Ibid.
166 For a brief mention of Swat's trade contacts with China, see Allchin and Allchin, 116.
167 Spate *et al.* (2017), 11: 7.
168 Allchin and Allchin, 115.
169 Ibid, 115–16.
170 Lone *et al.* (1993), 144.
171 NI Vavilov, op. cit., 360.
172 Allchin and Allchin, 80, 191, 264 & 276.
173 Cheng, op. cit., 97, 107, 115, 130–31, 137, 141 & 145.
174 Stacul (1989), 268.
175 Stacul (1992), 111–121.
176 Yatoo, and Bandey (2014), XXI: 37–44.
177 Ibid.
178 Shaffer (1978); Asthana (1975), 84–85.
179 Jarrige and Meadow, 130.
180 Mughal (1972), 8:36.
181 Piggot (1948), 4: 33–38; for Manda, see Joshi and Bala (1982).
182 Ibid.
183 Allchin and Allchin, 116; Asthana (1985), 204.
184 Mughal (1972), 8:36; Jarrige and Meadow, 130; Fairservis (1956), 45(2): 230.
185 Jarrige and Meadow, 130; Fairservis (1956), 45(2): 230.
186 Halim (1970–72), 7/8: 25–26; Dani (1970–71), 88–89; Joshi and Bala.
187 Fairservis (1956), 45(2): 230; AH Dani, op. cit., 88; Halim (1970–72), 7/8: 23; Khan (1965), 2: 82.
188 Singer, Holmyard and Hall (1954), I: 199.
189 Habib and Habib, 7.
190 Singer, Holmyard and Hall (1954), I: 199.
191 For details, see Asthana (1976), 173–89.
192 Sankalia (1975), 167; Allchin and Allchin, 163.
193 Ibid.
194 *Indian Archaeology – A Review* (1981–82), 25.
195 Sankalia (1969), 55–56.

196 Khan (1965), 2: 42–45.
197 Mughal (1972), 8:36.
198 Dani (1970–71), 144ff; Durani, op. cit., 133–138.
199 Asthana (1985), 97.
200 Mongait (1961): 97, 103–04, 116 & 122.
201 Chang, op. cit., 42 & 81; Groote 1951), 66; Singh (1974), 100 & 150.
202 Ibid, 167 & 190; Mellaart (1975), 190 & 191.
203 Hole and Flannery (1962), 24: 97–148.
204 Mellart, 72; Sharma, (1967), 242.
205 Gupta (1972), 89.
206 Ibid.
207 Loewe and Shaughnessy (1999), 160, 162, 166–67, 170, 178, 184, 189, 192, 196, 219–20, 225, 479, 727, 916, 918 & 927.
208 Allchin and Allchin, 116.
209 Ibid.
210 Ibid.
211 Loewe and Shaughnessy (1999), 916–18.
212 Dani (1983), 4. The following information on this subject is borrowed from Dani (1983), 91 and (1989) 90–91.
213 Dani (1989), 484, plate 4; Dani (1983), 53, pl. 34.
214 *Pakistan Archaeology*, (1965), II: 57, fig. 16(1) and plate XVII; (1970–71), V: 65–68.
215 Stein (1979), V: 30, note 30.
216 Dani (1989), 100–101.
217 Ibid. Also, see Dar (1984), 16.
218 Dar (1984), 16.
219 *Kin-lou-tse* of Yaun; quoted by Buddha Prakash; in: *Political and Social Movements in Ancient Punjab,* (Delhi, 1964), 47–48.
220 Prakash (1964), 47–48.
221 Ibid.
222 Stein (1907), 227–53.
223 Kalhana (1979), I: 108–11.
224 Penlebury (1939), 273.
225 *Nīlamata Purāna*, 205 sqq.
226 Abul Fazl (1869), II: 354.
227 Witzel (2008), 82.
228 Kalhana, III, 529–30
229 For ready references, see MA Wani (2004), 260–61.
230 Grierson (1903–22), VIII (II): 253.
231 Grierson (1903–22), VIII (II), Introduction.
232 Ibid.
233 Ibid.
234 *Nīlamata Purāna*, 4ff.
235 Ibid.
236 Akhtar Mohi-ud-Din (1998), 10.
237 Grierson (1903–22), VIII (II): 6.
238 Ray (1969), 31.
239 Quoted by Pollock (2006), 103.
240 Mukhopadhyay (2021), 8(193). This information has been borrowed from *The Hindu*, dated: 5 August 2021.
241 Fabian (1986).
242 Al-Biruni (1993), I: 207.
243 Ibid.

244 *Baharistan-i Shahi*, f. 46.
245 Basu and Pal, 73–80.
246 Witzel (2008), 50.
247 Ray (1969), 32–33.
248 Haddon (1925), 86.
249 Guha (1944), 23–26.
250 Iyer (1969), XIV.
251 Allchin and Allchin, 116.
252 Witzel (2008), 41.
253 Stacul, Swat, Pirak and Connected Problems (Mid 2nd Millennium BC) in: *South Asian Archaeology* (1989), 268
254 Buth, Bisht and Gaur (1982), VI: 41–45.
255 Ibid.
256 *Art Treasures of Jammu and Kashmir – A brochure* (1988).
257 Khazanchi and Dixit, 47–51.
258 Inden (2000), 77.
259 *Nīlamata Purāna*, 68–69.
260 Ibid, 207–208.
261 Ibid, 372–387.
262 Ibid, 231.
263 Ibid, 375.
264 Ibid, 881–946.
265 Abul Fazl (1869), II: 354.
266 *Mahāvamsa*, XII: 3.
267 *Nīlamata Purāna,* 388sqq.
268 Ibid, also vs. 575–581, 683–692.
269 Ibid, 239–242.
270 Sharma (2003), 12–30.
271 Kalhana (1979), V: 397–398.
272 Since exchange of goods and services was the only mode of transaction during the period, we have used the term "obtaining power" instead of purchasing power
273 *India Archaeology – A Review* (1980–81), 32; Buth, Bisht and Gaur, 41–45.
274 Naseem (1982), 175; Bandey (2009), 149; 201–2n47.
275 Meadow (1987), 881–916.
276 Khazanchi and Dikshit, 49.
277 Bandey (2009), 171.
278 Shali (2001), 117.
279 Ibid.
280 Ghosh (ed.), *Indian Archaeology 1964–65: A Review*, Faridabad, Archaeological Survey of India.
281 Hanley (1979).
282 For details about "Gandhara Grave Culture," see Antonini and Stacul (1972); Dani *et al.* (1967), III.
283 Antonini and Stacul (1972).
284 Jettmar (1961), I (105): 98–104.
285 Sharma (1992), I: 63–68.
286 Habib and Habib, 17.
287 Allchin and Allchin, 311–12.
288 MacDonnell and Conningham (2007), 151–159.
289 The term megalith is a Greek word. It is derived from mega (big) and lithos (stone).
290 Kaelas (1994), 1396–97.

291 Ibid.
292 Based on oral history.
293 Kaelas (1994), 1396–97.
294 Ibid, 1435–36
295 Stern (1970), 247–258.
296 Sarkar (1982), II: 49–55; Benerjee (1965), 40–67.
297 Ibid.
298 Hutton (1928), VII: 228–32.
299 Biddulph (1980), 57–58.
300 Dani (1989), 104.
301 About the transmission of trunnion axes from their distant sources Mughal says, "The trunnion axes are linked typologically with those known from the Mediterranean region, Europe, trans-Caucasia and northern Iran." Prof. Karl Jettmar observes that the occurrence of trunnion axes of western type in northern Pakistan indicates penetration of Caucasian elements into the steppes and eastwards in the Pamir and then in the Hindu Kush and the Karakoram. Quoted by Dani, op. cit., (1989), 105.
302 Shali (1993), 91.
303 Ibid, 94.
304 Hanley (1979).
305 For details about "Gandhara Grave Culture," see Antonini and Stacul (1972); Dani *et al.* (1967).
306 The principal sites so far published are Katelai I, Loebanr I, and Timargarha, all in Swat. The broad chronology of the graves appears to cover a wide spread. Katelai I produced five samples dated between 1500 and 200 BC; from Timargarha two samples gave dates of 1710 and 1020 BCE; while from Barama two samples were dated to 800–430 BCE. The graves consist for the most part of an oblong pit sometimes with dry stone walling and generally with stone slabs to form a roof. The pit was often dug in the floor of an upper larger pit, which was filled with soil and charcoal after the burial and often surrounded by a rough stone circle. Children's remains were sometimes placed inside a smaller cist with stone slabs for walls. The great majority contained inhumations with one or two skeletons. A minority of the graves contained cremated ashes, sometimes gathered in pottery cist, or 'box-urn' with flat lid, or large urn with a 'face' decoration consisting of appliqué and cut-out features. Some burials were of collected bones. The grave goods included large quantities of distinctive plain pottery, either buff-red or grey. Metal objects include those of copper or bronze and much more rarely objects of iron. Allchin and Allchin, 239–40
307 Allchin and Allchin, 239–240.
308 Dani (1989), 104.
309 Ibid.
310 For the continuities of earlier period, see Basu and Pal; Sharma (1967, 1968a, 1981, 1982); and Gupta (1972), 82–83.
311 Ray (1969), 35.
312 *Milandapanha*, edited by V Trenckner, (1928), 331.
313 Witzel (2008), 45.
314 Mc Crindle (1896), 69, 111–12.
315 Habib (2002), xx.
316 Ibid.
317 Ibid.
318 Iliffe (1953), 23.
319 Dar (1984), 187–88.

320 Iliffe (1953), 22
321 Dar (1984), 187–88.
322 Iliffe (1953), 22–23.
323 Dar (1984), 187–88.
324 Ibid.
325 N Dutt (1985), 5.
326 Bisht (1986), 56.
327 Kalhana (1979), I: 101–106.
328 Ibid, I: 102–103.
329 Si-Yu-Ki (1911), 1: 150.
330 *Mahāvamsa*, XII: 3.
331 Having published her *Asoka and the Decline of the Mauryas* in 1961, Romila Thapar was right then in saying that "unfortunately the region [Kashmir] has not produced any remains which can be dated with certainty to the Aśokan period" p. 131. But in the second edition of the book published in 2012, she does not make any change in her earlier stand (p. 166). Yet in the Afterward of the book, Thapar seems inclined to accept that Kashmir was a part of Aśokan empire as she says, "To argue that Aśoka described in the *Rājataraṅgiṇī* was not the Mauryan king but a petty ruler of Kashmir, would be rejected by most historians." (2012), 332.
332 *Indian Archaeology - A Review*, (1978–79), 70; (1980–81), 21; (1981–82), 16.
333 Ibid.
334 *Indian Archaeology - A Review*, (1981–82), 16.
335 Kalhana (1979), I: 107, 115–117
336 Ibid, I: 117–19.
337 Ibid, I: 118–120.
338 Ibid, I: 113.
339 Thapar, (2011), 236–37, 242.
340 Up to 1980–1981 about 450 NBP sites were found in different parts of India. Cf. Sharma (1983), 104–5.
341 Kautilya (1915), II (I): 60.
342 *Indian Archaeology - A Review*, (1978–79); (1980–81), 21; (1981–82), 16.
343 I know at least two villages carrying the name of Sangram. One is situated at Tral and another near Sopore.
344 For details, see Sharma (1983), 89 ff.
345 Thapar (2012), 173–227.
346 *Indian Archaeology – A Review*, 1981.
347 In the Gangetic plains too very few iron artefacts survived. Sharma (1983).
348 Sharma (1983), 92, 93, 117.
349 Waheed (2000), 77.
350 See Table 2.1.
351 Sharma (1983), 96.
352 Quoted by Alexis Sanderson (2015), 3.
353 For a vast difference in per unit productivity between rice and rain-fed crops in pre-modern Kashmir, see *Dastur al Amali Kashmir* known as *Tarikh-i-Kalan* written towards the mid of the nineteenth century.
354 For example, Semthan, which is the post-preliterate site, is situated comparatively at low level than Gufkral.
355 For details, see Sinha (1971–72).
356 Ibid. Also, see Sankalia (1952), 11.
357 *Indian Archaeology - A Review* (1978–79), 70; (1980–81), 21.
358 *Indian Archaeology - A Review*, 1981–82, 16.
359 Ibid.
360 Kalhana (1979), I: 102–3.

361 Si-Yu-Ki (1911), 150.
362 Kalhana (1979), I: 103.
363 Ibid.
364 *Indian Archaeology – A Review* (1980–81), 21.
365 For details, see Brown (1959), 5–6.
366 Brown (1959), 10. Fragments of stone pillars and stumps, indicating the existence of an 80-pillared hall, have been discovered at Kumrahar on the outskirts of modern Patna. They certainly attest the high technical skill attained by the Mauryan artisans in polishing the stone pillars, which are as shining as Northern Black Polished ware. Each pillar is made of a single piece of buff-coloured sandstone. Only their capitals, which are beautiful pieces of sculpture in the form of lions or bulls, are joined with the pillars on the top. The Mauryan artisans also started the practice of hewing out caves from rocks for monks to live in as shown by Barabar caves (Gaya Bihar).
367 Marshal and Vogel (1902–03), 141–184.
368 Ibid.
369 Dar (1984), 218–19.
370 Gupta (1969), 8–18.
371 *Indian Archaeology – A Review*, 1978–79, 70; 1980–81, 21.
372 Bleazby (1900).
373 I Ahmad (2002), 4:30.
374 Kalhana (1979), I: 104.
375 Ibid, III: 339–349.
376 For the archaeological importance of Pandrethan, see Sahni (1915–16), 41–61; Kak (1933), 33; Mitra (1977), 16–18.
377 To get an idea of the change which followed in the wake of early historical urbanisation in India, cf. Sharma (1968b), 61; also, see idem (1974), I: 101.
378 Sharma (1968b), 106–107.
379 The selection of the site on the river bank with backing of hills for the construction of cities was a Seleucid tradition. See Tarn (1938), 136–37.
380 Kautilya (1915), I: 19; Dhar (1981), 34–35.
381 Ibid.
382 Kalhana (1979), I: 120.
383 *Ancient Pakistan*, (1970–71), V: 65–68; *Pakistan Archaeology*, (1965), 2: 57; Sankalia (1975–76), 196.
384 For details, see Joshi (1999), 385–388.
385 Deambi (1985), 94.
386 Strabo (1903), XV: 1.
387 *Mahavamsa*, III, 3.
388 According to the Buddhist text *Divyavadana,* several monks of Tamasavana in Kashmir were invited by Aśoka to attend the Third Buddhist Council at Patliputra (*Mahavamśa*, xii, 834–36). Kalhana describes the establishment of several Vihāras in Kashmir during the reign of King Surendra, the predecessor of Aśoka, thus making us believe that Buddhism was introduced in Kashmir before Aśoka. Kalhana, I, 93–94.
389 *Mahavamsa*, XII, 834–36.
390 Dul-Va, 690; *Aśokavadana*, Introduction, 2; Ksemendra, *Avadanakalpalata*, palla, 70.
391 Watters (1988), 1: 261–262.
392 See Sahni (1915–16), 41–61; Kak (1933), 33; Mitra (1977), 16–18.
393 Kalhana (1979), I: 102–103.
394 *Si-Yu-Ki*, tr. Beal, I, 150.
395 *Dul-va*, op. cit.

3

A WORLD WITHIN A WORLD

Encounters With Cosmopolitan Ecumenes and Transculturation (From Greeks to Huns)

> Harwan tiles represent motifs suggestive of more than half a dozen alien civilizations of the ancient world, besides others which are indigenous and local.[1]
>
> Percy Brown

The eight odd centuries, which saw Kashmir's integration with five large empires built successively by the Central Asian powers, namely, Bactrian-Greeks, Śakas, Parthians, Kuṣāṇas, Kidarites and Huns, constitute one of the most formative phases of Kashmir history in that the culture of Kashmir was nourished by many great ancient cosmopolitan ecumenes following the intimate contacts with and immigrations of a variety of cultural groups from Central Asia—the hub of Greek, Persian, Indian, Central Asian and Chinese influences. This chapter discusses these contacts and the changes Kashmir underwent subsequently, allowing us to conceptualize Kashmir as 'a world within a world' besides justifying the term transculturation as it denotes a complex process of transformation unfolding through extended contacts between cultures, acknowledging also that cultural formations are always already hybrid and a dynamic activity.[2]

The Greeks in Kashmir and the Hellenistic Influences

In the preceding chapter, we observed *inter alia* that all along its history Kashmir was considerably influenced by the developments taking place on its immediate borderlands, particularly the north-west and the Punjab. History again repeated when around 200 BCE the Bactrian-Greeks crossed the Hindu Kush and occupied the Peshawar region and Taxila in the Punjab. Before we see how Kashmir was influenced by these developments, it seems pertinent to make a mention of the identity of the Bactrian-Greeks.

After the death of Alexander, the far-flung territories that he had conquered were divided among the powerful generals of his army. Accordingly, a Greek kingdom was established in Syria under Seleucus, which extended from the Euphrates to the Oxus and the Indus. Following in the

DOI: 10.4324/9781003367697-3

footsteps of Alexander, Seleucids established *satrapies* in the conquered territories and appointed *satraps,* who ruled the respective areas on behalf of the central authority. These were essentially military colonies comprising Greek soldiery headed by erstwhile Alexander's generals. One of these *satrapies* was established at Bactria, which lay in the region between the Hindu Kush and the Oxus. In course of time, the Greek rulers of Bactria, like other military colonies, developed their own hierarchical system which, with the passage of time, led to the assertion of their independence. This started happening right in the middle of the third century BCE. In 250 BCE Diodotus backed by his people revolted against Antiochus, the Seleucid king and finally Euthydemus succeeded in carving out an independent kingdom around 240 BCE. The assumption of power by Euthydemus coincides with the death of Aśoka and the gradual process of decline of the Mauryan authority in the north-west.[3] The Graeco-Bactrians gradually expanded southwards, occupying the Kabul Valley, the Peshawar region and Taxila in the Punjab.

After Euthydemus, his son Demetrius became the king of Bactria. He ruled between 200 BCE and 185 BCE. He is remembered for having created a great empire comprising southern Afghanistan, eastern Iran, Seistan up to the Indus, Jhelum and Kashmir.[4] Demetrius was succeeded by a chain of Indo-Greek rulers. Mention may be made of Eucratides, Menander, Antimachus II, Philoxenus, Apollodotus, Nicias, Hippostratus and Calliope also known in history by the name of Hermaeus. They ruled between 200 BCE and 55 BCE. They occupied a large part of north-western India, besides undertaking occasional expeditions to the Ganga basin and other parts of India. The Greeks, who made Bactria their ultimate home, belonged to a cosmopolitan world—an amalgam of Greek, West Asian, Central Asian, Indian and Chinese cultures—for which Bactria was known for centuries together.[5]

Evidence on Kashmir Under the Bactrian-Greeks

The fact that Kashmir remained a part of the Bactrian-Greeks (also called Indo-Greeks/Indus-Greeks)[6] is supported by a varied type of evidence. It is borne out not only by archaeological, numismatic, literary and anthropological evidence but also by place names. Period III at Semthan has revealed a deposit of 40 cm consisting of several floor levels. The important finds obtained from this period, which prove beyond doubt Greek settlements in Kashmir, are coins of Indo-Greek rulers, a distinguishing pottery, a clay seal depicting an Indo-Greek deity, a pot shard with an inscription in Greek which reads as "Dhamorai" or Dharmo (*rajai*), terracotta figurines clad in Greek dress and human heads with serene facial expression.[7] Writing about the Semthan terracottas with Hellenistic subject matter, John Siudmak says, "The most extensive class of locally produced sculpture is the series of small terracotta figurines and animals, predominately in Hellenistic style, discovered in excavations and as surface finds at Semthan, near Bijbihara."[8]

The coins that have been found at Semthan and other places of Kashmir belong to Euthydemus, Demetrius, Eucratides, Menander, Antimachus II, Apollodotus, Hippostratus, Lysias and Hermaeus. Even prior to the excavations, Semthan had yielded from the surface the coins of Indo-Greek rulers.[9] It can be argued that the coins might have been brought there by merchants and ultimately buried or lost. But, as we have seen, there is besides coins a variety of material evidence of Greek presence in Kashmir, which was found in association with the coins of the Indo-Greek rulers.

Coming to the literary evidence, we have a passing reference in *Rājataraṅgiṇī* mentioning that Kashmir was subjected to Indo-Greek (*mleccha*) invasion during the reign of Aśoka's successor, Jaluka, who, according to Kalhana, "expelled the *mlecchas* who oppressed the land, and conquered in victorious expeditions the earth upto the encircling oceans."[10] Whether Jaluka really expelled the Indo-Greeks or whether Kalhana tries to exalt the position of the ruler by portraying him as a great conqueror is a moot point. However, the fact still remains that no sooner did the Indo-Greeks occupy the North-West Frontier than Kashmir became the target of their covetous eyes and they not only invaded Kashmir but also occupied it, though temporarily, if we believe Kalhana whose authenticity about Jaluka as the successor of Aśoka is doubted by Romila Thapar and Michael Witzel. As mentioned earlier Thapar identifies Jaluka with Kunala; Witzel suggests that 'Jaluka in book 1 should be identified with Jaluka of book 2.'[11]

According to *Rājataraṅgiṇī*, Jaluka was succeeded by Damodara II.[12] Who was this Damodara II? Kalhana frankly admits his ignorance about his background.[13] Damodara of Kalhana is perhaps the famous Indo-Greek ruler, Demetrius (200–185 BCE) who, under the sweeping impact of Sanskrit language and culture from the second century CE onwards,[14] became Damodara in folk tradition – the only source of Kalhana for recording the early history of Kashmir.[15] According to Taran the kingdom of Demetrius included

> Afghanistan, Baluchistan, most of Russian Turkistan with some extension into Chinese Turkistan, part of North-West Frontier of India, the Punjab, much of the United Provinces with a small slice of Bihar, Sindh, Cutch, Kathiawar and the northern part of Gujarat.[16]

Indeed, a ruler, who had embarked upon such a policy of an ambitious scheme of conquests, could not be expected to have left Kashmir alone when its borders were contiguous with the Punjab and North-West Frontier with which the valley had always been closely related to.

Kalhana credits Demetrius [Sanskritised Damodara] of having constructed a long dam called Guddasetu "to bring water into the town which he had himself built on the Damodara – Suda [Damodara Wader]."[17] He is also said to have constructed dykes made of stones in order to guard against inundations.[18] It may be mentioned that the Greeks followed faithfully the Achaemenid policy of paying great attention to the maintenance and development of irrigation, a thing cultivated by Zoroastrian religion. Bactria, it should be remembered, was the traditional home of Zoroastrianism.[19] It is, therefore, no wonder to see Demetrius paying first-hand attention to constructing dams and canals in Kashmir and thus proving true to his rich heritage.

Another Greek ruler about whom we have literary evidence that he ruled Kashmir is the famous King Menander (155–130 CE). To quote Taran,

> A third fragment in Ptolemy gives the names of two provinces in Menander's home kingdom east of the Jhelum: Kaspeiria, which Ptolemy calls the upper Valleys of the Jhelum, Chenab, Ravi, and which would thus have corresponded to southern Kashmir.[20]

Also, according to *Milindapanha*, Menender (called as Milanda in the text) held discussions with Buddhist philosopher, Nagasena somewhere in Kashmir.[21] Perhaps the potsherd containing the inscription "Dhamorai" or "Dharmo (*rajai*)" discovered from Semthan refers to King Menander. Menender's legendary fame in Kashmir is attested to by the fact that the famous Kashmiri poet Kṣemendra in the eleventh century has a story about him, which is a transfer to him of a story first told about the great Kaniṣka two centuries after his death.[22]

The non-conventional sources such as place names, physiognomy and philology also substantiate the archaeological and literary evidence that Kashmir was a part of the Indo-Greek empire. Of these sources, place names mentioned in the following pages provide a rich and novel evidence.

Impact

A culture with which Kashmir had direct contacts for about one and a half centuries and, more so, which formed the *reference culture*, being the culture of the ruling class, it is quite natural to see it having left its deep impact on the life and conditions of the people. Ibn Khaldun anticipated the modern sociologists and social anthropologists by many centuries when he noted that "The vanquished always want to imitate the victor in his distinctive characteristics, his dress, his occupations and all his other conditions and customs."[23] Apart from the fact that Kashmir was ruled by the Greek rulers, who established a large number of Greek colonies in Kashmir and settled their own people in different corners of the valley, the capital of Indo-Greeks was also situated on the borders of Kashmir—first at Taxila and then closer at Sialkot (Śagala).[24] Thus Kashmir was face to face with a powerful culture.

Sadly, for want of adequate information, it is not possible to give a comprehensive treatment of Greek influences in Kashmir. What we shall be trying in the following pages is to piece together some stray reference scattered here and there in varied types of sources. This would, at least, give us an idea of the contribution of the cosmopolitan world of the Bactrian-Greeks to the cultural formation of Kashmir.

Immigrations and Settlements

The continuous streaming of people from the neighbouring territories and their settlement in the valley runs like a thread in the early history of Kashmir. But this phenomenon assumed intensity during the times when it remained a part of the great empires. Appointing their own people to important positions and stationing their own armies in the conquered territories were the important instruments employed by the conquerors to build empires. They also recognised the political importance of building local support structure as well as conquering the body and mind of the conquered people to consolidate the empire won by force. Thus alongside importing administrators and fighters from the mainland, the empire builders also encouraged the scholars, missionaries and the men proficient in various fields of their culture to settle in the conquered territories. The same is true of Kashmir when it became a part of the Indo-Greek empire. All those places of Kashmir, which bear the names ending in—hom (e.g. Sirhom, Monghom, Balahom, Chattarhom, Dirhom, Burzahom, Danihom, Bihom, Kanihom), were once Greek military colonies. *Hom* is Greek "*ium.*" As elsewhere, "*ium*" was associated either with the official who founded it or with some historical event or with some virtues or vices of the place.[25] Referring to a specific category of the Greek settlements in Asia, Taran says, "any place bearing a non-dynastic man's name, like Docimium, Zenodotium, Menidemium, Themisonium, was once a military colony which had named itself after the official who founded it."[26]

There are also many place names in Kashmir, which are essentially Greek names, for example, Kalaros (Gk. Cleros),[27] Methan (Gk. Meitona or Methone),[28] Odus (Gk. Edessa),[29] Anch (Gk. Antioch),[30] Sotur (Gk. Sotoer or Soteira),[31] Athan (Gk. Athena),[32] Zeus (Gk. Zeus),[33] Charus (Gk. Charis),[34] Ach (Gk. Achea),[35] Medur (Gk. Modura),[36] Aplun [Gk. Apallo],[37] Hamar, Hamari [Gk. Homer],[38] Pa'rgaum [Gk. Pergamum],[39] Memandar (Menendar),[40] Romoh (Gk. Roma, Riom),[41] Solun (Gk. Selena),[42] La'spur (after Lysias, the Greek ruler),[43] Āmon (Gk. Ammon),[44] Nicas (Gk. Nicias, the Greek ruler). Besides, there are some place names, which are essentially nick-names, given by the pre-Greek inhabitants of Kashmir to newly founded Greek settlements. Of such settlements mention may be made of Awanpur, a corrupt form of *yavanapura*, that is, the settlement of Greeks,[45] Poonzu, actually *punz* meaning monkey and Panzgum, meaning village of monkeys.

Even after the elapse of around 2,000 years since Greeks ruled Kashmir and despite an un-ending influx of varied ethnic groups into the valley and the consequent rampant inter-ethnic marriages, the physiognomy of the people of these places underlined by fair complexion presents a marked affinity with Greek physiognomy.[46] It may be noted that it was common among the Greeks to transfer the population from old Greek towns to new foundations.[47] Clearly, new ethnic and cultural stock was added to the already mosaic population of Kashmir during the Greek rule in Kashmir.

Coinage

The credit for the introduction of proper coinage in the Indian subcontinent, including Kashmir, goes to the Indo-Greek kings. They are the first to introduce inscribed coinage in the subcontinent. Their coinage bears their names, titles and epithets, effigies of themselves and deities besides the monogram and borders. Thus, they were the first to introduce the coins with the name of the issuer king including his ideology. The Greek coinage made such a powerful impact that it influenced the monetary types of the succeeding dynasties, namely, Scythians, Parthians and Kuṣāṇas. This is clear from their Greek script, Greek divinities and the Greek titles of the rulers.

The Greek coins have been found at various places in Kashmir. Alexander Cunningham was the first to discover many Greek and Scythian coins in the upper reaches of Jhelum Valley.[48] He was followed by GB Bleazby, who collected many Greek and Scythian coins from different parts of Kashmir.[49] Besides the coins of Indo-Greeks rulers, the coins of Philip II, Alexander, Diodotus and Euthydemus have also been found, which are probably commemorative coins, also known as "pedigree" coins—one of the innovations of Graeco-Bactrians.[50]

The following coin specimens (Figs. 3.2–3.10) show that in terms of coinage, Kashmir was a part and parcel of Indo-Greek monetary types. Adhering to the monetary system of their great ancestor, Alexander and his immediate successors, the Indo-Greeks, introduced bi-metallic coinage in silver and copper. The silver coins are didrachms and hemidrachms. With some exception they are all round and struck to Persian standard. Copper coins, square for the most part, are very numerous and are believed to have been on the standard of the local copper coins of Taxila.[51] Having issued coins by die-striking technique, which was earlier unknown in India, the Greek rulers placed portraits of the rulers on the obverse. Their coins mostly depict half portraits of their kings in diademed or helmeted head or bust on obverse and a series of Grecian deities or some of the symbols of their worship (the cap of Dioskouroi and the tripod of Apollo) on the reverse. The portraits on these coins are realistic and boldly drawn.

In Bactria, the Greek kings remained true to the traditional Greek Attic standard coinage with their reverses of monolingual legend, and the effigy of Greek gods and goddesses. But in India they made certain innovations to meet the demands of congruence and compatibility. First, they introduced a light-weight standard keeping drachma just a few grains more than punch marked coins. Second, they introduced a bilingual coinage with Greek inscriptions placed on the obverse and its translation in Prakrit written in Kharoshthi script on the reverse. Finally, besides displaying their own religious icons, the coins issued by the Greeks in India also represent Indigenous iconography—deities, animals and symbols.[52] Thus, while majority of the Greek coins found in Kashmir bear the effigy of Greek gods and goddesses, a few coins also represent Indigenous symbols. For example, the Apollodotus' coin reproduced here depicts bull in the reverse and elephant in the obverse. Bull is usually interpreted as Nandi, the sacred bull of Śiva. This shows transcultural appropriations of objects and images either for a will to perpetuate their rule in a different cultural setting or for an open religious system, where only circulation was required to remap cultural boundaries, rendering even religious images available for appropriation in the process.

Money currency, as we saw, was no doubt introduced in Kashmir by the Mauryas but the fact remains that it became wide spread only during the Indo-Greeks. That it was for the first time during the Indo-Greek rule that the Kashmiri people became aware of the money currency on a mass scale is substantiated by the fact that now onwards the Kashmiri Sanskrit scholars used the term *dīnārra*, (after Greek dinarius) for money currency in place of erstwhile *hār* (cowry).[53] The term *dīnārra* changed into *dyar* in Kashmir, which up to the present is used for money currency in the valley alongside the traditional term *hār*.

One irresistible conclusion that can be drawn from the monetisation of economy during the Indo-Greeks was a considerable growth in trade especially in the transregional trade of Kashmir. This is evidenced not only by the discovery of a large number of Greek coins, both copper and silver, but also by the fact that these belong to all the Indo-Greek rulers who ruled the north-west India. This growth in trade was obviously the result of some new phenomena that followed the Indo-Greek occupation of Kashmir: First, the Indo-Greek rulers connected Kashmir with Central Asia, Iran, Afghanistan and perhaps with China too. This is in addition to the maintenance of close relations with the Indian subcontinent. Secondly, the Indo-Greeks were accustomed to a particular life style, which would have exercised an additional demand for imports. Thirdly, the introduction of currency in a large scale obviated the problems that otherwise came in the way of external trade. While the punch-marked coins introduced by the Mauryas facilitated the circulation of commodities between Kashmir and the Mauryan empire extending up to eastern Afghanistan, the monetised tokens of the Greeks eased the movement of goods and services between Kashmir and a vast empire connecting Kashmir not only with the subcontinent but also with the Silk Route and through it with the globe. Significantly, the circulatory patterns of the Greek coins delineated monetary spheres of influence that were not necessarily coincident with boundaries of administrative and political authority.

Town Planning

Though archaeology has yet to unearth a Greek town in Kashmir, the impact of the Greek town planning is evident from the structure of temple complexes of Kashmir whose layout was designed in keeping with the three important features of Greek city—stone wall, imposing main gate and the main building at the centre.[54] The extensive use of stone masonry in the city walls, bringing acropolis within the city proper, projected main gate of the western origin, outwardly protruding round or square towers—all go to the credit of the Greeks.[55] Also, like the Greeks, we find almost all the subsequent rulers of Kashmir making use of natural factors such as the backing of the hills, gullies, ravines and rivers for strengthening the defence of the cities.[56]

Art and Architecture

It is well known that a new art emerged in Gandhara on account of the convergence of Greek and Buddhist art. This Graeco-Buddhist art is called Gandhara art. Although no specimen of the architecture and art of the period has so far been discovered in Kashmir, the later architecture and sculpture show that Greek forms had a profound impact on the art and architecture of Kashmir.[57] Many architectural features of Kashmiri temples, namely, columns of Doric order, pediments, trefoil arches, pilasters and cornice were borrowed from Greek architecture.[58] The S-shaped and other types of brackets were used in the Hellenistic world as early as the second century BCE.[59] Other motifs of unmistakable Greek origin are caryatids, acanthi, pedimental arches, carved door jambs, figures seated or standing under arches, birds perching on either side of arches and a host of other decorative motifs, such as meanders, vine scrolls, laurel leaves, garland bearers, atlantes and tritons.[60] We find in Taxila the art of stone dressing, stone-cutting, stone carving and stone-polishing achieving a tremendous progress under the Bactrian-Greeks.[61] The same could be true of Kashmir as well.

Greek art taught freedom to the artists of the East. In it, figures are shown in every attitude, face view, side view, even back view and in every kind of intermediate posture.[62] Frontality, which became a normal treatment of the figure during the Parthians, was an exceptional treatment in Greek art restored only for definite reasons.[63] That the Greek art left a profound impact on the art of Kashmir is clearly evidenced by the motifs stamped on the coins and Harwan tiles where the figures are shown in varied attitudes.[64]

Also, like the so-called toilet trays found in Gandhara,[65] we find in Kashmir trays, though made of clay, which like the Gandharan trays have bacchanalian scenes depicted within a circular space.[66]

Decorative scenes in circular space are also often encountered in Harwan tiles.[67] It may be mentioned that during the third-first century BCE relief decorations in circular space started appearing on ceramics of the type of Megarian bowls in Greece and Caelian Philae in Italy. And the decorations of the religious themes and other decorative motifs within circular space were common in both classical and Hellenistic periods.[68]

The Harwan tiles are also marked with Greek devices like cock and cock-fighting (Figs. 3.11 and 3.12) and the designs of the vine and floral scrolls.[69] Cock and cock-fighting motifs were common in both Classical and Hellenistic periods (Figs. 3.13 and 3.14).[70] The ancient Syrians worshipped the fighting cock as a divinity. The ancient Greeks and Romans associated the fighting cock with the gods Apollo, Mercury and Mars. And the sport of cock-fighting already existed in Rome around 450 BC.[71]

Pottery

The pottery of the Indo-Greek period, as found at Semthan, is distinguished by a thin fabric with bright red, orange or light slip.[72] The striking shapes are *thalis* (pans),[73] vases with out-turned and internally thickened rims, vessels with high necks and also goblets.[74] Intriguingly, the Greek "black ware" is missing. Terracotta finds are very rich in distribution and carry a wide variety of shapes.

Religion

Except for one ruler—the famous Menander—the Greek rulers continued to profess their ancestral heathenic pantheistic religion. This is evident from their coinage, which carries the portraits of Greek gods and goddesses or some of the symbols of their worship. Also, a clay seal has been discovered from Semthan, which depicts an Indo-Greek deity. It is presumed to be of Apollo.[75] The popularity of the Greek divinities can be seen from the monetary types of the Indo-Greeks, Indo-Scythians and Kuṣāṇas. The impact of the Greek gods and goddesses in the whole Orient was immense. Exemplifying it Osmund Bopearachchi says,

> As we know Heracles is similar to the Zoroastrian Verethraghana in Iran and Vajrapani in early Buddhist art in Central Asia and India. The iconography representation of Vajrapani in the early Buddhist art was a syncreticism of Heracles and Zeus. On the most of these images, Vajrapani is depicted wearing the lion's skin knotted at his neck, as on the Greek representations of Heracles, but instead of

> the club, his usual attribute, this faithful protector of the Buddha holds a thunderbolt which is the attribute, *par excellence*, of Zeus.[76]

Understandably the heathenic pantheistic religion of the Greeks would have further promoted polytheism and added more gods and goddesses to the heathenic pantheons that prevailed in Kashmir. Worshiping of images was so widespread among the Greeks that some scholars believe that idolatry was introduced into India by the Greeks.[77] It is pertinent to mention that image worship has no place in Vedic pantheon; nor its presence in former days is attested by the puranas.[78] The general disrespect for the image worshipping brahmanas in Smritis also suggests the exogenous roots of this institution.[79]

Buddhism also received state patronage for some time during the Greeks. According to *Milindapanha*, Menander was converted to Buddhism by the Buddhist philosopher, Nagasena, after a catechismal discussion on Buddhism between the two.[80] The questions posed by Menander are contained in *Milindapanha*, which means "Questions of King Milinda" (King Menander).

It may, however, be wrong to suppose that only two religious beliefs—Hellenistic religion and Buddhism—prevailed in Kashmir during the Indo-Greek rule. By contrast, people of many faiths lived side by side. In this respect, as is true of other matters as well, Kashmir was a part of the cultural complex of Gandhara where, besides Buddhism and the Greek religion, we find Śiva powerful in Pushkalavati[81] (Greek capital) and Viṣṇu strong in Taxila.[82] Having their centre at Bactra (Bactria), which was the traditional centre of Zoroastrianism, it is perhaps reasonable to presume that the Indo-Greeks might have greatly been influenced by this religion too. They were also influenced by sun worship which we find prevailing in Taxila.[83] A poem written not later than the first century BCE and addressed to Apollo is an early expression of the later belief that all deities merge in the sun.[84]

It is important to mention that Greeks were already influenced by Anatolian and Syrian religious beliefs. For example, we find one Greek making a dedication to Cappadocian goddess, Ma.[85] And there is a Greek epigram addressed to Apollo by the Syrian title Mara,[86] "Lord." *Ma* and *Mara* are commonplace words in Kashmir. *Ma* stands for Mother goddess and *mara* is a common term used by the Kashmiri Pandits to address someone with respect.

To sum up, the Indo-Greeks not only brought their own gods, goddesses and religious beliefs but they also brought with them many other beliefs prevailing in the Seleucid empire in general and Bactria and Gandhara in particular. Thus, with its own strong religious traditions, which were repeated by the Greeks, and the new beliefs brought by them, Kashmir became a hub of syncretic religion and culture. After all, the Greeks are known for their religious tolerance.[87]

Science

Indian astronomy and astrology greatly profited from the contacts with the Greeks. To quote Taran "one thing did come from Babylon to India during the Hellenistic period, the art of fore-telling the future by means of the stars."[88] It is significant to mention that the term *hora shastra*, used for astrology in Sanskrit, was derived from the Greek term *horoscope*.

Kashmir certainly benefitted by the Greek science. It was therefore natural that the Kashmir tradition should credit the Greeks with working wonders. According to the famous eleventh century CE polymath of Kashmir, Kśemendra, "Yavanas can make and fly aeroplanes."[89]

Language

The profound impact of Greek influence on Kashmir is also borne out by the Kashmiri language which still possesses some Greek words. For example, *kūr* (Gk. *kori* = girl), *piala* (Gk. *Phiali* = cup), *kukur* (Gk. *kokaras* = cock) and *gunnia*, that is, carpenter's L-shaped instrument for right angles (Gk. *gonie* = angle, corner).

Costume and Coiffure

While the Scythio-Parthian-Kuṣāṇa costumes served as the model for male attire of India including Kashmir from first century of the Christian era, the female dress showed more gravitation to Greek influences. The modern mode of wearing *sari* has evolved from the Hellenistic *chiton* and *himation* apparel.[90] The long loose tunic falling down the ankles worn by the Kashmiri panditanis has also most probably evolved from the *chiton* and *himation* as well as from the *kancuka*. The Greek dress assumed such a prestige that we find late in fifth-sixth centuries the Hindu goddesses dressed in *chiton* and *himation* (see Fig. 3.15). Both the apparels are loose enough, and the *himation* was arranged in such a way as to raise difficulty in distinguishing it from the tunic underneath. Such was, as a matter of fact, the most common way of draping as is delineated by the Gandhara artists.[91]

The terracotta female figurines found at Semthan provide valuable evidence on costume and coiffure informed by Greek influences (see Fig. 3.1). The following information is based on the detailed study made by John Siudmak on this subject. The female figurine,

> which is broken-off at the ankles, has short ear pendants of ribbed ovoid form, and hair cursorily indicated by cross hatching. The garment is a long, voluminous, heavily pleated and folded *chiton*, belted high on the waist, which falls around the feet.[92]

Another female figurine provides more details where

> a long *himation* is draped over the left shoulder and wrapped around the lower part of the body and the left arm, an edge held by lowered right hand. A notable feature is the beaded necklace, and the polygonal panel of beaded outline below that curves along the inside of the breasts.[93]

We also come across a semi-draped female figurine at Semthan. Though *humition* is draped, there is no *chiton*. The right shoulder and hips are exposed.

> The hair has a fillet, and a row of parted short curly hair lines the brow. . . . There is a short beaded necklace, a beaded and double-ribbed torque, and crossbands or *channvaira*. The latter device has a rosette medallion between the breasts.[94]

John Marshall has provided profuse evidence of the use of cross bands as a female adornment at Taxila.[95]

The headless male figurine found at Semthan also wears *himation* and *chiton*. The pleated and folded garment is draped over the left shoulder and falls to the ankles. "There is also detached bearded head. The short beard is closely trimmed and the ends of the moustache just overlap it. The forehead is creased, and the head is covered by a low conical cap, below which is a narrow row of stylised curls." Siudmak concludes saying

> Close parallels in dress {of the Semthan figuirines} can be found in the depiction of Greek subject matter on early "toilet" trays or pallettes, as well as on the slightly later proto- Gandhara stair raiser relief panels from the North-West with Helenistic subject matter which provide the only close comparison for the Semthan male garment.[96]

The Graeco-Roman arts bequeathed the floating scarf adoring a variety of female figures. These figures hold two ends of the scarf in their hands. This is what we exactly find in a Harwan tile which contains a motif of a dancing girl who holds the scarf in her two hands (Fig. 3.16). Such a motif can be traced back to Hellenistic art as early as the fifth century BCE.[97] Interestingly, the motif occurs on glassware from Begram and also on a toilet dish from Taxila.[98]

The popularity of an ornament comparable with the present day locket among the people of Kashmir is significant as it was well known among the Greeks who introduced it in Kashmir too (Fig. 3.17). Hellenistic impact on Indian Jewellery is evident from Taxila where the Hellenistic models such as the silver repoussé, the bust of Dionysus, acanthus design, a favourite Greek motif and use of pendants (again a Greek motif) in necklaces have been found.[99] These ornaments assumed so much prestige and popularity that we see the pendant forming an important ornament of the colossal figure of a Bodhisattva discovered at Harwan (Fig. 3.17). The art of granulation was also known in Greece from early time.[100]

The Śaka–Parthian Presence

And the Impact of Graeco–Iranian World

Around 75 BCE, the northern and western neighbourhood of Kashmir came under the occupation of a powerful Central Asian nomadic tribe—the Śakas. After having ruled for about half a century, they were replaced by yet another tribe of the same region namely, the Parthians who lived on the Central Asian frontiers of Iran. These developments were the direct result of the troubled conditions obtaining far away on the Central Asian frontiers of China. These unsettled conditions in Central Asia first affected the immediate neighbourhood of Kashmir and finally the valley too. Before we piece together the evidence to show the presence of the Śakas and the Parthians in Kashmir, it is pertinent to make a brief mention of their background to appreciate their impact on Kashmir.

"*Śaka*" was the name of a tribe, belonging to Andronovo culture, an ancient Iranian civilisation.[101] They lived in a portion of a vast area known by the generic name of Scythia. The Old Persian, Greek and Latin sources tend to locate the early habitat of the Śakas to the north or north-east of Sogdiana (Samarqand) and the Jaxartes.[102] This indicates that the area around the Lake Issyk Kul in Kirghizia, bordering Chinese Central Asia, constituted the Śaka country. They spoke a language which was related to the north Iranian group, which includes Sogdian and Pahlavika (Parthian Pahalavi).[103] They worshipped the sun and the bull.[104] Proficient in heavy armoured cavalry, Herodotus singles them out as one of the most advanced nations of the steppes.[105]

The Śaka invasion of India was the result of struggle for supremacy among the powerful Central Asian tribes. On account of the pressure faced by them from other Central Asian nomadic tribes, the Śakas were forced to leave their land and pour into Bactria. They snatched Bactria from Heliocles in about 135 BCE and subsequently occupied eastern Iran and Afghanistan too.[106] However, not long after this development, the Yueh-chis' (Kuṣāṇas) pressure put an end to the Śaka rule in Bactria. Having been forced to flee, they ultimately settled in or near Drangiana in south-western Afghanistan. This area finally came to be called Śakastan (present Sistan) after them. Since their expansion towards Iran and Central Asia was checked with all might by the Parthians and other Central Asian powers, the Śakas directed their invasions towards India.

There has been a controversy among the scholars regarding the route adopted by the Śaka invaders to occupy India. However, the startling discoveries made by AH Dani have resolved the controversy.[107] He found a large number of Kharoshthi inscriptions and rock carvings at the principal river crossings at Chilas, Gilgit and Hunza. These petroglyphs make it abundantly clear that the Śakas used Karakorum route for the ultimate occupation of Taxila though the subsequent waves of Śakas would have entered the Indus Valley from Sistan also. Thus around 75 BCE, the whole of the neighbourhood of Kashmir bordering its north and west had come under the Śakas, ready to penetrate into the valley. The Śaka power spread from Gandhara in the north to western India and upper Deccan, creating five centres of power, each under a particular branch of the tribe.

The first Śaka king in India was Maues or Moga who established Śaka power in Gandhara in about 75 BC. He was succeeded by Azes (also called Azes I), Azilises and Azes II. Another line of the Śakas was that of Vonones who ruled Kandahar and Baluchistan. Some coins carry the name of his brother, Spalahore, and his nephew, Spalagadama, showing that the Vonones either ruled in association with them or ruled as sub-kings of the Vonones. Since the other three branches of the Śakas with their headquarters in Mathura, western India and Deccan do not concern us, we are leaving them out.

The Indo-Scythian empire of the Śakas was conquered by a Parthian feudal family, which was pursuing the migrating Śakas. The founder of the Indo-Parthian empire was the Gondophares I. He was succeeded by Abdagases, Orthagnes, Pacores, Gondophares II, Sasan, Arsaces and Sanabares. According to the Takht-i-Bahi inscription, Gondophares ascended to the throne in 20 CE.[108] The Parthians were succeeded by the Kuṣāṇas around the mid of first century CE. The Indo-Parthian empire was spread over a vast area including Arachosia (Kandahar), Seistan, Sindh, Gandhara and the Kabul Valley.[109]

Nature of the Śaka-Parthian Culture

The Śakas and the Parthians belonged to almost the same culture. Both, as mentioned earlier, belonged to the Iranian race and both spoke Iranian language. Although the Parthians had made much cultural progress as compared to the Śakas, nonetheless by the time the latter reached India, they had achieved the same cultural level for which the Parthians were known. Having lived in the world dominated by the imperial Parthians (Arascids), the Śakas had got mixed up ethnically as well as culturally with the Parthians.[110] The resemblance in their culture was so close that a modern scholar believes that Maues was not a Scythian but a Parthian through and through.[111]

In support of his argument, he says that Maues and Azes issued Parthian types of coins such as "standing Poseidon," "king on horse back" (in which horse is not prancing) and "standing victory." Besides, their coin legends are the same as those of the Parthians and they also used Parthian title, *maharaja rajatiraja*[112] *(king of the kings)*. Though it would be incorrect to represent Maues and his successors as Parthians, it is beyond doubt that the Śakas were thoroughly influenced by the Parthian culture. The Parthian culture was basically a syncretic culture drawn from different sources. Yet, the Graeco-Iranian elements are prominent. To quote Koshelenko and Pilipko:

> Parthian culture developed through the interaction of a number of factors – the Achaemenid heritage, the conceptions of the Hellenistic period, the contribution of nomadic Parni, and the particular cultural traditions of the people who made up the Parthian state. The basic trend in the development of Parthian culture was the synthesis of Greek and local sources.[113]

Evidence of Śaka-Parthian Rule in Kashmir

Unlike the neighbouring Chilas or Taxila, no rock carving or inscription has so far been found in Kashmir to establish the presence of Śakas and Parthians in the valley. However, some precious coins belonging to Śaka and Parthian rulers have been found at different places in Kashmir, and many are preserved in SPS Museum, Srinagar and the Central Asian Studies Museum, University of Kashmir. Significantly, the number of Śaka coins found in Kashmir is only next to Kuṣāṇas—so large is their quantity.[114] It may rightly be asked: how the simple presence of coins can prove the political control of Śakas and Parthians over Kashmir? In response to this question, it can be safely argued that when the Śakas could reach as far as upper Deccan and western India and establish their rule there, how could Kashmir—the beautiful vale situated on the borders of Taxila, Gandhara and Chilas—the stronghold of Indo-Scythians—escape their empire-building agenda, especially when Kashmir was historically, geographically and culturally intimately related to its northern and western neighbourhoods.

Apart from the hordes of Saka coins found in Kashmir, the powerful Saka-Parthian presence is also established by a variety of evidence, both conventional and non-conventional. Among the conventional sources, archaeology provides a unique and rewarding evidence, some of which has already been brought to light by archaeologists and art historians. The motifs on some Hoinar tiles representing two winged lions locked in a fierce combat have a parallel in Iran at Qateh-Yazgrad, a Parthian site. It is reminiscent of ancient Mesopotamian tradition. Such motifs are reported to have come from Nuristan in Afghanistan as well, and have been often encountered in Scythian burials.[115]

The most important and often quoted archaeological site, Harwan (Srinagar), furnishes a wealth of information in favour of the Parthian association of the site.[116] The overall plan of the site, the design of the apsidal temple, the systems of construction, art and the motifs stamped on the tiles—the details of some of which have been given in the following pages—attest to the fact that it was originally a Parthian site though the lower terrace was subsequently converted into a Buddhist space. Fisher and Bhan have also given details of the similarities between the subjects and descriptions found at Harwan and many other Parthian sites beyond Kashmir.[117]

Despite having shown strong linkages between the finds obtained at the highest terrace of Harwan and many other Parthian sites elsewhere, Robert Fisher, however, believes that the site was originally occupied by the Ajivikas. This he suggests on the basis of the plaques with emaciated figures of ascetics surrounding the upper terrace that he identifies with Ajivikas.[118] We should not forget the fact that the Parthian sphere of influence was the cradle of Gnostic movement and that the Parthians were also influenced by the Greek and Indian cultures, which were known for manifold ascetic movements.[119] Also, it is well known about the Parthians that they were remarkably flexible in assimilating the cultures which they encountered with. Alexander's historians were struck by what they called 'naked philosophers' whom they found in Taxila.[120] The description of these ascetics figures prominently in their accounts. They used to go out naked and devoted to endurance by undergoing physical austerities and by exposing their bodies to sun and rain. They enjoyed considerable veneration among the people.[121] In Kalhana's *Rājataraṅgiṇī*, there is also a mention of 'naked mendicants' in Kashmir.[122] Though the reference is of later date, it was in all probability a continuation of old times as Kashmir has always remained culturally a part of Gandhara. Thus the Parthians confronted with a social and mental aura both within and without Kashmir, where ascetics were highly venerated, influencing them to absorb the Indian asceticism in their own culture, which was favourably disposed towards Gnosticism.[123]

Another important but less noticed fact that further links the site with Iranian culture is the name of the place where the site is located. It is called Harwan. It is composed of two words *h'ar* and *wan*. *Wan* means jungle and *h'ar* is derivative of Hara—the sacred hill in the Zoroastrian world view. According to the Zoroastrian belief about the world and its creation, the greatest mountain which grew from the earth was the high Hara, which encompassed the earth and kept growing.[124] It was believed that the stars, the moon and the sun, which were imagined to be below the vault of the sky, had their orbit around the Peak of Hara. According to the Mithra Yasht 51–52, Ahura Mazda together with the Amesha Spentas made a dwelling for Mithra on high Hara wherefrom he watches the whole world.[125] To be sure, like most migrants, the early Iranians seem to have applied old names to the new places.[126]

There is also another important religious place in Kashmir which is named after Hara. It is called Hari Parbat. Parbat in Sanskrit means hill. Hari Parbat is situated amidst the old Srinagar and has always remained a sacred spot. With the spread of Brahmanism, the place was integrated into the new tradition by weaving a new myth that it is the abode of Sharika Devi.[127] Sharika is a Sanskrit word meaning *meena*. In Kashmiri, it is called *ha'r*. Therefore it was made to believe that it is the mountain of *h'ar* (Sk. sharika). The myth also smacks of Zoroastrian influences. It is believed that the Hari Parbat is that pebble with which the goddess Sharika killed the demon, who lived in the lake Kashmir, was occupied by for millions of years.[128] And it became sacred not only because it is the pebble of the Devi but more so because she herself made it her abode so that the *dev* (demon) does not resurrect.[129] It may be mentioned that in Zoroastrian teachings, the demons are the followers of *drug*, "Falsehood" and they are the particular targets of divine wrath and were slain by thousands at the hands of various deities.[130] Thus not only here the *dev* is killed but also the goddess takes abode on the hill like Mitra on high Hara.

Prof. Gulshan Majid also finds Iranian presence in Harwan. To quote him:

> Most of the motifs like almond-shape leaves growing in water, ducks, aquatic flowers, *apsaras*, erotic human figures, garlands, the shells found in water, the pearls formed in water, flower pots and grape vines intimate that the goddess related to these forms is none other than the goddess *Anaheta*. It is possible that water must have been flowing over these tiles and this too is probable that sacrifices were made in the name of goddess *Anaheta* at the site.[131]

He also suggests linkage of Harwan with other places of Kashmir, namely, Harut and Marut (the Kashmiri variant of Harutat, the god of vitality and Marvitat, the god of preservation in Zoroastrianism) Hoynar and Hutmara (where Harwan like tiles have been found).[132] From the present stage of knowledge, it seems that tile work started at the closely placed sites of Doen Pather on the right side of river Liddar.[133] Is Don Pather the derivative of Doni par, the famous river of Central Asia with which the Parthians were accustomed to? Did the Parthians call Liddar after the famous Doni par? We leave it as an open question.

Besides, there are many place names in Kashmir which are related either to the Śaka and Parthian rulers, or Parthian cities or Parthian religion. For example, there is a famous village in Kashmir called as Ajas. Is this a Kashmiri variant of Azes? It seems so unless proved otherwise. Mention may be also made of the places, namely, Gund (after Gondaphares), Gous (after

Abdagases), Zewan (after Zeioneses), Dūr (after the famous Parthian city Dura-Europos), Aśh Muqam, Ash Ash Pur, Ash Much (after the pre-eminent Zoroastrian goddess, Aśi),[134] Hari Parbat, Harwan and Harwath (after the sacred Zoroastrian mountain, Hara).[135]

Coinage

GB Bleazby has recorded hundreds of Scythian and Parthian coins in his list of coins found in Kashmir.[136] These coins were also found at the famous archaeological site of Kashmir, Semthan, during the excavations in 1983.

For the most part the Indo-Scythians and Indo-Parthians retained the monetary system and devices of their predecessors—Indo-Greeks. They retained the silver denominations (tetradrachms and drachms) and square coppers of Indo-Greeks. After the Indo-Greek model, they minted in silver and copper, issued them by die-striking technique, put portraits of the rulers, their names and epithets, and imprinted them with bilingual inscriptions and figures of deities. Like the Indo-Greeks, the Indo-Scythians and Indo-Parthians issued bilingual coins—Greek inscription printed on the obverse and its translation in Prakrit written in Kharoshthi script on the reverse. Besides, their coins bear the Greek deities such as Nike, Pallas and Zeus on the reverse.

However, the Indo-Scythians and Indo-Parthians did not simply follow their predecessors; instead, they did make many modifications. One of the major changes which they brought was the introduction of a new motif, namely, mounted king in armour, holding an *ankuśa* (goad), a lance or a whip. Besides adopting this type invented by their ancestor Maus, the successive Indo-Scythian rulers also issued some new types, for example, Azes introduced a type which has a king riding on a two-humped Bactrian camel and holding an *ankusa*.[137] However they kept the reverse of the coins unchanged as they continued to carry Greek and Indian deities or their symbols. Azilises, the successor of Azes, issued a strikingly original Indian device—Abhisheka Lakshmi, that is, Lakshmi standing and facing a lotus flower with twin stalks and leaves, and on each leaf stands an elephant sprinkling water on the head of Lakshmi.[138]

The Parthians issued several coin types, but the "Nike" and "Horseman" type coins were most popular. On the "Nike" type coin appear both Greek and Persian deities. The "Bull" and "Camel" type coins in copper, which depict Bactrian camel and Indian bull are mostly known from Kashmir (Figs. 3.18–3.21). Such coins are attributed to the Parthian viceroy, Zeionses. The discovery of Zeionses' coins from Semthan and many other parts of Kashmir suggests that they were the most common type of Parthian coins in Kashmir.

The presence of Scythian and Parthian coins in Kashmir shows clearly that the commercial relations with the neighbouring countries, which

Kashmir had maintained for long, continued uninterrupted during the Śaka-Parthian period. They brought Kashmir closer to Central Asia, Iran and India through Dardistan and Taxila, which formed an important part of the Indo-Scythian empire. However, in the absence of any direct information, it is difficult to say anything about the commodity structure of the imports and exports except to draw a plausible inference that war horses and precious metals might have pressed for a great demand in Kashmir, for the employment of heavy armoured cavalry, and the use of gold, silver and bronze were the characteristic attributes of the Scythian and Parthian culture.[139] Kautilya mentions that the horses of the best breed were found in Kamboja (north Gandhara), Sindhu, Aratta (part of the Punjab) and Vanaya (Arabia or Persia), while the middling breeds came from Bahalika (Bactria) and Sauvira (lower Indus).[140]

Military Technology and Strategy

Like other nomadic people of Central Asia under whose constant pressure China, Europe, the Middle East, Iran and India lived up to the sixteenth century CE, the power of the Śakas was the cavalry, the availability of thousands of horses, the expansion of their armies and the abilities of their leaders.[141] The same is true of the Parthians as well. Herodian stresses that the Romans were invincible on foot and the Parthians on horseback.[142] The Parthians were unrivalled as mounted archers who were able to shoot while riding at full speed. Also, they pretended to flee, and suddenly turned round and aimed their deadly arrows at their pursuers. This is proverbial "Parthian shot.". It was as often quoted in literature as it is depicted in art.[143]

The arms of the Śakas and the Parthians were the bow and the arrow, the lance and the javelin, the dagger and the sword. They used helmets and armours.[144] Authors of the late antiquity have given us a vivid description of the horror felt by the Romans when they saw for the first time the Parthian archers completely encased in armour.[145] Flexible mail covered every limb, their faces were hidden behind masks and even horses were protected by mail.[146] The same is true of the Śakas. At more than 300 sites, fragments of scale armour were found in the western steppes.[147]

The first clear evidence of the impact of Śaka-Parthian military technology on Kashmir comes from Harwan tiles. These tiles show a horse fully accoutred and horseman in armour riding at full gallop and drawing his bow. On the right attached to the saddle hangs his quiver. These tiles contain Kharoshthi numerals and horsemen represented on the tiles bear heavy features, prominent cheek bones, narrow, sunk and slanting eyes and receding foreheads—a Central Asian physiognomy. The horseman appears in Parthian dress and Turkoman caps (see Fig. 3.22).

Architecture and Art

It is evident that the Śakas followed the Greek ideas in town planning and copied Greek prototypes in their architecture.[148] Subsequently, Indian influence becomes increasingly noticeable. The Parthian period witnessed more vigorously the re-emergence of Hellenistic art and architecture.[149]

> The legend of St Thomas, skilled in architecture and all types of work in wood and stone, being sold in Syria to a merchant called Habban and being brought to the court of Gondophares, is set against the background that skilled craftsmen from western Asia were commissioned to do work for the Parthians.[150]

Gondophares rebuilt Taxila after it suffered a great earthquake. He introduced new building methods including a strong form of diaper masonry.[151] The Parthians had also achieved great excellence in making fire-moulded tiles with pictorial variety.[152]

Although no building of the period has survived to us, it is abundantly clear that the development of syncretic architecture, which had started much earlier, received further impetus at the hands of Scythians and Parthians. The typical example of this is the moulded tiles of an extinct structure and the remains of an apsidal temple found at Harwan. According to Percy Brown, "the motifs of these tiles suggest the impact of half a dozen civilizations of the ancient world."[153] The diaper masonry, which we see having developed in Taxila under Gondophares, is seen as the main mode of construction at Harwan. Three different phases of building activity belonging to different ages have been noticed here. These are the pebble, the diaper pebble and the diaper rubble (see Figs. 3.23 and 3.24)—the system of construction we find in many buildings at Taxila.[154]

The overall plan of Harwan may also be due to Parthian influence. Like Harwan, the fire temple at Surkh Kotal (Bactria) is a terraced structure with a courtyard surrounding the main temple located on the highest level. Both Harwan and Surkh Kotal originally had a stairway leading to the centre of each terrace.[155] The apsidal temple preceded by an oblong hall has resemblance to the temple of Artemis—Nanaia at Dura-Europos (a famous Parthian site) and also with the apsidal structure of Sirkap, the Graeco-Parthian city.[156]

The Greek style of town planning and Graeco-Indian architecture, which received great advancement during the Śakas and the Parthians, left a deep imprint on Kashmir notwithstanding the politico-religious changes in Kashmir. The famous stone temples of sixth-seventh century Kashmir present a classic example of syncretic architecture with significant Greek elements.[157]

Amorous scenes, dancing and musical representation are seen on some tiles of Harwan. It may be mentioned that under the influence of Hellenistic culture, the art of bacchanalian scenes had thrived during the Parthians in north-west India. These were the favourite themes adopted for the decoration of the Buddhist stupas.[158] Referring to this fact in the context of Taxila, Dar says "The Hellenistic motifs during the Parthian period consist of pure Aphrodisiac and the Dionysiac scenes. This re-emergence of Hellenistic motifs during the Parthian supremacy is quite in keeping with other material excavated at Taxila."[159]

Art

In his pioneering and richly documented essay "Dura and the Problem of Parthian Art," Rostovtzeff distinguishes several features that characterise Parthian art. Chief among these is "the frontality" of human and animal figures whereby all figures in painting and sculpture are portrayed full face and in frontal representation, looking the beholder in the eyes: neglect of the body (in contrast to Greek art). Others are:

> Linearity of contour; painstaking depiction of details of dress, ornament, furniture and ethnic characteristics (oriental "verismus"); spirituality, in that the faces and features of gods or holy personages are made to appear celestial and ethereal, even without the help of a halo or radiant crown; repetition of the same figures with rigid ritual poses and expressions in the depiction of ceremonial and conventional scenes; and finally in scenes of hunt, combat or chase, portrayal of figures on horses at a flying gallop.[160]

The Parthian art seems to have been established in the course of the first century CE over "a large area of the eastern world from the Euphrates to China, from Siberia to India, from the highlands of Mongolia to the Bosphorus."[161] The evidence of the profound impact of this art on Kashmir is evident from terracotta tiles of Harwan and the terracottas found at Semthan and Ushkar. Harwan tiles present a typical example of synthesis of the Greek and Parthian art in that in the style of Greeks, figures are shown in every attitude and the head of the image is always shown in profile. And following the example of Parthian art, there is painstaking depiction of details of dress, ornament, furniture, ethnic characteristics, scenes of hunt, combat or chase, portrayal of figures on horses at a flying gallop (see Figs. 3.25, 3.26 and 3.27).

Ushkar is the best representation of Parthian 'frontality' as the figures are portrayed full face and in frontal representation looking the beholder in the eyes, and in contrast to Greek art there is neglect of the body (see Fig. 3.28). Another important Parthian feature we find at Harwan and Ushkar is that the holy personages are made to appear celestial and ethereal. It may also be mentioned that the most widespread form of artistic craft of Parthians was the fashioning of the terracotta statues.[162] And it is this that we find in Kashmir.

The Scythian art is well known for what is known as pure animal style. Harwan has provided a large number of tiles with animal motifs. Animal representation is both mythical and real. This includes besides galloping horse, long-horned deer, cows suckling their young, domestic cocks with foliated tails in roundels or in the centre of floral patterns, running or flying geese holding lotus stalks in their beaks, cock fighting, *makara* type of fanciful animals, lions and fish.[163] Semthan has also revealed a terracotta figurine of a lion. The lion, it may be mentioned, was very popular with the Scythians. Its popularity enhanced further with the conversion of Śakas to Buddhism as it was associated with Buddha—the Lion of the Śaka family.[164]

Religion

The epigraphic and numismatic evidence available on the Śaka and Parthian period suggests an atmosphere of remarkable catholicity in this period—the rulers showing equal regards towards Greek religion, Zoroastrianism, Buddhism and Brahmanism. Before their invasion of Graeco-Bactria, the Śakas as well as the Kuṣāṇas probably worshipped *Ahura Mazdah* as "God of heaven" with solar features and *Śvantā Armati* as "Goddess of earth."[165] They were acquainted with several categories of divine beings such as *daivas, yazatas* and *bagas*. They performed some sacrificial rites, and had different categories of priests.[166] With the conquest of Graeco-Bactrian territories, they were considerably influenced by a new religion, which was predominantly a synthesis of Greek and Iranian religious elements, and into which Indian religions had also carved a niche for themselves.[167]

As mentioned earlier, the coins of the Indo-Scythians and Indo-Parthians bear the portraits of Greek divinities, showing the profound impact of Greek religious tradition on them. Although no inscription of the period has survived to us, the inscriptions found at Taxila and elsewhere show the Śaka and Pahlava rulers depositing the Buddhist relics and constructing *vihāras*. The Taxila copper plate of Patika records the establishment of the relics of the Lord Sakyamuni and the founding of a *sangarama* by Patika, the son of Maue's kshatrapa of Chuksha.[168] From the period of Azes, we have growing evidence of the patronage bestowed upon Buddhism by Śaka rulers. The same is true of the Parthian rulers as well.[169] The Śakas and the Parthian rulers were also influenced by Brahmanism. We find Azilises introducing a coin type which bears the motifs of Abhisheka Lakshmi—strikingly original Indian device.[170] Gondophares also used for the first time the figure of Śiva on his coinage from the middle Indus provinces.[171]

Notwithstanding the tolerant attitude towards Buddhism, Brahmanism and Greek religion, and the influence these beliefs exercised on their world view, the Śakas and the Parthians also retained their own Iranian faith—Zoroastrianism, which left a deep imprint on the belief system of Kashmir. That Zoroastrianism spread in Kashmir during the period is amply borne out by some place names and beliefs and rituals of Kashmir. Of the place names, mention may be made of Mitar gom (village of Mitar after the Iranian divine being, Mitra), Mir (Mihr) Aur, Akhur (Ahura), Anich Dūr (Anahita Durra), Hari Parbat, the hill of Hara (Hara) and Harwan, the Jungle of Hara (Hara) and Vareh-haran (Varhran).

Besides the main gods (Ahura Mazda, Mitra and Varuna), the Indo-Iranian pantheon included nature deities who symbolised the sun, the moon and other luminaries, water, fire, wind and sky. Particularly prominent among these deities in Iran was the goddess of waters, *Aredvi Sura*, who is celebrated in the *Ābān Yasht* of the Avesta and to whom many Iranian heroes offered sacrifice.[172] Since in Kashmir every single water body—lake, river, stream and spring—is auspicious as each of them symbolises one or the other water deity, it is quite reasonable to say that though this belief was basically the result of the Naga cult, the most primitive form of worship of Kashmir, the association of Nag deity with water was further reinforced by Vedism and Zoroastrianism facilitating its ultimate appropriation by the brahmanic religion.

Another significant example of Zoroastrian presence in Kashmir is a very popular festival celebrated in South Kashmir. It is called *Frove*. It is held at the shrine of a popular Muslim Rishi saint of Kashmir, Zain ud-Din Rishi in the month of Āsid. The *Frove* continues for ten days. However, the most important event in which the whole populace of the area would participate, no matter even if they could not make it to visit the shrine, is what is known as *Z'ana Shah Sa'bun zool* (bonfire of Zain ud-Din Rishi). On this day immediately after the sun set, the people, young and old, would gather at some open space to burn *laisch* (the chips of pine wood arranged and tightly secured round a stick); and those who could not manage to have *laisch*, they would prefer to burn paddy grass, rather than to afford non-participation in this sacred ceremony—*Frove*.

What is the origin of *Frove*? Prof. Gulshan Majid rightly finds it in Zoroastrian presence in Kashmir. According to him, *Frove* is the derivative of *frover*, an Avestan term for soul; and the *frover* is rooted in the term *fravardin*, meaning honouring the dead.[173]

The time of *Frove* celebration in Kashmir is an additional evidence to substantiate the theory that the ritual is a vestige of Zoroastrianism that once exercised a powerful influence on Kashmir. To quote Gulshan Majid:

> The month of Acid in which the *Frove* is held, has a significant correspondence with the 9th month *Aciyadiya* of the old Persian calendar inscribed on the rock of Behistun by Darius (522–486 BC). *Aciyadiya* means to honour fire. In the Zoroastrian calendar it is replaced by *Atur* (*Adar*) again meaning the fire. If Nyberg

> is to be believed the year started with the month of Dadv and ended with the Atur. In this case the most important intercalary days fell between Aciyadiya (Atur) and Anamika – nameless month (Dadv). So *Farvardigan* ceremonies could well be held in Aciyadiya.[174]

While holding of *zool* (bonfires) is a common phenomenon associated with the *urus* celebrations of the Rishis, the folk heroes of Kashmiris, the question may be asked why the celebration of *Frove* is so strongly attached to one shrine only. The answer to this question may perhaps be found in the place-name where the shrine of the Rishi is located. It is known as "Aish Muqām." "Aish" is in all probability derived from Aśi, one of the most popular deities in Zoroastrianism; she is the goddess of reward, blessing, wealth and fortune. Portrayed as a noble and invincible maiden,[175] Aśi is one of the major Iranian deities venerated also in the Gathas.[176] Given the power of goddess Aśi, it is no wonder that her *fravasis* was frequently invoked with much veneration and she had gained wide popularity[177]—too much to be forgotten even after the religious changes. The only change that was gradually affected by time was that instead of goddess Aśi, *Frov* came to be held in the name of a new folk hero—Zain ud-Dīn Rishi. It is also significant to note that in the folk memory, Zain ud-Dīn Rishi is remembered to have occupied the cave after overpowering the dragons and monsters who had occupied it before him. Importantly, in Zoroastrian religion, dragons and monsters are recurrent adversaries.[178] And the *zool* (bonfire) held at the time of *Frove* symbolises the victory of Zain ud-Dīn over the dragons and demons.

Another popular ritual which, according to Prof. Gulshan Majeed, connects Kashmir with Zoroastrian Iran is what is known as *roohan posh* (flowers of souls). This ritual is being held in the month of *Vaihaik*. In this month, the Kashmiri Muslims remember their dead, visit their graves, sprinkle water over them and distribute backed loaves called *roohan tsuchi* (breads in memory of souls). It may be mentioned that the month of *Vaihaik* corresponds with the month of *Fravardin* of Zoroastrian calendar. It is on the 19th day of this month that Parsis remember their dead, offer wood to the fire and visit their towers of silence situated on the hills. And the custom of distributing *roohan tsuchi* has a close resemblance to the tradition of making ceremonial breads for distribution among the Parsis.[179]

Impact on Buddhism

While Buddhism—originally abstract and without images—started representing Buddha, Bodhisattvas, gods and demons under Greek influence, the Iranian Influences on Buddhism can be seen in the concept of Buddha

Maitreya, the most famous of the Bodhisattvas, who has messianic features reminiscent of Saoshyant, the Zoroastrian saviour.[180] It is this kind of Buddhism—Mahayana Buddhism—which became popular in Kashmir.

Sun Worship

The Śakas, as we saw, were basically sun and bull worshippers. It is believed that sun worship was introduced in India by a group of Magians who accompanied the Śaka invaders in the middle of the first century BCE and were priests.[181] Associated with their god Mit(h)ra were Aśi, Cista, Rashnu and Sraosha. His worshippers hoped for paradise (*Suryaloka*), which made this religion more readily acceptable to Viṣṇu.[182] In Kashmir we find sun worship a very popular cult, particularly among the Vaiṣṇavites, which was one of the dominant cults of Kashmir.[183] More importantly, there are many places in Kashmir, which are named after Mitra such as Mitar gom and Mir.

Agricultural Technology

Given the fact that agriculture was the mainstay of the economy of the valley, it is quite expected that the Śaka and the Parthian rulers would have introduced in Kashmir improved agricultural technology. It may not be without any interest to mention that one of the ploughs of Kashmir resembles Persian plough, *gajemeh*,[184] which was also widely used for rice cultivation in Caspian provinces.[185] In the neighbouring territory of Chilas, we come across a carved rock of Parthian period, which besides other things contains a carving of a human, carrying a plough on his shoulders.[186] The plough is quite identical with the plough commonly prevalent in Kashmir.

It is also quite probable that the technology of saffron cultivation was introduced in Kashmir during this period from Bactria, famous as *Bahlika*. It may be mentioned that in the ancient Indian literature, saffron was known as *Bahlikam* after the country of Bahlika where saffron grew in abundance.[187] Subsequently when Kashmir also became famous for saffron cultivation, saffron came to be known as *Kasmirajam*.[188]

Dress and Ornaments

The Śakas and the Parthians introduced certain new types of dress and ornaments, food habits, utensils, furniture, music, musical instruments, systems of reckoning dates, vocabularies etc.[189] Tailored garments first came into vogue in India about the beginning of the Christian era. The Scythian impact appears to have been the greatest in this respect. Of some new fashions that came into vogue in the beginning of the Christian era trousers or *janghatrana* is most remarkable. Originally, this dress had developed in Central Asia as a matter of necessity. To quote McGovern,

> By reason of their domestication of horse and adoption of horseback riding, the inhabitants of central Asia were forced to discard the loose skirt-like costume and to develop that ingenious piece of clothing that we call trousers. With the popularity of horse-riding it spread to other parts of the globe.[190]

The appearance of the mounted archer in the Indian battle field was a Scythian novelty, as it was common among them since the fifth century BCE.[191] Therefore, the Scythians were instrumental in introducing trousers in India as well as in Kashmir. Males and females with trousers is a ubiquitous motif on Harwan tiles.[192] The feet of the Scythians and Parthians were protected by supple leather boots.[193]

The triangle-collared and full-sleeved long tunic called *kancuka* in ancient India is considered to be a Scythian contribution to Indian dress.[194] This was the most popular mode of dress in Kashmir both among men and women (see Fig. 3.29). It seems that the proximity of Kashmir to Central Asia and the predominance of the Scytho-Parthian elements in its population popularised this dress there. In this context, it is remarkable that a long *kancuka* like garment was also in use in Dura Europos in the first century CE.[195]

The Scythians and the Parthians also introduced a short length, tight-fitting garment like a modern blouse, jacket and frock-like garments and the skirt. The fashion of using blouse, frock and trousers by women became popular in Kashmir (see Figs. 3.26 and 3.43).

The Scythians used caps, and the most common one was the peaked cap provided with flaps coming down over the ears.[196] For obvious reason in the subcontinent, the fashion first came into vogue in north-western India.[197] The conical cap with flaps popular in the Kashmir region (see Fig. 3.25) was clearly introduced by the Scythians from Central Asia.[198] The fashion of squat caps may have, however, come from Iran.[199] The fashion of wearing a *pattikam* (Kmr. *patka*) or fillet around the head was Iranian in origin.[200] Persian kings and commoners were fond of this dress, and subsequently the Sassanians patronised it. The Scythians and the *Su-li* people of western Turkistan also used this dress.[201] As a result of Scythian and Parthian influence, the fashion came into vogue in Kashmir[202] (Fig. 3.27). It became such an imitable fashion that we find the crown of Buddha with a flying *pattikam*.[203]

Śakas displayed shaven heads and long beards. Significantly, the custom of shaving the front part of the head was performed by both the Greeks and the Scythians.[204] This custom prevailed in Kashmir too as is evident from the Harwan tiles (see Fig. 3.45). The round and big ear rings worn by Harwan ladies were basically a Parthian fashion.[205]

Kuṣāṇa Kashmir: Confluence of Cultures

Around the mid-first century CE Kashmir became a part of the vast Kuṣāṇa empire, which extended from Central Asia to Mathura. The Kuṣāṇas originally belonged to the modern province of Kansu in Chinese Central Asia. They migrated westwards and passed through Kucha, Aksu and thence to modern Kyrgyzstan and ultimately subjugated north and south of Oxus. The Kuṣāṇa kingdom was founded around 29–30 CE by Kujula Kadphises and by the middle of the first century CE, he also subjugated Kabul, western Bactria, Gandhara, Taxila region and Kashmir.[206] Kujula was succeeded by Vima I Takto, who expanded the Kuṣāṇa empire up to Mathura. The other Kuṣāṇa rulers who ruled the empire successively are Vima II Kadphisis, Kaniṣka I, Huvishka, Vasudeva I, Kaniṣka II, Vasishka, Kaniṣka III, Vasudeva II, Shaka and Kipu Nanda. The Kuṣāṇas ruled their vast empire from Bactria which, as mentioned earlier, was the hub of cosmopolitanism forged on account of Persian, Greek, Chinese, Central Asian and Indian influences.

The literary and numismatic evidence testifies to the fact that Kashmir was incorporated in the Kuṣāṇa empire by its illustrious founder, Kujula Kadphises sometime after his conquest of Kabul, parts of western Bactria and north-west India. Recently a hoard of copper coins of Kujula Kadphises has been found from the ancient site of Tarakpura on Sopore-Bandipora route.[207] Bandipora route, it may be mentioned, was one of the main routes that linked Kashmir with Astor, Gilgit, Chitral, Yasin, Badakhshan and Central Asia on the one side and Yarkand, Kashgar, Khotan, Tibet and China on the other. In addition to this horde, there are 103 coins of Kujula Kadphises housed in SPS Museum, Srinagar—next only to Kaniṣka's in number.[208]

Earlier it was believed that Kujula Khadphises was succeeded by Vima Kadphises, known in Chinese sources as Yen-Kao-Chen. However, the startling discovery of the Rabatak inscription clearly demonstrates that Kujula Kadphises was succeeded by his son Vima Tak [to], and Vima Tak [to] was succeeded by his son Vima Kadphises.[209] Unfortunately about Vima Kadphises' reign in Kashmir, we have no evidence except for his one copper coin[210] and the inscription of Khaltse.[211] Vima Kadphises was succeeded by Kaniṣka I. The date of Kaniṣka's accession to power is a subject of great controversy. However, the recent evidence arrives at a date of CE 100/120–126/146 for Kaniṣka.[212] About Kaniṣka's rule in Kashmir, we have sufficient evidence—both numismatic and literary. The conventional evidence is also supported by place names and oral history. There are presently 572 Kuṣāṇa copper coins in the SPS Museum, Srinagar. Of them, 467 belong to Kaniṣka.[213] This is besides his two gold coins (out of total four) preserved in the same Museum.[214] Kalhana's *Rājataraṅgiṇī* not only refers to Kaniṣka as a ruler of Kashmir, but he also makes a mention of his building activities.[215] According to Kalhana, he built a town after his name and also constructed *mathas* and chaityas elsewhere in the valley.[216] Clearly, he refers to the same

Kaniṣka who is famous in history as a great patron of Buddhism. Hiuen Tsang, who visited Kashmir in the early seventh century CE found local traditions regarding Kaniṣka's rule still fully alive in the valley. And it appeared so true to the Chinese pilgrim that he faithfully recorded them in his travel account, particularly the holding of Fourth Buddhist Council by Kaniṣka.[217] The continued existence of a place called Kaniṣkapur (modern Kanispur) in district Baramulla, described as a foundation of Kaniṣka by Kalhana,[218] is a living evidence of Kaniṣka's rule in Kashmir.

Evidently, during the period of Kaniṣka, Kashmir attained unprecedented prosperity. This is abundantly clear from the Kuṣāṇa art treasures with Buddhist themes found in different nooks of the valley. Some sites are so distantly located that even today only an adventurer can reach them.[219] The huge quantity of Kaniṣka's coins so far retrieved in Kashmir further attests to this fact. No less significant evidence of Kashmir's emergence as a famous place of the Kuṣāṇa empire is Kaniṣka's decision to choose Kashmir as a venue for the Fourth World Buddhist Conference in preference to any other place of the vast Kuṣāṇa empire.

Besides Kaniṣka, *Rājataraṅgiṇī* refers to two more Kuṣāṇa rulers of Kashmir, namely, Juṣka and Huṣka.[220] Juṣka is in all probability Vasiṣka who succeeded Kaniṣka I in the 24th year of Kaniṣka Era and ruled for about four years.[221] It may be mentioned that Vasiṣka is also called as Vajheṣka in the contemporary records.[222] It is quite probable that he was known by this name in Kashmir. Yet by the time Kalhana wrote, Vajheṣka became Juṣka in the local linguistic environment. In addition to clubbing the building activities of the three Kuṣāṇa rulers (Kaniṣka, Juṣka and Huṣka) and the efflorescence of Buddhism during their rule, Kalhana writes exceptionally about "That wise king Juṣka, who built Juṣkapura with its Vihāra, was also the founder of Jayasvāmipura."[223]

Vasiṣka was succeeded by Huvishka, who was perhaps the brother of Vasiṣka. His reign marks one of the brightest periods of Kuṣāṇa history. He ruled for a long period of 34 years (between 28 and 62 of the Kaniṣka Era).[224] His coins from Kapisa [?] alludes to a vast Kuṣāṇa empire inherited by him from his father which he certainly preserved. A variety of his coins in gold and copper are equally suggestive of the peace and prosperity in his time. Huvishka's name figures among the three Kuṣāṇa rulers mentioned by *Rājataraṅgiṇī* to have ruled Kashmir.[225] He also credits him for having built a town Huṣkapura (Huvishkapura) after his name. The town survives in modern Ushkur,[226] a village about three kilometre to the south-east of Baramulla on the left bank of Vitasta (Jhelum). He also attributes to him and the other two Kuṣāṇa rulers the construction of stupas and mathas at Śuskaletra.[227] Huvishka's rule in Kashmir is also corroborated by his gold coin found by chance somewhere in the valley.[228] Like his father (Kaniṣka), Huvishka's coins also portrayed the divinities drawn from different pantheons,[229] although in the Indian environment, the tendency seems more towards the depiction of new brahmanical deities.[230] The solitary gold coin of Huvishka retrieved in Kashmir *inter alia* depicts *ankusa*, sun god and the legend Mioro.[231] This undoubtedly alludes to syncretic religious system promoted by Kaniṣka and his successors.

Huvishka was succeeded by Vasudeva I, the last great ruler of the Kaniṣka group of rulers. Vasudeva I was followed by Kaniṣka II, Kaniṣka III and Vasudeva II. We have no information about the rule of these Kuṣāṇa rulers in Kashmir. However, given the fact that up to Vasudeva II, Kuṣāṇas ruled the whole of immediate neighbourhood of Kashmir, it is quite reasonable to conclude that the valley of Kashmir would have also remained a part of Kuṣāṇa empire at least until they lost the north-west of India to the Sassanians around 262 CE. So far one gold coin of Vasudeva has been found in Kashmir, which still awaits scholarly attention whether it belongs to Vasudeva I or Vasudeva II. Besides, *Rajatarangini* refers to the name of a ruler Abhimanyu, who by all means seems an independent ruler but the one who had Kuṣāṇa affiliation.[232] As a true heir of Kuṣāṇas, he was favourably disposed towards Buddhism.[233] After him Kalhana makes a mention of the revival of traditional Naga worship at the hands of a local ruling dynasty whom he calls Gonandas.[234] If on the basis of the revival of Naga worship by the supposed Gonanda III we presume that Kuṣāṇas ceased to rule Kashmir after Abhimanyu, it seems that Kuṣāṇa rule continued a few years after it came to an end in the Peshawar region, which passed in the hands of Sassanians in 262 CE. Kalhana refers to five local rulers who ruled between the death of Abhimanyu and Kimnara (Kidara).[235] These five rulers probably ruled for not more than a century. As Kidarites occupied Kashmir around 410 CE, perhaps Kuṣāṇa rule came to an end there around 300 CE.

Kuṣāṇa Cosmopolitanism

Kuṣāṇa cosmopolitan ecumene was a remarkable synthesis of various cultures with which the Kuṣāṇas encountered right from their emergence on the borders of China through the establishment of a vast Central Asian empire, spreading up to the heart of India. Having lived in the neighbourhood of China, the influence of Chinese culture on them is quite understandable. They also learnt from many cultures they met during their long sojourn via Central Asia till they ultimately reached Bactria, the hub of Graeco-Iranian culture. For reasons of its splendour and fame as a great centre of cosmopolitanism, Kuṣāṇas made Bactria their permanent capital. Moreover, the routes that came under the control of the Kuṣāṇas connected China with West Asia and India, bringing the different cultures at their doorsteps. Kuṣāṇas had also trade and other relations with the Romans. With the expansion of their empire up to northern India, they tapped the resources of another great ancient culture. Thus, the Kuṣāṇa cultural horizon emerged from the cross-currents of six great cosmopolitan ecumenes of the time, namely, Chinese,

Central Asian, Iranian, Greek, Roman and Indian. Alongside these major sites, the regional cultures of their vast empire also cohered in the making and enhancing further its cosmopolitan character.

Immigrations and Settlements

The Kuṣāṇa rule, which lasted for about two and a half centuries in Kashmir, maintained the long established trend of immigrations and settlements in the valley. In fact, in no period of Kashmir history do we find so much widespread settlements of the newcomers as we come across during the Kuṣāṇas. Despite the fact that the spade of the archaeologists' has shown a superficial presence in Kashmir, still more than 50 Kuṣāṇa sites (see Table 3.1) have been identified so far, not only in the different nooks of the valley but also in its remote jungles.[236]

The immigrations and settlements were prompted by many factors. Of them the most important was the political compulsion of the empire builders who, in order to consolidate and perpetuate an empire created through conquest, needed a local support structure which in turn necessitated to have their own people settled in different parts of the empire. As these people had to act as props of the empire, their number was not only to be considerable

Table 3.1 List of Kuṣāṇa Sites in Kashmir

North Kashmir		
Balkot	Paran Pura	Kitshom
Buniyar	Shakkot	Malapur
Dattha Mandir	Tathamula	Singhpur
Lori	Patan	Wushkur (Ushkar)
Mahure	Baba Khaipur	Zainpur
Salamabad	Kalampora	Zandafaran
Silikot	Mamusa (Darwash bagh)	Zugiyar
Uri	Palhalan	Bambyar
Vrusa	Thapar	Pahli Pura
Shir Sirhar	Ahan	Gingal
Khunimoh	Sajwal	Manjgiran
Bunagantmula	Sarot	Naushahra
Drangbal	Seri Panditan	Naushahra (Pirniana)
Fatehgad	Kanispur	Khadayar
Huin	Dowarah	
Central Kashmir		
Gurwet	Harwan	Wanchdoor
Zakura		
South Kashmir		
Nagbal	Doen Pather	Hutmur
Kralchak	Takiyabal	Kutbal
Hoinar		
Shadi Marg	Semthan	Tengwani

but they had also to be from martial races, and well-trained in the techniques of the contemporary warfare.[237] In effect, the powerful land-owning tribes, known by the blanket term *damaras* in Kalhana's *Rājataraṅgiṇī*, who dominated the different parts of the valley and had become a serious cause of political uncertainty especially from the late ninth century CE, were these martial clans who settled in the valley from time to time under the patronage of the empire builders.[238] These settlers were backed up not only by their own physical prowess, numerical strength, well-knit tribal organisation and the advanced war technology of the time but, more so, by a strong economic power as they were allotted vast tracts of land giving birth to a powerful land owning aristocracy.[239]

Apart from encouraging the permanent settlement of their loyalists in the valley, the Kuṣāṇa period also witnessed the immigration of administrators headed by satraps who generally belonged to the royal family.[240] The Kuṣāṇa empire, as we know, was divided into provinces called Satrapies, and each province was under a provincial governor (Ksatrapa/Satrapa). To guard against the tendencies of localism, the Kuṣāṇas, like other empire builders, appointed their own people as governors and as highest state functionaries of their provinces. The Kuṣāṇa sites found at different places of the valley with strong evidence of aristocratic culture are obviously the foundations of Kuṣāṇa administrators posted at different places of the valley.[241]

For establishing an empire, a heavy and strong presence of army and administrative machinery in the provinces was not, however, sufficient *per se*; equally important was the cultural conquest of the conquered territories both for ensuring the consolidation of the conquest and satisfying the emotional state of the rulers. Thus alongside following the policy of settlement of martial groups and administrators in the valley, the Kuṣāṇas promoted the immigration of religious divines, technologists, craftsmen, artists and litterateurs. An idea of the immigration of religious divines of different persuasions can be had from different place names having association with Iranian and Greek religious cults, such as Mir (after Mioro), Mitra gam (after Mithra), Aharbal (after Ahura), Hardusho (after Ardoxoso), Nodo (after Oanindo), Pahru (after Pharro), Ash Much, Ash Muqam, Ash Pur (after Aśi), Harwan, Hari Parbat, Har wat (after Hara), Zeus (after Zeus), Aplun (after Apallo), Romoh (after Roma), Solun (after Selena) etc. Evidently these settlements came into existence around the shrines, temples, vihāras and mathas established by the rulers. The necessary concomitant of the establishment of a temple/matha/vihāra was the settlement of the priests at these places to perform the necessary rituals and to look after these institutions. Therefore, the more we come across the places having a nomenclature derived from the different religions promoted by the rulers, the more it speaks of the new religious settlements owing to the policy of the rulers to seek ideological conversion of the people and establish cultural unity of the empire for larger political interests.

While observing the settlement of the priests and preachers of different religious cults in the valley, one is particularly struck by the inflow of religious divines, missionaries and scholars belonging to Iranian cults and Buddhism. The strong presence of Zoroastrianism is testified by varied types of evidence including the place names after the Zorastrian gods and goddesses. The Magas—the worshippers of the sun god and the consecrators of sun images—who had their origin in Iran seem to have become an important section of Kashmiri society. The word *maga* was so popular in Kashmir because of the ubiquitous presence of these sun worshippers that the Muslim name Maqbool came to be known as *Maga* in Kashmir. The period also witnessed large-scale influx of Buddhist savants. According to Hiuen Tsang, Kaniṣka's decision to hold Fourth Buddhist Council in Kashmir was followed by more than 500 Buddhist scholars from different parts of Kuṣāṇa empire,[242] some of whom stayed in Kashmir permanently.[243] While narrating the Kuṣāṇa rule, the local sources mainly make a mention of the flourishing nature of Buddhism during the period. The efflorescence of Buddhism naturally attracted a large number of Buddhist savants and scholars from the neighbouring world to make Kashmir as their permanent abode.[244] Significantly the Buddhist monistic establishments found at different places of Kashmir are associated with material remains of Kuṣāṇa culture.[245]

The pouring of Kuṣāṇa technologists, artisans, artists and others into Kashmir and their permanent settlement in the valley is profusely substantiated by archaeological evidence. For example, the human motifs stamped on the famous Harwan tiles have unambiguous Central Asian physiognomy—receding forehead and slanting eyes.[246] They also wear Central Asian dress and ornaments.[247] This is besides the fact that the tile-making technology had strong parallels in China and Central Asia, and the motifs stamped on them bear the impact of many ancient sites of the world.[248] The tiles found at other places, such as Hoinar, Hutmur, Kutbal and Ahan, make it clear that the artists who were the brains behind the stamping of varied motifs on the tiles were well-acquainted with the Iranian and Central Asian cultures—so aptly these motifs portray the different cultural aspects and belief systems of the Kuṣāṇa world.[249]

Kalhana says that Huvishka, Juviṣka and Kaniṣka founded three cities, namely, Huṣkapura, Juṣkapura and Kaniṣkapura.[250] As was the practice of the time, these cities would have been mainly populated by the administrators, priests, scholars and urban artisans brought by the Kuṣāṇas with them. This is also substantiated by the various finds obtained from these Kuṣāṇa towns.[251] The famous Semthan site also bears out the settlement of new people belonging to Kuṣāṇa culture.[252]

The diaspora brought about significant changes in every sphere of Kashmiri life. It resulted in remarkable additions to the mosaic ethnic composition of Kashmiri society and the brahmanas' attempts to revisit the caste system to absorb these prestigious groups into varna system. With this, we find the emergence of hierarchically organised sub-groups among the higher castes and the conscious effort by the brahmanas to manufacture exalted pedigrees in favour of these groups to appropriate them into the brahmanical social system. *Nīlamata Purāna's* disdain for the "lower groups"[253] and subsequent attributions of rich ancestry to them[254] has to be viewed in the backdrop of the pressure exerted by the immigration of prestigious elements and their settlements in the valley, forcing the brahmanas to assimilate them into the varna order to broaden and strengthen its social base. The tailoring of high pedigree by the brahmanas for Durlabhavardhana—the founder of Karkota rule[255]—was not an innovation. They were essentially following a strongly embedded tradition which started immediately after the coming of Aryans and became pronounced between 200 BCE and 600 CE. That there were repeated influxes of powerful groups, who accompanied different rulers necessitating constant attempts to incorporate them in varna order, is also attested to by the fact that as late as the beginning of twentieth century, the brahmana society of Kashmir consisted of as much as 199 *gotras*.[256] These 199 *gotras* are essentially 199 kindred groups who streamed into Kashmir under the patronage of the rulers and eventually found a way into the higher social order. Yet these groups were hierarchically organised, some claiming higher positions vis-à-vis the others.[257] Indeed, with regard to flexible caste rules, which can be gleaned from the rise of low borns to high positions,[258] Inter-caste marriages,[259] absence of performing sati by the general masses[260] and ignoring the brahminical cannons on food and drinks,[261] Kashmir was an integral part of the north-west India, which was denounced by the orthodox *brahmanas* for their unorthodox beliefs and practices.[262]

It should, however, be remembered that with the coming of these people, we find each religious cult re-orienting itself by appropriating each other's deities, beliefs and customs to the much rude shock of the orthodox. This is clear from some statements made by Kalhana in the context of Mihirakula. Although the brahmana chronicler is unhappy with the Hun ruler for the atrocities he committed upon the people of Aryadeśa, he, however, softens his attitude towards him for he "re-established pious observances of this land which, overrun by impure Daradas, Bhuttas and *Mlecchas*, had fallen off from the sacred laws."[263]

The immigrations and settlements of the new people considerably increased the population of Kashmir and added a number of new villages to its existing list. It was the policy of the rulers to settle the newly arrived people in those areas which had to be brought under cultivation afresh with the help of the local people who were forced to internally migrate and settle in the newly occupied lands. The slave/labourer depicted on a tile of Harwan ethnically belongs to the category of superior groups stamped on the tiles of the site (Fig. 3.43). This shows that the immigrants had also brought sections of working class people with them. Yet, their number could not be obviously matched with the required work force needed for bringing new lands under cultivation.

The establishment of new settlements would have resulted in considerable increase in cultivated land and consequently a marked increase in gross domestic product to meet the needs of additional mouths. The fact, however, remains that the brunt of cultivating the new lands had to be borne by the working classes as the immigrants mainly belonged to noble class, administrators, priests, preachers, scholars and the urban craftsmen.[264]

Considering that the immigrants and settlers constituted the most prestigious section of the society, their culture became a 'reference model' for others to emulate for aspiring a respectable position in the society. Consequently, we find the new culture making profound impact on every sphere of life, an account of which is given in the following pages.

Religious Synthesis

Kalhana is not well informed about the religious aura under the Kuṣāṇas, which is why he makes us believe that Kuṣāṇas only patronised Buddhism.[265] Perhaps he was swayed by the popular Buddhist tradition, projecting the Kuṣāṇa period as the golden age of Buddhism, and Kaniṣka its greatest patron. While there is no doubt that Buddhism achieved great popularity at the hands of the imperial Kuṣāṇas, the fact, however, remains that the Bactrian religious tradition, which was an amalgam of Graeco-Iranian and Indian beliefs, remained the dominant religious tradition of Kuṣāṇas at least up to Vasudeva who got thoroughly Indianised.[266] Thus the prevailing syncretic and cosmopolitan religious tradition of Kashmir was not only securely preserved by the Kuṣāṇas but in their empire this multiplicity of items from different religions also "becomes more concentrated, more complex," to quote Harmatta.[267] This is abundantly clear from the numismatic and epigraphic evidence.

The first issue of the coinage of Kujula Kadphises has debased portrait and name of Hermeus on the obverse, and Heracles on the reverse, showing that the Kuṣāṇas still followed the Greek tradition. On the reverse, however, the legend is written in Kharoshthi, which reads as *Kujala Kasasa Yavugasa dhramathidasa* (of Kujala Kasa, the Kuṣāṇa Yabghu, who is steadfast in the law). The scholars have clearly shown that the epithet *dhramathida* means that Kujula Kadphises was a devotee of Śiva.[268] Nonetheless, Greek religious ideas and iconography remained important for the Kuṣāṇas. When after his victories Kujula Kadphises assumed the title *maharaja rajadiraja* (king of kings), he used the winged Nike as the reverse type of the issue.[269]

It is significant to note that of the six coin types issued by Kujula Kadphises, only one coin type has been retrieved in Kashmir. This is noticeable because, as mentioned already, a significant number of his coins have been found in Kashmir so far.[270] The obverse of this coin type contains a humped bull, *nandi pada* symbol and a debased Greek legend. The reverse has double-humped camel and a Kharoshthi legend[271] (Fig. 3.30). The depiction of bull is probably theomorphic representation of Śiva. Also, in Vedic mythology, the bull appears as *Vihana* of Śiva. The *nandipad* (bull's foot) symbol further substantiates the association of this coin type with Śaivistic pantheon.

The fact that all the hundred coins of Kujula Kadphises, so far found in Kashmir, belong to only one type showing king's tilt towards Śiva, makes it, at least, clear that in Kashmir he preferred to issue only this series obviously because Śaivism was the popular belief of Kashmir, and the king too had no ideological inhibitions to respond to the demands of Kashmiri society, for he, as we have seen, had already adopted the worship of Śiva though without any prejudice to other religions and cults of his empire. Evidently, Kujula issued different coin types for different societies taking into account their differing dominant religious traditions. As regards Kashmir, Śiva perhaps suited more than any other iconography.

The coin type of Vima Kadphises reported so far from Kashmir shows on its obverse the king offering at an altar and a legend in Greek showing his strong orientation towards Zoroastrianism and Greek culture. The reverse *inter alia* depicts Śiva standing with long trident in right hand leaning with left arm on bull (Fig. 3.31).[272] In fact, when Vima Kadphises assumed power, religious life of the Kuṣāṇas was characterised by two interesting features, namely, adoption of the forms of Greek religious art and Greek iconography—Kuṣāṇa gods lying behind the Greek iconographical garb of Zeus, Nike, Mithra and Heracles.[273] The other striking feature was the strong orientation towards Indian religions and the worshiping of Śiva in particular.

The accession of Kaniṣka ushered in remarkable changes in the religious life of the Kuṣāṇa kingdom. While Vima Kadphises preferred Śiva, Kaniṣka put Bactria and its Iranian religious cults at the centre of his religious policy. It should, however, be mentioned that as three Kaniṣkas ruled during the Kuṣāṇa period, the coin issues bearing the name of Kaniṣka can probably be divided among them though, according to some scholars, they predominantly belong to Kaniṣka I and Kaniṣka II. According to J. Harmatta and others, Kaniṣka, who is popular in the Buddhist tradition, was not Kaniṣka I but Kaniṣka II. They believe that while Kaniṣka I brought Iranian cults in the centre stage, Kaniṣka II's reign is marked by some more striking changes in the Kuṣāṇa pantheon as is borne out by the numismatic evidence.[274]

According to this understanding, the coins of Kaniṣka I depict mainly the Iranian gods, namely, Mioro, Mao, Oesho and Nana, albeit the importance of India and Indian religions, especially the worship of Śiva, remained unchanged. It should be mentioned that Kaniṣka has a reverse type representing Śiva with the name Oesho.[275] Harmatta ascribes to Kaniṣka II a new series of coins with a new category of divinities "who did not play any part earlier in the Kuṣāṇa coinage." They are, according to him, Pharro,

Manaobago, Ardoxso, Boddo, Orlagno/Oslagno and Lroasp. Besides these deities, we find all those Iranian divinities both Zoroastrian and local, which have been referred to in the context of Kaniṣka I.[276]

There are 467 coins in the SPS Museum Srinagar, bearing the name of Kaniṣka. However, we could identify the deities of only 133 coins. They are Mao, Mioro, Nana and Oesho on 48, Śiva with Nandi 10, Nana 45, Mypo 25, Oado 3, Manaobago 1 and Atsho 1 (Figs. 3.33–3.38). If we believe that Kaniṣka II's reign is marked by the appearance of new deities, then so far only one such deity, namely, Manaobago, has been identified on the coin issues bearing the name of Kaniṣka.

Given the paucity of sufficient evidence, it is difficult to arrive at a definite conclusion about the hallmarks of religious policy that separate Kaniṣka I from Kaniṣka II. However, one thing is certain: both of them showed catholicity towards all beliefs unlike the impression given by the tradition that Kaniṣka was only the upholder of Buddhism. For example, while on some of Kaniṣka's coins we find the motif of Boddo (Buddha), we also find on them the Iranian divinities both Zoroastrian and local, namely, Manao-Bago, Ardoxso, Oslango. Laroaspo, Pharro.[277] It is also not easy in the face of the mist and haze of controversial arguments to say which of them showed exceptionally greater interest in Buddhism. Yet, it is clear that one of them did bestow royal favour upon this faith.

Huvishka's coinage shows continuity as well as change in the religious attitude of the Kuṣāṇas. While he retained the Iranian deities, we come across the appearance of new gods, such as Skando (old Indian Skanda), Komaro (old Indian Kumara), Masseno (old Indian Mahasena) and even Ommo (old Indian Umā). Clearly, Huvishka enlarged the social base of his rule by recognising all the local cults alongside being strongly rooted in the Iranian religious tradition—the dominant religious tradition of Bactria during his time.[278] Unfortunately only one gold coin of Huvishka has been retrieved in Kashmir so far.[279] Yet this single coin also gives us a glimpse of the composite belief system of the Kuṣāṇas. On the obverse the king holds *ankuṣa* in left hand and sceptre in right hand. On the reverse is the sun god, halo of rays behind his head and the legend *Mioro*.[280] No doubt there is omission of Buddha from the reverse type of Huvishka; but it should not make us to believe that Huvishka was not a votary of Buddhism. *Rājataraṅgiṇī* portrays him as fundamentally a supporter of Buddhism.[281] That he also supported Buddhism is proved by the existence at Mathura of "the monastery of the Great king, the king of kings, the son of God, Huvishka."[282] Harmatta and others reason out the omission of Buddha saying that "his royal favour is seen in favour of the local cults absorbed by Buddhism."[283]

With the accession of Vasudeva, however, the trend changed from Iran-centric to India-centric religious stance. Although only a few coins of Vasudeva have been reported so far in Kashmir, they represent the new trend quite faithfully. The obverse shows the king offering with right hand at a small altar and long trident with fillet (?) in left hand. The reverse depicts two-armed Śiva with trident in left hand, a bull and Oesho.[284] It shows that during the late Kuṣāṇa period, Śaivism had taken the centre stage in terms of royal patronage, though without completely parting ways with Zoroastrianism.

Indeed, the period under discussion was underlined by syncretism and absorption. Religions were in constant interaction with one another, influencing and cross-fertilising themselves. Even if at some point of time we find some divinity becoming predominant, it is not difficult to see that it had already absorbed many features of other divinities and had assumed a syncretic character. For example, Śiva was the sole divinity used on the coins of Vasudeva, but the figure had apparently combined Greek, Iranian and non-Śaivite Indian elements.[285] Another typical example of religious syncretism is Buddhism, which was overwhelmingly influenced by Greek, Iranian and many non-Buddhist Indian traditions. While Greek religion gave this otherwise abstract religion a rich iconography with representations of Buddha, Bodhisattvas, gods, demons etc.,[286] among the Iranian influences on Buddhism may be counted the concept of Buddha Matreya, the most famous Bodhisattva, who has messianic features reminiscent of the Zoroastrian Soshyant.[287] Under the influence of many local sects, the traditional gods of the Brahminical religion were fitted into Buddhism. The Buddha ceased to be a dead teacher and was defied as a living god.[288] Gods like Avalokiteshvara and Manjushri were created to personify the great Buddhist virtues.[289] Evidently the gods of the theistic sects are thinly disguised in Buddhist symbolism.

On account of the influx of various religious beliefs and their cross-fertilisation of one another, there was no belief which could be scripturally called "puritan." It is, therefore, no wonder that the "pure" brahmanas of Kashmir pardoned the otherwise cruel Hun ruler, Mihirkula because he, according to Kalhana—the representative chronicler of the 'pure' brahmana tradition of Kashmir—purged Śaivism of accretions drawn from other traditions.[290]

Architecture

The written and archaeological sources point to a considerable building activity in Kashmir during the Kuṣāṇas. But, unfortunately, except for a few ruins, no edifice of the time has survived to us. Therefore, until the archaeologist's spade brings out an adequate evidence on the architecture of the period, we have to satisfy ourselves with merely drawing a sketch of it with the help of an extremely meagre material evidence supplemented by the insights from comparative history. Further, the available evidence pertains only to the religious establishments of the period. As such, the following account is one-sided as it excludes the domestic architecture of Kashmir, which always favoured wood, brick, mud and a sloped roof as a pragmatic response to the climatic challenges. On the contrary, the religious structures raised under the patronage of the Kuṣāṇa rulers and nobles were made of mud and stone, embellished with figurative tiles.

From the point of view of material and the pattern of its usage, the evidence about five types of structures has come to light so far. They are ordinary rubble stone style, diaper rubble style, pebble style, diaper pebble style and chip style. While the structure of the first four styles has been found at Harwan, the chip style has been encountered at Ushkur.

Rubble Stone Style: According to RC Kak, who excavated Harwan during the twenties of the twentieth century, the rubble stone structures "were at first sight scarcely distinguishable from the mud and mud stone walls of peasants' dwellings in Kashmir."[291]

Diaper-Rubble Style: According to this style, a number of large boulders were placed in one row with intervening spaces between each pair of them. These spaces were filled with smaller stones so that the entire façade presented a diaper effect (Fig. 3.24).

Pebble Style: In this style, walls had a core of rubble stones, which were plastered with mud; but their faces consisted of closely packed small pebbles fitted in the mud plaster. The pebbles are so carefully packed that after the lapse of two thousand years the portion of the wall that remained standing presents a very neat appearance.[292]

Diaper-Pebble Style: It consists of a series of large, smooth-faced irregularly shaped boulders placed at intervals of 6″ to 18″, the inter spaces being filled with small round or oval pebbles of 1″ to 2″ in diameter, providing a strikingly effective façade (Fig. 3.23). In Kashmir, diaper pebble facing was covered with a revetment of beautiful and elaborately moulded bricks as we find at Harwan.

According to RC Kak, ordinary rubble structures formed the oldest style, which was successively followed by pebble style, diaper pebble style and the diaper rubble style. It should be remembered that coarsed rubble masonry was the characteristic of the Greek and Śaka periods,[293] and the heavy diaper masonry was the trait of the Parthian and Kuṣāṇa periods.[294] At Taxila heavy diaper masonry had been introduced at Sirkap by the Parthians as in comparison to rough rubble masonry it was earthquake resistant.[295] With the coming of Kuṣāṇas, the diaper masonry was exquisitely augmented and widely introduced in other parts of the empire. Different stupas and monasteries at Taxila of this period were of the same characteristic.[296] The Kuṣāṇas were also known for introducing a semi-ashlar masonry in the hilly regions of their empire. About this style Marshall writes,

> the foundations of the walls are lime-stone rubble . . . but above ground level the walls are faced with the strong semi-ashler masonry

> which first came into fashion in AD second century and of which numberless examples can be seen among the Buddhist remains at Taxila dating from the second to the fifth century.[297]

We have seen that many faiths flourished in Kashmir during the Kuṣāṇas but, except for the Buddhist creed, evidence about the architecture of other creeds still awaits the archaeologist's spade. And even if Kalhana mentions the construction of a large number of Buddhist structures at Huvishkapura (Uṣkar), Juṣkapura (Zakura) and Kaniṣkapura (Kanispur), a little has survived to us and that too in the form of slender ruins. Yet the ruins and finds yielded by the excavators of these sites help us in constructing the broad features of the Buddhist architecture of the period.

Stupa

No stupa of the period has survived to us. We are, however, fortunate to have three votive terracotta plaques of the period bearing stupas in relief (Fig. 3.41). These were discovered at Harwan. Similar votive Buddhist stupa plaques in bronze have been found in Gandhara.[298] Significantly, the type of stupa found on the Harwan plaques is repeated in the ruined foundation at Harwan, Ushkur and Parihaspura. According to Robert Fisher, the Kashmir stupa was a towering edifice mainly due to the emphasis on the umbrellas and the multi-tiered base. Also, it often featured the use of free-standing columns at each corner of the platform. Regarding the shared history of this stupa type across multiple geographies, Fisher says,

> Reliefs of stupas with these same features are also known from Gandhara; and from the Mathura region at least one example exists. The latter (actually a Jain stupa) follows a similar arrangement with free-standing pillars and a stairway situated on a raised platform. It is thus difficult to determine whether the design of the Kashmir stupa originated in Kashmir, Gandhara or even Mathura.[299]

Chaityas

In Kashmir the earliest remains of chaitya (the Buddhist temple which houses the funeral mound of Buddha) have been excavated at Harwan, and it belongs to the Kuṣāṇa period. The Harwan chaitya is a large apsidal structure. It consists of a spacious rectangular antechamber with a circular sanctum behind. Though the style of Harwan chaitya conforms to the chaitya halls found in the Indian-subcontinent, it seems more closer to Sirkap chaitya style "because like Sirkap the row of free standing columns separating internal *pradakishina* path from the main hall is absent in Harwan caitya hall also, the pillars being replaced in both the cases by walls." Recently, BR Mani also found the ruins of a large structure at Kanispur, which, according to him, "seems to be an apsidal chaitya."[300]

Vihāra

Kalhana credits Kaniṣka, Huvishka and Juṣka with the construction of vihāras (*sangramas*) in Kashmir. The conventional arrangement of vihāra consisted of a series of cells enclosing three sides of a square courtyard. However, gradually at some places the cells were placed within the chaitya hall, and it was probably the latter type of vihāra which was constructed at Harwan and Ushkur.

Language

Alongside promoting various languages, namely, Greek, Persian, Bactrian and Prakrit, the Śakas and Kuṣāṇas are also known for appropriation of Sanskrit, and more so its use for the "public political purposes." Highlighting the significance of this 'innovating force,' Sheldon Pollock says,

> what is historically important is not so much that new power-seekers in the subcontinent began to participate in the prestige economy of Sanskrit – other groups had sought and found inclusion even in *vaidika* communities – but rather that Śakas, Kuṣāṇas and the poets and intellectuals they patronized, often Buddhist poets and intellectuals, began to expand that economy by turning Sanskrit into an instrument of polity and the mastery of Sanskrit into a source of personal charisma. If this kind of Sanskrit has a prehistory, no one has found it.[301]

Kashmir provides a typical example of the overwhelming influence of Sanskrit on Buddhist scholars as all the Buddhist literature produced during the period was written in Sanskrit paving the way for the influx of brahminical beliefs and symbols into Buddhism; which is why some scholars call the Kashmiri Buddhism as "Sanskrit Buddhism."[302]

Costume and Coiffure

The impact of "global" ecumene, which came to be forged in Bactria, the capital of all Central Asian empire builders from Bactrian-Greeks to Kuṣāṇas, is no less seen in the changes costume, coiffure, food and recreations underwent during the period with enduring consequences.

Costume

A significant contribution made by the Scythians, Parthians and Kuṣāṇas to the dress of India with remarkable functional implications, besides the equally important aesthetic value, is the introduction of tailored garments stitched tidy and tight in accordance with the form of the body. Before them, the customary dress was dhoti as lower garment and *uttariya* as an upper garment.[303]

Men's Dress

The male dress of the Kuṣāṇas generally comprised trousers, tunic, double breast jacket and long coat. Their head was often covered with a cap and feet protected with leather boots.[304]

The tiles and the coins so far found in Kashmir reveal two types of upper garments. First and the most prominent is a long tunic extending almost below the knees with wide bottom and tight waist. The typical example of this dress is depicted on Hutmur, Hoinar and Ahan tiles (Fig. 3.42). The figure drawn on them wears a long tunic with flares to the knees. It has wide bottom and tight waist. Evidently, it was designed and cut almost like the modern full sleeved skirt. This garment is also often encountered in Kuṣāṇa coins. The other type of upper garment was what is called in ancient Indian literature as *Kanchuka.*[305] Significantly, in the extant Harwan tiles we come across only this style of upper garment to the complete exclusion of the other type of tunic which we invariably find on the tiles found at Hutmur, Hoinar and Ahan. Perhaps it was basically a Parthian dress. A long *kancuka* like garment was also in use in Dura Europos in the first century CE.[306] Indeed, before becoming popular in the rest of India, the fashion had been in vogue in north-west India for some time; exactly similar coat patterns are met with at Gandhara in the second and third centuries CE.[307] *Kanchuka*, in terms of length, was of two types: one slightly longer than knees, and the other ending at the ankles.[308]

Besides popularising the aforementioned upper garments, the Kuṣāṇas also promoted wearing of trousers, which was first introduced in the Indian subcontinent by the Scythians and Parthians.[309] As expected, trousers first came into vogue in Gandhara[310] and subsequently spread to the rest of the subcontinent. The trousers used by men were of different types. However, two were most common. One was tight-fitting all along its full length; and the other was baggy in the middle and tight at the hem.[311] In Kashmir we mainly come across the former type—tight-fitting, full-length trousers.[312] Kuṣāṇas also popularised leather boots and leather leggings introduced by the Scythians.[313]

The Kuṣāṇas, like their immediate predecessors—Scythians and Parthians—popularised many cap types. The most typical Kuṣāṇa head dress was a conical cap worn by kings, soldiers and house holders.[314] This is known as *kulah* in Sanskrit, Persian and Hindi. Caps with domical shape and knobbed tops formed other types of *kulah* caps.[315] In one of the Harwan tiles, we find the mounted hunter wearing a conical cap with flaps coming down over the ears. The fashion of wearing fillet (Sk. pattikam; Kmr. patkha) around the head was basically a Persian dress,[316] influencing equally the Scythians, Parthians and Kuṣāṇas. It is important to note that the fashion first came into vogue in Kashmir where we find a mounted warrior wearing fillet.

It is, however, noteworthy that all men did not necessarily wear a head dress. In the tiles there are many figures without any head dress. A little portion of the male's forehead is shaven, and the remainder is grown long and combed curly falling on ears and neck (Fig. 3.45).

Before we close this discussion, it would be germane to say that the dress mentioned earlier was the dress of the rich. The poor just wore a loin cloth as depicted in Fig. 3.43. The right register depicts an upper class lady in costly clothes, and on the left is a water carrier, probably a slave, almost naked except wearing a loin cloth.

Women's Costumes

That a wave of new fashions characterised the Kuṣāṇa period is more adequately shown by the female dress of the period. Four types of women's costume are depicted on the Harwan tiles. One tile represents a graceful lady in her back view pose wearing a transparent robe (Fig. 3.43). The lady does not wear any head dress. Her hair is combed backwards and then looped to form a curved tail. She wears prominent ear rings. The robe consists of a long sleeved full-fledged skin tight blouse and a loose long skirt falling down on the ankles. The blouse is so akin to modern blouse and the skirt so identical in cut with modern *sari* from the waist downwards that to a common observer the figure looks quite a modern female figure clad in blouse and *sari* even if it is not full-fledged *sari* and the blouse is, unlike the modern blouse, full-sleeved. It is intriguing that the type of skirts that fall down on the ankles are invariably seen being slightly lifted upwards by catching a side of it. The portion that is caught is, however, so long that if left let loose it would form the tail of the skirt.

Harwan tiles frequently repeat the motif of a lady with the side view of her face and frontal view of body (see, for example Fig. 3.29). She wears a triangle collared full-sleeved long robe which is stitched skin tight above the waist and loose and long below it. It falls down on the ankles. And like the above lady, she also carries a vase of flowers/incense burner in her up-raised right hand and lifts slightly the back portion of her skirt with her left hand. She wears either a close fitted round cap or some sort of lowly turban like head dress.

Then we have a beautiful representation of frock, trousers and a scarf as a full-fledged lady's dress (Fig. 3.26). The tile portrays a dancer in the dancing pose. Although the head is presented in a side pose, rest of the body has been drawn in frontal posture. The upper garment constitutes a full-sleeved frock falling upon knees. The above-waist portion of the frock is stitched skin tight including the sleeves which are sewn in such a fashion as to give a folded look. The collar is round in shape and almost half-necked. The below-waist portion of the frock is comparatively loose and its two side hems slightly longer in size. The trousers also present a realistic picture of the specially designed trousers for dancers. These are tight and tied above the ankles and below the knees so that its middle portion gives a prominent baggy look with folds. It was a special design in itself. The dancer holds a long scarf in her two hands, waving it above her head rhythmically with her body movements. The scarf is not only long making her to catch it substantially above its hems, but it is also broad, and thus loosely folded while using for dance. The scarf was also probably used by throwing it over the shoulders to make frock-trouser dress a complete one.

Yet another type of female costume is delineated through the portrayal of a lady musician who plays a drum (Fig. 3.44). For upper garment, she wears a round collared full-sleeved tight-fitting short-sized costume. It looks like a modern round-collared medium-sized T-shirt. For lower garment, she wears trousers, which is neither baggy nor skin tight save its hems. The complete dress looks exactly like the modern T-shirt and trousers specially designed for winters. She does not wear any head dress; nor does she carry a scarf. Her hair is combed backwards to form a pony tail.

To sum up, the Central Asian contacts made an enduring impact on the dress of northern India including Kashmir. The conical cap (*kulah*) introduced by the Śakas and followed by the Kuṣāṇas assumed so much popularity in Kashmir that it became an identity marker of Kashmiri dress. The triangle-collared full-sleeved tunic, which in case of males fell slightly beneath the knees and in case of women slightly above the ankle, is perhaps the precursor of the traditional Kashmiri dress, *pheran*. Equally important is the introduction of trousers—baggy as well as tight, frock and scarf, which constitute a common dress of woman in the Punjab, as well as in Kashmir. So is the case with *sadi*, blouse and petticoat. The special type of trousers designed for the dancers continued to be used in the same fashion up to our own times. The belt, which was an essential part of Kuṣāṇa dress, formed an integral part of Kashmiri dress till late medieval times. The long skirt-type tunic with girdle stayed as a permanent dress with the people of Ladakh. The Irano-Hellanistic chiton and himation apparel also made a lasting impact. The best example of this is the typical *pheran* of Kashmiri Panditanis which, like chiton, is a long and loose robe falling down on the feet with folds and light-belted.

Coiffure: Along with the new kinds of dress and the fashionable modes of wearing them, some new hair styles also came into vogue following the contacts with the Śakas, Parthians and Kuṣāṇas. Such hair styles are frequently found in the figurative Harwan tiles. Perhaps the most fashionable hair dress was to style it curly. There is an often repeated portrait of a couple belonging to the ruling class, sitting in balcony and exchanging love (Fig. 3.45). The male is curly haired with a coiffure which looks like a net designed wig. A little portion of his forehead is occasionally seen shaven; and the curly-wig-net like hair falls on his neck concealing his ears too. He is clean shaved, not growing even moustaches. Significantly the custom of shaving the front part of the head was prevalent among the Greeks and Scythians.[317]

While the curly hair dress and shaving of the front part of the head seem to have been adopted by the Kuṣāṇas at Bactria under the influence of the predominant Graeco-Iranian culture, the Tokharian practice of shaving off the head as bald as the coot[318] was not given up. It was as much a respectable fashion as the newly adopted curly hair dress. In an exceptionally treated Harwan plaque, which contains the image of an ascetic in one register and a couple in the balcony in another register, the male's head is completely shaven off (Fig. 3.46). Clearly, among some sections, the practice of shaving off head had its roots in their belief system, because even the head of the woman in this case is shaven off except for the place where his/her top-knot sprouted, which was left long enough to fall back on the occiput. It is perfectly like the lock of hair (Kmr. *chaugh*) grown by the Kashmiri brahmanas till recently. Evidently, some sections of Central Asian immigrants had stuck to their ancestral practices without conforming to new fashions in the Bactrian environment. This was not, however, true for the majority.

The hair style of women was also of many types. Alongside showing the afore-mentioned upper class woman with her hair shaven off save growing a lock of hair at the head top (Fig. 3.46), the Harwan tiles show women in many hair styles. The upper class woman, shown in conversation with her curly haired husband in the balcony, has her hairs braided or they are curly dressed. The hair of a portion of forehead is combed sideways and that of the sides and the head top is tied with a ribbon. This top-knot hair style forms a hanging hair lock drooping behind the neck. As in the case of her male partner, a little of the front portion of his forehead and sides are shaven off (Fig. 3.45). The graceful lady shown in another tile (Fig. 3.43) also displays top-knot hair style forming a curved hair lock behind the neck. Another hair style that we come across thanks to Harwan artists is what is called as "pony hair style." A female musician is shown with a type of coiffure where she has gathered her hair and loosely tied it with a ribbon near the occiput. The hair is then ultimately shaped into a roundish bun that falls slightly below the neck (see Fig. 3.44). Can we still call it a "pony hair style?" Some women are seen wearing a close-fitted round cap or a piece of cloth (Fig. 3.29). This also obtained elsewhere in the Kuṣāṇa empire.[319]

Ornaments

The women represented on Harwan tiles have not been shown wearing a huge variety of ornaments; it does not, however, mean that only these few ornaments used by them were in vogue. For example, while we find terracotta hair pins, terracotta pendants and other ornaments at the Kuṣāṇa sites,[320] the use of the same is not encountered in any of the figures represented on the tiles. Unfortunately, except for Harwan, women representation has not been encountered at other sites so far save a dancer at Semthan and the newly discovered site—Kutabal. Indeed, had female figures been met with at other sites one could know more about the jewellery of the period as is true of the other themes.

The first thing that we observe from the study of human figures portrayed on Harwan tiles is that the ornaments were worn by both men and women. For instance, we see the curly haired couple wearing a neck ornament, like medieval *mukhta māl* or *guluband* (Fig. 3.45). It consisted of round-shaped buttons (of gold) strung on to (silk) and worn round the neck. Similarly the other couple with a net-like hair style are shown wearing ear rings (Fig. 3.47). While the prominently big and round earrings and *gulband* were worn by both men and women, we come across an ornament which was exclusively used by women. Worn by Harwan women, the ornament resembled with the present-day locket (Fig. 3.47).

The prominent earrings are ascribed to Iranian influences, and the locket-like ornament was well known in the Greek world[321] influencing the Scythians, Parthians and Kuṣāṇas, who popularised it in Gandhara as well as in Kashmir and other parts of the subcontinent.

Food and Drinks

Following the contacts with the Central Asians from the period of Bactrian-Greeks onwards, some marked changes occurred in the food and drinks of the people of Indian subcontinent especially in the areas of north-west, the Punjab and Kashmir, which were the citadels of Yavanas (Greeks), Pahlavas (Parthians), Śakas (Scythians) and Kuṣāṇas. Small wonder, then, the Mahabharata looks down upon them for having made sharp departures from tradition.[322]

The Central Asian rulers, including the Kuṣāṇas, popularised indiscriminate use of meat including beef.[323] The different kinds of animals and birds, namely, cow, sheep and poultry, that we come across in the Harwan tiles were most probably domesticated for obtaining meat, besides their other uses particularly helping in carrying out agricultural pursuits. Fish is also a favourite theme represented on the tiles, obviously for its food value. A common motif that we find in the tiles of the period is the scene of hunting deer; and the happiness which the hunter gets after having successfully aimed at the deer is also worth noticing. Although the Aryavarta brahmanas frowned at the Gandhara and the Punjab (Madradesha) brahmanas for eating meat, and regarded them "impure," meat-eating had become so much pervasive that even the "pure brahmanas" were also influenced by it. The best example of this is provided by Kashmir where all the brahmanas were meat eaters,[324] the habit of mind which has remained unchanged till date. The second major development that we find during the Indo-Greeks, Śakas, Parthians and Kuṣāṇas was the popularity of wine. This is evident from the pictorial representation of the period.[325] The Kuṣāṇas were experts in preparing wine from grapes, flowers and leaves.[326] Kashmir was one of the three important places where wine was brewed because of extensive grape cultivation, the other two being Bactria and Kapisa.[327]

Two other important additions made by the Central Asian diaspora in the culinary culture of Kashmir are the use of onion and garlic for which the people of Punjab and north-west including Kashmir received castigation from the brahmanical literature. As these vegetables owed their introduction to Central Asian influences,[328] that is why they were called *mlecchakanda*, a tuber liked by non-Aryans.[329] However, eating of these vegetables had assumed so much popularity that even a large section of the Kashmiri brahmanas could not maintain their resolution. Not surprisingly, therefore, when subsequently there was revival of orthodox Brahmanism in Kashmir, onion and garlic eating brahmanas were punished by depriving them of the state patronage.[330]

Music, Dance and Drama

The Central Asians including the Kuṣāṇas were great lovers of music, dance and drama. This is evident from the presence of such *ragas* as *Śaka, Abhira, Takka, Bhatta and Kamboja.*[331] Even as far as in Ajanta, musicians are dressed in Scytho-Kuṣāṇa style.[332] This is an indication to the extent to which music had been identified with the Central Asians. It is perhaps because of the wide participation of the Central Asians in music that made the Śastric tradition to look down upon the profession of music.[333] That the Central Asian people, especially the Kuṣāṇas, were famous for music and dance is evident from the reports of Chinese pilgrims who especially mention the proficiency of the people of Kuca and Khotan in this art.[334] This is also corroborated by the Indian lore which says "Gandhorvas, born of the beams of the moon and fond of singing and dancing, are mythological forms of the people of Kuca and the neighbouring Oases states of Tarim basin."[335]

It is, therefore, understandable that music and dance form one of the important themes of the figurative tiles found in Kashmir. In one of the registers of a tile is a representation of orchestra (Fig. 3.48). The orchestra consists of three musicians: one plays a flute, the other cymbals and the third, a pair of drums. The drums are placed in horizontal and vertical positions and played at the same time by the musicians.

On another tile is seen a standing female musician wearing body tight tunic and trousers. She plays on a double-sided drum which is slung over her left shoulder. The drum is small in size and cylindrical in shape. She plays its right side with a curved stick and the left with her hand. While playing the drum, she has been shown in a dancing pose (Fig. 3.44).

That dancing was a favourite art of the time is shown by a fantastic representation of a female dancer completely absorbed in dancing. Wearing a frock and typical trousers, which are being worn by the dancers till today, she is in a dancing posture with her left leg lifted towards the right side and waving over her head the long scarf she holds in both of her hands (see Fig. 3.26).

Drama

Stage theatre was introduced in northern India by the Greeks. As Kashmir also came under the political control of the Greeks, the introduction of stage theatre could be dated to those times. However, the first concrete evidence of its presence in Kashmir is provided by a tile found at one of the important Kuṣāṇa sites of Kashmir, namely, Hutmur (Fig. 3.49). The motifs stamped on the tile portray three humans, each wearing an animal face and tail, and all are in dancing posture. It reminds one of the traditional folk theatre of Kashmir where the *baghats* (folk stage artists) used to amuse people by disguising themselves in the shape of various animals and communicated through them the bitter realities of the time.[336]

Kidarites and Kashmir

Around 410 CE, Kashmir came under the rule of another Central Asian power called Kidara Kuṣāṇas. Ethnically the Kidarites were Huns; however, they came to be called as Kidarites after the name of the king (Kidara), who established the dynastic rule of this particular sub-group of the Huns. They are also called Kidara Kuṣāṇas because of having occupied the Kuṣāṇa country, and thus claiming to be the successors of the Kuṣāṇas.[337] The nucleus of the Kidarite state was the territory of Tokharistan (now northern Afghanistan and southern Uzbekistan and Tajikistan) and their capital was located at Bactria. The Kidara crossed the Hindu Kush and subjugated Gandhara in the beginning of the fifth century CE.

In the opinion of J. Harmatta, Kidaras' reign in Kashmir began approximately around 400–410 CE.[338] The main evidence of Kidarite occupation of Kashmir is numismatics. The Kidara coin type which, besides having a king standing on the obverse and a goddess seated on the reverse, bears the word Kidara written in Brahmi characters (see Fig. 3.50). Significantly enough, this coin type, including the legend Kidara, was adopted by the local rulers of Kashmir till as late as the ninth century CE. Unless this coin type had been in circulation for a very long time and unless it had assumed considerable popularity, it is difficult to understand why the successors of the Kidarites adopted the Kidara iconography and Kidara word on their coins. Damodargupta, the Kashmiri poet of the ninth century, also says that coins of his time were called *kidaras*.[339]

Certainly, the successors of the Kidarites in Kashmir followed a well-established tradition of the time, namely, retaining the honorific title of the preceding dynasty by the succeeding rulers. Just as the Kidara used to style himself on coins as *Kuṣāṇa 'Sahi* (king of Kuṣāṇas) for many years after the fall of the empire of the Kuṣāṇas, similarly the successors of Kidaras kept the name Kidara long after the Kidarite state had ceased to exist, especially when it was a high sounding title (Kidara meant hero, honoured, valiant) and was carried by an ethnic group to which they themselves belonged.

Harmatta also concludes that King Kimnara of Kalhana is actually King Kidara "whose reign in Kashmir must have been presumed already on the basis of historical considerations and numismatic evidence but who could not be identified in the text of *Rājataraṅgiṇī* hitherto."[340]

Impact

The Kidarites brought with them a cosmopolitan culture developed in Gandhara particularly under the Kuṣāṇas. It is noteworthy that the Kidarites had a close alliance with Sassanians for some time; and later on they occupied the Sassanian territories which the Persians had snatched from the Kuṣāṇas. Both these factors exposed the Kidarites to Persian influences, which is amply clear from the Persian iconography of their coins. As they were originally from Central Asia, and the nucleus of their power included a part of modern Uzbekistan, Tajikistan and Afghanistan with Bactria forming their capital, the Kidarites were deeply rooted in a culture which was an amalgam of Central Asian, Persian, Greek, Chinese and Indian civilisations. The Kidara coinage constitutes the principal evidence to testify this fact. The coinage they issued shows the inscriptions in Sogdian, Bactrian, Middle Persian and Brahmi. Their coins also display a wide range of iconography borrowing, as it reflects the world of Sogdian culture, official art of the Sassanians (fire altar between two standing figures) and the art of later Kuṣāṇas (Śiva in front of the bull).[341]

From the numismatic and other forms of evidence, it appears that like their predecessors, the beliefs of Kidarites had not yet developed into a rigid religious system. That is why they were receptive to different faiths—Zoroastrianism, Buddhism and Hinduism—they encountered in the lands they subdued; and it is this syncretic belief system that they exported to Kashmir too.

Kashmir's Contribution to Buddhism and Its Expansion

One of the great achievements of Kashmir, which gave it a pre-eminent position among the great nations of the ancient world, was its remarkable contribution to the promotion of Buddhist learning and its exemplary role as a relay torch bearer of Buddha dharma, spreading Buddhism to China, Central Asia and Tibet. Among the early prominent Buddhist scholars who earned for Kashmir a great name mention may be made of Dharmatrata (early third century CE), Harivarman (mid-third century CE), Skandhila (second half of fifth century), Sanghabhadra (fifth century), Vimalamitra and many others whose names figure in Tables 3.2 and 3.3. Significantly enough, the information in this regard has been mainly supplied by the Chinese and Tibetan sources, and the contribution of the Kashmiri scholars is also preserved in Chinese and Tibetan languages.

The contribution of Kashmiri scholars to Buddhism is manifold. First, they produced a vast literature on different disciplines of Buddhism, namely, its code of monastic discipline (*Vinaya Pitaka*), discourses attributed to the Buddha himself (*Sutrapatika*), scholastic exposition of the Buddhist philosophy (*Abhidharmapatika*), Buddhist meditation (*Ahyana*) and logic (see Tables 3.2 and 3.3). Second, the Kashmiri Buddhists did not only contribute to one school of Buddhism; they contributed to its different sects. While we find them promoting the early Buddhist canon (Hinayana) by expounding, translating and preaching its three *pitakas*—Vinaya, Sutra and Abhidharma from the view point of the Sarvastivada school, their contribution to Mahayana form of Buddhism is also outstanding, as is indicated by Appendix II. Third, the Kashmiri Buddhist scholars translated the Buddhist texts into different languages especially Chinese, Tibetan and various Central Asian languages (Tables 3.2 and 3.3). It is significant to note that while we have lost the Sanskrit originals, the entire Sanskrit canon is preserved only in large collections of Chinese and Tibetan translations. And last but not least, the Kashmiri monks preached Buddhism in different parts of China, Central Asia and Tibet, leaving a lasting impact on these lands besides considerably expanding the geographical boundaries of the Buddhist creed.

The emergence of Kashmir as a great centre of Buddhism during the Kuṣāṇas is borne out by both the literary and archaeological evidence. This is further corroborated by Kaniṣka's choice to hold the fourth World Buddhist Council in the valley.

Fourth Buddhist Council

According to Hiuen Tsang, the Fourth Buddhist Council was held in Kashmir under the patronage of Kaniṣka to reconcile the differing views and interpretations in the teachings of the Buddhist faith.[342] Having invited a large number of monks and learned men from all directions, finally 499 of them were carefully selected to sit in the conference to arrange the scriptures and to write an authoritative commentary on them.[343] The king himself accompanied the selected monks to the valley, which was preferred for the Council because of its favourable climatic conditions and also because it was free from too much sectarianism.[344] The Council was held under the presidency of Vasumitra—a venerable monk from central India.[345]

After protracted discussions for about six months, the Council drew up expository commentaries on *Tripitaka* (three baskets of the Buddhist scriptural writings—Sutra (sermons), Vinaya (discipline) and Abhidharma (metaphysics). The explanatory commentary written on Sutra was called *Upadeśa-śāstra.*[346] It ran into one lac *ślokās*. And the commentary written on Vinaya and Abhidharma was entitled as *Vibāsā-śāstra.*[347] According to Hiuen Tsang, Kaniṣka got the treatises inscribed on copper plates and enclosed them in stone boxes and deposited them in a stupa made for the purpose.[348] Hiuen Tsang adds that before leaving the valley, Kaniṣka, like Aśoka, gifted Kashmir Valley to the Buddhist sangha.[349] The holding of the Council in Kashmir has also been mentioned by Paramartha[350] and Taranatha.[351]

On account of hosting the Buddhist Council, Kashmir received a great importance among the Buddhist circles and attracted the attention of eminent Buddhist scholars and saints from different corners, some of whom made it their permanent abode. According to Kalhana, Nagarjuna—the great Buddhist scholar of South India—took abode in Kashmir at Sadarhadvana.[352] The other eminent scholars who visited Kashmir were Vasumitra, Parśva and Aśvagośa.[353] While sources are silent about Nagarjuna's participation in the Council, there is no doubt that the other three scholars played a leading role in it.[354] Subsequently we find Kashmir becoming an important centre of *Abhidharma* studies.[355] Certainly, Kalhana is silent about holding of the Buddhist Council in Kashmir, yet he does not find any other information about Kuṣāṇas, either available in his sources or worth to be recorded, except that Kashmir turned Buddhist and Buddhism reigned supreme during the reign of "Huṣka, Juṣka and Kaniṣka."[356]

Kaniṣka's Council is an important landmark in the history of Buddhism. It represents the rise of what is called Sanskrit Buddhism. The canonical texts and the commentaries drawn up at the Council were written in Sanskrit by the eminent Sanskrit scholars, namely, Ashvaghosha and Parshva.[357] Consequently all the subsequent discussions on them were also held in Sanskrit, making it the language of Buddhist thought and discussion all over the north as against the Kharoshthi or Brahmi script and Gandhari Prakrit language.[358]

The emergence of Sanskrit as the language of Buddhism had far-reaching consequences as it paved the way for creeping of Hindu theistic concepts into Buddhism.[359] The new orientation of faith at the hands of masterminds like Ashvaghosha, Nagarjuna, Vasubandhu and others was called by its followers as the Mahayana. And it was this school which found favour in Kashmir under Kaniṣka.[360] Having become the centre of Sarvastivadin Buddhism, the later orders and tendencies of northern Buddhism (comprising Northern India, Central Asia, China and Japan) are reworkings of this order of Buddhists.

Following the emergence of Kashmir as one of the highest seats of Buddhist learning, we see the students and scholars of Buddhism flocking to Kashmir from different parts of the neighbouring world, especially China, Central Asia and Tibet to learn at the great Buddhist seminaries of Kashmir. It is significant to mention that the great Kuchean Buddhist Scholar, Kumarajiva (344–413 CE), received education in Kashmir from the great Buddhist teacher Bandhudatta; and he completed his education from another great Kashmiri Buddhist scholar, Vimlaksa whom he met at Kucha.[361] Another famous Buddhist acharya to have received education from Kashmir was Buddhabhadra,[362] a contemporary of Kumarajiva. His teacher Buddhasena was an authority on Buddhist form of yoga in which the Chinese were very much interested. Another Kashmiri master of *dhyana* (Buddhist form of yoga) who attracted Chinese students to learn at his feet at the beginning of the fifth century CE was Dharmabhiksu. We also hear of the coming of Chinese monk Zhimeng to Kashmir with four of his companions around 404 CE.[363] In 420 CE, another Chinese monk, Fayong, came to Kashmir and spent more than a year there for studying the Sanskrit language and Buddhist texts.[364]

Apart from attracting students from distant lands of China, Central Asia, Tibet and other neighbouring territories, Kashmir played a leading role in spreading Buddhism far and wide. The exemplary passion of the Kashmiri Buddhist monks to spread Buddhism in the immediate and distant lands is evident not only from their unbending resolve to trudge up the death trap torturous routes ravaged by inclement weather but also from their enthusiasm to learn the mother tongues of these lands so as to translate the Buddhist texts in their own languages. It is largely because of their translations of Buddhist texts into Chinese, Central Asian and Tibetan languages that these monk-scholars of Kashmir outlived their enviable contribution to Buddhism, in terms of both developing its philosophy and expanding its geographical and demographic extent. The famous Sino-Indologists, PC Bagchi says:

> Kashmir takes the leading part in the transmission of Buddhist traditions directly to China. The number of Buddhist scholars who went to China from Kashmir in this period [third century CE to sixth century CE] is larger than those who went from other parts of India. Kashmir was the most flourishing centre of Buddhist learning in India in this period. It was the centre of the most powerful sect of northern India, the Sarvastivada.[365]

The famous Kashmiri Buddhist scholars who went to China and translated the Sanskrit Buddhist texts into Chinese included Sanghabuti (fourth century CE), Gautma Sanghadeva (fourth century CE), Punyatrata (beginning of fifth century), Dharmayasas (beginning of fifth century), Buddhayasas (beginning of fifth century), Buddhajiva (beginning of fifth century) Buddhavarman (fifth century), Vimalaksa (fifth century) and Gunavarman (fifth century).[366] A brief mention of their respective contributions is given in Tables 3.2 and 3.3. Certainly, this is indicative rather than exhaustive list of the Kashmiri monk-scholars who played an outstanding role in the transmission of Buddhist learning to China.

Relations between Kūci and Kashmir were very intimate during this period. According to recent studies, "these relations centered round the personality

Table 3.2 Some prominent Buddhist scholars of Kashmir who worked for the Spread of Buddhism in China and Central Asia

S.No.	*Name*	*Date*	*Place of activity*	*Contribution*
1.	Sanghabhuti	381 CE	China	Translated number of Buddhist texts into Chinese. The most important work among these was an extensive commentary on the disciplinary code, that is, *Vinaya Patika* of the *Sarvastivada* school.
2.	Gautama Sanghdeva	383–98 CE	China	Translated some Sanskrit texts into Chinese, namely, *Tridharmaka-Śāstra* and *Abhidharmahridaya Śastra* under the title *San-fa-tu-lun*. He also translated a number of important Buddhist texts. The Chinese version of *Madhyamāgamasūtra* was completed in 397–398 A.D.
3.	Punyatrata	399–415 CE	China	In collaboration with Kumarājîva, he translated in 29 sections the *Daśādhāya Vinaya*, (*Sarvāstivāda-vinaya*) under the Chinese title *Shih-sun-lun*.
4.	Dharmayaśas	405–414 CE	China and Central Asia	Translated *Strivivarta-vyākarana-sūtra* and *Śāriputrābhidharma Śāstra* into Chinese.
5.	Buddhayaśas	410–413 CE	Kashgar	He translated the following four Sanskrit works to Chinese. *Ākāśagatbha–bodhisattavasūtra*, *Dirghāgama*, *Dharma Gupta Vināya* and *Dharma Gupta Prātimoksha*.

S.No.	Name	Date	Place of activity	Contribution
6.	Vimalāksa	406–418 CE	Kūchā	In the Miracle Monastery of Kūchā, Vimalāksa studied *Vinaya* and acquired great fame as a Vinaya master. He translated a number of works and explained the translation made by Kumarajiva to Chinese scholars. In 413 he went to South China, where he spent rest of his life preaching Buddhism. Here he is said to have translated two works, one of them being the translation of *Daśādhāyavinaya.*
7.	Buddhajiva	From 423 CE till his death	China	Translated the three works of *Mahiśāsaka* school. Two of these works are *Mahiśāsaka Vinaya* and *Prātimoksha* of *Mahiśāsaka.*
8.	Dharmamitra	424–41 CE	Central Asia and China	He was a great teacher of the doctrine of *Dhyāna* or meditation and introduced a number of works on meditation in China. He is said to have translated 12 texts. *Ākāśagarbhabodhisattva—dhārani*—Sūtra is the only text available.
9.	Gunavarman	396–431 CE	Ceylon, Java, China	Propagated *dhamma* in Ceylon island. Converted the whole kingdom of Java into Buddhism. In China he is reported to have translated ten works (mainly on *Vinaya*) into Chinese. One of these was the *Bodhisattva—Carya-nirdśa.*
10.	Buddhavarman	c. 433 CE	China	Translated 60 chapters of Mahāvibhāshā-Śastra

Sources: Jean Naudou, *Buddhists of Kashmir;* PC Bagchi, *India and China;* PN Bose, *The Indian Teachers in China*; Advaitavadini Kaul, *Buddhist Savants of Kashmir: Their Contribution Abroad.*

Table 3.3 Kashmir's contribution to different Buddhist sects: A few examples

A—Hinayāna Buddhism

S.No.	*Author*	*Translated work*	*Language in which translated*	*Date*
1	Punyatrata in collaboration with Kumarājîva	*Sarvastivadavinaya* also known as *Vinaya Pitaka*	Chinese	404 CE
2	Vimalaksa	*Dasadhayavinaya*	Chinese	406 CE
3	Buddhayasas	*Dharmaguptavinaya*	Chinese	
4	Buddhajiva	*Mahiśāsaka-Vinaya* and the *Prātimoksa* of Mahisaska		

B—Mahāyāna Buddhism

1	Cha-Hou-Chêng (Kashmiri Scholar) in collaboration with Dharmaraksa	Yogācārabhūmi-śāstra	Chinese	284 CE
2	Dharmayaśas	Strivivarta-Vyākarana sūtra	Chinese	405–414 CE
3	Buddhayaśas	*Ākāśa-garbha-Bodhisattva-sūtra*	Chinese	410–417 CE
4	Dharmamitra	Bodhisattvadhārni	-do-	424–415 CE
5	Gunavarman	Bodhisattva-caryā-nirdeśa	-do-	396–431 CE

Sources: Jean Naudou, *Buddhists of Kashmir;* PC Bagchi, *India and China;* PN Bose, *The Indian Teachers in China*; Advaitavadini Kaul, *Buddhist Savants of Kashmir: Their Contribution Abroad.*

of Kumarajiva" whose association with the Kashmiri scholars was very intimate.[367] They collaborated with him not only in China but also in Kūci. Among the prominent Kashmiri scholars who worked in Kūci, the name of Buddhayaśa stands as the foremost. Chinese biographers have left a detailed account of his work in Central Asia. He first went to Kashgar and earned the great respect of the king who wanted him to live in the palace. Yaśa remained at Kashgar for ten years and then went to Kūci. From Kūci, he went to China to join Kumrajiva with whom he had worked at Kashgar.[368] Another Kashmiri scholar who worked in Kūci with Kumarajiva was Vimalaksa.[369]

Kashmir had also very close relations with Khotan since early times. There is immense presence of Indian elements, such as Prakrit in Kharoshthi script as administrative language and Śaivism at about the middle of the third century CE. MA Stein believes that the Indian elements in Khotan transmitted largely through Kashmir as there are racial traces of Kashmiri immigration in the region.[370] "Nevertheless," says Stein,

> I may note here I was frequently struck by a certain curious resemblance in general appearance of features between the Khotanese and the Kashmiris, a resemblance difficult to define yet all the more noteworthy on account of the unmistakable peculiarity of the type presented by the Kashmiris.[371]

Hiuen Tsang, Sung Yun, the *Pei Shih* and other historical texts, as well as the Annals of *Li-Yul*, unanimously say that Buddhism was introduced in Khotan by a Kashmiri *arhat*, Arya Vairochana (*p'i-pu-che-na*). According to them, he converted the king of Khotan who built a vihāra called Vairochana Vihāra, which is the oldest sanctuary of the territory.[372] The legend associated with the shrine of Palma (po-ch'ich-i) regarding the miraculous statue of Buddha from Kashmir indicates that Kashmir was credited with having supplied to Khotan not only Buddhism but also the Graeco-Buddhist art of Gandhara.[373] It is interesting to note that there is close resemblance between the Kashmiri legend and Khotanese legends regarding the drainage of lakes which were believed to have once occupied the present valleys of Kashmir and Khotan. The account of Khotan history opens characteristically with the Buddhist adaptation of a legend recorded by *Nīlamata Purāna*. "Buddha's stay on the mount of Goslinga seems to reflect the position taken on by Brahman and his divine host on the lofty peaks of the Naubandhna Tirtha in the mountains south-east of Kashmir."[374]

With Buddhism also travelled some iconographic hallmarks of Kashmiri Buddhists art to Central Asia, China and Japan. According to Paul,

> the elaborate pedestals consisting of rock formations on which the Buddhist deities are often made to sit are typically Kashmiri and are not encountered elsewhere in the subcontinent. Very likely these highly imaginative and stylized mountains are meant to represent Mount Meru. It would appear that the idea travelled north from Kashmir to Central Asia, China and Japan.[375]

To conclude, the human agents who created or translated the Buddhist texts and the Buddhist art and transmitted them to distant lands exemplify two things: the exemplary zeal of the premodern religions to expand their physical topography as much as possible and create dedicated missionaries to knit a common bond. Second, it shows "the mobility of routes and networks in contrast to the fixities of routes and territories."[376]

Huns and the Indic Turn (Sixth to the Beginning of Seventh Century CE)

The Huns constituted one of the deeply entrenched and immensely powerful Central Asian ethnic groups.[377] Yet, they were thoroughly influenced by Indian culture during their stay in the north-west and other parts of the subcontinent. This is evident not only from their personal names but also from their religious propensities as they were either Śaivites or Vaiṣṇavites or Buddhists. Since only one Hun ruler was Buddhist, it is no wonder that the period witnessed the ascendency of Brahmanism and Indian culture with enduring impact as Kashmir continued to remain gravitated towards the Sanskritic culture till the establishment of the Muslim sultanate in the early fourteenth century. Significantly, during the period under reference Kashmir was intermittently twice occupied by the Indian rulers which further contributed to the Indian acculturation of Kashmir. Clearly, the period saw a marked transition from an essentially syncretic culture with predominant Graeco-Persian and Indian elements to the formation of a new syncretic culture in an essentially Sanskritic crucible, though commercial and cultural contacts with the other parts of neighbouring world maintained their continuity.

However, it needs to be reiterated that the designs and textures of Indic culture, which had come to be forged by the beginning of sixth century CE, owed as much to trans-border networks as they owe to endogenous ingenuity and creativity, which synthesised the heterogeneous elements into a harmonious whole. Be it religion, religious cults, art, architecture, technology, languages, scripts, costumes, entertainments, ethnic mosaic of the population or cast system—all these and other elements of Indian culture were relationally constituted and therefore transborder in character.

In this new cultural configuration, one thing, however, remained constant, namely, the gateway to change remained unchanged. The changes flowed from the immediate west and north-west of Kashmir—the traditional intermediary landscape between Kashmir and the rest of the world. Robert E Fisher, the celebrated art historian, also finds Kashmir and Gandhara forming one single complex, which remained undisturbed by political changes.

> One plausible aspect of the early period that does emerge from the various literary sources, however, is the close connection between Kashmir and the area of west, Gandhara. Beginning at least with the Achaemenian Persians, around 500 BC, and continuing with the Greeks and Saka tribes, the region between Afghanistan and Kashmir was usually viewed as one cultural entity. The name Kashmir was not generally limited to the small Himalayan valley until times, in the early centuries AD. By the time of the Huna invasions, towards the beginning of the sixth century, which also encompassed both regions, Gandhara kings had used Kashmir as a refuge and likewise Kashmiri rulers could find temporary safety in the neighbouring area when needed. Despite invasions and wars, the commercial and cultural exchange between the adjacent regions continued without interruption. Even to earlier visitors, such as the Chinese monks of the seventh and eighth centuries, the cultures of the two regions still seemed to be essentially one.[378]

Fisher is joined by another art historian and critic, John Siudmak:

> Artistically both areas [Gupta empire in the South and Gandhara] had overshadowed Kashmir, although there is some evidence of direct Gupta influence, the predominant influence was from the north-west, either from Gandhara or from the post Gandhara tradition which survived in the region. This was natural given the geographical proximity of Gandhara to Kashmir and was generally the case historically. . . .[379]

Identical art forms were actually the off-shoot of identical political, religious and cultural developments, which occurred in Gandhara and Kashmir both before and after the Hun conquest.

Hun Conquest of Kashmir

The late fifth and early sixth centuries saw the beginning of Hun raids on Gandhara and subsequently on the whole of northern India.[380] Launching an offensive from the Punjab, Toramana, the leader of Huns conquered the whole of western India. Numismatic evidence indicates that Toramana ruled in Uttar Pradesh, Rajasthan, the Punjab and Kashmir.[381] His conquests brought with them the destruction of towns, villages and Buddhist monasteries.[382] In the time of Toramana, the Hephthalites in India began to operate independently of the Central Asian branch though the link between them does not seem to have been broken. Toramana's son, Mihirakula, intensified his father's efforts to conquer the whole of northern India and in this, he was highly successful. The account of *Cosmas Indicopleustes* confirms that the Hephthalites in India reached the zenith of their power under Mihirakula with their capital at Śakala[383] (Sialkot).

According to Biswas, the Huns occupied Gandhara under the command of a chief who subsequently became its governor. He was known by the Turkish title, Tigin (Lac-lin of Sung-Yun).[384] Biswas believes that Tigin is the father of Tormana and it is during Tigin's governorship of Gandhara that Kashmir was integrated with Hun empire.[385] The basis of this assumption is that there is a coin which is clearly inscribed with the word Tunjina and we also come across a ruler Tunjina in *Rājataraṅgiṇī*. However, as neither the identity nor the chronological sequence of the rulers as given in *Rājataraṅgiṇī*[386] tallies with the constructions of Biswas, his conclusion will continue to be a mere conjecture till it is substantiated by some solid evidence.

Kalhana mentions two rulers of Kashmir—Hiranyakula and Vasukula, respectively, as grandfather and father of Mihirakula.[387] The name of Hiranyakula has been read by Cunningham on coins closely resembling some of the issues of Mihirakula.[388] This clearly shows that Kashmir had come under the occupation of Huns much before Mihirakula. Perhaps Hiranyakula was the son of Toramana and brother of Mihirakula, and Vasukula was either the younger brother or the nephew of Mihirakula. Vasukula ruled Kashmir when Mihirakula was banished from India and was forced to take refuge in Kashmir.[389] The numismatic evidence suggests that Kashmir came under the occupation of Huns during the period of Toramana. According to Stein, the numismatic considerations based on the type and execution of these coins and the characters of their legend favour their attribution to Toramana, the father of Mihirakula.[390] Most importantly, Toramana coins have not only been found in large quantity in Kashmir but they also became model for later copper coinage of Kashmir. Kalhana attributes these coins to a later ruler whom he also calls Toramana. But Stein has convincingly refuted it saying:

> Since the very abundance of these coins appear to speak for their having been struck by a powerful ruler rather than an ill-fated pretender, it seems reasonable to conclude that the Toramana mentioned by Kalhana some seven hundred years after Mihirakula must have been a latter ruler and not the one whose coins became models for the latter copper coinage of Kashmir.[391]

Kalhana does not make any mention of Toramana, the father of Mihirakula. Instead, he places Toramana some 700 years after Mihirakula. Stein deconstructs Kalhana saying

> Either the Toramana of the chronicle is identical with the King of the White Huns, in which case Kalhana, or his authorities would be guilty of having placed the father some 700 years after the son. . . . Or the Toramana of the chronicle is another and later ruler, in which case the error of Kalhana or his authorities would lie only in the attribution of the coins.[392]

Biswas also cites a Jain Prakrit work, *Kuvalayamala* completed in 621 CE, in support of the view that Toramana reigned in Kashmir.[393]

Toramana, who enjoyed a vast empire and a successful career, probably died between 510 CE and 515 CE. He was succeeded by his valiant son, Mihirakula. However, soon after he brought the Hun power to its zenith in India, he faced a tough resistance from Yaśodharman of Mandasor and Baladitya of Magadha,[394] forcing him to be contented with a small empire comprising Gandhara, Sindh and Kashmir, which he had to re-conquer either from his rebellious family members or governors of Huns who declared independence after Mihirakula's waning power.

Mihirakula as Ruler of Kashmir

Around 530 CE, Mihirakula assumed the reigns of Kashmir kingdom and ruled till 544–550 CE.[395] From here he seems to have been engaged in endeavours to recover his lost dominions in the direction of the lower Indus.[396] Kalhana portrays him as a wicked and cruel despot who ruthlessly massacred the people. To quote the poet-chronicler verbatim:

> Mihirakula, a man of violent acts and resembling Kala (Death), ruled in the land which was overrun by hordes of *Mlecchas*. In him the northern region brought forth, as it were, another god of death, bent in rivalry to suppress the southern region which has Yama [as its guardian]. The people knew his approach by noticing the vultures, crows and other [birds] which were flying ahead eager to feed on those who were being slain within his armies' [reach]. This royal Vetala was day and night surrounded by thousands of murdered human beings, even in his pleasure-houses. This terrible enemy of mankind has no pity for children, no compassion for woman, no respect for the aged.[397]

When we read this description about Mihirakula together with Sung-Yun's graphic description of the interview, he had with this "cruel and vindictive" king in his camp on the borders of Gandhara[398] as well as with Hiuen Tsang's record of his [Mihirakula's] enmity against Buddhism,[399] it is clear that Buddhism faced a rough weather at the hands of Mihirakula. This is also supported by Kalhana. True, while portraying Mihirakula's violence, Kalhana does not expressly mention his special targets, yet our brahmana chronicler's attitude softens on the "terrible enemy of mankind" for he exterminated the other faiths and re-established the "sacred law."

> After killing the inhabitants of Āryadeśa he performed a terrible penance, and re-established pious observances in this land which, overrun by impure *Dāradas*, *Bhauṭṭas* and *Mlecchas*, had fallen off from the sacred law. . . . It was on this account that he bestowed a thousand *Agrahāra*s on Brahmans from the Gandhāra-land at Vijayeśvara.[400]

That Mihirakula was a Śiva is supported not only by Kalhana's aforementioned quote but also by his explicit mention that he founded at Srinagar a shrine of Śiva Mihiresvara.[401] Mihirakula's Śiva favouritism is confirmed by his coins, which clearly represent the royal standard surmounted by the bull, Nandi, the celestial mount of Śiva.[402] He inscribed coins with *Jayatu Vrsah* or *Jayatu Vrsadhvajah*. The *trisula* is engraved behind the king.[403] The Mandasor pillar inscription of Yaśodharman confirms Mihirakula's distinct leaning towards Śaivism. It refers to Mihirakula "whose head had never previously been brought into the humility of obeisance to any other save Śiva."[404] The Gwalior inscription of Mihirakula also depicts him as a devotee of Śiva.[405]

Successive Hun Rulers

Kalhana gives a long list of the Hun rulers who succeeded Mihirakula and ruled up to 620 CE with two brief interregnums. The list of Hun rulers who, according to Kalhana, succeeded Mihirakula is: (1) Baka, (2) Ksitinanda, (3) Vasunanda, (4) Nara II, (5) Akṣa, (6) Gopaditya, (7) Gokarna, (8) Narendraditya also called Khinkhila, (9) Yudhishthira I, (10) Meghavahana (the great grandson of Yudhishthira who lived in exile at the court of Gandhara), (11) Sresthasena (also known as Pravarasena and Tunjina), (12) Hiranya, (13) Toramana, (14) Pravarasena II, (16) Lakhana Narendraditya, (17) Ranaditya, (18) Vikramaditya and (19) Baladitya.[406] However, it should be mentioned that in between the Hun rule, Kashmir came twice under the occupation of two neighbouring rulers. First, after the forced departure of Yudhisthra; and second, before the accession of Pravarasena II. During the first interregnum, Kashmir was ruled by Pratapaditya I, Jaluka, Tunjina I, Vijaya, Jayendra and Samdhimat.[407] The second interregnum lasted for five years' rule of Vikramaditya who ruled Kashmir through his representative, Matrgupta.[408] Although, according to Kalhana, 22 Hun rulers ruled Kashmir (besides seven non-Hun rulers between them), coins of only a few Hun rulers have survived to us. They are Toramana, Hiranyakula, Mihirakula, Gokarna, Narendraditya also called Khankhila, Meghavahana, Tunjina, Pravarasena II and Lakhana.

Kashmir's Emergence as an Empire

During the Hun occupation, the political position of Kashmir witnessed an important development. It emerged as a great empire for the first time in its known history. Till Mihirakula was defeated by Baladitya and Yaśodharman around 530 CE, Kashmir was a part of the great Hun Empire, which extended from Kabul to western India. After the expulsion of Mihirakula from western India, the Hun empire squeezed to comprise only Gandhara, Sindh and Kashmir; the latter emerged its headquarters, and it was from there that Mihirakula tried to re-conquer his lost empire.[409] One of the successors of Mihirakula, namely, Narendraditya, who bore the second name Khinkhila and whose silver coin bears the legend *Deva Shahi Khingila*,[410] expanded the Hun empire up to Afghanistan. Biswas identifies Narendraditya Khinkhila of *Rājataraṅgiṇī* with the king whose name appears at the base of the stone image of Vinayaka (Ganesha) found in Kabul.[411] The king's name is recorded as *Parama-bhattaraka Maharajadhiraja Shri Shahi Khingala Odya* (tya) *na-Shahi*. Accordingly, Biswas concludes that the Kashmir empire included the Kabul Valley too.[412]

After mentioning the rule of about nine Hun rulers, Kalhana says that Kashmiri nobility installed a non-local, Pratapaditya, the relation of Vikramaditya on the throne of Kashmir.[413] According to Wilson, this Vikramaditya could be the ruler of Malwa.[414] He was followed by his five successors.[415] Although the identity of these rulers is shrouded in mystery, the paramount influence of Indian culture is markedly visible. This period is underlined by the settlement of Aryadeśi brahmanas in Kashmir and the consecration of shrines and mathas as well as the endowments of lavish *agrahara* grants in every nook and corner of Kashmir.[416]

Then again the local nobility restored the Hun rule by installing a scion of Yudhishthira, namely, Meghavahana on the throne of Kashmir.[417] With the installation of Meghavahana, not only the Hun rule was restored but also the relations with Gandhara became intimate as the two ruling dynasties—the Kashmiri Hun dynasty and the Gandharan ruling dynasty—were closely related. It must be mentioned that Meghavahana was brought up at the court of Gandhara where his grandfather and father had been living as guests of the ruling families since Yudhishthira (grandfather of Meghavahana) was forced by internal revolts to leave the country.[418] Among other things, Kalhana calls Meghavahana a *digvijaya*[419] (conqueror of the world). The popular belief gave him full credit for having even subjected the king of Lanka. This is shown by the fact that even during the time of Kalhana certain royal banners borne before the kings of Kashmir on their expeditions, known as *paradhvajah*[420] [banners from across (the sea)], were alleged to have been presented to Meghavahana on that occasion by the Lord of Lanka.[421] Giving due allowance for exaggeration, the fact remains that Meghavahana embarked on the policy of conquests, which was carried forward by his successors making Kashmir a great power in the late sixth and beginning of the seventh century CE with a brief interregnum of five years when, according to Kalhana, Kashmir came under Vikramaditya Harśa of Ujjayini who ruled Kashmir through his representative, Matrgupta.[422] According to Sexana, the ruler referred to by Kalhana here is Harśagupta, one of the later Gupta rulers.[423] The Hun rule was again restored by Pravarasena II, a scion of an earlier ruler of the dynasty, Pravarasena I, who had fled from the country and sought refuge somewhere in the neighbouring hill kingdom as, according to Kalhana, Pravarasena II marched towards Kashmir after conquering Trigarta (Kangra).[424]

Kalhana portrays Pravarasena II (c. 570 CE) as a great conqueror who vanquished Saurashtra (Gujarat) and recovered for Siladitya—Pratapasila, the throne of his father, Vikramaditya.[425] He is also said to have "brought back from Vikramaditya's residence to his own capital the throne of his own family which had been carried away by enemies."[426] Kalhana also attributes him to have repeatedly vanquished King Mummuni,[427] who perhaps ruled between Badakhshan and Tibet. The greatness of Pravarasena II is also attested to by his silver and gold coins, large-scale building activities,[428] foundation of modern Srinagar[429] and some remarkable technological introductions, such as building of boat bridges.[430] *Rājataraṅgiṇī* also presents the successors of Pravarasena II, namely, Yudhishthira I, Narendraditya, Ranaditya, Vikramaditya and Baladitya as mighty conquerors.[431] The latter also built a *matha* for the Kashmiris in the territory of Vankalas of unknown location.[432] That by the end of the Hun rule Kashmir had emerged a great political power is also substantiated by a notice in the Chinese Annals which mentions that around 627 CE, the Kashmiri rulers were controlling the route from China to Ki-pin, that is, the Kabul Valley.[433] Hiuen Tsang (631–633 CE) also found all adjacent territories on the west and north, down to the Takshashila, east of the Indus, Hazara, Salt Range and smaller hill states as tributaries of Kashmir.[434] Certainly, the emergence of Kashmir as a great empire was the contribution of Huns. The Karkotas who succeeded them carried the tradition forward as true heirs of their great ancestors.

Coinage

With the Hun occupation of Kashmir, we find the commencement of a new system of coinage, if not the advent of first independent coinage of Kashmir as Cunningham believed.[435] The issues of this coinage consisted of copper coins bearing the name of Toramana which, according to M A Stein, "are found to this day [late 1890s] in remarkable quantities all over Kashmir and the neighbouring regions."[436] It seems that Toramana collected the copper coins of Kidara Kuṣāṇas and re-coined them in his own name. It is significant to note that we have in the *Rājataraṅgiṇī* an important passage which distinctly mentions these coins. However, Kalhana wrongly attributes these coins to another Toramana, one of the latter rulers of the same dynasty whom Kalhana presents as an ill-fated pretender. "The very abundance of these coins," says Stein "appears to speak rather for their having been struck by a powerful ruler than by an ill-fated pretender."[437] It should also be remembered that the coins bearing the name of Toramana are not only available in abundance but they have also served as direct models for the later copper coinage of Kashmir, pointing to the same conclusion as arrived at by Stein. Significantly, this type was not only preserved by the Hindu rajas, we even find it in circulation late in the fifteenth century.[438] It is, therefore, small wonder that the copper coinage came to be popularly called as Toraman in Kashmir. Indeed, the coin type of only such a ruler can survive for so long a period of time and he would have laid the foundation of a powerful dynasty and earned a great fame. Toramana was such a figure. He founded a dynasty which ruled Kashmir not only till the assumption of power by the Karkotas in 620 CE; but the Karkota rulers, except for its founder, were descendants of Toramana through Angalekha, the daughter of last Hun ruler and the queen of Durlabhavardhana—the founder of Karkota dynasty which ruled up to 855 CE. More importantly, Kashmir emerged as a great empire during the Huns with no precedent in the annals of Kashmir.

As the copper coins with Toramana's name have been struck during a prolonged period, they, therefore, show differences both in execution and in characters of the legend. However, according to Stein, "the coin reproduced by Cunningham represents the best executed and probably earlier variety, and may be taken as a good specimen of the original type."[439] The obverse shows the figure of the standing king wearing short trousers, which gradually developed into the kilt or fustanella of curiously exaggerated dimensions we see in the later coins. To the left of the figure is the legend Sri Toramana in Brahmi character of about the fifth or sixth century. The reverse is occupied by the figure of the seated goddess with the letters *Ki-da-ra* written perpendicularly to the left. These letters are found in the same peculiar arrangement on the coins of Pravarasena and on all Karkota coins. They are undoubtedly copied from the coins of the Kidarite rulers.

True to their greatness, the Hun rulers, especially Meghavahana, Tunjina and Pravarasena, issued gold and silver coins.[440]

Cribb on Two Series of Kashmir Gold Coins

There exist two separate series of debased gold coins belonging to the Hun rulers of Kashmir. The recent discovery of a hoard of Kashmir gold series has, according to Cribb, resolved this anomaly as it helps us in understanding that one series was issued from Kashmir and the other from outside Kashmir in the Punjab and/or Kanauj. The new coins bear the names of *Śri meghamah* (Meghavahana), *Śri pravarasenah* (Pravarsena) and *tuysina* (Tunjina). Reports of the find-spot have been various and it is claimed to have come from Kashmir, Jammu, Himachal Pradesh or the Punjab.

On the examination of the coins of the new hoard, Cribb concluded as follows:[441]

All the coins are remarkably similar. The quality of the die engraving is as good as the best of Kuṣāṇa and Gupta coins. Like Kuṣāṇa and Gupta coins, the images are frontally postured; but there is one difference: while the head of the images of the Kuṣāṇa and Gupta coins is always shown in profile, that of Kashmir coins is with three-quarters turn. The representations are comparable with the surviving Kashmir sculpture of the period.[442] This coin type carries an unusual imagery, showing Śiva on the obverse. He is identified so by the trident he carries. This was a departure from the Kidarite prototype series of Kashmir coinage showing the king on the obverse and a deity on the reverse. There are elements of Kidarite/Kuṣāṇa design surviving into the Hun coins of Kashmir: they invariably depict a deity on the reverse. And the obverse figure of Tunjina and Tormana coins is shown placing offering on a small altar. The Kashmir coins are stylistically closest to Gupta coins. The presence of Viṣṇu conch on the waterpot next to the goddess on three of the types in the hoard and the lotuses held by her make it clear that the goddess had a Vaiṣṇavite association and "therefore should be identified as 'Sri".

Cribb, however, does not explain why this series was issued from outside. Yet it is not difficult to seek the reasons for the detachment of this series from Kashmir. In this regard, we have to consider the extent of the Kashmir empire during the period of the rulers whose coins have been found in the hoard as well as the strong inheritance of issuance of many coin series simultaneously. One may recall the Indo-Greeks, Śaka-Parthians and Kuṣāṇas, who issued different coin series in different regions of the empire to meet the demands of congruence and compatibility.[443] As discussed in the preceding pages, both Meghavahana and Pravarasena were great conquerors. Following the policy of the empire builders of the time, they seem to have issued a different coin series in the conquered land, probably in the Punjab, in search of seeking wider acceptability of their rule in an alien land by meeting the aspirations of the place having the followers of both Śiva and Vaiṣṇava cults. Except for the political expediency, there seems no other reason for issuing the series which substituted the motif of the king with an imagery of Śiva. After all, as we will see later on, Meghavahana was an orthodox Buddhist and Pravarasena was the follower of Vaiṣṇavism. The indication about the Buddhist association of king Meghavahana is also found in the coin depicting the goddess holding in her left hand a long stemmed lotus with a large blossom, in the form of *puranaghata*.

To conclude, the coins of the Huns began by copying the Sassanian type (Sassanian bust, fire altar or solar wheel). Later they were modelled after the Kuṣāṇa type (standing king on the obverse with the king's name and a seated goddess on the reverse) and then they gradually Indianised with Brahmi legends and symbols. While following the path of change, they, however, do not indicate a total departure with the past; instead, they point to a continuous story of absorption, and this time more of Indian traditions.

Religion

Though the revival of Brahmanism in Kashmir had begun not later than the fifth century CE, the Hun rule witnessed its ascendency following the patronage extended to it by both the Hun rulers and those who ruled between them. The contemporary play *Padataditaka,* written in the fifth century while ridiculing the Jataka tales, calls brahmanas 'gods on earth' (*bhumideva*). They are described as learned in the three Vedas and as students of grammar and logic. 'All of this' says Witzel "allows one to conclude that the Hindu organization of the social system, typical for the Gupta period in northern India, was well established in Kashmir by the late fifth century."[444] The Hun occupation of Kashmir, however, proved to be a decisive period in the saga of brahmanical religion's movement to becoming a dominant tradition. Minus one ruler, namely, Meghavahana, all the rulers of the period were either Śaivites or Vaiṣṇavas. With regard to cultic ascendancy, Śiva cult remained supreme until the assumption of power by Pravarasena II at the end of the sixth century CE. From Pravarasena II up to the end of the Hun rule, Vaiṣṇavism enjoyed royal patronage. Yet, except for Mihirakula, the rulers generally followed a tolerant policy towards the other faiths and cults. The later phase of the Hun rule, that is, from Pravarasena II onwards, is distinctively remarkable in this regard as we find them patronising equally all faiths and cults, though they were personally more gravitated towards Vaiṣṇavism. It was this legacy which was inherited by the Karkotas. Kalhana and other sources furnish a good deal of information about the religious propensities and activities of the rulers of the period, and the same is summarised later.

The Dominance of Śaivism

As mentioned earlier, Mihirakula was a devout Śaivite. This is attested to by the numismatic, epigraphic and literary evidence. His coins, besides being inscribed with *Jayatu Vrsah* or *Jayatu Vrsadhvajah*, are also engraved with *trisula* and bull[445]—the theomorphic representation of Śiva. The Mandasor Pillar inscription of Yaśodharman also confirms that Mihirakula was a devotee of Śiva. It refers to Mihirakula, "whose head had never previously been brought into humility of obeisance to any other save Śiva." Kalhana portrays him not only as a Śiva but also as a zealous follower of the cult. Besides this, Mihirakula also encouraged the influx of brahmanas into Kashmir by providing them land grants. According to Kalhana, he bestowed upon the brahmanas of Gandhara a thousand *agraharas* at Vijayesvara. Over his role of reviving Brahmanism, Kalhana forgives Mihirakula for his otherwise wanton cruelties he committed both within and without Kashmir.[446]

Śaivism continued to receive state patronage during the immediate successors of Mihirakula. Baka constructed the shrine of Śiva *Bakesa*.[447] Akśa founded the village of Akśavala (Achval) and settled the brahmanas there.[448] Gopaditya was more zealous in this regard. He settled the brahmanas at Khola (Khul or Kholi), Khagiha (Khag), Hadigrama (Adigam), Skandapura (Khandor), Samajasa (Shangas) and at other places and bestowed them these villages as *agrahara*s.[449] He also brought the brahmanas from Aryadeśa and "from auspicious countries" (*desebhyah punyebhyah*) and settled them in Gupkar (by establishing an *agrahara* called Gupagrahara (from which is derived the present name Gupkar), Vaścika (Vachi) and other *agrahara*s.[450] It may be significant to mention that the famous poet Bilhana's family was brought from Madhyadeśa by Gopaditya.[451] While the pure brahmanas received special treatment, those brahmanas who "had broken their rules of conduct" by eating garlic were punished by transferring them from royal headquarters to other places, namely, Bhuksiravatika (Buchvor) and Khasata[452] (?). He also forbade killing of animals except at sacrifices.[453] What is more, the king constructed the shrine of Jyesthesvara on what is called the Gopa hill (Gopadri).[454] His son Gokarna established the shrine of Śiva Gokarnesvara.[455] Narendraditya Khinkhila, the son and successor of Gokarna, consecrated shrines to Śiva Bhutesvara and founded a permanent endowment for the feeding of brahmanas.[456]

According to Kalhana, after Yudhishthira, the successor of Khankhila, Kashmir came under the rule of "Harśa and other foreign kings."[457] During this period too, Śaivism received preferential state patronage. Tunjina and his wife Vakpusta built the temple of Śiva called Tungesvara as well as the town Katika (Kai).[458] The queen established for brahmanas *agraharas* of Katimusa (Kaimuh) and Ramusa (Rōmūh).[459] Vijaya built a town surrounding the shrine Vijayesvara.[460] It is, however, during the reign of Samadhimat (Aryaraja) that Śaivism received unprecedented royal patronage. In this regard it is significant to quote Kalhana:

> This king's [Saṁdhimat's] court resembled the assembly of Śiva and was adorned by ascetics who carried ashes, rosaries made of Eleocarpus berries and knots of matted hair. The king never broke his vow to consecrate daily a thousand Śiva Lingas. . . . The revenue of the great villages which he gave as endowment for each Liṅga, has through the lapse of time become lost now-a-days to the Purohita corporations (*parṣad*). That great worshipper of Śiva made the earth great by [erecting] great [religious] buildings, great Liṅgas, great images of the bull [of Śiva] and great Triśūlas.[461]

Saṁdhimat *inter alia* constructed two famous Śiva shrines, namely, Saṁdhiśvara and Iśaśvara. While Saṁdhiśvara is unknown, Isasvara is, according to Stein, "the modern village and the Tirtha of Iśbar situated on the north-east shore of the Dal."[462]

Revival of Buddhism

With the accession of Meghavahana, who belonged to Mihirakula's line and was born and brought up in Gandhara, Buddhism became state religion. The very first thing which the king did was to impose a ban on killing of animals.

> At his very inauguration, the officials who had received an order [to this effect] proclaimed everywhere by the beating of drums the law against the killing [of living creatures]. The butchers who lost the livelihood on account of this ban were helped by grants from the state treasury. While Meghavahana did not force people to embrace Buddhism, the ban on killing was so sternly enforced that the followers of Śaivism had to use an effigy of animal in ghee at the sacrifice (*kratu*) and one in pastry at the "offering to the spirits" (*bhūtabali*).[463]

Kalhan's story of an angry brahmana, who was desperate to give to Durga the animal oblation to save his son from fever but could not do so because of blanket ban on killing of animals,[464] tends to smack of deep-rooted mentality in revolt against the new order.

The king founded new villages and established new *agraharas* obviously to settle the Buddhist priests whom he had brought from Gandhara. Of the new villages, which the king founded or endowed as *agraharas*, Kalhana specially mentions Mayustagrama and Meghavahana.[465] He also founded a monastery called Meghamatha.[466] During the period of Meghavahana, a number of vihāras and stupas were constructed by the ruling family. His queen, Amritaprabha,[467] built Amritabhavana 'for the benefit of foreign Bhikṣus.'[468] Ou'kong has also made a mention of this vihāra, and, he also stayed there.[469] According to Stein, Amritabhavan is survived by the present village Antabhavan, situated three miles to the north of old Srinagar.[470] Amritprabha also constructed a stupa called Lo-Stupa for his father's spiritual guide who had come from Leh.[471] Meghavahana's another queen Yqadevi built at Nadavana (Narvor) a vihāra of "wonderful appearance."[472] Indradevi, another wife of the king, built a vihāra, Indradevibhavana and a stupa.[473] Many vihāras "of renown" were built by his other queens, namely, Khādanā and Sammā under their own names.[474] According to Stein, Khadav Vihar is perhaps the present village of Khadaniyar.[475] However, the position of Sammavihāra is yet to be identified.

Revival of Śaivism as State Religion

According to Kalhana, Meghavahana's son and successor, variously named as Sresthasena, Pravarasena I and Tunjina II, was a Śaivite.[476] He constructed the shrine of Pravaresvara together with a 'Circle of Mothers' (*mātrcakra*). He also "consecrated various holy shrines" at the old capital, the present Pandrethan.[477] Kalhana does not reveal the religion of Hiranya, the successor of Pravarasena I, but it seems that he too was perhaps a follower of Śaivism.

Vaiṣṇavism as State Religion

Vaiṣṇavism became the state religion during the reign of Matrgupta,[478] who ruled on behalf of Vikramaditya of Ujjayini; and it continued to enjoy this position for a long period. All the rulers who ruled Kashmir from Pravarasena II onwards were Vaiṣṇavas. Pravarasena's strong Vaiṣṇava leanings have been covertly reported by Kalhana by portraying him a convert from Śaivism to Vaiṣṇavism through providential intervention:

> When he was first about to consecrate the [*Linga* of] Pravaresvara in pious devotion, the [image of Vaiṣṇu] Jayasvamin seated itself of its own accord on the base (*pīṭha*) after breaking the sacred diagram (*yantra*). This image [of Vaiṣṇu] was called by the king after the name of the architect Jaya who knew the auspicious time (*lagna*) which the Vetala had indicated. Owing to his [Pravarasena's]

> devoted worship the image of Vinayaka, [called] Bhimasvamin of its own accord turned its face from west to east in order to show that he was not averse to his city.[479]

Apart from having built the famous Viṣṇu temple—Jayasvamin—on or around Hari Parbat, Pravarasena built many other Viṣṇu temples in Srinagar. About one such temple, Kalhana says:

> In this city he, [who ruled] like Indra over the five races [of men], established [shrines of] five goddesses, who were designated by the word *śrī* as Sadbhavaśrī and so on.[480]

Kalhana also makes a mention of two other famous Viṣṇu temples—Vardhanasvāmin and Viśvakarmin—which stood 'at the limits' of his newly founded city (*Pravarapura*).[481]

Since the mother of Pravarasena came from a Buddhist family[482] and his maternal uncle Jayendra wielded an influential position during the period,[483] Buddhism received almost equal state patronage. Jayandra constructed the "illustrious" Jayandravihāra and the statue of the 'Great Buddha (*Brahabuddha*).[484] It is noteworthy that Hiuen Tsang, on his arrival in the Kashmir capital, stopped at Jayandravihāra, where he received instructions in the various śastras from the chief of the priests and spent most of his two years' stay (631–633 CE) in the valley in this vihāra.[485] The minister of Pravarasena, Moraka, also built a vihāra and named it after his own name—Morakabhavana.[486]

Buddhism also received state patronage during the reign of Pravarasena's successor—Yudhishthira. This is evident from the fact that Kalhana refers to only the construction of vihāras and chaityas during the period:

> His (Yudhisthira's) ministers, who bore the names Sarvaratna, Jaya and Skandagupta, obtained distinction by [erecting] viharas, caityas and other [pious] works. A minister of his was also Vajrendra, the son of Jayandra who made the village of Bhavaccheda famous by the construction of caityas and other (sacred buildings).[487]

Lakhana-Narendraditya, who succeeded Yudhishthira II, patronised both Vaiṣṇavism and Buddhism. He built the temple of Narendrasvamin. His two ministers—Vijra and Kanaka—were Buddhists; and they were "distinguished by pious deeds."[488]

As in the case of Pravarasena II, exactly in the same vein, Kalhana makes us believe that Ranaditya, the successor of Lakhana-Narendraditya, was basically a Śiva but he was miraculously converted to Vaiṣṇavism.

When the auspicious time *(lagna)* for the consecration [of Śiva images] was at hand, and when the king, being of the Śiva persuasion (Mahesvara), was just preparing to consecrate first the [Linga of] Raneśvara, the [image of] Ranasvaimin through the power of Ranarambha seated itself miraculously on the base pitha after breaking the sacred diagram (*yantra*).[489]

Besides constructing the famous Ranasvamin temple, the king also built the temples of Ranarambhasvamin and Ranarambhadeva in Srinagar and a matha for Pasupa [mendicants] on the hill of Pradyumna (Haraparvat, Srinagar).[490] He also built a temple dedicated to Viṣṇu in his form of Martanda or the sun.

He built at the village of Simharotsika a temple of Martanda which became famous everywhere under the name of Ranapurasvamin.[491]

Although the king was a devout Vaiṣṇava, there was absolute freedom of religion, and it is not uncommon to see people having faith in many cults simultaneously. For example, we find one of the queens of Ranaditya, Amritaprabha, building a Śiva shrine, Amrtesvara and at the same time placing "a fine statue of Buddha in the vihara which had been built by a wife of king Meghavana."[492]

About the cultic association of Vikramaditya and Baladitya—the last two rulers of the Hun dynasty—Kalhana is not forthcoming except saying that Vikramaditya built a shrine of Śiva, Vikramesvara by name[493] and Baladitya founded for *brahmanas* the *agrahara* of Bhedara and his wife, Bimba, constructed the shrine of Śiva, Bimbesvara.[494] These references tend to show the inclination of the last two Hun rulers to Śaivism. This seems doubtful because the daughter of Baladitya, Anangalekha, who became the queen after the death of his father, is portrayed by Kalhana a true heir of her predecessors in that she is shown having more gravitation towards Vaiṣṇavism and Buddhism.[495] The same is true of her husband and the founder of Karkota dynasty, Durlabhavardhana[496] who, being closely associated with the last Hun rulers, had obviously imbibed the religious propensities from his patrons and the courtly atmosphere, which propped him up from a petty position (*aśvaghāsakāyastha*) to becoming the king of a powerful empire.[497]

Religion, Patronage and the Emergence of New Villages and Towns

The period is marked by the emergence of a large number of new villages and towns—a direct consequence of the zeal of the rulers to brahmanise Kashmir with full state patronage. This is why we find Mihirakula bringing brahmanas from Gandhara and providing them lavish *agraharas* at Vijeśvara (Vijbror/Bijbehara).[498] Similarly Gopaditya settled *Aryadeśa* brahmanas at modern Gupkar and at other places and bestowed upon them the *agrahara*s.[499] While the political factor of enhancing the legitimacy of the rulers played a crucial role in extending state patronage to religion, the belief system of the time was no less an important factor in this regard. It was a well-established belief of the time that constructing of temples, mathas, tirthas, vihāras, stupas, chaityas and bestowing *agraharas* upon them and the brahmanas/bhiksus would obtain religious merit to the donee and help him/her in achieving the worldly goals. The lavish donations were facilitated by the strong financial position of the state accrued from the plundering raids, empire building based on tributary system and brisk trading activities. No wonder, then, there is hardly any ruler who did not construct shrines and gave away *agrahara* grants. This multicasual approach to gifts and gift exchanges is substantiated by Anthony Cutler's observation that with regard to premodern ritual practice, "aesthetic, economic and pious gesture do not inhabit entirely separate universes."[500]

Building of a shrine meant the simultaneous emergence of a new settlement, for its construction was accompanied by the settlement of its guardians—brahmanas/monks—who were bestowed with *agrahara* grants for the upkeep of the place of worship and also for their own maintenance. With the settlement of brahmanas or monks, it became necessary to settle the peasants and the professional groups to cultivate the land and render various services to the donees which for caste reasons they were unable to do themselves.

Of the villages and towns, which came into existence primarily because of the settlements of brahmanas under the patronage of the rulers, mention may be made of Mihirapura by Mihirakula,[501] Lavantosa (?) by Lava, Aksavala (Achaval), Khola (Khol or Khuli), Khagika (Khag), Hadigrama (A'dgom), Skandapura (Khandur), Samajasa (Shangas), Gupkar, Vascika (Vachi)—all by Gopaditya,[502] Katik (Kai) by Tunjina,[503] Mayustagrama and Meghavahana, by Meghavahana,[504] and Bhedara by Baladitya.[505]

Of the settlements, which emerged primarily because of the construction of *tirthas*/temples/vihāras and the consequential grant of *agraharas* to them and their custodians, mention may be made of the places which became famous after the shrine names, namely, Mihirisvara, Vijayesvara (Vij bror), Bakesa, Gokarnesvara, Bhutesvara, Sandhisvara, Isesvara (Ishber), Theda (Thed), Bhimadevi (Bran), Meghamatha, Amritabhavana (Antabhavan), Lo-stupa, Indradevibhavana, Khadanavihara (Khadinyar), Sammavihara, Bhimasvamin, Jyendravihara, Morakabhavana, Vardhanavamin, Visvakasman, Bhavaccheda (Bocch), Naredrasvamin, Vikramesvara and Bimbesvara.[506]

Besides the village settlements and foundations of many towns, the period is distinguished by the foundation of modern Srinagar by Pravarasena II. Kalhana has given a detailed description of the new capital:

> After the conquest of the world, while he resided in the city of his grandfather (Pravarasena I), there arose in him the desire of

> founding a town after his own name. He discovered that [measuring line] which the Vetāla had laid down, at the village Śārītaka at which the goddess Śārīka and the demon (*yaksa*) *Atta* resided. In this city he, [who ruled] like Indra over the five races [of men], established [shrines of] five goddesses, who were designated by the word *śri* as *Sadbhāvaśrī* and so on. This king had the 'Great Bridge' (*Brhatsetu)* built on the *Vitasā*. Only since then is such construction of boat bridges (*nausetu*) known. Jayendra, the maternal uncle of the king, caused the illustrious *Jayendravīhāra* and a [statue of the] 'Great Buddha' (*Brhadbuddha*) to be erected. The minister—*Morāka*—who had possession of *Simhala* and the other isles—built the *Morākabhavana*, a wonder of the world. The city at the limits of which stood the [temples of] *Vardhanasvāmin* and *Vīśvakarman* was once famous [as containing] 36 lakhs of houses.[507]

For the foundation of the city, Pravarasena constructed a long embankment around it to protect the low-lying portions of the city on the right river bank from the annual inundations from the Vitasta.[508] The durability and all-time relevance of this embankment can be had from its continued existence up to our own times, as the *suth* (Skr. setu) 'dyke' stretching from the west foot of the Takht-e-Sulaiman to the high bank of the Vitasta near the second bridge, is the same constructed by Pravarasena. According to Kalhana, the new city was built around the foot of Hariparvat (Skr. *Sarikaparvata*) and its limits were confined to the right bank of the river Jhelum, though Pravarasena is the first ruler of Kashmir to have introduced boat bridges, which originated in China. Having chosen a place for his new capital, which was guarded on all sides by water, it becomes quite clear that the Kashmiri kings continued to be guided by the Greek town planning using natural factors for strengthening the defence of the cities.

To conclude, Kashmir emerged a great political power for the first time in its known history during the Huns who, along with carrying the strong instincts of a martial race in their genes, were deeply influenced by Indian culture. With a large number of tributary kingdoms, Kashmir became an exceptionally great economic power pushing the transborder networks and the resultant flow of goods and the process of borrowing, imitating and emulating to new heights. That is why we find state-sponsored immigrations, introduction of new technologies, circulation of gold and silver coins and an unprecedented spurt in constructions including the foundation of villages, towns and a new splendid capital city replenished with innovations and dotted with temples/tirthas and brahmana settlements to superimpose Sanskritic beliefs and rituals.

Besides Sanskritising the valley and strengthening the legitimacy of the rulers as upholders of the socio-religious order, the *agrahara* grants helped in expanding agriculture by bringing new lands under cultivation. It may be mentioned that *agrahara* grants were not only of the type of surrendering state revenues to the grantees, they largely constituted the grant of uncultivated lands to be brought under cultivation by the grantees with the help of manpower provided to them by the state. Thus, when Kalhana tells us of the foundation of villages by the kings or the establishment of *agraharas* by them, he generally means the latter type of *agrahara* grant which was known as *Brahmadeya* in South India.

The emergence of temples and the bestowing of *agraharas* on brahmanas, temples, tirthas and monasteries was obviously the impact of the emergence of this phenomenon in the Gangetic northern India and subsequently in other parts of the subcontinent from the Gupta period onwards—a result of the growing importance of Bhakti and the influence of Puranic religion together with the compulsions of new ruling lineages as the construction and maintenance of temples had become an important agency of the political validation as well an effective device of acculturation.[509]

It is also from the Gupta period onwards that in the mainland India sculptural art began to get integrated with the decorative scheme of temple architecture. Small wonder, then, alongside the impact of Gandhara art and architecture, the sculpture and the stone temples of the period bear strong traces of Gupta influence[510] making Kashmir part of a vast cultural geography extending from Afghanistan to Sind. Referring to this fact in the context of Baramulla site of Kashmir, John Siudmak says,

> it is closely tied to the post-Gandhara tradition of the nort-west, comprising the ancient Gandhara region and parts of Swat and Buner. This school has long been recognized from the numerous Buddhist and Hindu miniature images found in the region. It is part of a generalized style which extended to Afghanistan, throughout the Punjab and probably as far south as Sind which absorbed many features of late Gupta art.[511]

The legacy of the Huns, underlined by the foundation and establishment of an empire with extended borders, growth of state power, increase in size of armies, an ambitious cultural project, expanded transborder networks, toleration, cosmopolitan society based on different ethnic, linguistic, cultural and religious groups, and a policy to maximise the human and economic resources, was carried forward with new zeal and zest by the succeeding rulers of Kashmir, the details of which are given in the following chapter.

Figure 3.1 Terracotta fragmentary draped Hellenistic female figurine (left). Terracotta figurine in Hellenistic style (middle). Terracotta semi-draped Hellenistic female figurine (right), Semthan.

(After Bhan, 2010)

Figure 3.2 Silver coin of Diodotus.

Obverse: Diademed head of the king to right.

Reverse: Zeus standing to the left and hurling thunderbolt. Greek legend, *basilious antinous*.

(SPS Museum Srinagar, Kashmir)

Figure 3.3 Silver coin of Euthydemus.

Obverse: Diademed head of the king to right.

Reverse: Hercules seated on rock holding a club whose lower end rests on palm.

(SPS museum Srinagar, Kashmir)

Figure 3.4 Copper coin of Eucratides.

Obverse: Helmeted head of the king to right; Legend in Greek

Reverse: Zeus standing to the left and hurling thunderbolt. Greek legend: *Basilious Antinous*.

(SPS museum Srinagar)

Figure 3.5 Silver square coin of Appollodotus.

Obverse: Elephant to right with Greek legend: *Basilious Apollodotus*.

Reverse: Bull to right; Kharoshthi legend: *Maharajas Apaladatasa*.

(SPS Museum Srinagar, Kashmir)

Figure 3.6 Copper coin of Appollodotus.

Obverse: Apollo standing, legend in Greek: *Basilious Apollodotus.*

Reverse: Standing tripod, legend in Kharoshthi: *Maharajasa Apaladatasa*

(Semthan, Bijbehara, Kashmir)

Figure 3.7 Silver coin of Menander.

Obverse: Helmeted bust to right, legend in Greek: *Basilious Basilion Menandrus.*

Reverse: Pallas standing left with shield; legend in Kharoshthi: *Maharajasa Rajdirajsa Menandrasa.*

(SPS Museum Srinagar, Kashmir)

Figure 3.8 Silver coin of Menander.

Obverse: Diademed bust to right, legend in Greek: *Basilious Basilion Menandrus.*

Reverse: Pallas standing left with shield; legend in Kharoshthi: *Maharajasa Rajdirajsa Menandrasa.*

(SPS Museum Srinagar)

Figure 3.9 Square copper coin of Menander.

Obverse: Elephant head to right, legend in Greek: *Basilious Menander.*

Reverse: Club upwards; legend in Kharoshthi: *Majarajasa Menandrasa.*

(Semthan, Bijbehara, Kashmir)

Figure 3.10 Silver coin of Hippostratos.

Obverse: Diademed bust of the king to right, legend in Greek: *Basilious Basilion Hippostratos.*

Reverse: King on horseback walking right, legend in Kharoshthi: *Maharajasa Hippostratasa*

(SPS Museum Srinagar)

Figure 3.11 Cocks fighting over what appears to be a lily bud.

Harwan, Kashmir (After Kak, 1933)

Figure 3.12 In central circle, a cock, with foliate tail; surrounded by circle of roundels; the whole within rectangular frame of pearls.

Harwan (After Kak, 1933)

Figure 3.13 Greek art Cock and band-cup.

(After Carr, 2017)

(After)

Figure 3.14 Greek Attic vase-painting with cock-fighting.

(After *Beazley, 1956*)

(After Beazley, 1956)

Figure 3.15 Durga or Maheshvari. Bejbehara.

(SPS Museum, Srinagar)

Figure 3.16 Motif of a dancing girl with scarf in her two hands.

Harwan Kashmir

(SPS Museum, Srinagar)

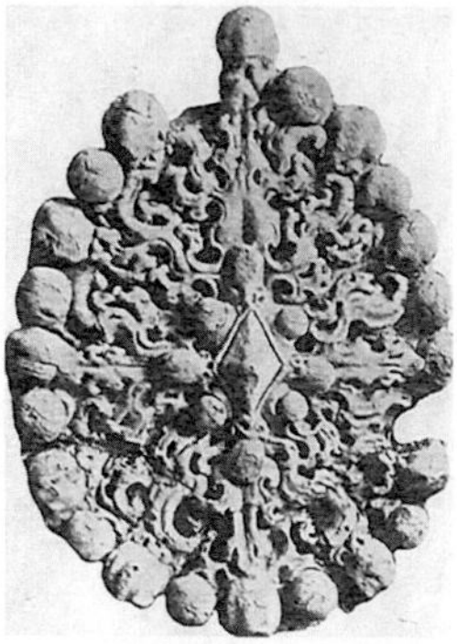

Figure 3.17 Woman wearing big ear rings and locket, Harwan (left); (b) Terracotta pendant from necklace of colossal figure of a Bodhisattva. Harwan (right).

(After Kak, 1933)

Figure 3.18 Silver coin of Azes.

Obverse: King on horseback, Greek legend: *Basilious Azoy*.

Reverse: Pallas standing to right with shield and spear, Kharoshthi legend: *Maharajasa Ayasa*.

(SPS Museum Srinagar)

Figure 3.19 Copper coin of Abdagases.

Obverse: King on horseback, a small symbol, Greek legend: *Basilious Abdagases*

Reverse: Zeus standing, holding sceptre, Kharoshthi legend: *Maharaja Abdagases*.

(SPS Museum Srinagar)

Figure 3.20 Copper coins of Zeinoses.

Obverse: King on horseback, legend in Greek: *Basilious Gondophares*.

Reverse: Śiva with trident, legend in Kharoshthi: *Maharaja Gondophares*.

(SPS Museum, Srinagar Kashmir)

Figure 3.21 Copper coins of Zeinoses.

Obverse: Elephant to right.

Reverse: Bull to right, legends in Greek and Kharoshthi: *Maharajadirajasa Zionosa*

(Semthan, Bijbehara Kashmir).

Figure 3.22 Fully accoutred horseman in armour riding at full gallop and drawing his bow.

Harwan, Srinagar (After Kak, Srinagar)

Figure 3.23 Wall of Apsidal Temple in Diaper-Pebble Style.

Harwan. (After Kak, 1933)

Figure 3.24 Triple base of Stupa in Diaper-Rubble Style, Harwan.

(After Kak, 1933)

Figure 3.25 Upper part of an archer wearing a conical cap, Harwan.

(SPS Museum)

Figure 3.26 A dancer wearing large ear rings and dressed in loose robe and trousers, with a long scarf held in both hands, which she waves over her head, Harwan.

(SPS Museum)

Figure 3.27 A huntsman with bow and arrow riding at full gallop, wearing a *pattikam*. Harwan.

(SPS Museum, Srinagar)

Figure 3.28 Terracotta heads, Ushkar.

SPS Museum

Figure 3.29 Left: Female figure wearing *kancuka*; Right: Standing soldier.

(SPS Museum, Srinagar)

Figure 3.30 Copper coin (local series) of Kujula Kadphises.

Obverse: Humped bull to right.

Reverse: Bactrian camel to right, legend not clear.

(SPS Museum, Srinagar Kashmir)

Figure 3.31 Copper coin of Vima Kadphises.

Obverse: King standing left, altar and trident on left. Club on right, Greek legend: *Basilious Basilion Vima Kadphises*

Reverse: Śiva standing with bull to right. Kharoshthi legend: *Maharaja Vima Kadphises*.

(SPS Museum, Srinagar)

Figure 3.32 Copper coin (local series) of Vima Kadphises.

Obverse: Elephant rider.

Reverse: Mao standing to left, legend in Greek: *Mao*.

(Turkhpur, Bandipura Kashmir).

Figure 3.33 Gold dinar of Kaniṣka.

Obverse: King sacrificing at altar, legend in Bactrian Greek: *Shaoano Shao Kanski.*

Reverse: Four armed Śiva, legend in Greek: *Oesho (Śiva) (SPS Museum, Srinagar, Kashmir).*

Figure 3.34 Gold dinar of Kaniṣka.

Obverse: King standing left, sacrificing at the altar and holding spear in left hand. Legend in Bactrian Greek: *Shaonano Shao Kanski*

Reverse: Athsho (god of fire) standing, legend in Greek: *Athsho*

(SPS Museum Srinagar Kashmir)

Figure 3.35 Copper coin of Kaniṣka.

Obverse: King standing to left, holding a trident in the left hand and offering with his right hand on the alter, legend in Bactrian Greek.

Reverse: Standing Mithra, legend in Bactrian Greek.

(SPS museum, Srinagar)

Figure 3.36 Copper coin of Kaniṣka (local series).

Obverse: King standing to left, holding a trident in the left hand and offering with his right hand on the alter, legend in Bactrian Greek.

Reverse: Standing Mao, legend in Bactrian Greek.

(Turkhpura, Bandipura, Kashmir).

Figure 3.37 Copper coin (local series) of Kaniṣka.

Obverse: King standing to left, holding a trident in the left hand and offering with his right hand on the alter, legend in Bactrian Greek.

Reverse: *Nanaia.*

(Turkhpura, Bandipura, Kashmir)

Figure 3.38 Copper coin (local series) of Kaniṣka.

Obverse: King standing to left, holding a trident in the left hand and offering with his right hand on the alter; legend in Bactrian Greek.

Reverse: Oado running to left.

(Turkhpura, Bandipura, Kashmir).

Figure 3.39 Copper coin (local series) of Huvishka.

Obverse: King riding on an elephant
Reverse: Deity standing to left, legend: *Mao*
(Turkhpura, Bandipura, Kashmir)

Figure 3.40 Copper coin (local series) of Vasudeva.

Obverse: King standing to left, holding a trident in the left hand and offering with his right hand on the alter, legend in Greek.

Reverse: Śiva standing with trident in right hand before the bull.

(Turkhpura, Bandipura, Kashmir)

Figure 3.41 Terracotta plaques showing miniature stupas.

Harwan (After Kak, 1933)

Figure 3.42 Tile with man and deer, Hoinar.

SPS Museum, Srinagar

Figure 3.43 Tile with man carrying pots and a women carrying a bowl, Harwan.
(SPS Museum, Srinagar)

Figure 3.44 Female musician Harwan.
After Kak

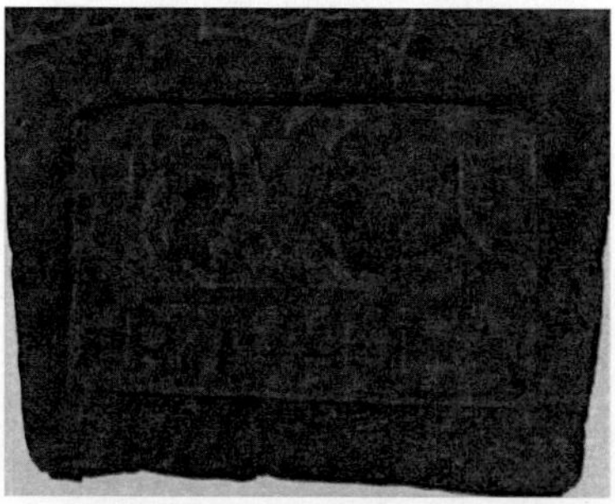

Figure 3.45 Tile with conversing couple sitting in the balcony. Harwan.
(SPS Museum, Srinagar)

Figure 3.46 Two pairs of men and women facing each other in a balcony.

Harwan (SPS Museum, Srinagar)

Figure 3.47 Women with net-like hair style, wearing big ear rings and locket like ornament.

Harwan (After Kak)

Figure 3.48 Upper register: three musicians. The one to left plays flute; the centre one, cymbals; and the third, a pair of drums.

Middle register: a mounted hunter aiming an arrow at a fleeing deer. In front, a tree and hind-quarters of galloping horse.

Lower register: a row of circular rosettes. Harwan

(SPS Museum, Srinagar)

Figure 3.49 Humans with animal face and tail, and in dancing posture, Hutmur.
(SPS Museum, Srinagar)

Figure 3.50 Base gold coin of Kidara Kuṣāṇas.
Obverse: King standing, legend in Brahmi: *Kidara*.
Reverse: Ardoksho.
(SPS Museum, Srinagar)

Figure 3.51 Toramana copper coins.
Obverse: Crude figure of standing king, legend in Gupta Bhrami, Shri Toramana.
Reverse: Crude figure of seated goddess, Ardoksho.
(Aishmuquam, Anantnag, Kashmir)

Notes

1 Brown (1959), 151
2 Flood (2009), 9.
3 For details about Indo-Greeks and their occupation of the north-west of India, see Taran (1980); Narain (1957).
4 Taran, 155.
5 Holt (1993), 2.
6 Ibrahim (1993), 3: 92.
7 Indian Archaeology – A Review (1980–81); also see Shali (1993); Siudmak (2013) 32–48: Agrawal (1998); Gaur (1987).
8 Siudmak (2013), 32.
9 Kak (1923), 58, 125–130.
10 Kalhana (1969), I: 115.
11 Witzel (2008), 53–54.
12 Kalhana, I: 153.
13 Ibid.
14 At least from the period of the Śakas and Kuṣāṇas, Sanskrit became the language of religion as well as the official language of Kashmir. The Tibetan and Chinese writers refer to many Sanskrit Buddhist literary compositions written during the Kuṣāṇa period. The Sanskrit continued to enjoy the position of official language and the language of dominant religion up to fourteenth century CE.
15 Sohini also suggests that King Damodara in the *Rājataraṅgiṇī* might be Demetrius. Sohini (1950), 36(1/2): 71–75. Quoted by Narain (1957), 44.
16 Taran (1938), 155.
17 Kalhana, I: 157.
18 Ibid, I: 159.
19 Taran (1938), 102–3.
20 Ibid, 238.
21 *Milindapanha*, 82–83.
22 Cf. Taran (1938), 267.
23 Ibn Khaldun (1978), 116.
24 Taran, 49.
25 Ibid, 11.
26 Ibid.
27 An allotment of land which carried with it the obligation to serve in the army was known as *cleros* in the Hellenistic period. See Taran, 7.
28 Maitona or Methone is Greek and Macedonian place name. Taran, 11.
29 Edessa is a Roman name. It was the name of some famous Greek towns. Taran, 11–12.
30 Antioch is a Greek name.
31 In Greek *soter* means "the saviour." It was a covetous title by which Appollodotus and Menander called themselves (Taran, 175). We also come across a Greek city by the name of Soteire in eastern Iran. Taran, 13.
32 Athena was a Greek goddess.
33 Zeus was a Hellenistic deity.
34 Charis was one of the famous Greek cities in eastern Iran. Taran, 13.
35 Achea was a Greek city in Iran. Taran, 13.
36 Modoura was a Greek goddess or nymph. Taran, 252.
37 Apollo was a Greek god.
38 Homer was the Greek poet and epic writer of ancient Greece.
39 Pergamum was the Greek place name. Taran, 179.
40 The Village Memender, situated near Shopian, is a corrupt form of Menander, the famous Greek King.

41 Roma was the Greek goddess.
42 Selena was the Greek goddess.
43 Lysias was the Greek ruler whose coins have been found in Kashmir. There are many villages named after the ruler. They are Lias in Shopian, Lasipur in Pulwama and Lasipur in Lolab.
44 Ammon was the Greek place name. Taran, 268. In Kashmir there is also a village called Amoon. It is situated in Kulgam Tehsil. While the Sanskrit writers called the Greeks yavanas after the Greek place name yonia, in Kashmiri a beautiful person/thing is called *yava,* a short form of yavana.
45 There are many villages named as Awanpora. I know at least three villages of this name. They are situated in Tral, Budgam and Lolab Tehsils.
46 Based on my field study of villages like Panzgaum.
47 Taran, 137.
48 Kak, (1923).
49 Bleazby, (1900).
50 Bopearachchi (2005), XXXII (1): 114.
51 Gupta (1969), 20–21.
52 Bopearachchi and Rahman (1995), 27–28. Nos. 131–140.
53 For the frequent references of 'dinnara' by Kalhana, see Kalhana (1979), III: 103; IV: 495, 617, 898; V: 71, 84 sq; 87, 89, 108, 116; VI: 38; VII: 163, 406 sq; 500, 950, 1118, 1220; VIII: 124, 151sq, 883, 3335.
54 For these salient features of Greek city, see Dar (1984), 32. And that temple complexes of Kashmir had these three distinctive features; see Fisher (1989a), 33–35.
55 Dar (1984), 32.
56 All the ancient and early medieval cities of Kashmir—Srinagri, Kaniskapura, Pravarapur, Pratapapura, Parhispura, Jayapidapura, Avantipura etc.—were built keeping in view the presence of these natural factors which helped in strengthening their defence, besides adding to their glory.
57 For details, see Pal (1989).
58 It is interesting that the specimens of Doric art have survived in Kashmir only. Dar (1984), 34 & note. For the impact of Greek architecture on Kashmir architecture, also see Cunningham (1848), VII: 241–327.
59 Fyfe (1934), 8, 148, 151, 152.
60 Marshall (1951), II: 699–728; Dar (1984), 35–36.
61 Dar (1984), 36.
62 Schlumberger (1983), 3 (2): 1051.
63 Ibid.
64 See Kak (1933), Plates XXII: 1, 2; XXIII; XXIV: 5/6; XXV: 8).
65 For Gandharan toilet trays, see Dar (1984), 99–143.
66 See Drabu (1990), plates 19 and 20.
67 Kak, Plates.
68 Walter (1896), 224–225, 256–61; Dar (1984), 103.
69 Kak, Plates XXX, XXXII, XXXVI.
70 For cock and cock-fighting designs in ancient Greek art, see Carr (2017); also visit: www.metmuseum.org/art/collection/search/247321
71 For details, see Hans (2014).
72 *Indian Archaeology– A Review* (1980–81).
73 Agrawal, 1998.
74 *Indian Archaeology – A Review* (1980–81).
75 Shali (1993), 120.
76 Bopearachchi (2005), 32 (1): 116.
77 We may recall that the cult of images and icons was promoted by Artaxerxes II (404–359 BCE) who, according to Berossus, the Babylonian priestly scholar

writing early third century BC, was the first to introduce the image-cult of "Aphrodite Anaitis" in the chief cities of the empire. Cf. Yarshater (1983), 3 (1): Introduction, XXV.

78 For details, see Chattopadhyaya (1937), 143; Kane (1941), II: 707; Cuningham (1879), 107; *Sāmba Purāna*, 29.2; quoted by Thapliyal (1979), 132–134.
79 Thapliyal (1979), 134.
80 *Milindapanho*, 82–83.
81 Dar (1984), 135.
82 Ibid.
83 Taran (1938), 39.
84 Ibid.
85 Ibid, 29.
86 Ibid.
87 Ibid.
88 Ibid, 386.
89 Levi, *Quid de Graecis*, 23; quoted by Taran (1938), 386.
90 Thapliyal (1979), 67.
91 See Ingholt (1957); Marshall (1951).
92 Siudmak, 33–34.
93 Ibid, 33.
94 Ibid, 36.
95 Marshall (1951), quoted by Siudmak (2013), 41.
96 Siudmak (43).
97 Hallade (1964–65), 15(1/2): 36–49.
98 Ibid.
99 Bhushan (1964), 57.
100 Marshall (1951), 618 and Pl. XXIII, 4.
101 Brentjes (1996), 4.
102 Mukherjee (1990), I (1): 1–2.
103 Taran (1938), 79.
104 Brentjes (1996), 4.
105 Leskov (1996), 7(1): 49.
106 See Puri (1994), II: 190–207.
107 Dani (1989), 118–122; See also Dani (1983), 62–66.
108 Bivar (1983), 3 (1): 197.
109 Gupta (1969), 25.
110 Mukherjee (1990), 1 (1): 3.
111 Leeuw (1949), 338–40.
112 Ibid.
113 Koshelenko and Pilipko (1994), II: 147.
114 Kak (1923). Also see SPS Museum Accession Register.
115 Bhan (1987), 77.
116 The site comprises three terraces with varied types of remains. These three distinct premises and terraces are away from each other by a few meters (approximately 100 m). Presently only the ruins of the upper most and the lower most terraces are visible. The ruins of the middle terraces are non-existent.
117 Fisher (1989), 5–8; Bhan (1987), 77; also idem (2010), 13.
118 Fisher (1989), 10–16.
119 For India, see Law (1940), 222ff.
120 Arrian, 7.2, vide, Dar (1984), 81.
121 Ibid.
122 Kalhana (1979), VII: 1094.
123 Yarshater (1983), 3 (1): ixvii-ixviii.
124 Ibid.

125 Ibid, 351.
126 The application of old names to new places was an established feature of Iranian society. See Ibid, 352.
127 Cf. Kak (1933), 87–88.
128 Ibid.
129 Ibid.
130 Yarshater (1983), 3 (1): 347.
131 Gulshan Majid (1997), 67.
132 Ibid.
133 Banday, (1992), 2.
134 For goddess Aśi, see Yarshater (1983), 3 (1): 345, 427, 465.
135 Yarshater (1983), 3 (1): 350–351.
136 Bleazby (1900).
137 Gupta (1969), 24.
138 Ibid, 25.
139 For an extensive use of gold and bronze by the Scythians, see Brentjes (1996), 5.
140 *Arthaśāstra*, II: 172.
141 Brentjes (1996), 5.
142 Kurz (1983), 3 (1): 561.
143 Ibid.
144 For details, see Brentjes (1996).
145 Kurz (1983), 3 (1): 651.
146 Ibid.
147 Vide, Brentjes (1996), 66–70.
148 Dar (1984), 31–32.
149 Ibid, 101.
150 Puri (1994), 205.
151 Ibid.
152 Fisher (1989a), 8–9.
153 Such are the Bharhut railing, the Greek "swag," the Sassanian foliated bird, the Persian vase, the Roman rosette, the Chinese fret, the Indian elephant, the Assyrian lion, with figures of dancers, musicians, cavaliers, ascetics and racial types from many sources as may be seen by their costumes and accessories. Brown (1959), 154.
154 Puri (1994), 205.
155 For Surkh Kotal, see Schlumberger (1983), 3 (2): 1044.
156 There is an intimate resemblance between the temple of Artemis—Nanaia at Dura Europos and the Surkh Kotal in Bactria. Dar (1984), 34. Since the Surkh Kotal temple resembles with Harwan in many ways, it is tempting to infer that the Harwan temple would have been similar to the temple at Dura as well.
157 See Cunningham (1848); Idem (1848), VII: 241–327; Fergusson (1876), 251–70.
158 Puri (1994), 205.
159 Dar (1984), 101.
160 Rostovtzeff (1935), 5: 155–304.
161 Ghirshman (1962), 280.
162 Koshelenko and Pilipko (1994), 147.
163 Kak, Plates XXII, XLII, XXVIII (17), XXIX, XXX, XXXII.
164 Dar (1984), 120.
165 Harmatta *et al.* (1994a), II: 315–316.
166 Ibid.
167 Ibid, II, 316–320.
168 Puri (1994), 206.

169 Ibid.
170 Gupta (1969), 25.
171 Puri (1994), 207.
172 Yarshater (1983a), 3 (1): 344.
173 Gulshan Majid (1996), 7: 62. In Zoroastrian religion, notwithstanding the dominated position of Ahura Mazda (the supreme god), individual deities, however, retain their powers and characters. They can aid those who worship them or frustrate and punish those who reject them. Thus Mitra and Aradvi Sura remain prominent, and the *fravasis* and *Xvaranah* (Divine fortune) continue to be important factors in human life as well as in world events. (Yarshater (1983a), 3 (1): 344). The *fravasis* were the souls of the departed. The *fravasis* were conceived as invisible powerful beings who could assist their kinsmen and ward off harm from them if properly commemorated with offerings and prayers. The *Fravardin* Yast (Yasht 13), devoted to the celebration of the immortal spirits of the dead (*fravasis*), enumerates in a long register the heroes of the faith from the beginning of the world to the end of time. The list includes the names of deities, mythical and legendry figures of the national history, the helpers of Zoroaster and many others whose *fravasis* have to be specially invoked. Accordingly, the Zoroastrians have in particular reserved a number of days to commemorate the dead. These days are collectively known as *fravardigan*, a festival that lasts for ten days. The first five days are more important as they belong to the righteous souls whose *fravasis* come to revisit the world during these days. The rest of the days of *fravardigan* are devoted to the recitation of relevant portions of the Gathas, worshipping of fire and offerings of *darun*, fruit, water and ghee. Gulshan Majid (1996).
174 Ibid.
175 Cf. Yarshater (1983), 345, 427, 465.
176 Yarshater (1983a), 3 (1).
177 Ibid.
178 Ibid, 347–348.
179 Gulshan Majid (1996), 7: 63.
180 Yarshater (1983), 3 (1): Xvii-Lxxvi. intro
181 Colpe (1983), 3 (2): 850–51.
182 Yarshater (1983), 3 (2).
183 Fisher (1989a), 36.
184 Waheed (2000), 78.
185 Ibid.
186 Dani (1983).
187 *Amarakośa*, II. 6. 124.
188 Ibid.
189 Mukherjee (1981), 112, 121, 122, 176, 200.
190 Mc Govern (1939), 2.
191 Herzfeld (1930), 5.
192 Kak, Plates XXIV, XXVII.
193 Borovka (1967), 26.
194 Mc Govern (1939), 17.1.
195 Ghirshaman (1962), pl. LIX.
196 In fact, one of the branches of the Scythians was called Śaka Tigrakhand, that is, Śakas with the peaked caps. Sen (1920), 93.
197 Ingholt (1957), Figs. 57, 287, 574.
198 Kak (1933), pls. XX, XXII.
199 Chandra, *Prācīna Bhāratīya Veśa Bhūsā,* 122; quoted by Thapliyal (1979), 56.
200 Rawlinson (1867), IV: 155; Sykes (1930), I: 368.
201 Chandra (1973), 11.

202 Kak (1933), pl. XXIX. 20.
203 Siudmak (1989), 51, Fig. 16.
204 Maisey, (1892), 32.
205 Fisher (1989a), 20.
206 Mukherjee (1988), 32–36.
207 *Indian Archaeology* – A Review, (1984–85), 144.
208 SPS Museum, Accession Register.
209 Sims-Williams and Cribbs (1996), 4: 75–142.
210 Kak (1923), 155.
211 Konow (1991), 79–81, XV/2.
212 Sims-Williams and Cribbs (1996), 4: 75–142.
213 Accession Register SPS Museum.
214 Kak (1923), 131.
215 Kalhana (1979), I: 168.
216 Ibid.
217 Hiuen Tsang (1911), 151–55.
218 Kalhana (1979), I: 168.
219 Sites like Doen Pather and Kutbal are situated at high altitudes having rocky tracks still unlinked by modern roads and transportation.
220 Kalhana (1979), I: 168–170.
221 Rosenfield (1967), 57; Mukherjee (1988), 92, 93.
222 Ibid.
223 Kalhana (1979), I: 169.
224 Mukherjee (1988), 92–99.
225 Kalhana (1979), I: 168.
226 Ibid.
227 Ibid, I, 170.
228 Kak (1923), 132.
229 Rosenfield (1967), 69–101.
230 Ibid, 76–77, 79, 92–95.
231 Kak (1923), 132.
232 Kalhana (1979), I: 174.
233 Ibid, I, 174–176.
234 Ibid, I, 185–187.
235 Ibid, I, 185–197. The five rulers mentioned are Gonanda III, Vibhisana I, Indrajit, Ravana and Vibhisana II.
236 An example of this is the sites, namely, Kutbal, Doen-Pather, Hutmur and Hoinar.
237 Kuṣāṇa tiles found in Kashmir portray well-built men, having strong physical prowess and often in possession of armour. The depiction of mounted archers indicates that Kuṣāṇas possessed a strong cavalry.
238 The word *damara* implies a feudal baron. They were powerful enough to play the role of kingmakers in Kashmir. It is because of their extraordinary fighting power and war tactics that Kṣemendra calls them the 'lion of the battle'. For details, see Stein (1979), II: 304–08.
239 Stein (1979), II, 304–308.
240 Kuṣāṇa administration was based on Satrapa system; and as a rule they sent Satraps and administrators to all parts and provinces of their empire. Cf. Puri (1965), 80–85; also see Mukherjee (1988), 342–349.
241 A significant example of this is Kutbal. This site, as mentioned earlier, is not only distantly located but also bears testimony to have been a place of considerable importance. The tiles found from this site indicate the presence of an urban culture for its being the headquarters of the local administrator.

242 Hiuen Tsang (1911), 152–156.
243 Nagarjuna whom Kalhana mentions to have taken up residence at *Sadarhavana* may have been one such Buddhist scholar, Kalhana (1979), I: 173.
244 Kalhana (1979), I.
245 Almost every site that has yielded Kuṣāṇa tiles has also yielded typical Kuṣāṇa pottery. For details, see Bandey (1992).
246 Kak (1933), 110.
247 Ibid.
248 Brown (1959), 155.
249 Bandey (1992), 10.
250 Kalhana (1979), I: 168.
251 Shali (1993), 121–128; Mani (2000), 10: 1–28.
252 Ibid, 121–122.
253 *Nīlamata Purāna*, 141 sqq.
254 Ibid, 388sqq.
255 Kalhana (1979), III: 489–490.
256 Kaul (1991), 86 sqq. Lawrence was, however, told of 121 *gotras* only. Lawrence (2004), 304.
257 Lawrence (2004); Kaul (1991).
258 Kalhana (1979), VII: 39–41, 203, 207–08, 285–91.
259 Ibid, V, 402.
260 Ibid, III, 123; V: 220–26; VI: 107, 195sqq; VII: 2334–37.
261 Ibid, I, 342–43
262 For details, see Thapliyal (1979), Chapter 4.
263 Kalhana (1979), I: 289–316.
264 This is evident from the categories of people realistically represented on the tiles. Except for one person, all others who are immigrants belong to either ascetic groups or aristocratic sections of the society or the urban artists.
265 Kalhana (1979), I: 168–178.
266 Harmatta *et al.* (1994a), 329.
267 Ibid.
268 Ibid, 318.
269 Ibid.
270 Kak (1923), 155.
271 Ibid.
272 Harmatta *et al.* (1994a), 318–319.
273 Ibid.
274 Ibid.
275 Rosenfield (1967), plate VIII. Coin Nos. 158, 159 and 160.
276 Harmatta *et al.* (1994a).
277 Ibid, 324.
278 Ibid, 327–328.
279 Kak (1923), 132.
280 Ibid.
281 Kalhana (1979), I: 168.
282 Luders (1961), 68.
283 Harmatta *et al.* (1994a), 327.
284 Kak (1923), 132.
285 Harmatta *et al.* (1994a), 329.
286 Yarshater (1983), 3 (1), Introduction, XXV.
287 Ibid, Introduction, Xvii-Lxxvi.
288 Ganhar and Ganhar (1956), 62.
289 Ibid.

290 Kalhana (1979), I: 312–316.
291 Kak (1933), 107.
292 Ibid, plate XVII.
293 Marshall (1951), I: 218.
294 Ibid.
295 Ibid, I, 63.
296 Ibid, 218.
297 Ibid, 219.
298 Fisher (1989a), 19.
299 Ibid, 22.
300 Mani (2000), 10: 1–21.
301 Pollock (2006), 72–73.
302 Ganhar and Ganhar (1956), 58–66.
303 Thapliyal (1979), 43.
304 Often on their coins and portrait statues Kuṣāṇa kings and nobles were seen wearing this kind of dress.
305 Thapliyal (1979), 59.
306 Ghirshman (1962), LIX
307 Ibid, pl. V.
308 Yazdani, *Ajanta,* pl. xxix; Sivaramamurti, *Amaravati Sculptures*, pl. IX, Fig. 15; quoted by Thapliyal (1979), 60.
309 Marshall (1951), I: 443.
310 Ibid.
311 Mani (1987), 76–78.
312 Kak, Plate XXIV, XXVII.
313 Borovka (1967); Ingholt (1957), pl. 420.
314 Ingholt (1957), 287, 574; Marshall (1951), 3: pl. 139; Rosenfield (1967), Pls. 10, 11.
315 Marshall (1960), pl. 17, Fig. 16.
316 Rawlinson (1867), 155, 160, 162; Also, see Sykes (1930), I: 365.
317 Maisey (1892), 32.
318 Kalhana (1979), IV: 178–79.
319 Mani (1987), Pl xii b.
320 SPS Museum, Srinagar.
321 Thapliyal (1979), 73.
322 Quoted by Thapliyal (1979), 83; For Kashmir, see Witzel (2008), 80.
323 Thapliyal (1979), 82–83.
324 Kalhana (1979), III: 5–7; Yule (1903), 1: 176–77; Witzel (2008), 79.
325 Marshall (1960), Pl. 62, Fig. 91. During the Kuṣāṇa occupation of Taxila, west Asian wines were in vogue there. The large two-handled amphoras make their appearance at Taxila in Kaniṣka's time, and these were certainly imported from west Asia where the Graeco-Roman amphoras were in common use. Marshall (1951), I: 406.
326 Kin-lou-tse of Yuan, quoted by Prakash (1964a), 224.
327 Mani (1987), 94.
328 *Mahabartha*, Karna P., 30–31; vide Thapliyal (1979), 83; Kalhana (1979), I: 342–43.
329 Vide, Thapliyal (1979), 97.
330 Kalhana (1979), I: 342–43.
331 Sarangadeva (1953), II (1): 21–23; Ganguly (1948).
332 Thapliyal (1979), 153
333 *Manusmrti*, III:153; vide Thapliyal (1979), 154.:

334 Legge (1877), 16; Watters (1988), I: 78.
335 Prakash (1964b), 231–32.
336 Based on oral history.
337 Zeimal (1994), III: 167.
338 Harmatta (1984a), 185–89. Also see Dani (1994), 167.
339 Dāmodaragupta (1944), 606.
340 Harmatta (1984a).
341 Dani (1994), 167.
342 Hieun Tsiang (1911), 151–155.
343 Ibid.
344 Ibid.
345 Ibid.
346 Ibid.
347 Ibid.
348 Ibid, 156.
349 Ibid.
350 Watters (1988), 279.
351 Taranatha (1970), 91.
352 Kalhana (1979), I: 175. Sadarahadvana is modern Harwan.
353 Ganhar and Ganhar (1956), 30–38.
354 Ibid.
355 Kaul (1987), 4–6.
356 Kalhana (1979), I: 169–170.
357 Ganhar and Ganhar (1956), 30–38.
358 Harmatta *et al.* (1994a), 324; also see Ganhar and Ganhar (1956), chapter, Sanskrit Buddhism, 58–66.
359 Ganhar and Ganhar (1956), 58–66.
360 Ibid.
361 Koul (1987), 57.
362 Bagchi (1950), 206.
363 Ibid, 67
364 Ibid, 68
365 Ibid, 37.
366 Ibid, 38–43, 203, 206, 207, 209, 211, 212, 218, 219, 220.
367 Ibid, 39.
368 Ibid.
369 Ibid, 22.
370 Stein (1907), 165.
371 Ibid.
372 Ibid, 164, 231.
373 Ibid, 118.
374 Ibid, 159–60
375 Pal (1989), VI-VII.
376 Flood (2009), 8.
377 From the mid-fifth to the mid-sixth century, Central Asia was ruled by the Huns. The Huns comprised different ethno-linguistic groups and are known by various names in various linguistic-cultural zones. The Chinese called them Hsiung-nu, the Persians Hyon as well as Heftal, the Europeans Hun, the Greeks Ephthalitae, the Armenians Hep't'al, the Syrians Eptalit and the Indians Huna. In the middle Persian, Byzantine and Indian sources we find two broad ethno-linguistic groups of Hun people, namely, Red Huns and White Huns. In the Indian sources the former are known as Hara Huna and the latter Sveta Huna.

It was the White Huns who invaded Persia and India. There is no definite opinion among the contemporary sources about the origin of the Huns. Some Chinese sources hold that they originated from Turfan; some trace their origin from southern Kazakistan and some regard them having descended from Great Yuch-chich. According to Gafurov the Hepthalities established a huge state structure even greater in geographic extent than that of the Kuṣāṇas, though it was more loosely knit and more unstable. For details, see Litvinsky (1994), 135.

378 Fisher (1989a), 29–30.
379 Siudmak (1989), 41.
380 Biswas (1973), 137.
381 Gupta (1969), 76–81.
382 Thakur (1967), 145–158.
383 Litvinsky (1994), 142.
384 Biswas (1973), 52–54.
385 Ibid.
386 In the *Rājataraṅgiṇī,* two rulers of Kashmir carry the name of Tunjina. The first one referred to by Kalhana is not included among the Hun rulers. According to Kalhana, he was one of the descendants of Pratipaditya, a relative of King Vikramaditya, and he ruled Kashmir as the third ruler of the line of Pratipaditya who assumed the throne as a vassal of Harsha. The latter occupied Kashmir following the internal disorder during the Hun ruler, Yudhishthira who was the eleventh Hun ruler to rule over Kashmir. Kalhana (1979), Book I and Book II. The second Tunjina ruled long after Toramana.
387 Kalhana (1979), I: 287–289.
388 Cunningham (1962), 114, pl. VIII, Figs. 9, 10.
389 Kalhana (1979), I: 289 and note.
390 Ibid, III, note 103.
391 Ibid.
392 Ibid.
393 Biswas (1973), 66.
394 Thakur (1967), 138.
395 Kalhana (1979), I: note 289.
396 Ibid.
397 Ibid, I: 289–293 vs. 306–307.
398 Hiuen Tsiang (1911), I: XIX sqq.
399 Ibid.
400 Kalhana (1979), I: 312–316.
401 Ibid, 306.
402 Gupta (1969), 79–80; plate 170; Smith (1972), 187–88.
403 Ibid.
404 Sircar (1965), 394, fn. 4.
405 Konow (1991), 162.
406 Kalhana (1979), I: 325–373.
407 Ibid, II, 8, 9, 11, 62, 63, 116.
408 Ibid, III, 125–129.
409 Thakur (1967), 163–185.
410 Cunningham (1894), 43, pl. III, Figs. V, VI.
411 Biswas (1973), 131–136.
412 Ibid.
413 Kalhana (1979), II: 5.
414 Wilson (1960), 34.

415 Kalhana (1979), II: 8 sqq.
416 Ibid.
417 Ibid, III, 2.
418 Ibid.
419 Ibid, 27.
420 Ibid, 78.
421 Ibid.
422 Ibid, III: 125–197.
423 Saxena (1974), 33.
424 Kalhana (1979), III: 285.
425 Ibid, 330.
426 Ibid, 331.
427 Ibid, III, 332–35.
428 Ibid, 336, sqq
429 Ibid.
430 Ibid, 354.
431 Ibid, 379 sqq.
432 Ibid, III, 480.
433 Remusat (1829), I: 212; quoted by Ray (1969), 44.
434 Tsiang (1911), I: 138, 143, 147, 163.
435 Stein (1979), II: 320.
436 Ibid, II, 319; Ibid, III, note 103.
437 Ibid, I, note, 103.
438 Ray (1969), 234, fn. 10.
439 Stein (1979), II: 319.
440 Cribb (2016).
441 Cribb (2016), 102 sqq.
442 For a detailed cerographic list of the coin series, see Cribb (2016), 89.
443 See Shrava (1985); Chattopadhyay (1967).
444 Witzel (2008), 55–56.
445 Kalhana (1979), I: note 289.
446 Ibid, I, 312–316.
447 Ibid, 329.
448 Ibid, 338.
449 Ibid, 340.
450 Ibid, 339–345.
451 Witzel (2008), 67.
452 Kalhana (1979), I: 342–43.
453 Ibid, I, 344. The action taken against garlic eating brahmans "falls into the same category as eating of garlic and onion is forbidden by the dharma texts (such as Manu)." Witzel (2008), 53.
454 Ibid, I, 341.
455 Ibid, 346.
456 Ibid, 347.
457 Ibid, II, 7.
458 Ibid, 4.
459 Ibid, 55.
460 Ibid, 62.
461 Ibid, 127–28, 132–33.
462 Ibid, 134n.
463 Ibid, III, 5–7.
464 Ibid, 82–93.

465 Ibid, 8.
466 Ibid.
467 She was from Assam. Witzel (2008), 55
468 Ibid, III, 8–9.
469 *L'Itineraire d'Ou-k'ong (1895)*, VI: 371sqq.
470 Kalhana (1979), III: n.9.
471 Ibid, 10.
472 Ibid, 11.
473 Ibid, 13.
474 Ibid, III, 10–11, 13–14.
475 Ibid, n. 14.
476 Ibid, III, 97.
477 Ibid, 99–101.
478 Ibid, 256, 263.
479 Ibid, III, 350–352.
480 Ibid, 353.
481 Ibid, 357.
482 Ibid, 355.
483 Ibid.
484 Ibid, 355.
485 Beal (1884), 69.
486 Kalhana (1979), III: 356.
487 Ibid, 380–81.
488 Ibid, 384.
489 Ibid, 453–54.
490 Ibid, 460.
491 Ibid, 462.
492 Ibid, 464.
493 Ibid, 474.
494 Ibid, 481–82.
495 Ibid, IV, 3–4.
496 Ibid, 5–7.
497 Ibid, III, 489.
498 Ibid, I, 312–316.
499 Ibid, 341.
500 Cutler (2001), 250.
501 Kalhana, I, 306.
502 Ibid, 340–43.
503 Ibid, II, 14.
504 Ibid, III, 8.
505 Ibid, 481.
506 Ibid, I, 306.
507 Ibid, III, vs. 336, 349–357, 99, 102–103
508 Ibid, III, 342 sqq; Stein (1979), II: 442–45.
509 Chattopadhyaya (2003), 153–71. Also, cf. Sahu (2013a), 179–215.
510 For details, see Pal (1989a).
511 Siudmuk (1989), 44.

4

EMPIRE AT THE FRONTIER

The Kashmir Empire and Cross-Cultural Networks (Karkotas to Loharas)

> Even in those lands which, indeed, to this day have not been seen even by the rays of sun, the command of this king [Lalitadatiya] met with no resistance.[1]
>
> —(Kalhana)

Making of an Empire

According to Ronald Inden, the early Hindu texts treated Kashmir a marginal, "barbarian country," at best a liminal part of India:

> Kashmir was a small country situated in the north and not in the Middle Region. Only two of her crossings appear to have had subcontinental standing among Vaiṣṇavas and Śaivas before the sixth or seventh century. The *Viṣṇusmriti*, a text of the north from that period and direct ancestor of the *VDhP* [*Visnudharmottara Purāna*], names Varāhaparvata and Kālodaka (together with Uttaramānasa) in a pan-Indian list of fifty-five *tīrthas* which it recommends for offerings to ancestors (*śrāddha)(Viṣṇusmrti 85*). The Vaiṣṇava text purporting to be still older (third to fifth centuries), *the Mahābhārata*, lists Kālodaka (together with other crossings near Haramukūta – Nandikuṇḍa, Uttarāmānasa – and the image of Nandīśvara) but makes no mention of Varāhaparvata (*Mahābhārata*, crit. edn., 13.26.56). Other passages, however, tell a different story. One lists the Kāśmīras and their hill neighbours, the Daradas (Dards) among the 'other northern barbarian peoples' and 'clans of Viaśyas and Sūdras living like Ksatriyas' (*MBh* 6.10.63–6). Another passage states that Arjuna vanquished the king of Kashmir during the Pāndava 'conquest of the quarters (*digvijaya*) (*MBh* 2.31.12–18). The Kashmiri king did come, along with other barbarians, to the Rājasūya (affusion into imperial kingship) (*MBh* 2.48.13), but did not participate in the greater war itself. So, from

DOI: 10.4324/9781003367697-4

the point of view of these early Hindu texts, Kashmir was at best a liminal part of India.[2]

However, from the third decade of the sixth century, there was a turnaround in the politico-cultural position of Kashmir. The kings of Kashmir transformed the valley from a "barbaric hinterland of India" to the "middle province" of an imperial kingdom. The process was started by the Hun ruler, Mihirakula around 530 CE. It was carried forward by his successors and reached to its apogee during the Karkota period (625–855 CE). For the first time in its known history, Kashmir emerged as an empire—the position which it retained until the tenth century with, of course, what Kumkum Roy says "fuzzy frontiers."[3]

The century preceding the Karkotas did not only witness Kashmir emerging as an imperial power, but it also, as we have seen, became a great centre of Brahmanism under the state patronage. Immigration and settlement of brahmanas, construction of *tirthas* and temples, and endowments of land grants to brahmanas and their institutions were the hallmark of the period. Following the repeated influx of people, the period is underlined by the establishment of a large number of rural settlements and towns crowned by the foundation of a new capital city which, according to Kalhana, was unparalleled in its bewitching attributes. Not surprisingly, therefore, the city (Pravarapura, modern Srinagar) maintained its position as the capital of Kashmir till date despite the attempts of a few rulers to shift it to other places. The preceding century is also remarkably known for the culture of catholicity and accommodation as except for Mihirakula, the predecessors of Karkotas patronised all the major beliefs of the time—Śaivism, Vaiṣṇavism and Buddhism.

It was this tradition of imperial polity and the culture of tolerance and accommodation that was inherited by the Karkotas. They did not only maintain the legacy they inherited from the latter Huns but also promoted it by providing an ideological basis to making Kashmir the Madhyadesha/Aryavarta[4] and by taking practical steps to qualify it for this coveted position. The ideological basis was provided by the two Puranas—*Nīlamata Purāna* (NP) and *Viṣṇudharmottara Purāna* (VDhP)—composed during the period. The NP which, according to Inden, was written during the period of Durlabhavardhana, the founder of Karkota dynasty, under the state patronage,[5] articulates the relationship of Kashmir to the Middle Region by ascribing it a divine origin, a creation of the brahmanical/brahmanised divinities.[6] According to the NP, "Kashmira is goddess Uma."[7] The NP insists that Kashmir was the goddess Uma when it was a lake, and it continued to be so when it became habitable after it got desiccated and the demon killed through the intervention of gods. Moreover, it is a place where all gods, goddesses, sages and in fact "the whole world [of divinities] have made their abode there";[8] all the wives of gods, the mothers of the gods, the hosts of Vidayadharas, Yaksas, seas and rivers (all went there)."[9] While the major gods—Brahma, Viṣṇu and Śiva—assumed the form of the mountain peaks, the wives and mothers of gods "assumed the forms of rivers."[10] As a result, all "the sacred waters, the oceans and the rivers went to Kaśmīra and her vicinity"[11]; and Kashmir became a "holy region" of all sacred places. There are "holy mountains," "holy rivers," "holy lakes" and "sacred temples" and "hermitages."[12] Devising a sacred geography parallel to madhyadeśa (middle region), the NP creates for Kashmir the most auspicious landscapes for which the Aryavarta stood apart as a sacred space, namely, Kailaśa, Ganga, Yamuna, Prayaga, Badarikaśrama and Varanasi.

> The Sindhu should be regarded as the Ganga and the Vitasta as the Yamana. The place, where there is the confluence of these two, should be regarded as equal to Prayaga.[13]

Ronald Inden and Mahesh Sharma believe that the NP was both an ideological and political instrument. According to Inden, the "complex author" of the NP, Durlabhavardhana and his court were engaged in transforming Kashmir into an imperial Vaişṇava kingdom.[14] Echoing the same impression, Mahesh Sharma says that by devising a sacred space parallel to the subcontinental cosmos, the NP was also mapping a political vision "for a Kashmir kingship that desired to rule over the entire earth, a nuanced way of devising hegemony over the seventh to tenth century north India."[15]

Inden, who has done a pioneering work on *Vişṇudharmottara Purāna* (VDhP) from the perspective of "medieval Hindu ideas of kingship," believes that it was composed during the period of Chandrapida Vajraditya and Muktapida Lalitaditya by a "complex author" comprising the king, his court and the Pancaratra preceptor of an imperial king. The text embodies a self-conscious narrative. "It is the working out of a Vaişṇava world vision that is also a Kashmiri imperial wish." It was both the product and the producer of the events in the seventh- and eighth-century Kashmir. "The 'conquest of the quarters' [as well as the temple building activities] that Muktapida undertook," says Inden, "was informed by the narrative and discursive contents of the VDhP, whereas the vision of the text was itself tailored to the situation."[16] That after studying the VDhP, Inden could see kings and rites inextricably bound up with the theology of the Pancaratra 'sect' of Vaiṣṇava as well as with an imperial political agenda; it is easy to understand why he captioned his article on the VDhP as "Imperial Puranas: Kashmir as Vaişṇava center of the world."

The elevation of Kashmir to the position of a great empire was not merely textual; the Karkota rulers took practical steps to make it so. Certainly, they had not to break a fresh ground in this regard. They had only to carry forward the strong tradition of empire building established by their predecessorsand imbibed by Durlabhavardhana, the founder of the dynasty, as the close associate of Huns being a functionary in their government.[17] More importantly, he got the empire through his wife, Anangalekha, the only issue of the last Hun ruler, Baladitya.[18] Durlabhavardhana gave a clear signal of carrying forward the traditions established by his predecessors, especially from Pravarasena II, by getting a prestigious pedigree manufactured for himself and for his dynasty claiming that he is the offspring of Karkota Naga,[19] one of the most venerated Naga deities of Kashmir. Given his humble origin, this was a conscious attempt at legitimising his rulership of an imperial kingdom. In an aura when family's royal roots entitled one to royal power, and the primogeniture was the normal mode of legal inheritance, the invention of mythical ancestry by the ruling family was aimed at exalting a line and to impose this consciousness on other members of the lineage group to assert its identity for legitimising its power and extending its place in political life through the falsification of its past, validating the family's right by means of a descent from a greatly venerated deity.[20] Another conscious exercise in this behalf was to get NP composed which, besides making Kashmir the domain of Nāgas (serpent deities), graduated the valley into a unique auspicious position—more auspicious than the Middle Region. Equally noteworthy is the fact that, according to Kalhana, Durlabhavardhana received the shower bath into kingship with the waters of the pilgrimage places poured out of golden jars,[21] a statement which, according to Inden, "to be read as a declaration that this king intended to establish an imperial kingdom."[22] That Durlabhavardhana and his court were ideologically convinced to follow in the footsteps of their predecessors is also evidenced by the fact that while the king built a Vaiṣṇava temple, his wife built a vihāra.[23]

Durlabhavardhana set out not only to carry forward the legacy he inherited but also to bequeath it to be pursued more vigorously by his successors. However, as Kalhana portrays all the later Hun rulers including the last ruler of the dynasty, Baladitya, as great conquerors, it is difficult to agree with the view suggesting that the surrounding borderlands of Kashmir, mentioned by Hiuen Tsang, were brought under Kashmir by Durlabhavardhana.[24] These lands, as we have seen in the preceding chapter, were already a part of the Kashmir empire. What seems probable is that Durlabhavardhana expanded the frontiers of the empire beyond the borderlands of Kashmir. Durlabhavardhana's victorious campaigns are also suggested by the construction of a temple he built in Srinagar which, according to Inden, was "presumably to mark his victory in establishing an imperial polity."[25] Arguing that building of an ideologically oriented empire had become the priority for the Karkotas right from the foundation of the Karkota dynasty, Inden says that the NP and the VDhP were as much involved in making Kashmir the centre of the Indic earth as the imperial project was in their composition.

> Durlabhavardhana may not have seen the VDhP completed at his court, but it is quite likely that the *Purāna* of Kashmir to which the

> VDhP was closely related, the *Nīlamata Purāna*, was completed at his court. That text, the regional and royal antecedent of the universal and imperial VDhP, also claimed to have been delivered to a king by a Brāhman sage. The author of the NP made Kashmir the centre of an imperial Theist kingdom consisting of the countries of the northern quarter of India.[26]

However, it was Lalitaditya who was the first ruler "to carry out the orders of *Viṣṇu* issued in the VDhP" and fulfilled the world vision by embarking on the policy of conquering the world.[27] He defeated the then greatest ruler of India, namely, Yaśovarman of Kanauj (Kanyakubja) and made his kingdom the tributary of the Kashmir empire, says Kalhana.[28] After conquering Kanauj, Lalitaditya was encouraged to embark on the policy of conquering the whole of India and he, according to Kalhana, made a triumphal conquest of Kalinga, Karnataka, regions of Kaveri and Gauda.[29] In fact, the rulers of a large part of India were presumably defeated one by one by Lalitaditya.[30] Kalhana writes with a deep sense of pleasure about the colossal Bodhisattva statues in bronze that Lalitaditya brought back with him from Magadha following its supposed subjugation.[31] "What is fascinating about this textual memory of a momentous transfer of an art work," says Shonaleeka Kaul, on the authority of art historians, "is that it tallies with the decided influence of the Pala school of Bihar on the famed Kashmiri Buddhist bronze industry, the best examples of which were commissioned by, and survive to this day in the monasteries of Tibet."[32] While 'reading' the symbolic content of the seizer of religious images during campaigns of military expansion or those being gifted to the powerful ruler, the modern scholars opine that with regard to seizer, the purpose was to deprive the homelands of their protective presence or to avail metropolitan pantheon of it;[33] and so far as being given as a gift, it is identified as "a metonymic" acceptance of "ritual subordination"[34] to forestall more aggressive engagements. From the perspective of the royal looters they, according to Richard Davis, employed the dislodged select images to "articulate political claims in a rhetoric of objects whose principal themes were victory and defeat, autonomy and subjugation, dominance and subordination."[35]

Stein doubts the authenticity of Deccan campaigns and regards Kalhana's account in this regard "merely a conventional elaboration of a popular belief which attributed to Lalitaditya the customary *digvijaya* of an Indian hero."[36] The same view is held by Sheldon Pollock. He says that just as Kalidasa modelled his account of the legendary Raghu on Samudragupta's Allahabad Pillar Inscription, similarly Kalhana's portrayal of Lalitaditya's conquest of the horizons is a reworking of Raghuvamsa's model for the *digvijaya* of King Raghu. This reworking was done not by Kalhana but by some unknown author of a *praśasti*, Kalhana used as a source.[37] Kumkum

Roy has also serious reservations about Kalhan's references to "grandiose *digvijayas.*"[38]

Though the corroborative evidence about most of his "conquests" is still lacking, the coins of Lalitaditya have been discovered at Kanauj, Banda, Faizabad, Nalanda and Monghyr.[39] This information was not available to Stein, who frankly admitted that "No coins of Lalitaditya have yet come to light."[40] It also needs to be considered that while narrating the southern, eastern and western "conquests" of Lalitaditya, Kalhana refers to geographical and cultural peculiarities of these regions.[41] Was this information handed down to Kalhana by oral history? Was it a mouth-to-mouth transmission of memories of those who participated in these campaigns? This is an open question. Yet, in his projection of Lalitaditya as a great conqueror whose sway extended to distant areas of India and Central Asia, Kalhana is also corroborated by non-local sources. *Chach Nama* (which is a Persian translation of the original Arabic chronicle written in the eighth century) says that in order to forestall Muhammad ibn al-Qasim (the famous Muslim general under whose command Sind was conquered) from launching aggressive campaigns against his kingdom, Rai Dahir, the then ruler of Sind, wrote a threatening letter to him, which provides a reminder of the widespread resonance of Lalitaditya's campaigns of conquest in India and Central Asia:

> If I had sent against you . . . the king of Kashmir who is the mighty possessor of a crown, kettle drums and standards, on whose royal threshold the other rulers of Hind have placed their heads, whose sway extends up to the whole of Hind and even the country of Makran and Turan, whose chains a great many nobles and grandees have willingly placed on their knees. . . . If I have sent these heroes against you, you could not have done the slightest harm to them.[42]

Referring to the equally important conquests made by Lalitaditya in the northern regions (*Uttrāpātha*), Kalhana says that the king vanquished the rulers of Kamboja, Tukharistan (upper Oxus Valley including Balkh and Badhakshān) and Tibet.[43] We have corroborative evidence which testifies to the accomplishment of these conquests by Lalitaditya. Kalhana refers to Śahi princes and Tukharas holding high positions in the Lalitaditya's government.[44] Indeed, defeating these territories, Lalitaditya brought the talent from these countries and appointed them to high positions.[45] Importantly, Al-Biruni makes a mention of the political festival, which was established by Lalitaditya at his capital city, Parihaspora, to celebrate the victory which he won over the Turks.[46] This festival was celebrated every year and continued for many centuries, at least up to the time of Kalhana who also makes a mention of this "permanently established great festival at Parihasapura" by Lalitaditya.[47] Without doubt, no event could outlive the celebratory character given to it by its creator for many centuries after his demise unless it was too momentous to the collective consciousness to allow it to be forgotten. Moreover, there are not only references to named people—Kambojas, Tukharas, Bhauttas, Dardas and Turuśkas in *Rājataraṅgiṇī*, but also mention about the salient attributes of the different regions conquered by Lalitaditya in *Uttrāpatha*.[48]

The emergence of Kashmir as a great power left a profound impact on the diversified aspects of Kashmir. The most important change which followed this development was that Kashmir underwent a remarkable technological and cultural transformation following the encounter of Kashmiris with a variety of cultures spanning a large area from *Dakṣināpatha* to *Uttrāpatha*. More importantly, it was customary among the conquerors of Ancient and Middle Ages to drain out the extraordinary talent in different fields from the vanquished territories to improve the statecraft and develop the technology, economy and culture of their respective capitals. So is true of the imperial Karkota rulers. Writing about this policy of Lalitaditya, Kalhana says, "He collected from different countries various wise men, as the wind collects masses of full-blown flowers from the trees."[49] This is also corroborated by the tangible references to the talent from different countries holding important positions in the administration of Lalitaditya. The primeminister of Lalitaditya, Cankuṇa, was a Tukharian,[50] and the five newly offices instituted by Lalitaditya, namely, high chamberlain (*mahāpratihārpīdā*), chief minister of foreign affairs (*mahāsamdhivigraha*), chief minister of the horses (*mahaśvasala*), high keeper of the treasury (*mahābhandāgāra*), and the chief executive officer (*mahāsādhanabhāga*) were held by Śāhi and other non-local princes.[51] The two other channels of contact with transformative effect were: the political integration of the neighbourhood with Kashmir facilitating the movement of people, ideas and commodities, and the affluence of Kashmir prompting the streaming of talent into Kashmir from the neighbourhood who in search of greener pastures found Kashmir a favourable destination.[52] Indeed, the enormous human and material resources enabled its rulers to make Kashmir a model country in every field. A glimpse of it can be had from the textual evidence provided by *Rājataraṅgiṇī*[53] and the ruined stone temples of the period, especially the Martand temple and the stone, bronze, copper and ivory sculptures of the time.[54] The ability to command resources on a transregional scale as a crucial enabling factor in building large edifices is affirmed by Ibn Khaldun (d. 1406) on the basis of historical knowledge and empirical evidence:

> The monuments of a dynasty are its buildings and large (edifices). They are proportionate to the original power of the dynasty. They can materialize only when there are many workers and united action and cooperation. When a dynasty is large and far-flung, with

> many provinces and subjects, workers are very plentiful and can be brought together from all sides and regions.[55]

Besides the precious human resource, Kashmir was almost flooded with wealth obtained both through plunder of the vanquished territories and through tributes paid by the feudatory chiefs. Drawing on the researches of Richard Davis[56] and Nicholas Dirks,[57] Flood says that spoils of wars and their distributions among those who participated in the war and reserving certain categories of plunder—including gold, silver, land, religious icons and royal regalia for the victorious ruler were common to South Asian traditions. These spoils were usually dispatched to the victor's capital for display, redistribution or donation to his temples, thus embellishing and extending the conqueror's power.[58]

Indeed, successful military exploits constituted an important source of revenue during the period of our study with the consequence of providing relief to local tax payers, according to Kalhana.[59] Referring to the treasure collected by Lalitaditya during the military raids and from the vanquished rulers, Kalhana says, "Then with the treasures obtained by his conquests he proceeded to his own land, as the lion goes to the mountain with his claws full of pearls [taken from the frontal protuberances] of the destroyed elephants."[60] It is after mentioning the treasure obtained by Lalitaditya from his conquests that Kalhana gives details of a large number of cities, towns, temples, mathas, viharas, stupas, and gold, silver and copper images and symbols constructed by Lalitaditya[61] as well as by the members of the ruling family and the ministers[62] including the enormous land grants endowed to them and to the religious class.[63]

The significance of the temple building activity by Lalitaditya after launching successful conquests can be understood in the context of the commandments contained in the VDhP according to which a king successful in battle was *inter alia* supposed to build temples. The construction of large and elaborate temples and the institution of a complete Pancharatra temple liturgy as its unifying theme were, according to Inden, the desire of the

> Pancaratrians and their king, successful in his conquest of the quarters of India. . . . to replace the old horse sacrifice with the installation of images (*surapratistha*) in a monumental Pancratra temple, an act that would make Pancratra Viaşṇavism preeminent, for the moment, among India's ways of life.[64]

The reworking of the Pancharatra order of Vaişṇavas that appears in the VDhP is, according to Inden, "the ancestor of most of the orders of Vaişṇavas that arose later throughout the subcontinent."[65] The temple style, which the VDhP recognised as emblematic of universal rule in the Kashmir environment, was a new composite style to distinguish it from the general style elsewhere in India so as to have the effect of making Kashmir as the universal centre.[66]

Another important step taken by Lalitaditya to make Kashmir as the Middle Region of an imperial empire was the construction of his new capital, Parihāsāpura, near the confluence of the Vitasta and Sindhu—the former being homologous with the Yamuna and the latter with the Ganga, and the confluence of the two Prayaga as enunciated by the NP. The Puranas, as we know, defined the Middle Region as the one which is drained by the Ganga and its tributary the Yamuna; and which is blessed with the confluence of the two—Prayaga, a major Vaiṣṇava place of pilgrimage. Thus Lalitaditya did not only conquer Kanyakubja (Kanauj), the political centre of this Middle Region, but he and his court "filled out this homology by making Parihāsāpura a new Kanauj."[67]

Jayapida is the only known ruler of the Karkota dynasty to have followed in the footsteps of his illustrious predecessor in building a large empire.[68] However, according to Kalhana, his ambition remained a dream as except for overpowering the ruler of Kanauj[69] (who obviously seems to have declared complete independence from Kashmir after Lalitaditya), he had to face reversals after reversals including imprisonments, even though he went as far as Bengal and Nepal in pursuit of maintaining the tradition of his grandfather.[70] The adventure seems to have proved so expensive that Jayapida had to take drastic retrenchment measures to the great displeasure of land revenue grantees.[71] Nevertheless, the military campaigns in different parts of India won Jayapida many friends in the Indian subcontinent who helped him in his difficult times, and they were duly rewarded by him by appointing them to high positions when he regained his empire. For instance, Jayadatta was bestowed with the highest position of *pañcamahāśabda*[72] and *Āca*, the son-in-law of lord of Mathra was the king's chamberlain.[73] The most intimate contacts, however, came to be established with Bengal as Jayapida's chief queen, Kalyanadevi, was from a royal family of Gauda[74] (Bengal). Jayapida was so much attached to her that he made her the chief chamberlain (*mahāpratīharapīda*).[75] Like his predecessor, Jayapida also utilised his military adventures for searching talent and luring them to settle down in Kashmir. To quote Kalhana, "The king searched for and collected all scholars to such an extent that in the lands of other kings there was a dearth of learned men."[76]

Besides expanding the frontiers of the empire inherited by them, the Karkotas entered into diplomatic relations with China to safeguard their empire from the impending dangers. From the Annals of the Tang dynasty, it seems that Kashmir and China had close diplomatic relations for they looked at each other as natural allies against the emergence of any new power on their borders. The Tang Annals make a mention of Chandrapida (*Tchen-to-lo-pi-li*) of Kashmir who applied in 713 CE to the Chinese emperor for aid against the Arabs.[77] We know that the Arabs were posing a serious threat to Kashmir at that time. In 713 CE when Muhammad ibn al-Qasim, the Arab general, occupied Multan, he marched towards the frontier of Kashmir called *Panj Nihayat*.[78] The threat to Kashmir was averted as the general was recalled by the Caliph Walid (705–715) to his court.[79] Considering the threat of Arab invasion, Chandrapida's appeal to China for help makes sense. Indeed, there is chronological compatibility between the threat and the request. The Annals also record that about the year 720, the emperor granted Chandrapida the title of king[80] pointing to further improvement in their mutual friendly relations. Even Lalitaditya approached the Chinese for military help against the powerful Tibetans when Lalitaditya's forces were exhausted after prolonged Indian campaigns. According to the Tang Annals, Muktapida Lalitaditya (*Mu-to-pi*) sent a diplomatic mission to China during the reign of Emperor Hiuen Tsang (713–755 CE), requesting for an alliance against the Tibetans, and the dispatch of a Chinese auxiliary force, which was to encamp in the midst of his country on the shores of the Mahapadma Lake[81] (the Vular Lake). Lalitaditya offered to find provisions for an army of 200,000 men and reported that in alliance with the king of central India, he had blocked the five routes of Tibet.[82]

Karkota kings also believed that no empire can be built and sustained without ensuring internal stability. This is clear from an unambiguous observation made by the "composite author" of the NP: "the strongly rooted kings are destroyed here due to internal dissensions." It is therefore quite natural to see them treating all the religions and beliefs equally, the details of which have been given elsewhere in this chapter.

The 28 years' glorious rule of the illustrious founder of Utpala dynasty, Avantivarman (855–883 CE), is not known for military exploits; instead, it is distinguishingly famous for having brought immense economic prosperity to Kashmir by enormously increasing the agricultural produce of the country following the construction of a network of canals, reclamation of water-logged areas, and establishment of a huge number of new rural settlements, dredging Jhelum and reinforcing its banks to prevent the occurrence of floods.[83] After giving a detailed account of the work done by Avantivarman's famous irrigation and flood control engineer, Suyya, whom Kalhan calls Lord of Food (*annapati*), the poet-chronicler says:

> Neither Kāsyapa nor Samkarşaṇa (Bhalabhadra) bestowed those benefits which the virtuous Suyya produced with ease in that land. Suyya who possessed accumulated religious merits, achieved in a single birth that holy work which Vişṇu accomplished in four incarnations, viz. the raising of the earth from the water, the granting of it to worthy Brahmans, the construction of stone dykes in the water, and the subjugation of the [Nāga] Kāliya. There, where previously from the beginning of things the purchase price of a Khāri rice was two hundred Dinnaras in times of great abundance, in that very

> land of Kaśmīr henceforth-O wonder! – the Khari of rice came to be bought for thirty-six Dinnāras.[84]

As a result of the financial prosperity of the kingdom, the king could devote himself to developing the other basic structures of the empire, especially the human resource.[85]

Unlike Avantivarman, his son and successor, Samkaravarman (883–902 CE) embarked on the policy of conquests. *Rājataraṅgiṇī* gives an exaggerated account of the numerical strength of his army, which was further swelled "from place to place by the troops of feudatory chiefs."[86] Yet, the narrative of actual conquests seems a matter-of-fact account as the victorious campaigns remained restricted within the neighbouring polities. According to Kalhana, he defeated the ruler of Trigarta (Kangra) and the ruler of Gurjara, (Gujarat, the Punjab),[87] who "gave up to him humbly the Takka land preserving his own country."[88] From the account of Kalhana, it seems that during the period of Samkaravarman, the neighbouring territories of Kashmir extending from Kangra to the Punjab and the territories on the banks of the Indus (Sindhu) up to Urasa (Hazara)[89] were again re-conquered and made tributaries of Kashmir. Samkaravarman's policy of retrenchment and the imposition of new taxes including 13 kinds of corvée exacted from the villagers for carrying loads of the army clearly show that these military exploits affected adversely the state exchequer and the common people.[90] However, the Utpalas maintained the supremacy of the kingdom of Kashmir over its neighbouring territories. During the reign of Gopalavarman (902–904), the son and successor of Samkaravarman, the Kashmiri army is seen vanquishing the rebellious Śahi of Udabhāndapura and installing a loyalist, Toramana, on the throne.[91]

It is with the death of Gopalavarman that we, for the first time, learn from Kalhana about the "confederacy" formed by a section of 'feudal barons' called Tantrians who were "strong enough to punish or favour the rulers of this [land]."[92] And it is also for the first time, that unlike the past, we find the ruler "relying on the Ekangas (another group of feudal barons) and the goodwill of the Tantrians,"[93] for ruling the country. This turn in the kingship of Kashmir created such a chaos that hardly any ruler could restore peace till Kashmir was devastated by the Mongol invasion in 1320 CE. Consumed by the internal revolts, no ruler could evidently assume the stature of the "universal conqueror" which, though being the wish of Kalhana, could not be ascribed to any ruler from the beginning of the tenth century onwards. The Kashmir *mandala* was shrunk within the confines of its mountain ramparts, occasionally seeking allegiance from the petty rulers ruling the medley of small principalities situated in the mountains around the valley. They were, however, a constant source of trouble for Kashmir. That is why Kalhana *inter alia* puts these words in the mouth of Lalitaditya which he supposedly told his successors for maintaining the independence of the kingdom.

> Those who dwell there in the [mountains] difficult of access, should be punished, even if they give no offence, because, sheltered by their fastness, they are difficult to break up if they have (once) accumulated wealth.[94]

Nonetheless, it goes to the credit of rulers who, despite being confronted by recurrent revolts and rebellions, maintained the policy of developing the different sectors of the mandala by drawing on the resources of immediate and distant neighbours besides patronising the local talent. As a result, Kashmir became a great centre of learning, which ushered in a new era of "cultural circulation" in which Kashmir became an imitable model. And what is no less important is that, although from the beginning of the eleventh century the kingdom was surrounded by a "hostile" neighbour who supposedly was also culturally "the Other," the Kashmiri rajas learnt to be practical, threw the borders open and maintained the age-old commercial and cultural relations with their neighbours, even receiving them with open arms to enrich the country from their resources. The result was that towards the mid-twelfth century, Kalhana found Kashmir unique in intellectual and material prosperity which, to borrow his poetic language, "could not be found even in heaven,'[95] though he was aware of the imminent decline of Kashmir owing to 'internal dissensions."[96]

Kashmir as a Centre of Learning

A distinctive feature of early Kashmir which, like its natural beauty, became a defining character of its identity, regardless of the vicissitudes of history, was its remarkable excellence in learning, thanks to the phenomenal patronage of the rulers. The state patronage not only promoted the local talent but also attracted the talent from outside making the valley a hub of great minds. In the mid twelfth century, when Kashmir was riven with internal conflicts, Kalhana referred with pride to some special attributes of Kashmir, and he gave learning the first place among them:

> Learning, lofty houses, saffron, icy water and grapes; things that even in heaven are difficult to find, are common here.[97]

Hiuen Tsang, who visited Kashmir more than 500 years before Kalhana, was also impressed by its high culture of learning. He recorded: "They love learning and are well instructed. Since centuries learning has been held in great respect in this kingdom."[98] In fact, it was because Kashmir was widely known as a great centre of Buddhist learning that attracted this famous pilgrim to Kashmir during the early years of Karkota rule and he stayed there for two full years—a longer halt than any other place which he visited during his 16 years' wandering throughout the whole length of India and Central Asia.[99] He dwells with evident pleasure on the recollection of the learned conferences with the Kashmiri Buddhist scholars, though at the time of Hiuen Tsang's visit to Kashmir, it was not Buddhism but Brahmanism which, according to him, was the 'sole thought' of the Kashmiri rulers and the people at large.[100]

After Hiuen Tsiang's visit, we not only notice a further development in the field of learning, but it entered into a golden era. The number of institutions and scholars multiplied, the quality of scholarship improved and the field of study diversified.[101] True, the basic cause of this unprecedented development was the rulers' passion to see Kashmir as a great seat of learning; nonetheless, the emergence of Kashmir as a prosperous empire lubricated the process. It attracted the talent from the neighbouring countries to settle in the greener pasture—Kashmir—and flourish under the patronage of its knowledge-loving kings. The zeal of the rulers to develop every branch of knowledge can be gauged by the fact that, according to Kalhana, Lalitaditya "collected from [different] countries various wise men, as the wind [collects] masses of full-blown flowers from the trees."[102] Similarly the scholar-king, Jayapida "searched for and collected all scholars to such an extent" that, in the language of the poet-chronicler, "in the lands of other kings there was a dearth of learned men."[103]

Not only religious learning flourished on account of the liberal grant of *agraharas* the Karkota rulers endowed upon the brahmanas, bikshus, and their institutions, but also Kashmir became a great centre of litterateurs, grammarians, scholars of poetics, architects, civil engineers, artisans, craftsmen, physicians, scholars of law and experts in public administration.[104] *Rājataraṅgiṇī's* celebration of the achievements of some selected rulers clearly demonstrates that among the core components of royal obligations, distinction and civility was the promotion of learning. It was as much important for the ruler to develop the country technologically and promote secular and religious learning as it was to ensure political stability and social and spiritual order. Referring to the relationship between culture and power in Kashmir, Sheldon Pollock says,

> clearly for Kalhana at least the stories of the kings Abhimanyu and Jayapida . . . convey a sense of the central place of royal patronage in the fostering of systematic Sanskrit knowledge especially philological knowledge. They thus testify to the larger paradigm at work concerning the correlation of grammatical and political correctness.[105]

No wonder then, Kashmir became the land of Śarada (the goddess of learning). Also, it was because of the patronage extended to the connoisseurs of the then advanced architecture and civil engineering that it became possible to construct great stone temples and cities. The experts of irrigation technology introduced lift irrigation worked out with water wheels;[106] the astronomers installed an observatory;[107] the physicians of repute from other countries were given almost the status of ministers;[108] the genius in law framed comprehensive law codes[109] and the veterans in public administration were imported from outside to introduce new institutions as well as to man them.[110]

Jayapida—the scholar-king—was the leading Karkota ruler who showed an exceptional interest in making Kashmir a great centre of learning. Although Kalhana criticises Jayapida for revoking some *agraharas* and imposing land revenue on *agrahara* grantees,[111] he fully acknowledges his contribution to learning. From Kalhana it seems that notwithstanding Kashmir's fame as the 'homeland' of knowledge, yet at the time Jayapida took over as the ruler of Kashmir, it (knowledge) had taken 'cover in far-off lands,' that is, the position of Kashmir as a distinctive cultural centre was lost to other lands. And so had happened to the scholarly tradition of studying Patanjali's *Mahabhasya*, to the extent that "The king recruited exegetes from abroad to reinstate the text [curiously] in the place where it belongs."[112] The king not only brought from abroad competent expositors for rejuvenating the study of Patanjali's *Mahabhasya*,[113] but he himself also received instructions from a master of grammatical science called Kṣīra;[114] and he attained such a position as a scholar that he came to be called 'Pandita Jayapida' (learned Jayapida).[115] Writing in the mid-twelfth century, Kalhana says, "So much [great] was his fame from the title of scholar than from that of king, that notwithstanding his various faults it has not faded like other [things] subject to time."[116] Jayapida had such a passion for making Kashmir a great centre of learning that he almost hunted for scholars in the whole neighbourhood of Kashmir and attracted so large a number of them to serve in Kashmir that, according to Kalhana, it caused "dearth of learned men" in the "lands of other kings."[117]

According to Kalhana Jayapida honoured the scholars so much that even the princes approached them for getting positions in the government.

As the king was attached to the learned, the princes who came to serve him and desired to reach his presence frequented the houses of scholars.[118]

Certainly, Jayapida is the first known ruler of Kashmir who attached maximum value to scholarship making it a top priority of the state programme, massively funded and personally "led by the king giving Kashmir," in the words of Yigal Bronner, "a cultural hegemony."[119] This is *inter alia* evident from the fact that the king bestowed coveted positions upon the scholars and paid them huge salaries. Impressed with the scholarship of Thakkaya, the king co-opted him into his staff and "made him prosper."[120] Bhatta

Udbhatta, "the writer on poetics, was appointed king's Sabhapati (Chief Pandit) with a daily allowance of one lakh dīnnāras."[121] Damodragupta, a famous poet, was his chief councillor.[122] Vamana, the grammarian and "others [were] his ministers." And Monaratta, Sankhadanta, Cataka and Samdhimat were his court poets.[123] According to Kalhana, Jayapida was so much interested to see legal luminaries coming from foreign countries to his kingdom that "when he saw in his dream the sun rise in the west, he thought that [some] exalted teacher of law had luckily entered his land."[124] About the steady stream of scholars during the period of Jayapida and their diversity and quality, Bronner writes:

> [T]he inflow of academics was so massive that it left all other lands with an acute brain drain (*vidvaddurbhiksa*). Indeed, the list of scholars and authors appointed and recruited by Jayāpīda stands out in quantity, quality and diversity. Consider, in this context, the boost to the disciplines of grammar and logic given by Kṣīra and Dharmottara, respectively, the thriving of poetry – note the plethora of poet laureats named by Kalhana and the powerful position enjoyed by Damodra Gupta, whose *The Madam's School of Thought* (*Kuttanimata*) is given a mention of honour – and the growing preeminence of literary theory under the leadership of Vāmana and, more important, Bhatta Udbhata, who is made 'president of the Royal Academy' (*sabhā* pati) and whose profound impact on Sanskrit poetics is yet to be acknowledged by modern scholars.[125]

Luther Obrock also expressed his wonder over the extraordinary passion Jayapida demonstrated in making Kashmir a great centre of learning.

He lures scholars from all over the Sanskrit-speaking world offering huge salaries and royal prestige. The roster of the intellectuals in his employ reads like a who's who of ninth-century South Asian letters: the Buddhist logician Dharmottara, the rhetorician Udbhaṭa and satirical poet Damodara are among the most famous. His lack of Kannauj resonates in Kashmir as he aggressively fosters his own court as the new centre of Sanskritic culture. What Yaśovarman's court was to eighth-century India with such luminaries as Bhavabhūti and Vākpatirāja, so was Kashmir to become under the patronage of Jayāpīḍa.[126]

As a matter of fact, due to favourable courtly milieus of the Karkota rulers in general and Jayapida in particular, Kashmir became an international centre of learning. On the authority of a contemporary source, Louis Massignon writes:

> Qashmir [Kashmir], under the Karkutaka [Karkota] dynasty, had become an important intellectual center where Hindus and Turkish

> Buddhists of the neighbouring and allied state of Gandhara mingled with foreign scholars.[127]

It is, therefore, no accident that in Kashmir "the fervid creativity in the production of literary theory that was to have such a powerful influence across all of India" began from the eighth century.[128]

Like Lalitaditya and Jayapida, Avantivarman, the illustrious founder of the Utpala dynasty, was a great patron of learning. He and his prime minister, Sura, were so much passionate to promote learning that he made the leading scholars of the time members of the King's court. Writing with great delight, Kalhana says:

> The minister Sūra, by honouring learned men with a seat in the [King's] Sabha, caused learning, whose flow had been interrupted, to descend [again] upon this land. The scholars, who were granted great fortunes and high honours, proceeded to the Sabha in vehicles (litters) worthy of kings.[129]

Indeed, it was a commonplace occurrence in ancient and medieval times that the fame of a ruler as a patron of learning attracted scholars from distant lands to his court. In the words of a medieval Sanskrit chronicler, such rulers were like 'the Kalpa tree,' who attracted the people of accomplishments "from distant countries like bees."[130] And the same situation prevailed during the period of Avantivarman. Not surprisingly, therefore, Avantivarman's court was humming with the presence of great literary figures and scholars of repute. Of them Kalhana has made a mention of Muktakana, Śivasavamin, Anandavardhana and Ratnakara.[131] While all of them were reputed poets, Anandavardhana's fame rests principally on his celebrated *Dhvanyaloka*, a treatise on the Science of poetics.[132] Other reputed rhetoricians of the period are Rudrata, Mukula and Induraja.[133] That during the period Kashmir attracted scholars, poets and other learned people from different corners of the neighbouring world can be inferred from the fact that Induraja, the famous rhetorician of the time, was actually from Konkan, and he had migrated to Kashmir obviously after hearing the munificence of Kashmiri rulers towards the men of letters.[134] Undoubtedly, the patronage of learning and tolerance of different faiths made Kashmir a popular meeting place for scholars and saints belonging to different countries and beliefs. The author of the celebrated work, *The Passion of al-Hallaj* (originally in French), quotes the contemporary sources saying that the court of Utpala rulers had become a great centre of intellectual debates in which foreign and local scholars took part and held discussions "on the Thura (Torah), the Injīl (Gospels) and the Zābār (Psalms)";[135] not surprisingly, therefore, it was during this period around 895 CE that the famous mystic of Islam, Mansur al Hallaj, visited Kashmir to take benefit of the argumentative environment of Kashmir, though the details of his activities are not known.[136]

It was also during the period of Avantivarman that, according to Kalhana, "Bhatta Kalatta and other Siddhas descended on the earth for the benefit of the people."[137] Bhatta Kallata was the disciple of Vasugupta, the founder of a branch of "Kashmiri Śaivism" called *Spandaśastra*. The work of Bhatta Kallata expresses the secrets of the theory and practice of Śaivism as taught by the Śiva—Sutras supposed to have been revealed to Vasugupta (725–790 CE).

Samkaravarman, the son and successor of Avantivarman, was also a great patron of learning. Two great litterateurs of the period were Bhallata,[138] the author of the well-received work, *Bhallatatasataka* and Jayanta Bhatta,[139] the author of three extant works on *Natyaśaśtra*. As a result of the court patronage, the talent from the neighbouring world continued to pour in—a trend which was further nourished by the liberal mindedness of the ruler. We find a *domba* singer coming to Kashmir "from abroad"[140] and the king taking his two "sweet-eyed" daughters, Hamsi and Nagalata into his seraglio,[141] and even raising Hamsi to the rank of chief queen[142] and her father, Ranga being bestowed with an *agrahara* grant to the much resentment of the orthodox brahmanas.[143]

In 939 CE, the Utpala dynasty came to an end, and in the absence of any scion from the royal line, the wife of the preceding king recommended one Yaśaśkara, her supposed son for the throne.[144] The brahmanas, after being impressed by his eloquence, he had learnt by studying "abroad" for many years, approved his candidature.[145] Having himself received education from 'abroad' Yaśaśkara showed considerable interest in making Kashmir an international centre in Hindu learning. To facilitate the study of foreign scholars and students in Kashmir, Yaśaśkara built grand *māthas* to provide free boarding and lodging to them. About one such *mātha,* Kalhana says:

> The king being fond of endowments, built on a piece of land which had belonged to his father, a *Matha* for students from Aryadeśa who were devoting themselves to [the acquisition of] knowledge.[146]

The extraordinary position of this *matha* can be inferred from the fact that its superintendent was bestowed with royal insignia "with the exception of mint-dies (*tanka*) and the royal seraglio."[147]

According to Rajatarangini, Yaśaśkara also settled some Brahmins on the banks of Vitasta and bestowed upon them *agraharas:*

> On the banks of the Vitasta, he granted to brahmanas 55 agraharas furnished with various implements.[148]

These brahmanas were in all probability scholars of repute from Aryadeśa where Yaśaśkara had developed personal connections during his studies.

This is besides the fact that Yaśaśkara's fame as a great patron of learning would have by itself attracted the fortune seekers from different corners to settle in Kashmir.

Didda's long rule of around 50 years (958–1006), including the period of her regency, is remarkably known for maintaining the position of Kashmir as an international centre of higher learning. This is indicated by her construction of maṭhas and monasteries for the accommodation of "foreign" students:

> She (Didda) built further the [temple of Viṣṇu] Diddasvamin, together with Diddapura and a *Maṭha* for the residence of people from Madhyadeśa, Lata (Gujrat) and Saudotra (?). . . . She . . . built a Vihāra with a high quadrangle as an abode for Kaśmīrians and foreigners (daiśika) . . . and a *Maṭha* for the residence of foreign Brahmans.[149]

The earlier phase of Harśa's reign (1089–1101) has been portrayed by Kalhana as the period of efflorescence in different languages, poetry, music, dance, dress, cosmetics, coiffure, court etiquettes, delivery of justice, pleasure gardens and the like thanks to Harśa's love for learning, extraordinary talent in 'all sciences of knowledge', passion for glamour, beauty and entertainment; and consequently his hunt for talent and search for his likings in other cultures. Kalhana repeatedly mentions Harśa's distinguishing abilities in the field of knowledge:

> Knowing all languages, a good poet in all tongues, and as a depository of all learning, he became famous even in other countries. . . . Surely, not even Brahaspati is able to name clearly all the sciences in which he was versed. Even to this day, if one of the songs which he composed for the voice, is heard, tears roll on the eye-lashes even of his enemies.[150]

Bilhana, the famous poet of the time, whose reputation spread to far-off lands, and was patronised by the rulers of Karnataka, also praised Harśa for his poetic skills by which he "surpassed even Srihara."[151] He also refers to his power of composing sweet songs in all languages.[152] As a result of his passion for certain arts in particular and love for learning in general, Harśa patronised with uncommon liberality the scholars, poets, singers, dancers and others "distinguished for good qualities"—the reputation which spread to distant lands and which, according to Kalhana, made Bilhana to repent for having left his country even though he was holding a high position and was held in high esteem by the Chalukya king, Vikramaditya Tribhuvanamalla famous as Parmadi:

> The king [Harśa], who was the crest- jewel of the learned, adorned men of learning with jewels, and bestowed upon them the privileges

> of [using] litters, horses, parasols etc. Bilhana, who had left Kaśmir in the reign of King Kalaśa, had been made by Parmādi, the lord of Karnāta, his Chief Pandit (*Vidyapati*) and when travelling on elephants through the hill-country of Karnata, his parasol was borne aloft before the king. When he heard that the liberal Harśa was like a kinsman to true poets, he thought even so great a splendour a deception.[153]

The leading courtiers of Harśa, according to Kalhana, were the scholars, poets, musicians and singers, and the main activity of his court was "attending meetings of learned men, musical performances and dances."[154] True, Harśa patronised all those who possessed some kind of distinguished ability which attracted a variety of talent from different countries. To quote Kalhana:

> He took [into his service and] assigned salaries to persons distinguished for good qualities and valour who had arrived from various countries, and whom his greedy father had left unnoticed.[155]

Among the later rulers covered by *Rājataraṅgiṇī*, Kalhana specially mentions Jayasimha, because not only he ruled for a pretty long time (1128–1149 CE), but, more so, he also showed remarkable interest in state-building, especially in promoting learning. He bestowed hereditary land grants of considerable value on the scholars of repute, and even constructed spacious houses for them.

> From morning to evening one does not see him do one act for which men of experience do not give the direction. In the black darkness of ignorance, learning had shown forth at intervals in the passing lightning flashes of fortune [coming] from such clouds as Jayapida and other [royal patrons]. He, however, has given permanent brilliancy to the picture of his virtue which is of wondrous variety, by bestowing wealth, which lasts like the radiant light of a jewel. He has made scholars and their descendants owners, as long as the planets, the sun and moon should last, of villages possessing an abundance of unimpaired fields. The houses he has constructed for men of learning raise their terraces to such height that the Seven Ṛṣis (the Great Bear) come to see them as they are towering above their heads.[156]

Considering the enviable patronage extended by the rulers to education and scholarship, it is not difficult to understand why Kashmir became a great seat of learning, and thus came to be venerated as "Śardadeśa" (the land of the goddesses of learning) and 'Saraswati' (goddess of knowledge).

In the beginning of the eleventh century, the renowned Muslim scholar, Al-Biruni, found only two great centres of "Hindu learning" in India. One was Kashmir and the other, Banaras.[157] Al-Biruni is also supported by Damodaragupta, the author of *Kuttanimata* who, however, mentions three centres of learning—Kashmir, Banaras and Patliputra—"one travels for the sake of learning."[158] Writing around the year 1087 CE at the court of Chalukya king, Vikramaditya VI, in Kalyana (northeastern Karnataka), the famous Kashmiri peripatetic Pandit and author, Bilhana[159] wrote with pride, "It seems that those who really delight in poetry are close kin to the saffron flower, for I have not seen a trace of them anywhere else since I left Kashmir, Saraswati's country."[160] Around 63 years after Bilhana in 1149–1150, the celebrated historian of Kashmir, Kalhana, wrote with the same pride about the exceptional greatness of Kashmir in the field of learning: "Learning, lofty houses, saffron, ice water and grapes: things that even in heaven are difficult to find are common here."[161] This was not merely a poetic conceit. Kashmir had achieved such a distinctive position as a centre of excellence in the Sanskrit cosmopolis that the outside scholars would consider it a privilege to receive Saraswati's seal of approval. We are even told that the celebrated poet Srihara came to Kashmir for seeking the acceptance of his poem.[162] Al-Biruni also furnishes similar information in the context of Kashmir's distinguished position in grammatical science, which, "has always been a focal point of study in Kashmir."[163]

> I have been told that the last mentioned author [Ugrabhūti, the author of *S'ishyāhitdvritti*] was the teacher and instructor of Shah Anandapala, the son of Jayapala, who ruled in our time. After having composed the book he sent it to Kashmir, but the people there did not adopt it, being in such things haughtily conservative. Now he complained of this to the Shah, and the Shah, in accordance with the duty of a pupil towards his master, promised him to make him attain his wish. So he gave orders to send two lakh dirham and presents of a similar value to Kashmir to be distributed among those who studied this book. The book became the fashion and highly prized.[164]

It is also interesting to learn from Al-Biruni that the first person who undertook the great task of explaining the *Veda* and committing it to writing was a Kashmiri brahmana:

> They did not allow the *Veda* to be committed to writing, because it is recited according to certain modulations, and they, therefore, avoid the use of pen, since it is likely to cause some error, and may occasion an addition or a defect in the written text. In consequence it has happened that they have several times forgotten the *Veda* and lost it. . . . This is the reason why, not long before our time,

> Vasukra, a native of Kashmir, a famous Brahman has of his own account undertaken the task of explaining the *Veda* and committing it to writing. He has taken on himself a task from which everybody else would have recoiled, but he carried it out because he was afraid that the *Veda* might be forgotten . . .[165]

This statement about the mastery of Kashmiri brahmanas over the Vedas is also corroborated by *NP*, which calls the Kashmiri brahmanas *Vedavedangaparaga*.[166]

Al-Biruni's sources credit Kashmir for having been the originator of the famous alphabet *Siddhamatrika*:

> The most generally known alphabet (of India) is called Siddhamatrika, which is considered by some as originating from Kashmir.[167]

Kashmiris had also devised their own calendar. Al-Biruni made a thorough study of this what he calls "Kashmiri calendar."[168] This calendar had achieved such a respectability that the people of Multan had also adopted it.[169]

Another innovation of Kashmiris was their own numerical signs:

> The people of Kashmir mark the single leaves of their books with figures which look like drawing or like the Chinese characters, the meaning of which can be learned by a very long practice.[170]

No less distinctiveness of Kashmir in the field of learning was that it produced the first work of real history in South Asia in the middle of the twelfth century.

Maintaining its glorious history of making path-breaking contributions to philosophy, language and literature, Kashmir became 'home to a series of revolutions in systematic thought (*śāstra*) and literature (*kaya*) both' from the middle of the ninth century. It is therefore no wonder that lovers of learning flocked to Kashmir in large numbers and Kashmiri authors and their texts were much sought after in different parts of the subcontinent, thanks to courtly milieus—the glamorous centres of cultural life—and the multitude of different channels of cultural flows. The great master-rhetoricians, grammarians and philosophers, namely, Vamana, Rudrata, Udbhata, Mammata, Ruyyaka, Bhatta Tauta, Jayanta Bhatta, Anandavardhana, Abhinavagupta, Mankha, Bilhana and Kṣemandra elevated the position of Kashmir as a great centre of highly sophisticated philosophico-linguistic theories, such as dhavāni, the science of poetics (*alamkārāśāstra*), the model poetry and Śiva philosophy. In the words of Sheldon Pollock, "A new philosophical-religious aesthetics was elaborated by the eleventh century Kashmiri scholars, namely, Bhatta Nayaka, Bhatta Tauta and Abhinavagupta, to name a few, which transformed Sanskrit literary theory fundamentally and permanently."[171]

Struck by the immense contribution of Kashmir to Sanskrit learning John Nemec says, "Indeed the bibliography of Kashmiri contributions, one feels, is practically asymptotic to that of premodern Sanskrit learning *tout court*."[172] The contribution of Kashmiri scholars "cover the gamut of fields of Sanskrit learning from Dharmaśāstra to philosophical writings to *vyākaraṇa* and other technical literatures, to works of *belles letters* in a range of genres, and, of particular note, to the *alaṃkāraśāstra*."[173]

Though not fully in agreement with Bilhana's "melancholy verse," the poet included in his *Vikramāṅkadevacarita* to demonstrate unparalleled position of Kashmir in the field of learning,[174] Whitney Cox admits that the "fervid literary creativity in the Southern peninsula" from the late eleventh century to the late thirteenth century was largely the contribution of the learned culture of the valley of Kashmir disseminated in the Peninsula by both Kashmiri scholars, poets and traders and by the southerners themselves who visited Kashmir to learn at the feet of its renowned Pandits and gurus, and to procure the copies of the texts produced in the Saraswati's country:

> We can feel some empathy for Bilhana, still, he was not being entirely fair, or accurate. The late eleventh century was a time of fervid literary creativity in the southern peninsula; but more important, this was a creativity fueled in a great many ways by the learned culture of the Valley of Kashmir itself. Though we know more about Bilhana's career than perhaps any other (and though he was a poet of genius), he was only a single player in the much wider drama of the dissemination of this culture. The abundant surviving evidence of this dissemination presents us with a centuries-long collective effort to import and domesticate the many discrete sectors of the learned culture of Kashmir. Authors like Bilhana found themselves and their works met with interest throughout the peninsula, while in turn southerners made the long trek northward to study and return with fresh copies of the texts they studied there.[175]

Cox further says that Kashmiri texts were as actively incorporated by authors writing in the Dravidian Vernaculars as they were by those working exclusively in Sanskrit. The reputation of Kashmir as a great centre of Sanskrit teaching continued till the thirteenth century. It is therefore no wonder that "around the turn of the twelfth century a great number of recently composed Kashmirian texts" were studied in the South.[176] The presence of a huge number of these texts in the South and their much more serious readership in the peninsula in comparison to their place of origin can be gleaned from the fact that the texts of Kashmiri origin on poetics and Śaiva religion, which are not now extant in the north, are available in the South. That these texts were much more intensively studied in the South than the "Kashmirian hot house" is evident from their receptions and adaptations by the southern authors aptly termed by Cox in a fascinating trope, *Saffron in the Rasam*. It must, however, be mentioned that although the South was more indebted to the contribution made by Kashmir to philosophy, literary theory and literature, some of the scholarly productions at the southern hands, of course, composed by reworking of Kashmiri sources in a self-conscious way, also attracted the attention of the Kashmiri scholars; and these were transformed in the same way as was done by the authors of the South. Among them mention may be made of *Mahārthamanjarī* by Mahesvarānanda composed in Chidambaram (Tamil Nadu) in the later part of the thirteenth century on Śiva religion:

> Unlike the great majority of South Indian Sanskrit works of this period, the MM [*Mahārthamañjarī*] managed to find an audience in the far North, in fact in Kashmir itself, an audience that produced the text many times over – of the surprisingly large number of manuscripts that survive of the MM, most are from Kashmir, written in either the Śāradā script or the local version of Devanagari. What other manuscripts survive are from the far South and no place else to my knowledge (there are no Gujarati, say, or Bengali script manuscripts). And these two regions, Kashmir and the deep South, are home to two massively different versions of the *Mahārthamañjarī*, a northern and a southern recension.[177]

Before concluding, it is necessary to mention that the Ghaznavid and Ghurid conquests of India did not have any adverse impact on Kashmir's distinguished position as a centre of learning; instead, it left a positive impact on the learning landscape of Kashmir in that, according to Al-Biruni, "Hindu Sciences have retired from those parts of the country conquered by us [the Muslims] and have fled to places which our hand cannot yet reach, to Kashmir, Banaras, and other places."[178] This is also substantiated by Sheldon Pollock. He says:

> In Kashmir . . . the production of most major forms of Sanskrit court poetry ceased after the twelfth century, but this seems to have resulted from internal processes of civic disintegration unrelated to the Central Asian powers, whose control over the Kashmir Valley was not consolidated until the fifteenth century, who infact sought thereafter, with only mixed success, to revitalize Sanskrit culture.[179]

Alongside having the fame of being a great centre of Hindu learning, Kashmir was also famous as a great seat of Buddhist learning. Though the Karkotas were Vaiṣṇavas, they were fairly disposed to all faiths, including Buddhism. Together with constructing temples and mathas, they also built vihāras and monasteries.[180] The result was that Kashmir saw the rejuvenation of Buddhism, which had begun during the later Huns and received further fillip at the hands of the Karkotas attracting the Chinese lovers of Buddhist learning to Kashmir. The Emperor of the Yang of the Sui dynasty (605–616 CE) sent a mission to Central Asia and India. The mission was entrusted to Weijie (Wei-tsie) and Du Xingman (Tu Hsing-man). We are told that they went to India by the upland route and visited, besides various kingdoms of Central Asia, a number of places in India including Kashmir.[181] Unfortunately, the account of their journey is not extant. Hiuen Tsang and Ou-k'ong considered their visits to India incomplete without making an academic and spiritual sojourn to Kashmir. They spent there a good deal of time. Hiuen Tsang stayed for two years and Ou-k'ong stayed for four years to satisfy their yearnings for higher studies at the feet of Kashmiri scholars.[182] Significantly, they were much impressed by the Kashmiris' love of learning and the great achievements they had made in the field.[183] Indeed, in the words of Walter Slaje, "from the seventh to the tenth centuries, Kashmir exercised a strong attraction for pilgrims from central Asia and from east Asia, when also the production of logico-epistemological works and commentaries reached its peak in this country."[184] Slaje also quotes a Central Asian itinerary, drawn on in the tenth century, which mentions an overwhelming presence of Buddhist sites on the routes from Tarim Basin to Srinagar (*Adhisthana*). About the Buddhist monasteries in Srinagar at that time, this Khotanese itinerary by an anonymous contemporary says, "there is a large monastery with a *dharmaraja* (stupa) and 500 rock cells, smaller monasteries are countless."[185]

Besides attracting the lovers of learning to Kashmir, the Buddhist monks of Kashmir took Buddhism to China, Khotan, Kutch and Tibet; translated the Buddhist texts into Chinese and other languages, leaving a lasting impact on these lands besides considerably expanding the geographical boundaries of the Buddhist creed. It is quite probable that the same relationship would have been obtained between Kashmir and Afghanistan, where Buddhism had become the dominant tradition by the time of Karkotas. This is substantiated by a passing reference in the *Itinerary* of Ou-k'ong mentioning that a number of Buddhist sacred places were founded in Kashmir by the royal family of the Tou-kiue (Turks).[186] Though it is impossible to say with certainty where this Turkish dynasty ruled, one is tempted to think of the area from Tukharistan through Kabul Valley to Upper Indus. Lalitaditya's military adventures in Central Asia and his fame as a tolerant ruler also accounted for the influx of talent from Central Asia. It is remarkable that his prime minister was a Tukharian Buddhist,[187] and many of his leading ministers were Śahis.[188]

The scholarly and missionary activities of the Kashmiri Buddhist savants in the neighbouring world continued after imperial Karkotas. More importantly, it was during this period that in the spread of

Buddhism in Tibet, the activities of the Kashmiri Buddhist missionaries intensified with no precedence. Indeed, in the context of cultural interaction and borrowings, the relations between Kashmir and Tibet are not older than the seventh century when the king Songtsen Gampo (d. 649) sent his minister, Thonmi Sambhota, to Kashmir to learn writing and adapt it to the notation of the Tibetan language.[189] Since then, Kashmir acted as an unfailing source of inspiration for Tibetan Buddhism. The activities of Kashmiri Buddhists in the propagation and development of Buddhism have been divided into two phases. The first phase is what the Tibetans call "the First Propagation." It started under Songtse Gampo and his successors and continued until the persecution of the Buddhist monks by Glan Dar-ma in 840 or 901. During this phase Kashmiri monks propagated Buddhism and accomplished the enormous task of translating the Buddhist texts into Tibetan.[190] The second phase which began around 980 is called the Later Phase Propagation of the law. During this phase the contribution of Kashmir is distinguished by its role in the diffusion of logic and Vajrayana.[191] Among the most famous Buddhist scholars who went to Tibet, took part in the first and second propagation of Buddhism and translated the Buddhist texts into the Tibetan language in collaboration with Tibetan scholars, mention may be made of Dharmākaradatta (eighth century), Ananta (ninth century), Jinamitra (ninth century), *Dānaśila* (ninth century), *Sraddākaravarman* (tenth century), *Ratnavajra* (tenth century), Guhyaprajna, Noropa, Bodhibhadra, Jnanasribhadra, Janardana, *Lakshmi* (eleventh century), *Subhūtiśriśānti* (eleventh century), Mahājana, Suksmajana, Prahitabhadra, Bhavjaraja, Kumarasri, Tilakalasa, Kanakavarman (eleventh century), Jayananda, Kumaraprajna, Gunākaraśribhadra, Sugataśri (eleventh to twelfth century), Śākyaśribhadra, Śākyaśri, Sarvajñāśriraksita and Dharmādhara.[192]

Since Tibetan Buddhism, especially that of western Tibet (which then included most of Ladakh, Zanskar and portions of Himachal Pradesh), was largely inspired by Kashmiri Buddhism, it is no wonder that, according to the famous art historian, Pratapaditya Pal, there is so close similarity between Tibetan wood and metal sculpture and the stone and metal sculpture of Kashmir that it is difficult to distinguish them from each other.[193] Pal has no doubt that the sculptors of these art objects were either Kashmiri artists or those who were influenced by the Kashmiri art. To illustrate his view, he quotes wood Maitrya (eleventh century Ladakh), exquisitely carved entrance to the Dukhang (eleventh century, Alchi Ladakh) and the like. Of the bronzes, Pal cites the bodhisattva in brass (western Tibet (eleventh century)) in the Rockefeller collection, spirited representation of a yama or yamari, a charming goddess and a magic dragger showing strong Kashmiri influences. Pal also discerns influences of Kashmiri style paintings on the surviving murals in the monasteries of Ladakh, western Tibet and Himachal Pradesh.

While there is no doubt that court patronage played a larger role in making Kashmir a reputed centre of learning, many factors helped to accomplish this royal project. Among these were relative peace (till the beginning of twelfth century), contact, circulation, toleration and material prosperity owing to global trade.[194]

Commercial Contacts

Despite being surrounded by a ring of mountain ramparts, Kashmir had commercial relations with distant and neighbouring territories thanks to a number of passes which gave passage to and from the valley to meet the demands for imports and exports. The bordering territories of Kashmir were dotted with mercantile emporia through which Kashmir was commercially connected with the globe. Of these important trade entrepots, mention may be made of Leh towards the east; Askardo, Gilgit and Hunza towards the north; Multan towards the west; and Taxila, Bust, Ghazni, Bamiyan, Kabul and Balkh towards the north-west.[195] These frontier towns, which were conduits for raw materials, high value goods and human agents, ultimately connected Kashmir with Central Asia, west Asia, China, Russia and Europe. From the Indus Valley, access could be had more direct to the sea routes. Undoubtedly, Sind was a transregional nexus before 1000 CE when the sultans of Ghazni reconfigured the cultural and political landscape of the eastern Islamic world.[196] Kashmir's maritime connections through Sind is perhaps borne out by the arrival of great mystic of Islam, Mansur Al-Hallaj, via Daybul around 895 CE to take part in religious debates for which the Kashmir's reputation had reached far and wide.[197] The relation between commercial networks and the flow of religious ideas and their human carriers is underlined by Finbarr Flood on the basis of profuse contemporary evidence:

> There can be little doubt that maritime connections between Sind, Egypt and the Persian Gulf played a role in these realignments [sectarian changes in Arab Sind] facilitating the relatively rapid transmission of potentially seditious ideas and the human agents who propagated them.[198]

It is true that the political relations between Kashmir and its borderlands were far from stable during the period of our study, but the vagaries in political relationships had little impact on the flow of goods and human agents. The abortive bids of the Arabs to conquer Kashmir aroused equal and opposite reaction in Kashmir as we shall see in the following pages. But the situation normalised when the Arabs gave up incursions against the valley. The Kashmiri rajas reciprocated the gesture by providing all conceivable facilities to the Muslim merchants, who were operating in the neighbouring commercial towns of Kashmir, to lure them to conduct Kashmir's external trade. We are told that the neighbouring Kabul was a typical city populated as it was by Muslims, Jews and Hinduwān (Indians). Most of them were traders involved in transregional trade. Same is also true of the coastal areas of Sind.[199] Evidently, the composition of the mercantile community of the other commercial towns on the route stretching from Balkh to Kabul, Gardez and Ghazni through the Gomal Pass to the Indus Valley would have been the same as in Kabul and Sind. According to Kalhana, the Karkota king Vajraditya "sold many men to the *Mlecchas* and introduced into the country practices which befitted *Mlecchas*."[200] Clearly, Vajraditya would have prompted some local people to embrace Islam and Judaism so that the mercantile community coming from the neighbouring trading entrepots is encouraged to conduct business without being hampered by any personal inconvenience. The same policy was followed by the *Zamorin* of Calicut.[201] And it is this policy which Kalhana translates as "Vajraditya sold many men to the *Mlecchas*."

That according to *Rājataraṅgiṇī* Vajraditya "introduced into the country practices which befitted the *Mlecchas*" connotes the same religious freedom and other faith-related special facilities, which were globally provided to the traders at that time. The Hindu merchants doing business in the ports of southern Iraq constructed their own shrines and placed an idol of Zun in the Iraqi port cities of Basra and Al-Uballa.[202] Around the same time mercantile communities of Hindus and Muslims were constructing temples and mosques in the ports of southeastern China.[203] The Iraqi and Persian Muslim merchants trading in western India were provided with neighbourhood mosques and Friday congregational mosques.[204] Al-Muqaddasi mentions that the minority Muslim population of both Kabul and Kanauj were administered by an independent authority. Similarly Muslims living under Rashtrakutas were governed by Islamic law and administered by a *qadi*.[205] Being an integral part of the global culture, which treated the mercantile community as a favoured category regardless of ethnic, religious, linguistic and spatial considerations, it comes as no surprise to see the Kashmiri rajas favourably disposed towards the non-local traders in particular and the mercantile community in general, making Kashmir a meeting ground of transborder merchants dealing with variety of goods.[206] *Rājataraṅgiṇī* also refers to the existence of a prosperous section of local traders participating in transregional trade during the eighth, ninth and tenth centuries.[207]

When the Ghaznavids wiped out the Śhahi kingdom and also posed a threat to Kashmir, the Kashmiri rajas again closed the borders not allowing anyone to enter into the valley, not even the Hindus whom they did not know.[208] However, once the threat of invasions was averted, the Kashmiri rulers, like their predecessors, revived their age-old established ties with the neighbouring mercantile emporia. Not surprisingly, therefore, we see a thriving foreign trade and a prosperous local and non-local trading community during the eleventh and first half of twelfth century,[209] the period about which Kalhana furnishes details on the basis of the testimony of his near contemporaries and on what he personally witnessed.

From the mid sixth century when Kashmir emerged as a powerful empire there are, as we have seen in the preceding chapter, clear indications of unprecedented prosperity in Kashmir, expansion and enhancement of transborder networks; and circulation of technology, art, ideas and human agents—all cumulatively suggesting the phenomenal growth in size and volume of Kashmir's foreign trade. Barring coinage (gold and silver coins used for external trade), the evidence to this effect is, however, mainly circumstantial till the assumption of power by the Karkotas. From the Karkota period onwards, there is direct evidence that Kashmir was an important constituent of mercantile cosmopolis comprising India, Middle East, West Asia, China and Central Asia, leading to the emergence of a rich trading community which, besides importing and exporting the goods, acted as a powerful agency of cultural exchange.[210] There were many reasons for this development. The first and the foremost factor in this regard was the emergence of Kashmir as a vast empire extending on the one side with the Silk Route and on the other with the Indian plains. According to the Chinese Annals, at the time of the accession of Karkotas to power, Kashmiri rulers controlled the route from China to Kabul.[211] Hiuen Tsang, who visited Kashmir in 631 CE, found all adjacent territories on the west and south down to the plains, subject to the sway of the king of Kashmir.[212] In expanding the frontiers of Kashmir empire, Lalitaditya broke all previous records. The creation of a vast empire evidently facilitated the movement of goods and offered a vast market to the traders.[213] At the same time, for maintaining the vast empire, a well-equipped large army and a sizeable bureaucracy was a prerequisite. To that end, it was necessary to recruit a large number of people and also to import more horses and elephants as well as raw material for making arms.[214] Clearly, besides directly giving impetus to foreign trade, the creation of a vast empire also increased the number of people with a good purchasing power. The exposure of the ruling class and the soldiers to different cultures during the long period of their conquests in India and Central Asia, about which we have graphic information in *Rājataraṅgiṇī*, created a demand for these peculiarities in Kashmir.[215] What is more important, the riches, which the Kashmiri rulers obtained by plunder and tribute while denuding the neighbourhood, enormously enriched the treasure of Kashmiri rulers leaving a direct impact on boosting trade. The riches, on the one hand, generated the need for luxuries exercising a demand for foreign goods, and, on the other hand, it enabled the ruling class to create the symbols of their grandeur and greatness, increasing the number of buyers or further enhancing their purchasing power. The wealth earned from war also encouraged the rulers to give land grants liberally to religious institutions[216] and their guardians,[217] which expanded as well as enriched the middle and upper classes.

Although we don't have a full picture of the imports and exports of the period, we are informed that in Kashmir there were "merchants of different wares coming from all regions."[218] The sources are replete with the liberal use of gold, silver and copper in making images and statues of gods, goddesses and the Buddha.[219] The richest even possessed lamps formed of jewels (*manidipika*).[220] Since these metals, except for a small quantity of copper, were not locally available, they were obviously imported from neighbouring countries. Importation of war horses from different neighbouring territories, namely, Yarkand, Tukharistan and Kamboja had increased manifold during the period.[221] The use of China silk is corroborated by both the literary and the sculptural evidence.[222] It is, therefore, no wonder that Kashmir had become a meeting ground of foreign merchants. Evidently, the business opportunities in Kashmir were so alluring that some of the foreign merchants made Kashmir as their permanent abode.[223]

The best example of the increasing trading activity of the period is the presence of a prosperous trading class. Nona, a merchant from Rohtak, who subsequently settled in Kashmir, was so rich that even the King Durlabhaka–Pratapaditya II, with whom he had developed a close friendship, was 'astonished by his extravagance and huge wealth.'[224] Kalhana draws a comparative portrayal of the lifestyle of the King and that of the rich merchant, Nona:

> Once the king invited him (Nona) in a friendly way to the royal palace, and honoured him for one day with polite attention such as befit a king. When the king with kindness enquired in the morning as to his being comfortable, he said that the soot from the lamps had caused him headache. When the king was once in turn invited by him, and stopped at the [merchant's] house, he saw [there] at night lamps formed of jewels (*manidipika*).[225]

Nona also built a *matha* called Nonamatha for the accommodation of the brahmanas who visited Kashmir from his homeland—Ruhitaka[226] (Ruhtak).

A section of the trading class became so influential because of enormous wealth that we find some of them entering into the fold of nobility by affecting a serious breach in the citadel of hereditary land-owning dominated ruling class. They were not the ordinary administrators of *vaisyas*; instead, they were the semi-independent rulers ruling the outlying regions. Since it is an important information, it is tempting to quote Kalhana verbatim:

> Nara and other merchants who were in possession of spotless horses and owned villages, ruled *Darvabhisara* and the neighbouring regions, setting up [their own] thrones.[227]

The most important items which figured in the commodity structure of the imports were related to the defence needs, namely, horses, elephants, saddles and iron for making war weapons.

Cavalry[228] was central to the tactical viability of the army of the period, and therefore essential for the strength and stability of the state, which is why the import of horses was the chief item in the commodity structure of Kashmir's foreign trade. This is also borne out by the details we find on cavalry in the sources besides the direct references regarding the drain the import of horses caused on the state exchequer.[229] The *Lokaprakaśa* speaks of a veterinary doctor, a specialist in horse diseases and an expert in the science of horses and cows.[230] It further lists various breeds of horses and their stables.[231] The horse trainers (*Aśvaśaliya*) received largesse from the king.[232] It appears that they purchased horses for the state, maintained them and trained them for their use in wars. The importance of cavalry can also be inferred from the fact that Kṣemendra devotes most of his work, *Nitikalapatru,* to the varieties of horses, their respective qualities, movements, diseases and the heavily armoured cavalry.[233] The rulers of Kashmir were very keen to enrich their army with the best breed of horses and the import of such horses must have cost the state exchequer exorbitantly. Writing about Saussala (1112–1120 CE) Kalhana says, "Being fond of new works and of possessing many horses, the artisans and foreign horse dealers grew rich under him."[234] Both literary and archaeological evidence confirms that the superiority of cavalry determined the political fate of a ruler or those who contested for the throne.[235] *Rājataraṅgiṇī* gives a vivid picture of the use of mounted archery in the battles and a breathtaking number of cavalry forces of the rulers.[236] Therefore, RS Pandit rightly remarks that "the twelfth century was pre-eminently the century of the knight and the steed, both rider and mount being protected by armour in Kashmir as in other lands."[237] Horses were also gifted to the favourites and brahmanas.[238] Regarding the direction of supplies, we have evidence that the war horses were imported from Kamboja (eastern Afghanistan), and Balkh and Badakhshan.[239] There is also mention of yearly import of horses from "Sindhu, Afghanistan, Bactria and Sogdia areas."[240] It seems that a selected breed of horses was imported from Khotan and Yarkand and then was made to inter-breed locally to produce a good stock.[241]

In addition to horses, elephants were also an important part of the army.[242] Lalitaditya and Jayapida maintained a huge elephant corps. Not surprisingly, then, one section of *Nitikalapatru* is devoted to the description of elephants and their characteristics. The areas which were the main source for the supply of elephants were Kalinga, Gauda (Bengal), Vindhya Pradesh and Assam. The Himalayan belt too supplied elephants.[243]

Another important category of imports was precious metals—jewels, gold and silver—and lesser valued metals, namely, copper and iron. To possess as much precious metals as possible either in solid form or in the form of jewellery, images, vessels or currency was a crucial necessity for earning prestige and maintaining authority. Thus hoarding and bequeathing a treasure of precious metals was an important attribute of sovereignty. Citing the reason for not handing over the treasure to his son (Harśa), King Kalasa argues:

> That I have not handed over to you the treasure of your grandfather and my own, for that you should not blame me till you hear the reason. I keep the treasure because I bear in mind that a king without means falls under the will of his own people as well as of his enemies.[244]

It was the fad of the royalty to possess jewels and jewellery, and have images of worship made of jewels. When Kalasa set on fire the stores of his father (king Ananta), only a few things could be recovered of which Kalhana specially mentions a *linga* made of jewel. The queen Suryamati sold it to the wealthiest traders of the time, namely, Takkas for 70 lakhs of dinars.[245] The royalty had become so familiar with the jewels that they could not be deceived about their intrinsic value. Writing about Kalasa, Kalhana says:

> No seller of goods could cheat him as he purchased jewels and other things personally and according to their intrinsic value.[246]

Perhaps Takkas and similar international businessmen traded with jewellery. Jewels were most probably brought from Central Asia, especially from Badakhshan, which continued to be the supplier of jewels to Kashmir into the late medieval period as the term *La'li'Badakhshan* (jewel of Badakhshan) is in common usage in Kashmir. That Kashmir was an important market of jewels is also substantiated by the place name Lal Bazar (the market of jewels) in the outskirts of Shahr'i Khas (historic Srinagar).

In terms of quantity, the most important precious metal, however, was gold purchased by the rulers for storing in their treasure houses, to buy the support of the kingmakers, and to make vessels, jewellery and idols besides giving away their own weights in gold as a work of piety.[247] That building of vast treasures of valuables, and manufacturing of new vessels and jewellery of gold and silver by every new ruler was customary of the time, it is significant to quote Kalhana who seems favourably disposed to the idea of grinding of these valuables into the powder to be distributed by the succeeding ruler among the brahmanas—the practice sanctioned by the brahmanical tradition and legitimised on the basis of notions of purity, pollution, shame, courage, human feelings and piety.

> How is that these kings, when they went to the other world, were not masters of the gold, the supplies, the valuables and other [property]

> which they had stored up in their treasure houses? How is it that the king [who came after them] did not feel ashamed or think of their purity, when they ate from the vessels which the other [kings] had left behind? Who does not feel misgivings when he sees the marks of the names of bygone kings on the big silver bowls [resembling skulls]? Who could delight in necklaces, cursed and unholy, which have been torn from the neck of the dying [king] when the sling of death had passed over it? Who does not feel his heart shrink when he touches those ornaments which former [kings] have left behind, after defiling them in their death struggle with the hot tears of misfortune? Reflecting thus, the king had the gold and other [valuables] ground into powder, and distributed this to Brahmans with his own hands as porridge (*karambhaka*).[248]

When Kalasa set on fire the stores of his father "so much gold and other valuables the king got out from the ground below the heaps" that, according to Kalhana, "its mere mention nowadays [Kalhana's own days] engages our curiosity."[249]

Not only the king but the whole rich section of the society invested in purchasing gold ornaments. Indeed, in early times the acquisition of ornaments in gold and silver was the only popular form of effecting investments. It was the royal privilege to mark the gold according to quality and price which served to bring to light the savings of the people. It was a kind of assay for articles of gold which enabled the officials to estimate the private means of individuals. According to Kalhana, during the reign of Ananta, Haladhara, the prime minister, abolished this practice "knowing that succeeding kings would endeavour to seize through punishments and other means this accumulated wealth."[250]

No less demand for gold, silver and copper was exercised by making images of these precious metals by the rulers, their family members, ministers and the wealthiest class. It was a practice in which each ruler wanted to set a record not to be broken by others to outlive his/her memory and seek legitimacy besides satisfying his psyche by doing an act of piety. All in all, it became an imitable model for the members of royalty, councillors and the richest section of the society. Writing about the images made of gold, silver and copper by the richest king, Lalitaditya, Kalhana says:

> The glorious silver image of Viṣṇu, *Parihāsakeśava* shone like the god [Viṣṇu], when flooded by the strong light of the pearls during his sleep on the ocean. The famous [image of] Viṣṇu *Muktākeśaca*, made of gold, shone as if it had taken its lustre from the many stamina of the lotus [rising from Viṣṇu's] navel. Clad in a golden armour, the [image of Visnu] *Mahāvarāha* shone forth like the sun when he puts on his radiant light to overcome the darkness in the

> world below. He had a silver [image of the] god Govardhanadhara made, which was white as if [coloured] by the streams of milk [flowing] from[his] herds of cows. Into the image of *Muktākeśava*, he put eighty-four thousand tolakas of gold. And collecting as many thousands of Palas of silver, that pure-minded [king] made the famous [statue of] *Parihāsakeśava*. With just as many thousands of Prasthas of copper he made the glorious [statue of] the 'Great Buddha' (*Bṛhadbuddha*) which reached upto the sky.[251]

And writing about the queens and ministers who followed in the footsteps of the king, Kalhana says:

> The ladies of the seraglio, his ministers and princely attendants, consecrated there in hundred images [of gods], wonders of the world. His queen Kamalavati, she who founded Kamalahatta, put up the large silver image of Kmalākeśava. His minister Mitraśarman, too, put up the Śiva-[Linga called] Mitreśvara. The king of Lata, called Kayya, made the famous [shrine of Viṣṇu] Kayyasvamin. The Tuhkhara Caṅkuṇa, who founded the Caṅkunavihāra, made a Stupa loftier even than the mind of the king, and golden [images of the] Jinas.[252]

Gold in dust and coins, and silver ingots and coins were traditional items of imports from Chinese Turkistan.[253]

Copper and iron were also in considerable demand. Besides making images of copper, the metal was used for coinage and for manufacturing vessels. Iron was meant for manufacturing weapons of war and agricultural tools. While perhaps some demand of copper was met locally from the newly discovered copper mines in Kamarajya (Kamraz),[254] iron in large quantity was imported from Central Asia and India.

Among other imports, mention may be made of China silk, betel leaves and spices. The use of China silk (*Cinansuka*) was a fad among the royalty and richest section of the society. It was also bestowed as a robe of honour.[255] It seems that there was a brisk trade between China and Kashmir as China did not only supply to Kashmir its specialties, but we find even ordinary beads from China being sold in Kashmir markets.[256] It is now an established fact that shawl manufacturing in Kashmir dates back to the ancient period, though clear mention of this technology in Kashmir has been first made by the eleventh-century polymath of Kashmir, Ksemendra.[257] Since shawl wool continued to be imported from Tibet and the neighbouring territories of Central Asia till late times, the same would have been obviously true during the period of our study.[258]

Another category of important imports in terms of quantity and impact is betel leaves and spices. The taking of betel was so lavish in the courtly culture that King Ananta (1028–1063 CE) became bankrupt due to their reckless offering at assemblies, functions, festivities and festivals. The situation reached to such a pass that Ananta had not only to give up almost the whole revenue of the country to the betel trader, but he had also to pawn his diadem and the throne to him as a security for more money which was due to him.[259] It was the Queen Suryamati who saved the honour of the country when she got back the emblems of regal dignity by liquidating the debt from the savings of her own treasury.[260] Betel, "*nagarakhanda*" and "other ingredients" were supplied to the king by a trader, Padmaraja, from Malwa who wielded considerable influence in the court.[261] Though the import of betel was a huge drain on the treasury, it continued to be a royal luxury. Writing about King Uccala's (1101–1111 CE) prodigious distribution of betel in the assemblies and at festivals, Kalhana says, "Not even king Harśa showed such extravagance in offering betel [at assemblies] and such splendour as he did."[262] For maintaining their freshness betel leaves were placed in specially constructed wells.[263]

Kalhana and Kṣemendra also refer to the marketing of spices and cosmetics, namely, pepper, asafoetida, ginger, collyrium and sandal paste,[264] which were obviously imported from India. In terms of volume of trade, salt ranked first among the imports as it was the basic need of all rich and poor. No doubt it was also imported from Central Asia but the major supplier was the Punjab, which transported it through Hirpura–Bimbar route. Considering the volume of salt imported through this route and its brisk transportation throughout the whole year (except for the winter months), it is no wonder that this route came to be called Salt Route (*Lavanasarāni*) and it led to the emergence of colonies of labourers, inns, *tirthas* and monasteries on the route.[265]

Barring a few casual references, sources are silent about the exports from Kashmir. From a passing reference in *Rājataraṅgiṇī*, it becomes quite clear that Kashmir exported victuals to far-off lands, and in this trade Kashmiri traders took active part. While narrating the events of eleventh-century Kashmir, Kalhana refers to one Jayaka who, by selling victuals as a trader to far-off regions, became in course of time a rival to the lord of wealth (*Kubera*).[266] The victuals were most probably saffron, rice, oil, honey etc. Kashmir was so much famous for saffron and its export that it came to be called in Sanskrit literature outside Kashmir as *Kaśmira* or *Kaśmiraja*.[267] A guild of South Indian merchants, calling itself the Five Hundred Masters of Ayyavole, mentions saffron especially among the goods it had in trade in the Kannada and Tamil countries.[268]

More importantly, Kashmir also exported flowers to India as they were considered important for religious rituals. According to Al-Biruni, "Every day they brought there (Somnath Temple) a jug of Ganges water, and a basket of flowers from Kashmir."[269]

Evidently, the merchants not only exchanged goods between Kashmir and the neighbouring world, but they also constituted an important agency to transmit and diffuse ideas and cultures, and thus contributed significantly to the formation of a trans-regional culture that was the early culture of any region including Kashmir. Writing about the role of trade (here especially the role of saffron trade with Southern Peninsula), in transmitting Kashmiri Sanskritic culture to Southern reaches of the subcontinent, Cox says:

> It was along the same routes that saffron travelled southward – and perhaps in the same caravans or even the same parcels – that the textual culture of Kashmir went global within the Indic world of the early second millennium, with massive and palpable consequences.[270]

Apart from educational and commercial contacts with the outside world, there were many other channels which knit Kashmir and the neighbouring world together and buttressed the cosmopolitan legacy Kashmiris inherited from their ancestors. These different modes would be discussed in the following sub-heading.

Inflows and Connectivity

One of the commandments contained in the NP to be followed by the people of Kashmir is to welcome immigrants from different directions: "All the people immigrating (to Kaśmira) from the other directions, should be honoured."[271] Immigration is also expressly referred to in a discussion appended to the rules concerning the royal consecration.[272] Clearly, the NP was reflecting a fundamental reality of Kashmir, namely, the contribution of inflows and contacts to the making of Kashmir, which is why honouring the incoming people finds a mention among the canons contained in the *Purāna*. As the NP was, according to Inden, written under the auspices of Kārkota king, Durlabhavardhana and his court,[273] this injunction was reflective of one of the important aspects of the state policy of the time. This was not, of course, any innovation considering that the history of Kashmir is all about the history of immigrations, settlements and contacts. What is, of course, new was that this policy assumed the status of a religious dictum to facilitate building Kashmir as an empire, and to construct a new capital to rival Kanauj, which necessitated attracting a variety of talent by extending liberal patronage. This is what Lalitaditya did practically by collecting "from different countries various wise men, as the wind collects masses of full-blown flowers from the trees,"[274] according to Kalhana. This policy was facilitated by the creation of a vast empire, which, on the one hand, made Kashmir financially richer among its neighbouring territories and, on the other, made movement of people far easier than before. The Kashmir empire, with its fabulous wealth and enormous opportunities of employment and patronage, also attracted the fortune seekers from distant lands. It is, therefore, no wonder to see great luminaries belonging to diversified fields thronging Kashmir and making it a model country in science, technology, town planning, architecture, art, statecraft, governance and philosophy, a reference to which has been given in the preceding pages of this chapter. Suffice it to recall that the ancestors of the famous literary and philosophico-religious figures of early Kashmir, namely, Abhinavagupta and Bilhana came from Madhyadeśa, and those of Abhinanda hailed from Gauda.[275]

Unlike Lalitaditya, Jayapida failed as a conqueror. But the military campaigns in different parts of India won him many friends in the Indian subcontinent who helped him in his difficult times, and they were duly rewarded by him by appointing them to high positions when he regained his empire. For instance, Jayadatta was bestowed with the highest position, *pañcamahāśabda,*[276] and *Āca*, the son-in-law of lord of Mathra, was the king's chamberlain.[277] The most intimate contacts, however, came to be established with Bengal as Jayapida's chief queen Kalyanadevi was from a royal family of Gauda[278] (Bengal). Jayapida was so much attached to her that he made her the chief chamberlain (*mahapratiharapida*).[279] Like his predecessor, Jayapida also utilised his military adventures for searching the talent in different fields and luring them to settle down in Kashmir. To quote Kalhana, "The king searched for and collected all scholars to such an extent that in the lands of other kings there was a dearth of learned men."[280]

In the preceding chapter, we have also seen that Buddhism forged intimate contacts between Kashmir and the neighbourhood, especially with China, Central Asia and Afghanistan. This spatial perforation was bound to exercise mutual influences in different aspects other than religion besides exercising a demand for each other's achievements and specialties in different fields, especially when we consider that China was the home of technological innovations, and Kashmir was also famous for some special products. Though the paucity of evidence prevents us from constructing a picture of it, we know that the knowledge of building of boat bridges—an innovation of China—was introduced in Kashmir during the preceding dynasty,[281] and the use of China silk (*cinanasuka*), if not sericulture—a special contribution of China to human civilisation—was common among the upper classes.[282] A typical example of the impact of Chinese and Central Asian cultures on Kashmir is the sculpture of the period, a glimpse of which is given elsewhere in this chapter.

Considering that the Kashmiri Buddhist missionaries took the message to China, Khotan and Kucha besides attracting the lovers of Buddhist learning from far off places to learn Buddhism in Kashmir, it is quite probable that the same relationship would have obtained between Kashmir and the other parts of Central Asia including Afghanistan where Buddhism had become a dominant tradition by the time of Karkotas. This is substantiated by a passing reference in the *itinerary* of Ou-k'ong, where it is mentioned that a number of Buddhist sacred places were founded in Kashmir by the royal family of the Tou-kiue (Turks).[283] Though it is impossible to say with certainty where this Turkish dynasty ruled, one is tempted to think of the area from Tukharistan through Kabul Valley to Upper Indus. Lalitaditya's military adventures in Central Asia and his fame as a tolerant ruler also accounted for the influx of talent from Central Asia. It is remarkable that his prime minister was a Tukharian Buddhist,[284] and many of his leading ministers were *Śahis*.[285]

From the sixth century CE onwards the contacts with the Indian subcontinent extended and deepened beyond precedence. Mihirakula not only inaugurated the era of campaigns in India, bringing the tradition down to Karkotas, but also revived Brahmanism with great fanfare. Barring very few exceptions, all the rulers then onwards were either *Śaivites* or *Vaiṣṇavas* making Brahmanism the dominant tradition of Kashmir. It was during the period of Karkotas that the *Purānas* were written to construct hegemony and dominance of Brahmanism. While the *Nīlamata Purāna* Sanskritised the geography of the valley, its cosmologies, beliefs and rituals, the *Viṣṇudharmotra Purāna* was involved in making Kashmir the centre of Pancarātra Vaişņavism and devising temple space for images whose iconography it standardised. As the Hindu *tirthas* and the centres of learning were spread over the whole of the subcontinent including Kashmir, it is no wonder to see a regular movement of pilgrims[286] and seekers of knowledge[287] between Kashmir and the different parts of the subcontinent for whose accommodation the state as well as the resourceful individuals built *mathas*.[288]

The monistic Śaivism, famous today as "Kashmiri Śaivism," was started by Trambakaditya who lived near the Kailaśa mountain.[289] This is why it is also called Trayambaka School.[290] His son Samgramaditya went to Kashmir and settled there somewhere in the seventh century.[291] In the following pages we would see that the "Kashmiri Śaivism" was inspired by a variety of gurus who emerged in different parts of India. Yet, this philosophy received unprecedented intellectual support in Kashmir as most of the scriptures and treatises of this school were written in Kashmir;[292] and it is for this reason that it is called "Kashmiri Śaivism" though some modern scholars are of the opinion that the term is something of a misnomer because "it is both overly specific geographically and overly general doctrinally."[293]

The relations between Kashmir and the Indian subcontinent had become so intimate that the matrimonial ties between the Kashmiri ruling families and the ruling families of different kingdoms of the Indian subcontinent had become a commonplace affair. Even though furnishing such information was beyond the subject matter of the chronicles and other types of sources, there is a passing mention of these relations in a non-local chronicle, namely, *Chach Nama* and an incidental mention in *Rājataraṅgiṇī*. While the former makes a mention of the matrimonial relations between the ruling families of Sindh and the ruling families of Kashmir,[294] the latter refers to these relations with the ruling family of Bengal.[295] The existence of such relations with the Śahis and the kingdoms around Kashmir was a routine affair in the early Kashmir.[296]

Like their predecessors, the Utpalas also won "global" fame for making Kashmir a meeting place of international scholars—the details of which have been given in the preceding pages of this chapter. Avantivarman, the founder and the most famous ruler of Utpala dynasty, is also famous for great works of architecture and art for which he seems to have employed engineers and artists well-versed in Indian and Sasanian art and architecture.[297] As a result of the court patronage, the talent from the neighbouring world continued to pour in—the trend which was further nurtured by the liberal mindedness of Samkaravarman, who, as we have seen, treated a talented immigrant outcaste family on a par with upper caste/class local people.

Yaśaśkara, who was enthroned for being well-versed in religious education received in Aryadesha, had deep connections with mainland India. It is therefore understandable that besides providing adequate facility to "foreign students" for receiving higher education in Kashmir without any difficulty, Yaśaśkara also settled brahmanas coming from India on the banks of Vitasta and bestowed upon them *agrahāras*.[298]

Kşemagupta's reign (950–958), especially his marriage with Didda, the daughter of Simharaja, the lord of Lohara, and the daughter's daughter of the Śhahi king, Bhimapala proved of significant importance especially in the context of linking Kashmir intimately with Lohara and Śhahi kingdom, leading to the influx of people and culture from these lands and the lands that bordered them. The people of Lohara and Śhahi kingdom assumed masterful positions in the valley to the much resentment of existing nobility. Kalhana writes disapprovingly, "The lavish Kşemegupta took thirty-six villages from the burnt Vihara, and gave them into the tenure of the Khasa ruler."[299] After Kşemagupta, the trend of monopolising the important offices and looting the wealth by the Lohara officials exacerbated:

> The wicked Jayagupta, who was the favoured associate of Udayaraja, the queen's brother, was in charge of the Aksapala [office]. In company with him, other officials of cruel character plundered Kashmir in consequence of the sins which this [land] had accumulated.[300]

In this political and cultural configuration, Didda's role was predominant. Being the daughter of Lohara and daughter's daughter of Śhahi ruler, she was emotionally gravitated to these lands—the sentiment which translated into her preferential patronage to the people of Lohara and Śhahi family, the acme of which reached when she transferred the throne to her nephew in 1003 CE. It should be mentioned that Queen Didda was not only an iron lady but she ruled for a longest period in the known history of early Kashmir if we consider that she was the real power behind the throne of her husband, Kṣemagupta (950–958), as well as during the rule of his son, Abhimanyu (958–973), and grandsons, Nandigupta (972–973), Tribhuvana (973–975) and Bhimagupta (975–980), before she directly assumed the reins of the government in 980 CE and ruled up to 1003.

During her half a century rule, the people of Lohara and Śhahi kingdom assumed dominance to such an extent that Tunga, who became the prime minister (*sarvadhikārin*) under Didda, was, according to Kalhana, a herdsman of buffaloes from a village of Parnotsa (Punch).[301] He came to Kashmir along with his five brothers and was employed as letter carrier (*Lekhahārkara*);[302] he captivated the heart of Didda who ultimately made her the prime -minister.

Besides occupying important positions in the administration and entering into matrimonial relations with the royal family, the Śhahis also showed considerably interest in promoting Vaiṣṇavism in Kashmir without however being prejudicial against the other cults and faiths. Bhima Śhahi, the maternal grandfather of Didda, built the temple of Bhimakeśava[303] in Kashmir which, according to MA Stein, can be recognised with the temple of Bumzu.[304] Indeed, under the influence of Śhahis and Loharas, Vaiṣṇavism was the royal cult during Didda's ascendency. "Under the name of her father, Simharaja," says Kalhana, "She (Didda) created the illustrious shrine of Simhaśvamin."[305] However, like a true Vaiṣṇava, Didda was tolerant of other faiths as we find her building vihāras alongside temples.[306] Given her keen interest in the promotion of learning, the period witnessed a great momentum in the inflow of "foreign students" and "foreign" brahmanas generated by the state patronage.

In preference to a Kashmiri, Didda raised her nephew Samgramaraja of Lohara to the rank of Yuvaraja[307] paving the way for his becoming the king of Kashmir in 1003. The foundation of the rule of Loharains further cemented the ties between Kashmir, Lohara and the Śhahi kingdom—the latter extended from modern Afghanistan to the Punjab. During the period of Samgramaraja (1003–1028), the Śhahi kingdom was subjected to Mahmud of Ghazni's invasions culminating in its extinction. Trilochanpala, the last independent ruler of Śahi dynasty, sought the help of Samgramaraja against Mahmud;[308] and, as expected, the Kashmiri ruler sent a large army for help[309] though it proved inconsequential as the Kashmiri army was not acquainted with the "Turkish warfare."[310] The extinction of Śahi empire had important consequences for Kashmir. It led to a large influx of people from the erstwhile Śhahi kingdom.[311] Among those who opted to run away and seek shelter in Kashmir were the members of the ruling dynasty and the religious class.[312] The members of the ruling dynasty and the commanders of the empire were appointed to high positions.[313] Now onwards,

Palas became an important group of Kashmiri nobility.[314] The *Pals* who constitute a segment of Kashmiri population are obviously the descendants of the *Palas* of our time. This can be further substantiated by the physiognomy of the present population of *Pals* even if a thorough intermixing of ethnicities took place during the intervening 900 years. Kalhana disparagingly refers to three Śahi princes—Rudrapala, Diddapala and Anangapala—who were actually ruling the country during the early years of Ananta's rule (1028–1063):

> Most dear to him (King Ananta) were Rudrapala and other Śahi princes who exhausted the kingdom's revenue by the large salaries they drew. Though receiving from the king one and a half lakhs [of *Dinnarās*] daily for his maintenance, Rudrapala yet never got rid of his money troubles. Diddapala, though he drew daily eighty thousand [Dinnaras] from the king, could yet not sleep in peace at night. Anahgapala, [that] vetala, who was the king's favourite, was ever planning the breaking up of golden statues of gods. Rudrapala protected those who robbed [others] of their property and lives, and was a safe refuge for thieves, *Candalas* and the like. Kayasthas who were Rudrapala's intimates, oppressed the people. The foremost among them, the famous Utpala, founded a *Matha* for the blind. What more need be said of the king's affection for him [Rudrapala]? He himself had married the elder daughter of Inducandra, the lord of Jalamddhara, the moon faced Asamati, on account of her beauty, the same who built a *Matha* called after herself at Tripuresvara. He then married her somewhat younger sister, the queen Suryamati, to the king.[315]

About Kalasa, the son and successor of Ananta, Kalhana, writes with disdain: "Four arrogant princes (*rajaputra*) from the Śahi family, Bijja, Pitharaja, Paja and another were his favourites."[316] Besides the members of royal family and sections of the ruling class, the learned brahmanas also flocked to Kashmir. While referring to the forcible flight of the Hindus from the erstwhile Śahi empire after its occupation by Mahumud, Al-Biruni mainly mentions Kashmir and Banaras as preferred destinations of these migrants. Since these migrants were mainly learned persons in Hindu sciences, Kashmir's position as an outstanding centre of Hindu learning was further enriched by this wave of immigrations.[317]

Kalhana says that Suryamati, the queen of King Ananta, built *matha*s with *agraharas* and bestowed 180 *agraharas* on "learned brahmanas" at Vijayesvara.[318] Since Suryamati was the daughter of the royal family of the erstwhile Śahi kingdom, and she was the most beloved queen of Ananta upon whom she wielded enormous influence, it is most probable that the *matha*s were constructed for and *agraharas* bestowed upon the brahmanas who were migrants from Gandhara and the Punjab.

Mahmud's invasion and extinction of the Śahi empire, his abortive bids to conquer Kashmir[319] and the refugees' "inveterate aversion towards the Muslims"[320] no doubt created antagonism against all foreigners to the extent that according to Al-Biruni, the Kashmiri rulers did not allow anyone to enter their land.[321] Yet the compulsions of the realities of life forced the Kashmiri rulers to be pragmatic. A powerful Muslim empire was created on the borders of Kashmir. It spread over an area with which Kashmir had intimate economic and cultural relations. It was therefore unrealistic and counterproductive to continue hostilities with it. Moreover, Mahmud's invasion and the failure of the Śahis, including the Kashmiri army, to face it had exposed the military weakness of Kashmir. To prepare the country to face any challenge to its sovereignty, it was necessary to update its military technology and tactics of warfare for which it was dependent on the Turks—now the Muslim Turks who lived on its borders. It is, therefore, no wonder that we find the Kashmiri rajas opening up borders to the Muslims and employing them in the army. Ananta (1028–1063), Harśa (1089–1101), Bikśacara (1120–1121) and Jayasimha (1128–1149) had a good number of "Turuśka captains" in their armies.[322]

Kashmir's intimate relations with distant lands and immediate neighbourhoods are also indicated by the mention of a "foreigner," named Dullaka who was very close to king Ananta, and a rich trader from Malwa who was supplying betel leaves and other ingredients to him. We are also told of the "evil habits which the wretched foreigners had taught" to King Kalasa (1063–1089 CE).[323] Kalhana also informs us about the "Turuśka girls born in various distant regions,"[324] being bought by a Kashmiri trader, and an artist from "Turuśka country" knowing the craft of making a parasol of gold or putting gold on copper.[325] Kashmir's trans-border linkages are also borne out by the employment of a brahmana Kaśin from Karnata (Karnataka) in the nobility of Kalasa; and the latter's[326] introduction into "this country (Kashmir) the taste for choral songs (*upangagita*) and a careful selection of female dancers as customary in other lands."[327] The same conclusion becomes irresistible from the warm reception which an influential Kashmiri noble (Bijja) received from different rulers of India though he was then an exile.[328]

Harśa (1089–1101 CE), the famous connoisseur king of the time, patronised all those "persons distinguished for exceptional talent" which attracted a variety of 'eminent persons' from different countries.[329] As a result, we find remarkable cultural changes in Kashmir. Leaving part of the details to the following pages, we will discuss here only his fad for South Indian fashions and the interest he showed to introduce them in his courtly life. According to Kalhana, "People appeared in his assembly hall with waving palm-leaves, adorned with big forehead-marks of sandal ointment" and his ladies "wore long garlands formed by their hair-braids into which were [woven] golden Ketaka leaf."[330] Kalhana also refers to Sephali flowers bound up with their locks, the pendants they wore over their forehead marks, the joining of the corners of their eyes with their ears by a line drawn with collyrium, short jackets with short sleeves and the typically long nether garments like a *lehanga* so commonly used in the South.[331] All this clearly points to the considerable influence of the fashions of southern India, especially Karnataka, on the costume, cosmetics and coiffure of Kashmir during the period of Harśa.

Harśa showed so much liking for importing from Southern Peninsula whatever appealed to him that he also "introduced a coin-type (*tanka*) copied from that of Karnata (Karnataka)."[332] According to M. A. Stein, Cunningham has described the actual coins to which Kalhana refers here. They are of gold and bear Harśa's name.[333] Their type is quite different from that maintained through the "whole of the Hindu coinage of Kashmir." And, "the fact of the coins being made in imitation of those of Karnata (Karnataka) is fully corroborated by the coins of that country."[334]

Indeed, one of the best examples, which sufficiently demonstrates that the people of Kashmir looked much beyond their mountain ramparts and drew on the resources of others to develop the different sectors of their *mandala* alongside exporting their own assets to enrich the reserves of others, is the trade-off between Kashmir and Dakśina (South India). According to Michael Witzel, the immigration expressly referred to in *Nīlmata Purāna* in a discussion appended to the rules concerning the royal consecration point to early immigration from South India; "In connection with Pancaratra Brahmans and the Taittiriyesvara, this might even point to early immigration from South India as, by this time, only South Indian Brahmans belonged to this Yajurveda School, with exception from Assam." '[335] Tirumular, the earliest of the Siddhas of Tamil Nadu assigned to the second half of the seventh century, is believed to have come from Kashmir.[336] Siddhas, it may be mentioned, were anti-ritual, anti-ceremonial and anti-caste.[337] In return the South transmitted to Kashmir what is called Dakśinacāra, which was essentially a brahmanical cult. We also find Kashmiri brahmana settlers in the south of Madurai (Tamil Nadu). "This movement" says Witzel, "was connected with the spread of Śaivism."[338] However, the evidence also shows that the emigration of Kashmiri brahmanas to South India was also connected with the spread of Vaiṣṇavism. In this context, it is important to mention that the Vaiṣṇava Saraswats of Karnataka, who trace their ancestry to Kashmir, sing the following verse in their evening *sandhya: Sarawati mahamaya kashmira-puravasini; stadresamantat tam saraswata mahamunium* (we bow to Saraswati, who is the great *maya* and resident of Kashmir, and also to the great sage Saraswata residing in the neighbourhood of *Satadri*).[339]

Kashmir's close connections with Karnataka can also be gleaned from the fact that the famous poet of Kashmir, Bilhana, found Karnataka the best place for patronage; and the Chalukya king, Vikramaditya Tribhuvanamalla appointed him as his chief pandit distinguished by the grant of a "blue parasol and a mast elephant."[340] The poet wrote verse biography of his royal patron, the *Vikramānkadevacarita*.

The intimacy and depth of these relations can also be gauged from the fact that we find a brahmana from Karnataka being inducted in the nobility of Kalasa.[341] In the preceding pages, we also gave a detailed account of the exchange of knowledge between Kashmir and South India during the eleventh, twelfth and thirteenth centuries.

Although the post-tenth century CE reeled mostly under fratricidal and feudal wars, the political, economic and cultural relations with the outside world continued without much disturbance thanks to the compulsions of real life. The relations with the Indian rulers were so strong that Queen Asamati took secretly the endangered prince Bhiksacara to Deccan and he grew up there; the ruler of Malwa "kept him like his son."[342] The king Uccala (1101–1111 CE) came to know of this from the "envoy who had returned from abroad."[343] The wars made the contenders of throne to recruit the outsiders or to seek their support, even if many of them were Muslims. Referring to Bhoja's hiring of Muslim support, Kalhana says with much disdain: "He (Bhoja) was delighted in looking at them as they climbed down from the mass of mountains talking an unknown tongue and growing familiar by kind treatment just like monkeys."[344] The war-torn conditions not only led to the recruitment of foreign fighters by the warring factions but they also increased the demand for war horses. Kalhan's statement that the "foreign horse dealers grew rich under Sussala (1121–1128)"[345] can be understood in this context.[346]

During the reign of Jayasimha, who reigned for a considerable period (1128–1154), Kashmir witnessed the revival of cultural activity after he restored "cold peace." He, his family and the ministers patronised the scholars, built vihāras, *mathas* and temples, and "settled here [Kashmir] Brahmanas from the Indus region and numerous Dravidas."[347] Kalhana also mentions Jayasimha's friendly relation with the rulers of Kanyakubja (Kanauj). Mankha in his *Śrikanthacarita* not only corroborates Kalhana but also furnishes additional evidence in regard to Jayasimha's relations with different kingdoms of the subcontinent. In his description of the Sabha of scholars organised by Alamkara (Superintendent of treasury and chief justice under Jayasimha), Mankha mentions that among the persons present were Suhala, the ambassador of Govindachandra, the king of Kanyakubja and Tejakantha, the ambassador sent by Aparaditya, the lord of Konkana.[348]

With the domination of Śaiva and Vaiṣṇava Brahmanism for more than 500 years with full state patronage, Kashmir emerged as one of the great centres of Hindu learning and pilgrimage of the Peninsular India. The other parts of the subcontinent, needless to say, were also dotted with the most notable sacred Hindu tirthas and centres of learning. As a result, a two-way traffic between Kashmir and the rest of the Indian subcontinent, for pilgrimage and knowledge, became the hallmark of relations between Kashmir and the rest of India. The pilgrimage of Kashmiris, especially the richest class to Gaya, Ganga, Yamuna, Kurukshetra, Banaras, Prayaga and other important *tirthas,* is understandable,[349] but what is most surprising is that the *tirthas* situated in the remotest parts of Kashmir were not only known to the people of far-off places of India such as Bengal and Malwa, but they also had a profound faith in them. We know from Kalhana that the *tirtha* of Śarada situated in the upper Kishanganga Valley had assumed such a considerable renown that it attracted devotees from Bengal.[350] Even Al-Biruni heard that this *tirtha* was "much venerated and frequented by pilgrims."[351] More importantly, the King Bhoja of Malwa (1011–1055 CE), who is also famous as "one of the most extraordinary figures in the history of literary culture in India,"[352] was such a fervent devotee of another distantly located *tirtha* of Kashmir, Papasudana at Kapatesvara (the modern Kothar), that he got the enclosure of the sacred spring of Papasudana constructed through a trader of Malwa, Padmaraja, who was trading in Kashmir.[353] What is more, the king of Malwa had taken a vow "that he would always wash his face in water from the [spring of] Pāpasūdana Tirtha," and this was made possible with the help of Padmaraja.[354]

The contacts between Kashmir and the neighbourhood were not, however, a one-way affair. There is considerable evidence of Kashmiris travelling to different parts of the distant and immediate neighbourhood for various purposes. We have seen that the Kashmiri Buddhist missionaries travelled to different parts of China, Central Asia, Tibet and the immediate borderlands of Kashmir for preaching and dissemination of Buddhist creed. We also know the brahmanas of Kashmir going to different parts of India, even to deep south for patronage. For example, the poet Bilhana (ca. 1100 CE) travelled widely in northern and western India before he got due patronage from Vikramaditya, the Chalukya ruler of Kalyana. We also come across the name of Pandit Sothala who became the chief of the royal chancellery (*Śrikaranadhipa*) under the kings Jaitrapala and Bhillanna of the Yadava dynasty at Devagiri (Daulatabad) in ca. 1200 CE.[355] Many of them left the valley in search of relieved conditions in contrast to occasional hostile courtly milieu at home.[356] The emigration and settlement of Kashmiri brahmanas in Tamil Nadu in connection with the spread of Śaivism are substantiated by the inscriptions at the Tiruvallesvara temple, south of Madurai (Tamil Naidu), built under the Pallavas.[357] We are also told about a Kashmiri trader who became "god of wealth" owing to the trade in victuals in foreign countries.[358]

Contacts With Muslims

From the beginning of eighth century Kashmir came face to face with Islam as by 713, Arabs had reached close to the borders of Kashmir and the whole Central Asia came under the sway of Muslims by the end of eighth century. In 713 when Muhammad ibn al-Qasim, the Arab general, occupied Multan, he marched towards the frontiers of Kashmir called *Panj Nihayat*. But the threat to Kashmir was averted as the general was recalled by the Caliph Walīd (705–715) to his court.[359] Later sometime after 757–758, Hishām bin Amir al Taghlibi, the Arab governor of Sind, also made an attempt to conquer the valley.[360] But owing to its natural frontiers, he could not make it. Balādhuri is supported by no local evidence in his claim that Hishām conquered the valley.[361] That Kashmir remained under a great threat of Arab invasion during the first half of the eighth century is also substantiated by the Annals of the Tang dynasty, from which we learn that the king of Kashmir, Chandrāpida, sent an embassy to the Chinese court to invoke its aid against the Arabs, who were threatening his territories from the north.[362] Perhaps Lalitaditya (eighth century) too had an encounter with the Arabs in the northern regions of what today is Afghanistan. While mentioning Lalitaditya's wars against Tukharas who lived in the upper Oxus Valley including Balkh and Badakhshan, Kalhana makes us believe that he defeated Mummuni thrice.[363] Who is this Mummuni? One thing is clear that he is portrayed as a formidable power.[364] Levi identifies Mummuni with the title of the Khalifa, Amir al-Mu'minin.[365] It seems so as the earliest Arab incursions into the Kabul Valley occurred by the 650s and the northern and western regions of what today is Afghanistan had come under Arab control by the early eighth century.[366] Since the campaigns and conquests by the Arabs were launched in the name of Amir al-Mu'minin, and the credit of conquests was also given to him, therefore, the term Amir al-Mu'minin became a commonplace in an aura when Arabs were making rapid strides in the immediate neighbourhood of Kashmir, paving the way for the entry of the term in Sanskrit vocabulary (like Yavana and Turuśka), and used by Kalhana many centuries after the Arab domination of Kashmir's borderlands as a generic term not only for the Arabs but also for powerful non-Indian, non-Turk, conquerors and empire builders of his not much distant past.[367]

The policy of confrontation and resistance between the Kashmiri rulers and the Arab power on its borders was, however, a contingent phenomenon because Kashmir was heavily dependent on its neighbourhoods for its very survival. That is why we find the Karkota rulers favourably disposed towards the Muslim traders and immigrants.[368] As the neighbouring towns of Sind and Multan and the frontier towns along the trade routes to Iran and Central Asia were polyglot emporia containing ethnically and religiously heterogeneous population, with marked presence of Persian traders, both Muslims and Jews,[369] the Kashmiri rulers provided them all the faith-related facilities to promote Kashmir's foreign trade.[370] And to make Kashmir a real cosmopolitan realm, the Kashmiri rulers encouraged inflow of all religions and their human agents, encouraging the great mystic of Islam Mansur al Hallaj to visit Kashmir in 895 to take benefit of the court-sponsored argumentative ethos of Kashmir and the fluidity of confessional identity.[371] Small wonder, then we are told of a Kashmiri ruler making a written request to the Arab amir of Sind around 883 to send him *hindyah* translation of exegesis (*tafsir*) of Islamic law.[372] In fact, by 850s the Arabic language and the Islamic learning had made significant impact in the immediate neighbourhood of

Kashmir. This is borne out by a foundational text dated 857 from the Tochi Valley in Waziristan. It is inscribed in both Arabic and Sanskrit[373] "attesting to an overlap between the dominant Islamic and Indic linguistic ecumenism of the period."[374] By tenth century Persians had also made deep inroads into the cultural landscape of Kashmir's borderlands.[375] This was partly because of the thriving trade with Iran and Central Asia, and partly because of the rapid expansion of the Ghaznavid power. The Ghaznavids who belonged to Persianate-Islamic culture brought Kabul Valley and north-west up to the Punjab under their control in early eleventh century. Immediately after the conquest of Kashmir's borderlands by Ghaznavids, the influx of Muslims assumed an unprecedented scale. This is borne out by the presence of hundreds of Turk Muslim commanders in the armies of eleventh- and twelfth-century Hindu rajas of Kashmir.[376] Being members of the great power of the time, they were also the carriers of the then reference cultural model—a touchstone for the rulers and elite of Kashmir to reach at self-appraisals. Kashmiri non-Muslim elite also got an exposure of Islamic culture in the Punjab and north-west of India where, interestingly enough, Al-Biruni interacted with them in a relieved condition though according to his own admission, the Hindus had left the areas in panic after their conquest by Mahmud of Ghazni. Indeed, it was from the Kashmiri brahmanas that Al-Biruni collected information about Kashmir while making sojourn of Peshawar, Multan and the Punjab to collect material for his *Kitāb fi tahqiq-i-mali 'l-Hind*.[377]

The subsequent period of Kashmir history is poorly recorded until we reach the beginning of the thirteenth century and hear from Marco Polo about the presence of *saracens* [Muslims] in Kashmir who, according to him, used to slaughter animals for the non-Muslims.

> The people of the province [Kashmir] do neither kill animals nor spill blood, so if they want to eat meat, they get the *saracens* [Muslims] who dwell among them to play the butcher.[378]

This clearly shows that following the establishment of Muslim power on its borders, the Kashmiri rajas had very prudently engaged with the Muslim rulers of the neighbourhood and encouraged the immigration and settlement of Muslims in the valley as a part of this engagement. Without any doubt during the premodern times, borders of Kashmir were not normally closed to foreign adventurers and prospective settlers. This is how Syed Sharf–Ud-Din Bulbul Shah, the Suhrawardi saint from Turkistan, Shah Mir from Swat, Rinchan from Ladakh and Langar Chak from Dardistan (who subsequently played a decisive role in shaping the history of Kashmir) arrived in Kashmir during the reign of Suha Deva (1301–1320 CE) and were given state patronage.[379] However, on account of the political instability, the borders were left unguarded paving the way for Mongol invasion called Zulju's invasion in 1320 CE, which caused havoc in the valley and shattered the ramshackle rule of the Hindu rajas.[380] It was Shah Mir who along with Queen Kota Rani saved Kashmir from another invasion Kashmir had to face within a few years after the Zulju's invasion. The heroic role of Shah Mir paved the way for the establishment of Muslim Sultanate by Shah Mir whom the contemporary Sanskrit chronicler Jonaraja calls "saviour" for bailing out Kashmir from civil wars and invasions.[381]

Making of Cosmopolitan Kashmir

Considering the nature of our sources, the trans-border connections of Kashmir, outlined in the preceding pages, are only a silhouette, an illustrative rather than exhaustive account of the extent and depth of these relations. Still it is sufficient to prompt us to ask the question: In what ways did these inflows and connectivities impact the society of Kashmir? Though we are conscious of the multidimensional effects of linkage and flow, we have chosen here only a few sites which help us in gauging the extent to which the movement of people and ideas led to the formation of a dynamic, plural and composite culture.

Replenishment of the Ethnic-mosaic of Population

We have seen in the foregoing chapters that the history of Kashmir is the history of immigrations and settlements. This process continued during the post-sixth century period, even receiving more momentum if we rely on the available evidence. The sources contain significant information, though scattered and fleeting, about the immigrations and settlements from distant and immediate neighbourhoods at the initiative of the state under its ambitious project of empire building or making the country to rival "Madhyadeśa" and other great cultural centres they had heard about while keeping themselves abreast of the happenings in the neighbouring world. We have also seen people flocking to Kashmir on their own in search of fortune. What is notable is to see people coming from distant lands, namely, Dravida (Tamil Nadu), Karnataka, Maharashtra, Gujarat, Bengal, Uttar Pradesh, Haryana, the Punjab, Himachal, Gandhara, Sind, Afghanistan and Oxus Valley.[382] Besides this, there were repeated influxes of people from the entire bordering territories from Gilgit-Baltistan to Swat Kohistan called Dardas; and from Muzaffarabad to Kishtwar called Khasas. As these people belonged to different ethno-cultural backgrounds and were generally "distinguished people" belonging to the upper strata of the society, mostly the brahmana caste, the brahmana community of Kashmir got stratified into a number of *gotras* (ethnic groups), each forming an exogamous group because the brahmanical religion, as practiced in Kashmir, prohibits marrying within the kindred group. Even as late as the twenties of the twentieth century, the number of gotras among the Kashmir brahmanas was as large as 199,[383] which sufficiently points to the large-scale immigrations of brahmanas from different directions. Significantly, as per the tradition, there were only six *gotras* originally.

What is more, as the brahmanas came from different places which the brahmanical sources grouped in a hierarchical order in accordance with differing adherence to the standards of brahmanical purity, the brahmana community got divided into different strata with varying status, for example, those who belonged to "Aryavarta" were "pure" brahmans, and therefore the most prestigious of all. But those who came from Gandhara were "impure" and therefore lowest in esteem.[384] Besides the brahmanas, the other "people of quality" were also in demand; mention may be made of artists, craftsmen and other professionals of repute, and those who belonged to martial groups. The latter were the most sought after people by kings, ministers and "feudal barons." Since they were powerful enough to leave consequential impact on the thinking of the ruling class, Kalhana condemns them—Bhuttas, Dardas, Mleechas, Turuśkas, Khasas, Loharas etc.—for polluting Kashmir and its value system.[385]

Proliferation of Cults

Inflow of people with varied religious and cultural backgrounds together with Kashmiris' exposure to different religious discourses during their sojourn to different "hot places" of its neighbouring world led to four major and interrelated developments in the religious space of Kashmir, namely, proliferation of cults and their hybridisation, flexibility in *Varnaśramadharma*, the formation of a syncretic dominant tradition, and innovation in religious traditions.

In the preceding chapter, we have seen that from the third decade of sixth century, Śaivism and Vaiśnavism became the dominant traditions of Kashmir. Yet, besides Śiva and Viṣṇu there were many other minor gods and goddesses in the pantheon of these dominant sects. The most important of them include Surya, Kartikeya, Ganesha, Agni, Lakshmi, Durga, Ganga, Yamuna and Kamadeva.[386] Moreover, none of the two major dominant traditions was monolithic; instead each of them was split into many sects with stark divergencies and differences in their respective beliefs and practices. For example, Śaivism, which was the dominant tradition from the tenth century, was divided into many sects having hardly anything in common save that all of them regarded Śiva as the Cosmic overlord. Broadly there were three types of Śaivites who may be classified as semi-Vedic, non-Vedic and anti-Vedic. The semi-Vedic Śaivites were those Śaivites who followed the Vedic and *Smarta Puranic* norms plus many aspects of Śaivism, namely, the Mother Goddess cult, lingam worship, carnivorous diet etc. However, as adherents of *Vedas* and *Smarta Puranic* norms, they were the believers of *Varnāśramadharma*, authority of the *brāhmanas*, idol worship, theism and pantheism, rituals and ceremonies.[387] Among the semi-Vedic Śaivites may also be counted what may be called the renouncers, who, according to Marco Polo

> live in communities, observe strict abstinence in regard to eating, drinking and the intercourse of the sexes and refrain from every kind of sexual indulgence in order that they may not give any offence to the idols whom they worship.[388]

The non-Vedic Śaivites were the Tantric Śaivites who relied more on *Tantras* than on the *Vedas*. The Tantric Śaivism of Kashmir also known as "Kashmiri Śaivism" is essentially an absolute monistic philosophy based on 64 *Śaiva Āgamas*.[389] This absolute non-dualistic philosophy posits that there is only one absolute reality called *Paramaśiva*.[390] It belittles the worth and value of pilgrimage, worship of the gods and the like of *vrata, tapa, tirtha, devācārnādishu*.[391] It also emphasises that God should be meditated upon as one without hands, feet, belly or limbs and only as *Satcitananda* and *Prakāsha*.[392] To "men of little intelligence God seems to dwell in icons or symbolic diagrams (*pratimāsu alpabuddhīnam*)."[393] Telling of beads or recitation of the names of God and singing of hymns of praise "are worship of a low kind while offering of oblations into sacrificial fire (*hōma*) and *pūja* are even lower than the low kind of worship (*japastutih syādadhamā homapūjādhamādhamā*)."[394] In the same vein, it does not see any worth and value in austere penance. More emphasis is laid on yoga rather than on ritual.[395] Also, there is no room for discrimination on the basis of caste and sex so far as initiation in Śaivism is concerned.[396]

The Tantric Śaivites were also divided into different sects on the basis of the different *ācāras* followed by different groups. The main *ācāras* were *Daksina ācāra, Samaya ācāra, Vama ācāra*, *Kaula ācāra*, *Mata ācāra* and *Trika ācāra*.[397] The last one of these was predominantly popular among the Śaivas of Kashmir. The use of five *makārās* (wine, meat, fish, roasted corn and sex) was essentially prescribed in *Kaulācāra*[398]—the *ācāra* whose popularity in Kashmir was only next to *Trika ācāra*.[399] *Trika ācāra*, however, agrees with the *Kaula* view that the limitless divine self-bliss can be experienced through sensual enjoyments. The use of *makarās* has been recommended in couplets 69–74 of the *Vijnānabhairava*, an important scriptural work on the *Trika* system.[400] Abhinavagupta, the famous exponent of Kashmiri Śaivism, maintains that an aspirant can have access to the limitless divine bliss called *jagadānanda* through an experience of sensual enjoyments.[401] *Vamācāra* prescribed an excessive use of intoxicants without any element of modesty in its practice.[402] While *Kaulas* used *makārās* in closed compartments called *Kaulācāra*, *Vamācārins* took it publically.[403] *Daksinācāra* prohibits the use of such objects.[404] The *Mata ācāra* has a position in between the *Kaula* and *Trika ācāra*.[405] However, each of these sub-sects was a mix of different beliefs and practices so aptly summed up by the famous dictum, "internally a Kaula, externally a Śaiva and in social practice a follower of the Veda" (*antaḥ kaulo bahiḥ śaivo lokācāre tu vaidikaḥ*).[406] Writing about the distinct number of Viśnu images in the famous Sun temple of Kashmir, Martand, Robert E. Fisher remarks,

> Were it not for the traditional popularity of the sun-god cult in north-western India and the name of the temple being Martand, this structure might today be judged to have been dedicated to Vishnu, so prominent are the images of that deity.[407]

The occurrence of dissent, difference and counter-voice in any learned society, which is also connected with different centres of learning, is quite normal, and, therefore, does not necessarily prompt one to search for any direct evidence for its sources. However, we have tangible evidence that many beliefs intersecting, contradicting, destabilising and modifying each other were introduced from outside along with human agents. For example, the monistic Śaivism was introduced in Kashmir by Samgramaditya somewhere in the seventh century CE. Samgramaditya was the son of Trambakaditya who lived near Kailaśa mountain. That is why monistic Śaivism is also called the Trayambaka School.[408] Abhinavagupta, at whose hands monistic Śaivism reached to its perfection in the tenth-eleventh century, says that the 'sage who gave the light of true knowledge' to him was Śambhu Nātha of Jalandhara.[409] Śambhu Nātha's preceptor and grand preceptor were Soma Natha and Sumati Natha, respectively, who lived in South India.[410] Kaula ācāra begins with Maheshwarananda alias Gorakhanatha. The present Kauls of Kashmir believe that Maheshwarananda was their ancestor who came from Maharashtra.[411] The anthropological study of the Kaul population of Kashmir would easily connect it with either Maharashtra or Bengal. The originator of Kaula system of Yoga was, according to Abhinavagupta, the sage named Machhanda alias Matsyendra Natha of Assam.[412] Dakśinācāra, which was essentially brahmanical, had its roots in South India as the name indicates. We are also told by Jayanta Bhatta, in his *Nyayamanjari* and in more detail in his *Agamadambāra*, about the arrival of a new tantric sect, Nilambra, which caused a great uproar in Kashmir.[413] Kalhana mentions that the "wretched foreigners" taught Kalasa "evil habits."[414] If we read it together with Kalasa's basest licentiousness and drinking of wine without moderation in the company of his tantric guru,[415] it becomes amply clear that the "wretched foreigners" referred to by Kalhana, were the gurus of Vamācāra, which discounted any external worship of the deity and resorted to five Ms (*pancamakāras*) namely *madirā* (wine), *matsya* (fish), *māṁsa* (meat), mudrā (roasted corn) and *maithuna* (coitus with beautiful women).[416] Also, Mankha, Jayanta Bhatta, Ksemendra and Jonaraja disapprovingly refer to the impressive presence of atheists.[417] Indeed, the atheists of Kashmir were not a unique body of non-believers. They were an integral part of pan-Indian tradition. In this regard mention may be made of Carvākās.[418]

Flexible Varṅāśramadharma

The nature of *Varnāśramadharma* in Kashmir is a subject of interesting debate. SC Ray opines that in Kashmir there were neither such castes as *kśatriya, vaiśya* and *śudra* nor intermediary castes between the *brāhmanas* or other lower castes as we find in other parts of the subcontinent.[419] This contention has been convincingly refuted by Krishna Mohan, who on the authority of Kalhana refers to the existence of not only *kśatriyas, vaiśyas* and *śudras* but also 64 intermediary castes.[420] *NP* explicitly refers to the existence of four castes, and that too among the special features of Kashmir.[421]

While there is no denying the fact that Kashmiri society was divided into four castes plus outcastes like *dombās* and *ćandālās*, it is, however, true that there was no strict adherence to the four-fold classification and caste segregation in practice, as we find occasionally low castes occupying high positions,[422] high castes marrying low castes[423] and only *dombās* and *ćandalas* being considered impure.[424] Though not a rule, it alludes to considerable flexibility in caste system. Probably this phenomenon can be attributed to the resilience of local traditions should we bear in mind that Aryans had to accommodate the local beliefs in their liturgy and also to give a place to the local leaders in their pantheon. Also, Tantricism, which pervaded all the beliefs of Kashmir, considered caste system blasphemous.[425] The influence of Buddhism and Islam together with the infiltration of diverse ethnic groups might have also acted as powerful contributory factors to blunt the caste system.

That *Varnāśramadharma* had to make compromises because of the influx of non-brahmana immigrants is also substantiated by Kalhana who says that "the pious observances of this land had fallen off from the sacred law" because of its being "overrun by Dardas, Bhuttas and Mleechas."[426] The same factors accounted for the absence of any regard for *sati* among the general populace,[427] eating of beef by some *damaras*[428] and inter-religious matrimonial relations.[429]

Formation of a Syncretic Dominant Tradition

Indeed, Brahmanism faced a serious challenge at the hands of non-conformist forces—both theistic and atheistic, but these forces could only affirm rather than displace the dominant tradition.[430] With kings and upper castes (exceptions apart) as its supporters, Brahmanism continued to be the dominant tradition. Yet, in the presence of a host of alternative beliefs, it would be naïve to think the dominant tradition remaining immune from the environment reverberating with many narratives. Nor could any belief in human history afford to resist the demands of practical life. This is the reason that we see, in the words of Kalhana, the "ignorant gurus revising the traditional doctrines by texts of their own,"[431] "taking of arms by brahmanas,"[432] drinking of wine by brahmana gurus while singing their chants,[433] and conjugal life of ascetics and their possession of lands.[434] And this is also the reason that Kalhana is unfailingly worried about the fluid social milieu, structured along non-brahmanical lines. He is particularly annoyed with choosing of rulers, officials or wives from diverse social categories, and fluidity of sexual relations and distortions in the use of brahmanical institutions.[435] The pressures of complex realities gave birth to what the Kashmiri brahmanas would call *deśaguna*, literally meaning a virtue of the country, technically connoting a compromise, a concession to the circumstances. That all the Kashmiri brahmanas were meat eaters and that they even employed Muslims for slaughtering animals are justified on the ground that it is based on *deśaguna*.[436]

The two dominant cults, Vedic Śaivism and Vedic Vaiśnavism, present an interesting picture of religious syncretism. Drawn from various sources, the pantheon of Vedic Śaivism comprises Śiva, Viṣṇu, Surya, Bhairava, Ganesha, Kamadeva and Shakti under various names alongside the Vedic gods.[437] Referring to the continuity of this syncretic tradition over the *longue durée*, the eminent social anthropologist and the Kashmiri Pandit, TN Madan says: "Kashmiri Brahmans today are Smartas, that is, worshippers of Shiva, Shakti and Vishnu, and upholders of the householder tradition. Domestic puja comprises of the panchayat (so named) of Ganapati, Surya, Vishnu, Shiva and Devi."[438] The deep-seated impact of tantricism on Vedic Śaivites can be inferred from their appropriation of many tantric rituals which together with the Vedic rituals came to be recognised as fundamental principles in achieving union with Śiva. In this regard mention may be made of their concept of Śakti in its various forms, the *Lingam* worship, the awakening of *kundalini* by yoga, the idea of deities presiding over the different parts of the body and their outward symbolic representation by means of mystic diagrams, the different *ācāras* followed in worship, the recitation of mantras, the necessity of rituals, the spiritual discipline in company with women etc.[439]

Initially the two Viṣṇava cults, Bhagvatas and Pānchrātras, were non-Vedic and anti-brahmana. Later on the followers of these cults identified their respective deities with the Vedic Viṣṇu. *NP* mentions "with reverence the Bhagwatas, the Brahmanas and the Pānchrātra system" pointing to the synthesis of Vedic and Viṣṇava cults. We even find the Viṣṇavas offering meat to the goddess Śāradā hinting at the same conclusion of comingling of different gods and goddesses.[440]

The best example of the emergence of syncretic dominant tradition is *Nīlamata Purāna,* which places Viṣṇu and Śiva in a complementary relationship;[441] accords reverential position to Buddha and Sakyas;[442] and, more importantly, makes the local Naga divinities and even the Piśacas next to none of the divine forces to be worshipped as per the liturgical procedure laid down by Nīla, the Naga king who is represented virtually as an emanation of Viṣṇu himself.[443]

Innovations in Religious Traditions

The emergence of a myriad of cults, the binary opposition between the dominant tradition and dissent, the *Puranic process* and the resultant hybridisation of dominant tradition all point to the same conclusion that religion was not something a bundle of fixed attitudes which could not be reformulated, changed or even challenged in the light of new experiences and novel problems. The fluid religious scenario substantiates the assertion of John Nemec that the "religious traditions of Medieval South Asia were nothing if not innovative in idea and practice."[444] Basing his argument on the writings of the most prominent authors associated with "Kashmiri Śavism" namely, Somananda (ca. 900–950), Utpaladeva (ca. 925–975), Abhinavagupta (ca. 975–1025) and Jayaratha (early thirteenth CE), Nemec says, "the authors in question explicitly wedded themselves to the notion that novelty, the production of something new, was not only acceptable, but was an asset to their religion."[445] Nemec quotes Utpaladeva's own concluding remark on his completed text:

> Thus I set forth this new (*nava*), easy path as it was explained by my distinguished teacher (Somananda in the Śastra, entitled Śivadṛṣṭi).[446]

One of the new paths is outlined in the 18th chapter of the *Mālinīvijayottaratantra* authored by Abhinavagupta. This new path is not only non-conformist, seeking a partial rupture with the past, but it is also an umbrella site offering shelter to all, an open path, inviting everyone to walk on it:

> There is no purity here, nor impurity, no consideration of what is to be eaten, etc. there is no duality, nor non-duality, and no (requirement to perform) acts of devotion to *liṅga*, etc. There is similarly no (requisite) abandoning of those [acts], nor the (required) renunciation of material possessions, nor gain any (requirement regarding the) accumulation of material possessions. There is no (requisite) maintenance of twisted locks of hair [*jaṭā*], of (smearing oneself with) sacred ashes, or the like, nor any (requisite) abandoning of the same. And as regards the performance or non-performance of vows, etc., and entrance into sacred places, etc. [i.e., *kṣetras, pīṭhas*, and *upapīṭhas; see* TĀ 4.259cd and the TĀV thereupon], the observance of rules of action, and (those rules associated with) initiatory name, initiatory lineage [*gotra*], or the like [i.e., according to the lodge (ghara) and the like of the initiate; see TĀ 4.267cd], whether the form, sectarian marks, and so on be one's own or another's – nothing is prescribed here regarding these, nor, contrariwise, prohibited. Absolutely everything is performed here [according to the rules of the *Mālinīvijayottara*], and, contrariwise, omitted. Yet, this (alone) is necessarily enjoined here [in the *Mālinīvijayottara*], O Goddess, that the wholly pleased yogin must fix his consciousness [*cetas*] on reality; and he should therefore act only in accordance with that [reality (*tattva*)], whatever that may be for him. Moreover, the one whose consciousness [*citta*] is fixed on reality, partaking even in the pleasures of the senses [*viṣaya*], is not touched by bad consequences, just as the petal of a lotus (is not affected) by water. The yogin who has great

understanding [*mahāmati*] is the one who is similar to the person who, armed with mantras that counteract poison and the like, is not deluded by the poison even while devouring it.[447]

That innovation was commonplace during the period is evidenced by the proliferation of multiple *śastras* which were supplementing as well as competing with one another. This is marked even among different branches of non-conformist Śaivism. For example while agreeing with Shaman Hatley, Nemec says that Abhinavagupta "while allowing for an innovative social institution that ignores caste distinctions, it also synchronizes such practices with the caste-based Brahmanical structures that were not, historically speaking espoused in the Kula-Kaula branch of *Śavism*." Similarly, according to Alexis Sanderson what is offered by Abhinavagupta is a "Vertical" model of authority and innovation, as opposed to the more radical, "horizontal" model found elsewhere in the *Śaiva* traditions which more fully unshackled themselves from Brahmanical norms.[448] The religious scriptures introduced by "particular agents in particular historical moments . . . allowed for, indeed anticipated, the emergence of new exceptional rules, new texts, to respond to the new challenges begging resolution."[449]

Architecture and Sculpture: A Site of Entangled Histories

The Karkota period, especially the reign of Lalitaditya, saw the zenith in the development of art and architecture at the hands of great masters—both local and non-local—liberally patronised by the king, members of the royal family and the wealthy ruling class. According to written evidence, Lalitaditya and other kings of the time constructed a huge number of Hindu and Buddhist structures.[450] However only a few of them have survived to us, and those too are in ruinous conditions. Of the important sites of archaeological value are Martand, Parihaspura, Ushkur, Tapar, Bunyar, Pandrethan, Naran Nag, Letapura, Kakpura and Avantipura. Although in ruinous conditions, both the Hindu and Buddhist architecture and art point to two important facts: One that, like philosophy, literature and religion, Kashmir's contribution to architecture and art is "not just profound but totally disproportionate to its geographical size."[451] Second, the architecture and art exhibit a successful blend of foreign and Indigenous elements thanks to the presence of artists of different cultural backgrounds.

Stone Temples

"Of all the artistic remains in Kashmir," says Robert Fisher, "none is more distinctive than the stone temples. The typical Kashmiri temples exhibit a unique blend of foreign styles and native creativity that resulted in an architectural tradition notably different from others in the subcontinent."[452] The special features of the brahminical stone temples of the period include double pyramidal roof; triangular pediment enclosing a trefoil niche; fluted columns with Doric and Ionic capitals; a wood or stone "lantern" ceiling and cloistered courts.[453] Of the European styles which filtered through west Asia and Gandhara and played an important role in the development of Kashmiri stone architecture, mention may be made of columns of Doric order, pediments, trefoil arches, pilasters, dentil and cornice. All these architectural features were borrowed from Greek architecture through Gandhara—the hub of Graeco-Indian cultural synthesis. An important architectural feature of the stone temples, borrowed from wooden models of Parthian origin, is the formation of intersecting cross-members, popularly called the "lantern" ceiling.[454] The dominant decorative motif throughout the famous Sun temple (Martand temple built by Lalitaditya) is the distinctive architectural niche. It is believed to have been derived from Gandhara.[455] The cruciform terraced structure surrounded by monks' cells commonly found in Kashmiri Hindu stone temples originated from Gandhara Buddhist monuments and practically adopted in the construction of Buddhist monastic establishments at Ushkur and Parihaspur.[456] The Indian influences can also be found in such motifs as water pot, lotus flower and lotus petals on cornices of capitals, geese, parrots, *yakshas, garudas* and *gandharvas.*

Writing about the Avantisvami temple built by Avantivarman, Fisher says,

> Nearly all the pilasters [of the Avantisvamin temple] are decorated with a rich variety of motifs, some native to India; others reflecting West Asian taste, as found upon Sassanian silver: roundels that enclose lotuses, geese, mythical creatures, paired humans, birds and flowers as well as numerous geometric patterns that all together give these ninth-century monuments a livelier quality than was possible with the older, fluted columns of Karkota temples.[457]

Buddhist Architecture

Almost the whole Buddhist architectural wealth has become extinct. Yet the ruins of Ushkur and Parihaspur provide a clue to the history of Kashmiri Buddhist architecture featuring four stairs, high plinth and cells built into the enclosure. Lalitaditya created a new composite structure by bringing the stupa inside the vihāra and adding monks' cells to the surrounding wall—exactly like the temples of the time with the central shrine and courtyard surrounded by arcaded walls.[458] The same Buddhist architectural configuration is found in Taxila site of Bhamla and in the Rawak vihāra of Khotan. Interestingly all these sites are roughly of the same date in "Trans-Indus" regions, namely, Central Asia and Afghanistan including Kashmir.[459]

Sculpture

Like architecture, the sculpture of the period is also characterised by a synthesis of heterogeneous style, giving birth to a new school of sculpture, which is represented by in all the versions of the time—terracotta, stone, metal and ivory. Referring to the syncretic character of the sculpture of the Karkota period, Stanislaw Czuma says:

> A new school of sculpture evolved there under the auspices of the Karkota dynasty, which came into prominence sometime during the seventh century, while a related style flourished in the adjoining territory of today's Afghanistan under the patronage of the foreign Hindu Shahi dynasty. Since Kashmir was once an integral part of vast empire, it is not surprising that the Gandhara tradition to a great extent formed the roots of the Kashmiri style. Gandhara is, however, but one factor contributing to this complex style, which is equally strongly influenced by the plasticity and spirituality of Gupta art. Iranian motifs combined with Central Asian and Chinese elements are also frequently present. The Stuccos of Fondukistan and the terracottas of Akhnur and Ushkur provide probably the closest stylistic parallels and are frequently cited as precursors of that style . . . the Kashmiri school absorbed all those [foreign] influences and transformed them into an idiom that is uniquely Kashmiri. The style thus created is characterized by great elegance and sophistication, with slightly elongated figures that exhibit the naturalistic modelling of Gandhara and the sensuality of Gupta art.[460]

Underlining the linkages of Kashmiri sculpture with its vast neighbourhood, Czuma says that the textile patterns found on some of the bronzes represent the classic designs of the period, found from Afghanistan through the Himalayas to Chinese Turkistan.[461] He further says that all the images of the Buddha display a facial type that has "at once affinities with faces found in Central Asian paintings – such as at Qizil or Kucha – as well as in the art of Tang China."[462]

John Siudmak found a number of features in the Buddhist stone sculptures recovered from the Cankun Stupa at Parihaspura which are common in the art of Buddhist Central Asia and China.[463] The complete standing Buddha is "the classical Buddha type of Kashmir." It wears a three-part crown formed of crescents within which are motifs of flowers, and the crown is tied with flying ribbons.[464] This "unusual crowned Buddha," says Fisher, "has close parallels, in the treatment of the crown, from central Asia and China, especially at Yun Kang, which is certainly of early date."[465] The heterogeneous influences on Kashmir bronze have also attracted the attention of Pratapaditya Pal:

By and large, the early Kashmir bronzes of the sixth-seventh century reveal vestiges of the Gandhara tradition as well as influences of Gupta aesthetic. This is clearly evident in two small but charming bronzes of the seventh century. One represents the Hindu god Ganesha and the other Buddha Sakyamuni. In both bronzes, the pedestals are clearly derived from Gandhara images. Plain, moulded rectangular bases are common in Gandhara bronzes, while thrones supported by animals and atlantes are frequently encountered in Gandhara stone images. The stylish elegance and swagger of Ganesha, using his battle-axe like a walking stick, as well as the suave modeling of the Buddha, are on the other hand features that are typical of Gupta period sculptures. The plain circular nimbus of the Buddha, however, is a survival of the Gandhara tradition and continued to be popular with Kashmiri sculptors well into the Utpala period.[466]

The Kashmiri Language—A Repository of the Culture of Encounters

Like any other language of a linguistic cultural region, the Kashmiri language is a mine of information about the valley's past, especially its evolution and growth as a cultural realm owing to its repeated encounters with the neighbouring world. The word fund of the language is so hugely derived from a variety of sources that it has become a dynamic text capable of generating many meanings simultaneously. No wonder then, some scholars consider it to have been derived from Sanskrit,[467] some regard it as an independent branch of the Aryan Language,[468] some trace its origin to Dravidian languages or having been influenced by them,[469] and some even believe that it has descended from the Hebrew language.[470] Indeed, if the linguists would re-look at the issue and examine the word fund of the Kashmiri language in the light of major and minor languages spoken in its immediate and distant neighbourhoods during early Kashmir, a multitude of new theories would flow from it. After all, Kashmir had intimate connections with the Mediterranean world, East Asia, Russia, Central Asia, West Asia and the Indian subcontinent since the hoary past. To be sure, the early culture of Kashmir is the extension and juxtaposition of the salient elements of all these cultural centres. With cultural changes also occurred linguistic changes, making the Kashmiri language basically a loan-oriented language. Since it has been studied in the background of Dardic, Sanskrit, Hebrew and Dravidian languages only, the equally other important sources of the language await a collaborative effort of the linguists and historians belonging to different linguistic-cultural regions.

The archaeology, history and anthropology show it unmistakably that till the close of the fifth century CE, the sources of Kashmiri culture, and thereby of the Kashmiri language, were numerous and multi-directional. However, from the mid of the sixth century till the end of thirteenth century, the fountainhead of the culture of Kashmir and, by implication, of the Kashmiri language was mainly Indian culture, especially the Brahmanic religion and the "language of the gods" (Sanskrit). That is why, without any exaggeration, every second word of the present Kashmiri language is either of Sanskritic origin or pressed into a Sanskritic garb,[471] though more than 600 years have elapsed since Sanskrit and Sanskritic culture lost the official patronage and the position of being the language and culture of the mass religion. This is the main reason that some scholars believe that the Kashmiri language originated from Sanskrit. George Grierson, who does not regard Kashmiri as a Sanskritic form of speech, however, admits that "the greater part of its vocabulary is now of Indian origin and is allied to that of the Sanskrit Indo-Aryan languages of northern India."[472] It should, however, be noted that like the pre-sixth century era when the Kashmiri language was influenced by the neighbouring regional and sub-regional languages alongside the languages of major cultural centres, in the similar vein after the post-fifth century Indic turn, Kashmiri culture and its popular language, Kashmiri were also influenced by the regional cultures/languages of the subcontinent alongside Sanskrit, the language of the high culture. After all, there were not only repeated influxes of people from different linguistic-cultural regions of India, but Kashmir had also intimate cultural and economic relations with distant regions of the subcontinent reaching up to the deep south. The influence of regional languages of India has been so significant that Mohammad Yusuf Taing, a Kashmiri scholar, believes that there is a close affinity between the Kashmiri and Dravidian languages.[473] Similarly SK Chatterji opines that "the Indo-Aryan Prakritis and Apabhramsha from the Midland and from northern Punjab profoundly modified the Dardic basis of Kashmiri language."[474]

Encounter With Islamic Cosmopolitan Ecumene:

Around 883 CE, the Arab amir of Sind, 'Abd Allah received a letter from the then ruler of Kashmir requesting to arrange for him a *hindiyah* (Hindavi or Sanskrit) version of exegesis (*tafsir*) of the law of Islam.[475] It is not surprising should we consider that right from the Arab control of Sind and Multan in the beginning of eighth century Kashmir was face to face with Islam. Initially the Kashmiri rulers were under great threat of Arab incursions forcing them to enter into alliances with the powers in the neighbourhood to checkmate the Arab advancement.[476] As Kashmiri rulers had matrimonial and diplomatic relations with the ruling family of Sind,[477] Kashmir became a safe place for asylum seekers including a fugitive Arab commander and his corps.[478] However, once the fear of invasion was allayed, the Kashmiri rulers realised the significance of being pragmatic and sent the feelers of befriending the Arabs who were occupying the borderlands of Kashmir, the most crucial lifeline of the valley.

The Kashmiri rajas did not only throw the borders open to Muslims but they also gave them all the facilities to conduct hassle-free trade between Kashmir and the neighbouring world.[479] In this regard it may be mentioned that Arab and Persian merchants, both Muslims and Jews, operated in the coastal areas of Sind.[480] By the early eighth century, the northern and western regions of what today is Afghanistan also came under the control of Arabs. As a result, by the ninth century, the Arabic language and Islamic learning had made such deep inroads into the erstwhile Sanskritic frontier societies of Kashmir that a foundation text dated 857 from the Tochi Valley in Waziristan is inscribed in both Arabic and Sanskrit.[481] Given the contacts of Kashmir with the Arab Muslims since the beginning of the eighth century and the dominant Islamic ecumene in its immediate neighbourhood together with the friendly relations of knowledge-loving rulers of Kashmir with the Arab amirs, it is no wonder to see one of them approaching the amir of Sind in the later quarter of ninth century for a *hindiyah* translation of an exegesis of the laws of Islam.

Meanwhile, the evidence of significant Persianate-Islamic influences in the neighbouring Multan has come down to us. We are told that in addition to Arabic, comprehensible Persian (*farsiyyati mafhumat*) was spoken in Multan in the tenth century obviously because of its position as a terminal of the Khurasan trade.[482] According to the contemporary sources, tenth-century Kabul was populated by Muslims, Jews and Hinduwān (Hindus).[483] The Muslim traders operating in Sind and Kabul were both Arabs and Persians.[484] That they, alongside Jews, traded in Kashmir is borne out by Al-Biruni who says that no one, not even a Jew or Hindu, was allowed to enter Kashmir during the Ghaznavid incursions on Hindu Śhahi kingdom,[485] which extended from Kabul to the Punjab. However, when the Ghaznavids of Afghanistan established their empire on the north and western borders of Kashmir, the Kashmiri rajas, while taking a cue from their predecessors, realised the significance of being pragmatic in their relations with a formidable neighbour, and thus whole-heartedly owned the Muslim Turks leading to an unprecedented influx of the Persianate-Islamic background Muslims into the valley. Given that from the beginning of eleventh century the balance of power shifted in favour of Persianate background Ghaznavids making Persian and the Persianate-Islamic culture "prestigious imitation" in the Ghaznavid Indian empire influencing Kashmir too, it comes as no surprise to see a learned Kashmiri, Tilak proficient in Hindavi and Persian which enabled him to get entry at the court of Ghaznavid ruler, Sultan Mas'ud (1031–1041) as a translator (*mutarjim*).[486]

There is no doubt that with the Ghaznavid control over the west and north-west borderlands of Kashmir in the beginning of eleventh century Kashmir's encounter with Persianate-Islamic culture increased exponentially to the extent that we find Muslim Turks holding commanding positions in the armies of Ananta (1028–1063), Harśa (1089–1101), Biksukara (1120–1121) and Jayasimha (1128–1149).[487] The impressive presence of Muslim Turks in the courts of the Hindu rajas of Kashmir presupposes the impact of Persianate-Islamic culture on the courtly milieus, a glimpse of which we have in Kalhana's description of the cultural project of the connoisseur King Harśa.

In the preceding pages we have discussed that following his disposition for glamour and aesthetics, Harśa introduced into Kashmir, especially in his courtly life, the salient attributes of exotic cultures which satisfied his special tastes. He was also perhaps impressed by the stories of grandeur of the Sassanian courts which had also impressed the Muslim rulers.[488] Indeed, the Sasanian courts had become imitable models for the Muslims since the "Abbasid caliphs who modelled much of their court culture on that of the Sassanian kings"[489] whose territories they had inherited. The Ghaznavids, who ruled just on the other side of Kashmir's western and north-western borders, faithfully followed this tradition of their predecessors.[490] And as the Kashmiri rajas had intimate relations with the Ghaznavid courtly milieu through the Turuśka captains[491] and artisans[492] they recruited and the Turuśka concubines they had in their seraglio,[493] it is no surprise that Harśa modelled much of his court culture on that of the Sasanian kings creating a common bond rooted in the etiquette and rituals of kingship. This is what one can gather from the information we have about his splendid palaces, pleasure gardens and, more so, about "the lustre of his new sovereignty" which he displayed by issuing a dress code and other related instructions to his courtiers. To quote Kalhana:

> The very numerous palaces of the king show forthwith wonderful splendour, having golden amalaka ornaments and buildings which reached to the clouds. In his Nandana grove there were all trees only the wishing trees (*Kalpadruma*) absent as he had put them to shame by his liberality. . . . Nobody in his court was seen without brilliant dress, without gold ornaments, with a small following, or without a resolute bearing. At that gate of the king's palace at which people from various nations presented themselves, the riches of all countries seemed always to be piled up. In the king's palace, councillors, chamberlains and other [attendants] moved about without number, adorned with golden chains and bracelets. While thus displaying the lustre of his new sovereignty, the king regarded the opinion of Vijayamalla just as that of a Guru. . . . The king who was free from jealousy, introduced into his land elegant fashions, just as the spring [brings flowers] into the forest. Formerly people in this country had, with the single exception of the king, worn their hair loose, had carried no head-dress and no ear-ornaments. In this land where the commander-in-chief Madana, by dressing his hair in

> braids and the prime minister Jayānanda, by wearing a short coat of bright colour, had incurred the king's displeasure, there this ruler introduced for general wear a dress which was fit for a king. When some of his ministers had got themselves up in brilliant finery, he, without feeling jealous, got his own female attendants to swing lights (*ārātrīka*) around them.[494]

Aural Stein notes the likelihood that the "change of fashion here referred to have had something to do with the customs (of the Muslim Sultanates to the west)."[495] Finbarr Flood shows firm inclination to agree with Stein because during "the eleventh and twelfth centuries the Turkic amirs and Sultans who dominated the eastern Islamic world provided the models for court cultures from Armenia to Afghanistan."[496] Also, the Hindu rajas of Kashmir showed no qualms to emulate the Turks as is shown by the employment of a Turk Muslim artisan to gild the parasol (*chatr*) covering the central icon of a Śiva temple.[497] Flood even believes that the artists who painted Alchi frescoes showing *inter alai* Muslim robes hailed from Kashmir.[498]

Harśa was also probably influenced by the much circulated stories of proverbial justice of some Sasanian and Muslim rulers, especially Khusrau Anu Shirwan (531–578 CE) and Harun al-Rashid (786–809 CE). While the circulation of the stories of justice of Harun al-Rashid by Muslims is understandable, what is more significant is that they played an important role in propagating the just rule of Anu Shirwan by telling and retelling these stories in their Arabic and Persian works perhaps to use it as one more tool in an overwhelmingly Persianate environment to realise the Islamic ideals of kingship in which the dispensation of justice features prominently. After all, it is the Muslims who popularised him by the title of Naushirwān-i'Adil—Naushirwan, the just—the popularity which perhaps also travelled to Kashmir through contacts with the Muslims both inside and outside the valley and impressed Harśa who was known for emulating the exotic.[499] Thus, to ensure that justice is done to the victims, especially to the powerless who had no access to the court, Harśa, like Anu Shirwan,[500] introduced a novelty of putting up bells (at his palace gate) the ringing of which would facilitate the speedy delivery of justice by the king himself:

> At the palace gate (*Siṁhadvara*) he hung up great bells in all four directions, to be informed by their sound of those who had come with the desire of making representations. And when he had once heard their plaintive speech, he fulfilled their desire [as quickly] as the cloud in the rainy season[fulfils]that of the Cātaka birds.[501]

Apart from employing people regardless of their ethnic/religious/spatial backgrounds by the two neighbours—Ghaznavids and Kashmiri rajas, there was a continuous movement of people between Kashmir and the Muslim ruled neighbourhoods for political, commercial and religious purposes. Even many Kashmiris settled in the Muslim ruled neighbourhood,[502] and a good number of Muslims from proximate neighbourhoods made Kashmir as their permanent abode giving birth to a colony of Muslims in Srinagar.[503] The intimate encounter with the Islamic culture was pregnant with making vital impact on Kashmir, but we have only a few fleeting references in the sources as it was not the subject of interest for Kalhana to whom everything non-brahmanic was abominable; nor did it arouse the curiosity of other contemporary Sanskrit writers of Kashmir. Yet a glimpse of this impact can be had from the usage of a few Sanskritised Persian terms by Kalhana, namely, *divara* (Pr. *dabir*), *ganja* (Pr. *ganj*), *ganjawara* (Pr. *gangwar*) and *Hammira* (Pr. *Amir*).[504] The appropriation of the terms of the "other" sets the process of "internalization" of the other or "othering" of the self, a movement of accommodation of the culture that it represents.[505] Moreover, it points to a long history of contact Kashmir had with the Persianate-Islamic culture. As rightly noted by Flood, "The synchronic deployment of the name presupposes a diachronic history of engagement through which the appropriated term acquires its desirable qualities".[506] Kalhana refers to a powerful faction of kingmakers, Lavanyas "taking cow's meat in the lands of *Mleechas*"[507] testifying to their not mere outward public self-representation but a thorough absorption into the dominant Persianate-Islamic culture of the neighbourhood with which the prestigious sections of Kashmir—rulers, nobles, elite and the traders—had intimate relations.

Indeed, cosmopolitan of all sorts was considered an asset for the state. That is why we find the borders being left open to religious preachers. Kśemandra, the famous polymath of eleventh-century Kashmir, makes a casual but intriguing mention of the presence of "Muslim singers" (*mleccha gayānah*) in Kashmir.[508] It is intriguing because the writer refers to the "Muslim singers" in the context of a courtesan who refuses to accept fee from her clients "for fear of *mleccha gayānah* who wandered the streets."[509] These *Mleccha* singers were in all probability the *manāqib khawāns* or *fadā'il khawāns*, who besides singing in praise of Allāh extolled the virtues of 'Ali (in case of being Shi'is) and the other companions of the Prophet (in case of being Sunnis) in the streets and bazaars of Iran and Central Asia as a propaganda technique to spread their belief and influence.[510] The *manāqib khawāns*, it may be noted, existed in "Iraq" since the Būyid period (932–1055 CE).[511] These "*Mleccha singers*" of the Sanskrit scholar had gained so much prestige and influence because of their exemplary piety that the courtesans (who otherwise freely indulged in prostitution under the very nose of local religious *gurus* and state authorities) refused to entertain the clients at their sight.[512]

That by the beginning of the thirteenth century Muslims formed an important section of the Kashmiri population and that Persianate Islamic culture had made great strides are further borne out by a recently discovered copy of the Qur'ān written by one Fateh Allāh Kashmiri in 1237 CE.[513] It is written in such a fine style and form that according to Muhammad Yūsuf Teng, "it would have taken hundreds of years to the Kashmiri Muslims to attain such a proficiency in Arabic script."[514] What is more significant about this copy of the Qur'ān is that it also contains a Persian translation. The Qur'ān with Persian translation, *inter alia*, unmistakably proves the increasing presence of Muslim preachers and their activities in the valley many centuries before the establishment of the Muslim Sultanate.

Significantly enough, of a very few facts, which Marco Polo chose worth recording about Kashmir, is the existence of a section of Muslims in Kashmir who worked as butchers for Kashmiri non-Muslims:

> The people of the province [Kashmir] do not kill animals, nor spill blood, so if they want to eat meat they get the *saracenes* [Muslims] who dwell among them to play the butcher.[515]

It is puzzling to notice only Muslims playing butchers for Kashmiri non-Muslims, especially when we know that animal sacrifice (*pasu-yaga*) and eating of meat (*mamsa*) were among the main rituals of Tantricism[516]—the popular religious philosophy of Kashmir much before the birth of the Prophet of Islam—which left a deep imprint upon Kashmiri Brāhmanism.[517] The veracity of Marco Polo's evidence cannot be questioned because it still holds good. The Kashmiri *brāhmanas* are meat eaters all and sundry; but they do not kill animals themselves; instead, they employ Muslims for the purpose. Then the question arises as to who acted as butchers before the *saracens* (Muslims). There can be no other answer save the one that some local group performed this job. It is, therefore, irresistible to conclude that probably the entire section of the local butchers had embraced Islam by the end of the thirteenth century. They had a socio-psychological temptation to embrace Islam as they belonged to some lower social group—the stigma that they could not live down, particularly after the revival of Brāhmanism in Kashmir. The fact that the butchers were assigned a lowly station in the society is further substantiated by the fact that because of the stable mental framework this group does not still command a much respectable position in Kashmiri society, although in the new social system, they felt elevated as is indicated by the prestigious *krāms* (surnames) as *Ganaie* assumed by the butcher group of Kashmir after embracing Islam.[518] The second plausible inference can be that with the introduction of Muslim butchers by the prestigious Muslim immigrants, the Kashmiri Hindu upper class would have preferred the Muslim butchers to local ones, forcing the latter to adopt the new faith that ensured the security of their hereditary calling.

Although there is evidence to suggest that the Muslim preachers continued to be present in Kashmir, only the name of a Suhrawardi saint, Sayyid Sharaf al-Dīn commonly known as Bulbul Shah, has survived to us. He came to Kashmir during the reign of Suhadeva.[519] His name was rescued from falling into oblivion by one of his most extraordinary achievements. He was instrumental in converting the reigning Buddhist ruler of Kashmir, Rinchana (1320–1323 CE) to Islam. And in order to pay tribute to his memory, Rinchana (now Sadr al-Dīn) constructed a *khānaqāh* after his name and endowed it with a rent-free land grant.[520] The *khānaqāh*, which is the first known *khānaqāh* of Kashmir, became so famous that the *muhalla*, where it was built came to be known as Bulbul Langar.[521] Besides the *khānaqāh*, Sultān Sadar al-Dīn also constructed a Jami Mosque in his newly built capital Rinchanpura (Srinagar).[522]

Considering that Sayyid Sharaf al-Dīn came all the way from Turkistan trekking through the difficult and inhospitable mountainous terrain to propagate Islam in an alien and non-Muslim land, and also bearing in mind that he belonged to the institutional phase of Sūfism characterised by *pīr-murīd* relationship, it can be safely inferred that the Suhrawardī saint would have been accompanied by a big group of *murīds* (disciples) and *khudām* (ancillary staff) as was commonplace with every religious mission of the time.

The conversion of the ruler to Islam marked a turning point in the history of Islam in Kashmir. Not only did Islam now receive political patronage but also became a "reference group culture"—a status-improving way of life, as the Muslim was elevated from a *mleccha* to a monarch. This is besides the fact that the conversion of the ruler would have validated the religious superiority of Islam vis-à-vis other religions of the period with obvious consequences. In this connection, it should be borne in mind that Rinchana embraced Islam after having discussions with the Hindu, Buddhist and Muslim religious personages of the period.[523] All in all, therefore, Rinchana's conversion to Islam was followed by the conversion of a large number of people including his Hindu prime minister, Rāwanchandra[524], who also happens to be the predecessor of a very influential noble family of Chandān, famous as Rainas in our sources.[525]

The streaming of Muslims into Kashmir continued unabated till the Muslim Sultanate was finally established in 1339. One among the lately arrived immigrants was Shah Mir, the future founder of the Muslim Sultanate in Kashmir. Coming from the royal family of Swāt, he along with his tribe entered Kashmir around 1313 and was bestowed with a land grant and an important position in the administration by the then ruler, Suhadeva (1301–1320).[526] Thus the Muslim Sultanate, which finally came into existence in 1339, was not the result of any military conquest of Kashmir by the Muslims, but was founded by a Muslim immigrant, Shah Mir, who, along with many other Muslim settlers from the neighbouring Muslim-ruled territories, had settled in the valley and shown exemplary qualities of leadership to bail the people out of centuries of misrule and recurrent foreign invasions prompted by the internal chaotic conditions of Kashmir. Such a role as this made Shah Mir a popular hero, winning for him titles like "saviour of the people,"[527] and that too from the die-hard *brāhmanas*. To be sure, Shah Mir occupied the throne and founded his dynastic rule primarily with the help of local nobility and people at large. Thus conversions to Islam, which took place in Kashmir especially during the reign of the Shah Mir dynasty (1339–1561), were conversions with a difference in the sense that there was no room for using force as the basis of the political authority of early rulers of the dynasty rested on the support of local "feudal" lords who constituted their nobility, army and bureaucracy and who were mainly non-Muslims until gradually brought under the fold of Islam.

Rājataraṅgiṇī *in the Context of Persianate Islamic Historiography*

At all hands, Kashmir is recognised as a unique place in the history of Sanskrit literature. This is so because Kalhana's *Rājataraṅgiṇī* (river of kings), written in 1149–1150 CE, is often considered as the first work of real history writing in South Asia. Many doyen historians, namely, AL Basham and Romila Thapar attribute this special feature of Kashmir's history to her contacts with central and west Asia where much before Kalhana, history writing was an established academic activity.[528] This assertion has been further elaborated recently by Jesse Knutson,[529] who sees Kalhana's *Rājataraṅgiṇī* informed by Persianate tradition especially the *Shahnamah*, the magnum opus of the great tenth-century Persian poet, Firdawsi. The basic features which, according to Kuntson, set the Rājataraṅgiṇī apart from other historical works of Sanskrit making him (Knutson) to proclaim that it "was modelled, at least in outline", on the Shahnamah, are as follows:

a) The concept of scientific accuracy and exhaustiveness [which Kalhana shows while narrating the events of his contemporary and near contemporary times] are probably direct imports from a Persianate tradition, exemplified in large part by Firdawsi's tenth century Shahnamah
b) Like Rājataraṅgiṇī, in Shahnamah "each dynasty begins auspiciously, then falls into moral and political decline."
c) "The template of rise and fall can be found in earlier Sanskrit works, such as, Kalidasa's Raguvamśa, yet in the latter work it is a cycle rather than tight concentric cycles, as in Kalhana and Firdawsi.
d) "The notion of history as exclusively coincident with kings, their cycles of prosperity and perdition, connects it [Rājataraṅgiṇī] to broader Islamic traditions" which had their roots in pre-Islamic Persian historiographical tradition, imported into Muslim historiography via translations of Sassanian historical works. The direct weight of "the Iranian, and then broadly Islamic concept of history . . . is felt in a unique way in the Rājataraṅgiṇī, even in the very title 'River of Kings', which could be read as a nod to Firdawsi."

Thus "Kalhana's work represents, as all previous scholars have more or less recognized, Sanskrit kavya's reconciliation with something far beyond itself." The *something* is Persianate Islamic historiography which orders past by reigns of rulers and revolves history round kings and courts.

This argument deserves a much fuller study, especially in light of the recent study of *Rājataraṅgiṇī* by Obrock who stresses that "Kalhana's historiography is a particularly regional development" arisen "through the fortuitous coincidence of several literary precedents, and remained a very Kashmiri form with a very Kashmiri genealogy."[530] Obrock, while arguing that Kalhana was influenced by Kashmiri Kathā genre, agrees that "Kalhana did not slavishly adhere to the Kashmiri Kathā's genre; rather he drew upon, adapted, and in the end transcended its expectations."[531] Was it just a "fortuitous coincidence" that Kalhana transcended the expectations of Kashmiri Kathā or was it due to some powerful exogenous influence that prompted Kalhana into its reworking? Obrock needs a further elaboration on this point by taking note of the arguments advanced by Knutson.

Tolerance

All said and done, it would not have been possible for Kashmir to emerge as a cosmopolitan space, and a great centre of learning, a site of innovations and a hub of technologies, crafts and commerce without having a tolerant ambiance to become a meeting place of different communities, races, religions and cultures. Although the Karkota rulers were Vaiṣṇavas, they were no less well disposed towards the other faiths. Alongside building Vaiṣṇava temples, the kings, members of the royal family and the ministers also built Śiva temples, vihāras, stupas and caityas. While Durlabhavardhana built a Vaiṣṇava temple, his wife Angalekha built a vihāra. The most famous in this regard is Lalitaditya who, besides making a Buddhist and a Turk, Cankuna, one of his cabinet ministers, built a large number of religious structures for all the faiths prevalent in Kashmir then. For example, about the caityas, vihāras and statutes of Buddha constructed by Lalitaditya at Parihaspura, his newly constructed capital, Kalhana says:

> That king, who was free from passions, built the ever-rich *Rājavihāra*, with a large quadrangle (*catuhśālā*), a large Caitya, and a large [image of the] Jina (Buddha). . . . With Just as many thousands of Prasthas of copper he made the glorious [statue of] the 'Great Buddha' (*Brhadbuddha*) which reached upto the sky. . . . He built the quadrangle (*catuhśālā*) and the sacred shrine (*caitya*), in each case with such expenditure that his five structures were alike [as regards cost]. . . . By this very [king] was built also the wonderful and famous Kayyavihāra, where subsequently the Bhiksu Sarvajhamitra resided, who appeared as another Jina. . . . The Tuhkhara

> Cankuna, who founded the *Cankunavihara*, made a stupa loftier even than the mind of the king, and golden [images of the] *Jinas*.[532]

So is true of Jayapida, about whose catholicity Kalhana says, "That pious (king) set up three Buddha images and a large vihāra, and built in the town [Jayapura, built by him] a [shrine of] Jayadevi."[533]

The *Nīlamata Purāna* (NP), written under the auspices of the founder of the Karkota dynasty, is emblematic of exemplary co-existence, tolerance, assimilation and accommodation promoted by the Karkota rulers. We believe that NP is actually an instrument of legitimacy to pietistic cosmopolitanism, a serious patronage textual exercise to reconcile the contradiction between belief and practice. As rightly observed by Inden, the NP "placed Viṣṇu and Śiva in a complementary relationship, and did so to the extent that it [is] sometimes difficult to tell which is superior."[534] Alongside co-opting the entire range of Vedic–Puranic gods and goddesses, the NP devised new divinities to accommodate the diverse sects and practices, creating a new divine hierarchy. It, therefore, comes as no surprise to see NP acknowledging the venerating position of the Buddha and assigning him, the Nāgas and the Pisaca leaders a dignified position in the brahmanic pantheon. Considering pietistic entanglements between different faiths and the difficulty of distinguishing between heterodoxy and orthodoxy, one is reminded of Cemal Kafadar's suggestion that frontier belief

> should be conceptualised in part in terms of a "metadoxy", a state of being beyond doxies, a combination of being doxy-naïve and not being doxy minded, as well as the absence of a state that was interested in rigorously defining and strictly enforcing an orthodoxy.[535]

True to their open-mindedness, the Karkota rulers demonstrated in practice what their textual instrument intends to convey its readers and listeners. The patronage extended by them to the people of different faiths who visited Kashmir as students, pilgrims, traders, asylum seekers or fortune hunters is a case in point. Hiuen Tsang was personally received by Durlabhavardhana,[536] and he was provided all support to make his two years' stay in Kashmir comfortable. Ou-k'ong was also at home during the full four years he spent in Kashmir. He supplies significant information about the steady increase of *sangrāmās* in Kashmir since the departure of Hiuen Tsang from the valley.[537] The increase of 200 *sangrāmās* since the time of Durlabhavardhana is quite understandable, keeping in view the patronage which Buddhism received from the Vaiṣṇava rulers of Kashmir for more than two centuries in between the visits of Hiuen Tsang and Ou-k'ong.[538]

And, as a modern scholar says, "Note also that Kalhana portrays an intellectually pluralistic and highly diverse picture of Jayāpīda's court, with Vaidikas, Buddhists and possibly even Caravakas inhabiting the same realm."[539]

No less important is the warm reception and patronage the Karkota ruler, Vijraditya, accorded to the Arab fugitive commander, Muhammad Alāfi, who sought asylum in Kashmir after he and his patron Jasiah failed to repulse the Arab invasion of Sind. The reigning Karkota ruler not only gave asylum to Muhammad Alāfi and his corps but he also received him like a king and bestowed upon him a territory and allowed him to practice his religion freely. Since it is significant information pointing to a remarkable broad-mindedness of the Karkota rulers, it would be in the fitness of things to quote the contemporary Muslim chronicler verbatim:

> When Jaisiah received the news of the approach of the Arab army, he lost no time in leaving the place with his valuables and his family, and passing through a sandy desert, he came to Chankan and Ura, Okayah belonging to the province of Jitor. There Alāfi separated from him, and proceeded to the province of Tākiah, and thence, with the intention of taking shelter with the king of Kashmir, came to the frontier of Rāwim, close to Rāwistān. The country was all a desert and an extensive plain. From there he wrote letters to the king of Kashmir whose capital was situated further up in the midst of hills, protesting his sincerity, and praying for a refuge. The Rānā of Kashmir, after reading the letters, ordered one of the towns, in the skirts of Kashmir, known by the name of Shakalbār to be granted to Alāfī. Later on when Alāfī paid a visit to the Rānā, the latter gave 50 saddled horses and 200 valuable robes of honour as presents to his companions. Alāfí then asked Jehm son of Samah Shāmī to go with him and remain in the alienated town of Shakalbār. When Alāfī went again to pay a visit to the Rai of Kashmir, the latter again received him with due honour and distinction, and made gifts to him of an umbrella, a chair and a palanquin. Such honour, according to the prevalent custom of those days, was accorded only to kings. He then sent him back with honour and éclat to the land assigned to him, which was situated in a valley. After some time Alāfī died at Shakalbār and was succeeded by Jehm son of Samah, and his line survives up to this time. He built many mosques and enjoyed great respect and dignity at the Kashmir court.[540]

We also learn from Kalhana that Vajraditya (eighth century), "Sold many men to the *mleechas*, and introduced in the country various practices which befitted *mleechas*."[541] These *mleechas* were in all probability Muslims because the different races, ethnicities and religious groups residing in the neighbourhood of Kashmir were called by Kalhana by such names as Khasās, Bhuttas, Dards, Tukhāras, Kambojās, Śāhis and Turuśkās.[542] The only non-traditional group, which had recently entered into the neighbourhood of Kashmir and was also posing a threat to it, was the Muslims—the fact we have discussed in the preceding pages of this chapter. Therefore, to earn the goodwill of the Muslim neighbour as well as to benefit from their trading activities Vajraditya seems to have, like Zamorin of Calicut, encouraged some non-Muslims to embrace Islam to ease the problem of Muslim traders.[543] It is perhaps this policy of Vajraditya which has been twisted by Kalhana saying "Vajraditya sold many men to the *mleechas*, and introduced in the country practices which befitted *mleechas*." Since the Muslims needed religious freedom to live according to their own life style, and as the same was granted by Vajraditya, the brahmana chronicler was offended by the ruler's permission to the Muslims to live according to their own beliefs and practices. Indeed, providing faith-related facilities to the traders by the rulers was a global phenomenon during the Early Middle Ages. In this regard it is worth quoting Flood,

> The circulations and interactions within the ninth and tenth century world system to which the numismatic evidence attests included communities of faith. The construction of mosques for minority communities of Muslims in the territories of the Gurjara-Pratiharas and Rashtarakutas offers one example, and reports that Indian merchants placed an idol of Zhun (whose principal shrine was located in southern Afghanistan) in the Iraqi port cities of Basra and al-Uballa another. During the same period, mercantile communities of Hindus and Muslims were constructing temples and mosques in the ports of south eastern China.[544]

Considering the cosmopolitan courtly milieus providing a consequential site for cultural production based on accommodation, tolerance and dignity to all irrespective of caste, creed and class, it is not fortuitous to see a leather tanner not allowing the state officials to construct a temple for the king by removing his hut and the king, Chandrapida reprimanding the officers for acting arbitrarily without getting the consent of the tanner.

> When the work on his [king Chandrapida's] temple of *Tribhuvanasvāmin* was to be begun, a leather tanner refused to give up his hut which was on the suitable site. Though he had often promised it to those in charge of the new building he, obstinate by nature, would not allow the measuring lines to be laid down. When thereupon they went to the lord of the earth and reported the matter, he considered them to be at fault, not the tanner. He told them: "Shame upon the inconsiderate conduct of those who began the construction of the new [temple] without previously asking that [tanner]. Stop the building, or have it erected elsewhere! Who would stain a pious work by taking away another's land? If we, who are to look after right and wrong, do unlawful acts, who should proceed by the right path?"[545]

The culture of tolerance and accommodation cultivated for many centuries, and nourished by the Karkotas, became finally the Kashmir ethos. It is, therefore, no wonder that for the pleasure of his minister, the founder of Utpala dynasty, Avantivarman (885–883 CE) "bore himself [outwardly] as a worshipper of Śiva, though he was [in reality] from childhood a worshipper of Viṣṇu."[546] In his newly built capital, Avantipura, he built both—the shrine of Viṣṇu, Avantisvamin, and the temple of Śiva, Avantiśvara.[547]

However, the most significant information provided in this regard by non-local sources, puzzling even a modern mind, is the debates held on world religions in the courts of Utpala rulers[548] which also attracted the famous mystic of Islam, Al-Hallaj to visit Kashmir and take benefit of the freedom of expression and argumentation sponsored by the courtly milieu of Kashmir.[549] No less remarkable is that around the same time a ruler of the region between upper and lower Kashmir reportedly wrote to the Habbarid amir 'Abd Allah requesting an exegesis (*tafsīr*) of the law of Islam to be rendered into *hindiyah* (perhaps Hindi or Sanskrit). The translation was done by an Iraqi living in Mansura but who had been raised in al-Hind and was familiar with its languages.[550] The veracity of this evidence is easy to establish as it coincides with the moment when, as mentioned earlier, Kashmir had become a court-sponsored space of deliberations on major religions of the world, clearly pointing to an ambiance of tolerance, religious pluralism, freedom to preach one's faith and the mutability of religious identity. The liberal environment of the period is also indicated by Kalhana's mention of a *domba* singer coming to Kashmir "from abroad"[551] and the king Samkaravarman (883–902 CE) taking his two "sweet-eyed daughters," Hamsi and Nagalata, into his seraglio,[552] and even raising Hamsi to the rank of chief queen[553] and her father, Ranga, being bestowed with an *agrahara* grant, to the much resentment of the orthodox brahmanas.[554]

The presence of a myriad of cults and their open activities, even though some of them were seeking rupture with the tradition and some were even atheists,[555] testifies beyond doubt that with regard to the tolerance of difference, the early medieval state of Kashmir was as large-hearted as any liberal model state of present times. The image of the state becomes brighter should we also note that the rajas who, though being adherents of the dominant tradition, recruited the Muslims in army, and that too on covetous positions.[556]

This was not, however, operating in only one direction. The recruitment of Muslims in the armies of Hindu rajas of Kashmir finds contemporary counterparts in north-western India where we see the Hindu generals and soldiery serving under the Ghaznavid Sultans. The best documented of these is Tilak, a Kashmiri Hindu who went to Ghazni to seek patronage at the court of Sultan Mas'ud (1031–1041). Tilak, who is said to have written excellent Hindavi and Persian, began his career at the court as a translator (*mutarjim*) with the Indians before rising to become the commander of the Indian contingent (*Sipahsalar-i Hinduyan*). He reached high office and was conferred with honours including khilat, banners, a parasol and drum.[557] Tilak not only led Ghaznavid campaigns against his co-religionists but also undertook punitive expeditions against rebellious Muslim Turks on behalf of the Ghaznavid Sultan.[558] The employment of Muslims by the Hindu rajas and Hindus by the Muslim rulers alludes to an important scenario of the time—that when it was a question of state-building or improving one's position, cultural, ethnic and religious boundaries were evidently permeable and porous. Second, as both the state and the people of Kashmir and those of its borderlands demonstrated identical mentality, it further substantiates the fact that Kashmir and its proximate neighbourhood belonged to the same cultural horizon which is a relatively common limitrophe phenomenon.

Indeed, an important characteristic of the frontier societies is circulation of religious affiliation, fluidity of confessional identity, religious patronage and practice, pietistic entanglements—in fact "metadoxy"—and the absence of a state keen in enforcing orthodoxy.[559] The same is true of Kashmir, a typical frontier society. Unsurprisingly, therefore, we see Muslims, even the religious preachers trekking up the hills for choosing Kashmir as their abode or as missionary destination centuries before the Muslims brought it under their political control. Evidently it was through this agency that around 883 we see a ruler of Kashmir so much impressed by Islam that he requested the amir of Sind to render for him the exegesis (*tafsir*) of the laws of Islam in *hindiyah* (perhaps Hindavi or Sanskrit).[560] It was around the same period that the celebrated mystic of Islam, Mansur al Hallaj also set foot in the valley to take advantage of the argumentative religious aura of Kashmir.[561] In the eleventh century we find the Muslim missionaries singing devotional songs in the streets and bazaars of Kashmir. They had made such an impact on the society that the courtesans refused to entertain their clients at their sight.[562] The Persianate-Islamic culture had got such a favourable environment in Kashmir because of pragmatic "orientation to power" that we find a Kashmiri brahmana so well-versed in Persian language that around 1030, he was employed as translator at the court of a Ghaznavid ruler.[563] By the beginning of thirteenth century there were a sizeable number of Muslims in Kashmir who, according to Marco Polo, were employed by the non-Muslims for slaughtering animals.[564] This important example of co-existence, interdependence and concession to pragmatism maintained continuity over the *longue durée* as the Muslims still continue to slaughter sheep/goat for their Kashmiri Pandit brethren who (before their migration) were carnivorous without exception.

Among the late-comer Muslims were Sayyid Sharaf al-Din Bulbul Shah and Shah Mir. Both of them came to Kashmir during the reign of Suhadeva (1301–1320), who extended royal favours to both of them. While the former only needed freedom to preach his religion, the latter was inducted in nobility and endowed with land grant. Their name was rescued from falling into oblivion by their historic role. Bulbul Shah was instrumental in winning the Buddhist ruler of Kashmir, Rinchana (1320–1323) to Islam, and Shah

Mir founded the Shah Mir dynasty after playing a decisive role in saving Kashmir from an impending Mongol invasion, compelling even an orthodox Sanskrit chronicler to exclaim "Strange, this believer in Alla (Allah) became the saviour of the people."[565] Clearly, the early Kashmir is marked by such a remarkable type of religious pluralism and freedom of religion that even many modern societies are unable to imitate it. This phenomenon was the direct result of Kashmir being basically a space of inflows facilitated by its borderlands which because of their locational advantage connected Kashmir with the outer world. As a result, on the one hand, Kashmir became a cosmopolitan society and, on the other, it and its borderlands shared an identical cultural horizon including the ethnic mosaic of population. This fascinating story of entangled histories between Kashmir and its borderlands is discussed in the following chapter.

Notes

1 Kalhana, IV: 339.
2 Inden (2008), 537–539.
3 Roy (2003), 52–56.
4 The Ganga Valley comprising present Uttar Pradesh and Haryana is known as Madyadesha (Middle country) or Aryavarta in Sanskrit sources. During early medieval period, it was the heartland of social and cultural norms with Kanauj as its most important political centre.
5 Inden (2000), 76–77, 82.
6 *Nīlamata Purāna*, 141 sqq.
7 Ibid, 252, 262, 283–84
8 Ibid, 194.
9 Ibid, 156–58.
10 Ibid, 243.
11 Ibid, 244.
12 Ibid, 24–25 sqq.
13 Ibid, 305–307.
14 Inden (2000), 54, 76–78
15 Sharma (2008), 139.
16 Inden (2000), 26, 30.
17 Kalhana, III: 489.
18 Ibid, III, 494 sqq.
19 Ibid, III, 529.
20 For fuller discussion of the social logic of the genealogical history, see Spiegel (1983), 43–53.
21 Kalhana, III: 528.
22 Inden (2000), 75.
23 Kalhana, IV: 2–6.
24 Devahuti (1983), 72–73
25 Inden (2000), 75.
26 Ibid, 76–77
27 Ibid, 83–84.
28 Kalhana, IV, 133 sqq.
29 Ibid, IV, 146 sqq.

30 Ibid, IV, 146sqq. Also, see Saxena (1974), 56–81.
31 Ibid, IV, 259.
32 Kaul (2018), 111.
33 Porter (1993), 18.
34 Davis (1997), 54.
35 Ibid.
36 Stein (1979), I: 90.
37 Pollock (2006), 241–242
38 Roy (2003).
39 Saxena, 61
40 Stein (1979), I: 88.
41 Kalhana, IV: 147 sqq.
42 Kūfī (1979), 87.
43 Kalhana, IV: 163–79.
44 Ibid, IV, 142–43, 211, 215–16.
45 Ibid, IV, 245.
46 Al-Biruni (1993), II: 178.
47 Kalhana, IV: 242.
48 Ibid, IV, 165 sqq.
49 Ibid, IV, 245.
50 Ibid, IV, 215.
51 Ibid, IV, 142–43.
52 Ibid, IV, 11, 142–43, 209, 211, 245–46, 325. According to Abhinavagupta, his ancestors had come from Uttar Pradesh and settled in Kashmir during the reign of Lalitaditya. Abhinavagupta, 37–38, 39; quoted by Pandit (1977), 25. Kalhana makes a mention of Gadhipura having been vanquished by Lalitaditya. Gadhipura is a name of the town Kanyakubja, the present Kanauj derived from its legendry king Gadhi; Kalhana, Book IV; and Stein's note 133. There is a place name Gadhapur (in Tral) and Gadha mohalla (in Down Town, Srinagar); and surname Gadha in Kashmir. Did Gadhapur and Gadha mohalla come into existence because of the settlement of the people from Gadhipura?, and are the Gadhas of Kashmir the immigrants from Gadhipura during the period of Lalitaditya? These are open questions which perhaps can be solved with the help of anthropologists.
53 Kalhana, IV: 181–217.
54 See Pal (1989).
55 Ibn Khaldun (1967), I: 143.
56 Davis (1993), 27–28; idem (1994a), 301; idem (1994b), 166.
57 Dirks (1982), 100.
58 Flood (2009), 28
59 Kalhana, IV, 620–24.
60 Ibid, IV, 176.
61 Ibid, IV, 181 sqq.
62 Ibid, IV, 207 sqq.
63 Ibid, IV, 181 sqq.
64 Inden (2000), 60.
65 Ibid, 546.
66 Ibid, 86–87.
67 Ibid, 85.
68 Kalhana, IV: 404 sqq.
69 Ibid, IV, 471
70 Ibid, IV, 421 sqq, 514 sqq.

71 Ibid, IV, 629 sqq
72 Ibid, IV, 512.
73 Ibid, IV, 513.
74 Ibid, IV, 460–62.
75 Ibid, IV, 485.
76 Ibid, IV, 493.
77 Stein (1979), I: 124, fn. 45.
78 Kūfī, 160; Balādhuri (1866), III: 440.
79 Balādhuri, 440; Kūfī, 160.
80 See Stein (1979), I: 124, fn. 45.
81 Ibid, I, 130–131, n. 126.
82 Ibid, I, 130–131, n. 126.
83 Kalhana, V: 78–117.
84 Ibid, V, 113–117.
85 Ibid, V, 32–34.
86 Ibid, V, 140.
87 Ibid, V, 143–44.
88 Ibid, V, 150.
89 Ibid, V, 216–217.
90 Ibid, V, 165–177.
91 Ibid, V, 232–33. Udabhāndapura was the ancient capital of Gandhara. It was situated on the right bank of Indus. For details, see Stein (1979), II: 336–339.
92 Ibid, V, 248.
93 Ibid, V, 249
94 Ibid, IV, 346.
95 Ibid, I, 42.
96 Ibid, IV, 845.
97 Ibid, I, 42.
98 Hiuen Tsang (1911), I: 148 sqq.
99 For the table of dates for Hiuen Tsang's *itinerary*, see Cunningham (1871), 563 sqq.
100 Hiuen Tsiang, 148 sqq.
101 Ou-k'ong, 341 sqq; quoted by Stein (1979), II: 355–56; Kalhana, Book IV.
102 Kalhana, IV: 245.
103 Ibid, IV, 493.
104 Ibid, IV, 142–43, 215–16, 245, 488–498. The famous eleventh-century poet of Kashmir, Bilhana, says that his ancestors had come from Madhyadeśa. Bilhana (1965), xviii–73. The poet, Abhinanda (tenth Century), the son of Jayanta Bhatta, traces his ancestry from Saktisvamin, a minister under Lalitaditya who was originally an inhabitant of Gauda (Bengal). Ray (1955), 31 (3): 243.
105 Pollock (2006), 172.
106 Kalhana, IV: 191.
107 Massignon (1982), 178–180.
108 Kalhana, IV: 216.
109 Ibid, IV, 46, 498.
110 Ibid, IV, 142–43, 215.
111 Ibid, IV, 620 sqq.
112 Ibid, IV 488. For details, see Bronner (2013), 167–76.
113 Ibid, IV, 488.
114 Ibid, IV, 489.
115 Ibid, IV, 489.
116 Ibid, IV, 491.

117 Ibid, IV, 493.
118 Ibid, IV, 492.
119 Bronner (2013), 171.
120 Ibid, IV, 494.
121 Ibid, IV, 495.
122 Ibid, IV, 496.
123 Ibid, IV, 497.
124 Ibid, IV, 498.
125 Bronner (2013), 169.
126 Obrock (2015), 61.
127 Massignon, 178–80.
128 Pollock (2006), 81.
129 Kalhana, V: 32–33.
130 Śrivara (1898), 151.
131 Kalhana, V: 34.
132 See Anandavardhana (1974).
133 Ray (1969), 191–196.
134 Ibid.
135 Massignon, 178–180.
136 Ibid.
137 Kalhana, V: 66.
138 Ibid, V, 204
139 Ray (1969), 196.
140 Kalhana, V: 359.
141 Ibid, V, 360.
142 Ibid, V, 387.
143 Ibid, V, 397–98.
144 Ibid, V, 468–475.
145 Ibid, V, 476.
146 VI, 87.
147 Ibid, VI, 88.
148 Ibid, VI, 89.
149 Ibid, VI, 300, 303–304.
150 Ibid, VII, 610, 941–42.
151 Bilhana, xviii, 64–66.
152 Ibid.
153 Kalhana, VII: 934–37.
154 Ibid, VII, 934–44.
155 Ibid, VII, 611.
156 Ibid, VIII, 2392–2396.
157 Al-Biruni, I: 173.
158 *Kuṭṭanī-mata Kāvya*, V, 172–73.
159 Bilhana mentions his travels to Mathura, Kanyakubja, Varanasi, Dahala, Dhara, Somanatha and the southern states. Witzel (2008), 84, n. 208.
160 Vide, Cox (2016), 177. Bilhana makes repeated mention of Kashmir as a centre of learning. For example, "In every house [of Kashmir] Sanskrit and Prakrit words sound charming like the mother tongue of even women"; "the unparalleled glory of the educational institutions is cause for fame." For details, see Witzel (2008), 84.
161 Kalhana, I: 42.
162 See Granoff (1995), 361.
163 Witzel (2008), 83–84.

164 Al-Biruni, I: 135–36.
165 Ibid, I, 126–27.
166 *Nīlamata Purāna,* 15.
167 Al-Biruni, I: 173.
168 Ibid, I, 391; II: 8–9.
169 Ibid, I, 391; II: 8–9.
170 Ibid, I, 174.
171 Pollock (2006), 105–06.
172 Nemec (2020), 285–86.
173 Ibid, 286 n5.
174 Cox, 177.
175 Ibid.
176 Ibid, 180.
177 Ibid, 191.
178 Al-Biruni, I: 22; See Witzel (2008), 84
179 Pollock (2006), 492. Also, see idem (2001), 392–426.
180 See Kalhana, Book IV.
181 Bagchi (1950), 70.
182 See Hiuen Tsiang, 148 sqq; *Ou-k'ong (1895)*, VI: 341 sqq.
183 Bagchi, 70.
184 Slaje (2007), 186.
185 Skjaervo (2002), 524–526, quoted by Slaje (2007), 186–87.
186 Ou-k'ong, VI: 341 sqq.
187 Kalhana, IV: 211, 215.
188 Ibid, IV, 142–43.
189 Naudou (1980), 21.
190 For details, see Naudou, Chapters II and III.
191 Naudou, Chapters V to VII.
192 Ibid, Chapters II, III, V to VII.
193 Pal (1989a), 117–135.
194 Also, see Nemec, 255, n. 4.
195 Khuihami, I: 243–267; Hamdani (1986); Anon (1962), 103; Ibn Hawqal (1967), 450; Al-Muqaddasi (1967), 304; Minorsky (1980), 88, 108, 110; Bosworth (1994), 63; Collins and al-Tai (1994), 268. Quoted by Flood.
196 Flood, 18–19.
197 Massignon, 178–180.
198 Flood, 19.
199 Anon, 103; Kramers and Wiet (1964), 435; Ibn Hawqal, 450. Vide Flood.
200 Kalhana, IV: 397.
201 Qureshi (1984).
202 Bosworth (1984).
203 Clark (1995).
204 Flood, 21.
205 Ramhurmuzi (1883–86), 142–44, 161; Al-Mas'udi (1962), I: 187; Maclean (1989), 71.
206 Kalhana, IV: 11.
207 Ibid, IV, 712.
208 Al-Biruni, I: 206.
209 Kalhana, VII: 494–95; VIII: 73, 493.
210 Ibid, IV, 11–12.
211 Remusat (1829), I: 212. Quoted by Ray (1969).
212 Hiuen Tsiang, 136, 143, 147, 163.

213 Kalhana, IV: 11.
214 Ibid, IV, 405–407, 415.
215 For the description of the peculiarities of different neighbouring regions, see Kalhana, IV: 147 sqq, 165 sqq.
216 Kalhana, IV: 5, 9, 181 sqq.
217 Ibid, IV, 5, 9, 181 sqq.
218 Ibid, IV, 11.
219 Ibid, IV, 196–203.
220 Ibid, IV, 15.
221 Ibid, IV, 165–66, 415–417.
222 *Kuṭṭanī-mata Kāvya,* 343. Also see Harwan Tiles.
223 Kalhana, IV: 11–16.
224 Ibid, IV, 16.
225 Ibid, IV, 13–15.
226 Ibid, IV, 12.
227 Ibid, IV, 712.
228 The cavalry was called *hayasena* and the rider *hayaroha*. The commander of the mounted soldiers was known as *ayasenapati* or *hayapati*. One who commanded 10,000 (*ayta*) horses and 1,000 men was known as the lord of horses (*asvapati*).
229 Kalhana, VII: 735–737.
230 *Lokaprakaśa*, 4.
231 Ibid, 11–12.
232 Kalhana, VII: 188, 198; *Lokaprakaśa*, 11.
233 *Nitikalpataru*, 98, 120.
234 Kalhana, VIII: 735–737.
235 Ibid, IV, 415–17; VII: 371, 1360; VIII: 1094.
236 Ibid, IV, 415–17; VII: 371, 1360; VIII: 1094.
237 Pandit (1968), 612.
238 Kalhana, IV: 415–17.
239 Ibid, IV, 165–66
240 *Padatataditaka,* 41, 5, vide Witzel (2008), 71, n. 142.
241 *Lokaprakaśa*, 11.
242 For details, see Drabu (1986), 234–35.
243 Drabu (1986), 234–35.
244 Kalhana, VII: 644–45.
245 Ibid, VII, 414.
246 Ibid, VII, 509
247 Ibid, V, 16; VI: 339; VII: 211–12, 407, 416, 714, 756, 773–774, 818; VIII: 265.
248 Ibid, V, 11–16.
249 Ibid, VII, 416.
250 Ibid, VII, 211–12 and Stein's note.
251 Ibid, IV, 195–198, 201–203.
252 Ibid, IV, 207–209, 211.
253 Warikoo (1996), 119.
254 Kalhana, IV: 617.
255 *Nīlamata Purāna,* V. 335. Also, see *Samayamātrikā*, quoted by Chandra (1973a), 183.
256 *Samayamātrikā*, quoted by Chandra (1973a), 183.
257 Chandra (1973), 236.
258 Bernier (1914), 419.
259 Kalhana, VII: 194–95.

260 Ibid, VII, 197.
261 Ibid, VII, 190–97.
262 Ibid, VII, VII, 71.
263 Ibid, VI, 19.
264 Ibid, VII, 1221; VIII, 141.
265 *Samayamātrikā*, quoted by Chandra (1973a), 183.
266 Kalhana, VII: 494–95.
267 Varahamihira, XIV. 29sqq. *Amarakośa*, II, 6.124.
268 Vide, Cox, 179.
269 Al-Biruni, II: 104.
270 Cox, 180.
271 *Nīlamata Purāna*, 872–73.
272 Witzel (2008), 60–61, 66.
273 Inden (2000), 76–77, 82.
274 Kalhana, IV: 245.
275 Pande (2018); Bilhana, xviii, 73–79.
276 Kalhana, IV: 512.
277 Ibid, IV, 513.
278 Ibid, IV, 460–62.
279 Ibid, IV, 485.
280 Ibid, IV, 493.
281 Ibid, III, 354.
282 *Kuṭṭanī-mata Kāvya*, 343.
283 Ou-k'ong, VI: 341 sqq.
284 Kalhana, IV: 211, 215
285 Ibid, IV, 142–43
286 Ibid, IV, 324–25.
287 Ibid, IV, 11–12.
288 Ibid, IV, 11–12.
289 Pandit (1977), 18.
290 Ibid.
291 Ibid.
292 Ibid, 31.
293 Dyezkowski (1987), 222–23.
294 Kūfī, 40.
295 Kalhana, IV: 460–62.
296 Ibid, VI, 176–77; VII: 956; VIII: 1443.
297 Fisher (1989a), 40.
298 Kalhana, VI: 89.
299 Ibid, VI, 175.
300 Ibid, VI, 287, 288.
301 Ibid, VI, 318–20.
302 Ibid, VI, 318–20.
303 Ibid, VI, 178.
304 Ibid, VI, fn. 177–78.
305 Ibid, VI, 304.
306 Ibid, VI, 303.
307 Ibid, VI, 355.
308 Ibid, VII, 47.
309 Ibid, VII, 48.
310 Ibid, VII, 49–51.

311 Ibid, VII, 144–152; Al-Biruni, I: 22.
312 Ibid, VII, 144–152.
313 Ibid, VII, 144–152.
314 Ibid, VII, 144sqq.
315 Ibid, VII, 144–152.
316 Ibid, VII, 274.
317 Al-Biruni, I: 22.
318 Kalhana, VII: 180–84.
319 Between 1014 and 1012 Mahmud of Ghazni made two attempts to conquer Kashmir, but he failed both the times owing to the strong fortress of Loharkot and bad weather. Gardizi (1928), 73–79.
320 Al-Biruni, I: 22.
321 Ibid, I, 206.
322 Kalhana, VII: 188, 1149; VIII: 885–87, 919–93, 2264.
323 Ibid, VII, 519.
324 Ibid, VII, 520.
325 Ibid, VII, 528.
326 Ibid, VII, 675.
327 Ibid, VII, 606.
328 Ibid, VII, 560.
329 Ibid, VII, 611.
330 Ibid, VII, 927, 928–931.
331 Ibid, VII, 928–31, 945.
332 Ibid, VII, 926.
333 Ibid, VII, note 926.
334 Cunningham (1894), 34, pl. V. 22–23.
335 Witzel (2008), 66, n. 126.
336 Meenakshi (1996), 128–29
337 Ibid, 111–134.
338 Witzel (2008), 68, n. 133.
339 Nazki (2014), 36.
340 Kalhana, VII: 935–37n.
341 Ibid, VII, 625
342 Ibid, VIII, 225–228.
343 Ibid, VIII, 230.
344 Ibid, VIII, 2766.
345 Ibid, VIII, 493.
346 The instability also made the Loharas insecure in Kashmir and they drained the wealth out of Kashmir to their home land (Lohara) which they were unable to forget. Kalhana writes about Sussala "the king in his avaricious greed was daily accumulating fresh treasure and sent all his riches to the hill of Lohara." He again says: "He sent into [the castle] of Lohara, masses of gold which resembled the 'gold mountains' (Meru), after having made them into gold bricks (ingots)." Kalhana, VIII: 639.
347 Kalhana, VIII: 2395–2444.
348 Mankha, xxv, 102, 110sqq.
349 Kalhana, VI: 252, 254–55 and note, VII: 1008, VIII: 2220.
350 Ibid, IV, 324–325.
351 Al-Biruni, I: 117.
352 Pollock (2006), 105–114.
353 Kalhana, VII: 190–93.

354 Ibid, VII, 190–93.
355 Witzel (2008), 69. For more details on Kashmiris in foreign services, see idem (2021).
356 Kalhana, IV: 631, 635–637, 639; VIII: 2227
357 Witzel (2008), 68.
358 Kalhana, VII: 494–95.
359 Kūfī, 193–94; Balādhuri, 440.
360 Balādhuri, 445–46.
361 Ibid, 446.
362 For details, see Stein (1979), I: 124, fn. 45.
363 Kalhana, IV: 107.
364 Ibid, III, 332; IV: 107.
365 Levi (1895), 351.
366 Marquart and de Groot (1915); Bosworth (1965); Habibi (1967), 75–76; Bosworth (1973); idem (1984), 6–7; Wink (1996), 1: 112–28; Kuwayama (1999), 29–35, 66–67, 72. Quoted by Flood.
367 Kalhana, III: 332
368 Ibid, IV, 397.
369 Anon, 103; Kramers and Wiet, 435; Ibn Hawqal, 450.
370 Kalhana, IV: 397.
371 Massignon, 178–80.
372 Ramhurmuzi, 2–4.
373 Habibi (1954).
374 Flood, 42.
375 Al-Mas'udi (1861–77), I: 207; Kramers and Wiet, 318; Ibn Hawqal, 325; Al-Muqaddasi, 479–80; Collins and al-Tai, 420–21.
376 Kalhana, VII: 188, 1149, VIII: 885–87, 919–23, 2264.
377 Stein (1979), II: 259–60, n 46; also see Sachau (2015), xx.
378 Yule (1903), I: 167.
379 *Bahāristān-i Shāhī*, f. 7a, f.7b, f.46; Malik, 34–35, 37–38.
380 Jonarāja (1898), 1718; *Bahāristān-i Shāhī*, ff.5ab; Malik, 35.
381 Ibid, 26.
382 Kalhana, I: 307, 341–343; IV: 142–43, 512, 513, 460–62; V: 89; VI: 300, 303–304; VII: 80–84, 144–52, VIII: 2395, 2444; Kūfī, 40; Al-Biruni, I: 22; Pandit (1977), 18, 27; Witzel (2008), 72, 81.
383 Koul (1991), 86 sqq.
384 Kalhana, I: 307, 341.
385 Ibid, I, 312–316.
386 For details, see Ray (1969), 180–84.
387 For these practices of the Vedic Śaivites, see *Nīlmatāpurāna*; *Rājataraṅgiṇī*, *passim* and *Lalla Vaakh*.
388 Yule, I: 167.
389 Pandit (1977), 188.
390 For details about 'Kashmiri Śaivism,' see Pandit (1977); also idem (1997); Chatterji (1962).
391 Kularnava Tantra, ix; quoted by Kaul (1973), 16.
392 Kaul (1973), 16.
393 Ibid.
394 Ibid.
395 Pandit (1977), 189.
396 Ibid.
397 Ibid, 201, 206, 207.

398 Ibid, 206.
399 See Drabu (1990), 176–77.
400 Vide, Pandit (1997), 119.
401 Pandit (1977), 155.
402 Ibid, 207.
403 Ibid.
404 Ibid.
405 Ibid.
406 Cited by Nemec, 292, 303.
407 Fisher (1989a), 36.
408 Pandit (1977), 18.
409 Ibid.
410 Ibid.
411 Ibid, 27.
412 Ibid, 30.
413 Quoted by, Witzel (2008), 72.
414 Kalhana, VII: 519
415 Ibid, VII, 293, 305, 523, 684.
416 Drabu (1990), 174–77.
417 See Wani (2004), 94.
418 Dasgupta (1976), 69.
419 Ray (1969), 86.
420 Mohan (1981), 211–12.
421 *Nīlamata Purāna*, 14–16
422 Kalhana, V: 390 sqq; VII: 39–41, 203, 207–8, 285–291
423 Ibid, V, 361–67
424 Ibid, V, 402.
425 Drabu (1990), 149, 162, 182–83; also see Nemec, 299–304.
426 Kalhana, I: 312–16
427 Ibid, III, 123; V: 220–26; VI: 107, 195; VIII: 2334–37; *Samayamātrika*, 11, 21.
428 Ibid, VII, 1232.
429 Jonarāja, 26–27.
430 See Wani (2004), 87–96.
431 Kalhana, VI: 11.
432 Ibid, VI, 9.
433 Ibid, VI, 10.
434 Ibid, VI, 10.
435 For details, see Roy (2010), 142–164.
436 Bühler (1877), 28; Witzel (2008), 79; Yule, 167. *Nīlamata Purāna* also makes it obligatory that *Śraddha* should be performed with meat. *Nīlamata Purāna*, 485–86.
437 For details, see Drabu (1990).
438 Madan (2008), 3.
439 Drabu (1990), 82.
440 Vaid Kumari, I: 156–57, 165.
441 For example, it not only included a rule for the main liturgical work of the Śivas, the Śivaratri, but also told its listener to perform it in accord with the procedure declared for Viṣṇu's four monthly sleep, *Nīlamata Purāna*, 527–33.
442 *Nīlamata Purāna*, 710–12.
443 Ibid, 351–75.
444 Nemec, 283.
445 Ibid, 284–85.

446 Ibid, 297.
447 Translated by Nemec, 304.
448 These observations were received by Nemec from the two scholars as personal communications. Nemec, 309, n54.
449 Nemec, 309, 314.
450 Kalhana, Book IV and V.
451 Pandit (1968), 12.
452 Fisher (1989a), 29.
453 Coomaraswamy (1965), 143.
454 Fisher (1989a), 38.
455 Ibid, 36.
456 Ibid, 28.
457 Ibid, 40.
458 Ibid, 22–23.
459 Sarkar (1966), 66.
460 Czuma (1989), 62.
461 Ibid, 65.
462 Ibid, 67.
463 Siudmak (1989), 51.
464 Ibid, Fig. 16.
465 Fisher (1989a), 25.
466 Pal (1989b), 80.
467 Among the scholars who consider that Kashmiri language has originated from Sanskrit, mention may be made of LB Bowring, John Cristop, Gerard Fussman, MP Edgeworth, Dr. Buhler, Ram Chandra Ambe, TN Ganju, SN Tickoo, BN Kala, PN Pushup, SK Toshkhani and BB Kashru. For details, see Altaf (2014).
468 See Grierson (1919), VIII: 235–253.
469 Akhtar Mohiud-Din (1991), II: 58; Teng (1988), 86–87. Also see Munawar and Shouq (1992), 16.
470 Ahmad (1999); Kashmiri (1988); Hajni (2013), 83–111.
471 Stein (1979), II: 371–373.
472 Grierson, 253.
473 Teng (1988).
474 Chatterji (1963), 256.
475 Ramhurmuzi, 2–4.
476 Kūfī, 193–94; Balādhuri, 440, 445–46. For details, see Stein (1979), I: 124, fn. 45.
477 Ibid, 28–29, 40, 87.
478 Ibid, 160.
479 Kalhana, IV: 397.
480 Anon, 103; Kramers and Wiet, 435; Ibn Hawqal, 450.
481 Habibi (1954).
482 Al-Mas'udi (1861–77), I: 207; Kramers and Wiet, 318; Ibn Hawqal, 325; Al-Muqaddasi, 479–80; Collins and al-Tai, 420–21.
483 Anon, 103; Kramers and Wiet, 435; Ibn Hawqal, 450.
484 Flood, 17.
485 Al-Biruni, I: 206.
486 Bayhaqi (1971), 523–24; Elliot and Dowson (1990), 125–34.
487 Kalhana, VII: 494–95; VIII: 73, 493.
488 Bosworth (1975), IV: 183–84.
489 Flood, 7.
490 Bosworth (1975), IV: 183–84.
491 Kalhana, VII: 188, 1149; VIII: 885–87, 919–23, 2264.

492 Ibid, VII, 528.
493 Ibid, VII, 520.
494 Ibid, VII, 881–884, 921–25, 938–39.
495 Ibid, VII, 923n.
496 Flood, 69.
497 Kalhana, VII: 528.
498 Flood, 68–69.
499 In this regard, it is important to mention that, according to Kalhana, Harśa had "hundreds of Turushka captains in his army." Kalhana, VII: 1149
500 For Khusrau Anu Shirwan's *Zangir-i-'adl* (Rope of justice), see Rawanbakhsh (2007).
501 Kalhana, VII: 879–80.
502 Bayhaqi, 523–24; Elliot and Dowson, 125–34.
503 See Wani (2004), 50.
504 Kalhana, V: 177; VII: 47–69, 119, 125–26; VIII: 131.
505 Stewart (2001), 276.
506 Flood, 258.
507 Kalhana, VII: 1232.
508 Vide, Chandra (1979), 184.
509 Ibid.
510 Bausani (1968), V: 293.
511 Ibid, V, 293.
512 For details, see Dāmodaragupta's *Kuttanīmatam*; *Kṣemendra's Narmamālā* and *Samayamātrkā*.
513 For details about this MS copy of the Holy Qur'ān, which is preserved in the Jammu and Kashmir Academy of Art, Culture and Languages, Srinagar, see Teng (1988), 6–7.
514 Teng (1988), 6–7.
515 Yule, I: 167.
516 Drabu (1990), 97, 143.
517 See Ibid, 143.
518 Almost the whole hereditary butcher section of Kashmiri society carries the *krām* of Ganaie, which originally belonged to the class of scribes. That Ganaie was a blanket term for scribes during medieval times, see Diddamari (1998), 84. During our period, Ganaie was a noble tribe of Kashmir. Sayyid 'Ali, f.9a.
519 Sayyid Sharaf al-Dīn was the disciple of Shah Ni'amat Allāh Fārsī, who in turn was the disciple of Shaikh Shihāb al-Dīn Suhrawardī (1144–1234). Sayyid Sharaf al-Dīn was originally from Turkistan. And as directed by his preceptor, he arrived in Kashmir during the reign of Suhadeva. He passed away in 1326 and is buried in Bulbul Langar in Srinagar. *Bahāristān-i Shāhī,* f. 7a; Malik, 37–38; Mishkāti, ff. 44a-45a.
520 *Bahāristān-i Shāhī,* f. 7a; Malik, 37–38; Mishkāti, ff. 44a-45a. According to Muhammad A'zam Diddamarī, the eighteenth-century chronicler of Kashmir, the *khānaqāh,* was functioning normally up to the end of the Sultāns. Diddamari, 66.
521 The *muhalla* is today called Bulbul Lankar.
522 *Bahāristān-i Shāhī,* f. 7b; Malik, 38. Although the original mosque was gutted in fire, mosques, however, continued to be built on the original site and invariably carried the name of the original mosque, viz. *Rinchoo Masjid*. The present mosque which, too, stands on the original site is also famous by this name.
523 For the fact that Rinchana had discussions with the religious divines of different faiths, see *Bahāristān-i Shāhī,* ff.6b, 7a; Malik, 37. To undermine Rinchana's

conversion to Islam, Jonarāja has fabricated the story that the *brāhamana* Devasavami refused to initiate him into Hinduism on the ground that he was a 'Bhotta' (Tibetan Buddist) and, therefore, unworthy of such initiation (Jonarāja, 20–21). Thus Jonarāja vainly tries to make us believe that there was no scope for conversion from Buddhism to Hinduism and that Devasavami was the only religious authority in Kashmir to initiate someone to Hinduism.

524 Bahāristān-i Shāhī, f.7b; Malik, 38.
525 Malik, 41.
526 Jonarāja, 15; *Bahāristān-i Shāhī*, f. 46; Malik, 34–35
527 Ibid, 26.
528 Basham (1961), 57; Thapar (1983), 61; also see Roy (2010), 108.
529 Knutson (2015), 281–93.
530 For details, see Obrock (2015), 32.
531 Obrock (2015), 37.
532 Kalhana, IV: 200, 203, 204, 210, 211.
533 Ibid, 507.
534 Inden (2000), 78.
535 Kafadar (1995), 73, 76, 82.
536 Li and Beal, 68–69.
537 Ou-k'ong.
538 See Kalhana, Book IV.
539 Bronner (2013), 169–70.
540 Kūfī, 160.
541 Kalhana, IV: 397
542 Ibid, I, 312–16; IV: 144, 165, 166, 179; VII: 217, 773; VIII: 2887.
543 Vide, Qureshi (1984), 2, fn. 5.
544 Flood, 26–27.
545 Kalhana, IV: 55–60.
546 Ibid, V, 43.
547 Ibid, V, 45.
548 Massignon, 178–80.
549 Ibid, 178–80.
550 Ramhurmuzi, 2–4, quoted by Flood, 44.
551 Kalhana, V: 359.
552 Ibid, V, 360.
553 Ibid, V, 387.
554 Ibid, V, 397–98.
555 See Pandit (1977); idem (1997); Kaul (1973); Drabu (1990). Also, see Wani (2004), 88–96; Nemec.
556 Kalhana, VII: 494–95; VIII: 73, 493.
557 Bayhaqi, 522–24; Flood, 78.
558 Ibid, 497; also see Flood, 78, 264.
559 Kafadar, 73, 76, 82.
560 Ramhurmuzi, 2–4; Flood, 44.
561 Massignon, 178–180.
562 Chandra (1973), 184.
563 Bayhaqi, 523–24; Elliot and Dowson, 125–34.
564 Yule, I: 167.
565 For details, see Wani (2004), 195–98.

5

SHARED HISTORY

Kashmir and the Immediate Borderlands

> The finds of various early sites of Swat, Potwar region and Kashmir leave no room to doubt that they belong "to a single complex."[1]
>
> —(Allchin and Allchin)

> That Kashmiri language has a Dardic basis is a matter of which no philologist can have any doubt.[2]
>
> —(George A Grierson)

> As in architecture, so also in Kashmiri style sculpture, the routes lay in Gandharan sculptural tradition.[3]
>
> —(Pratapaditya Pal)

The history of Kashmir is closely intertwined with its immediate neighbourhood. These neighbourhoods played manifold roles in shaping the history of Kashmir. The population of Kashmir largely comprises the immigrants and settlers from bordering regions. They played a central role as commercial and cultural entrepots between Kashmir and the distant markets and cultural centres. The strength and weakness of Kashmir depended upon the level of control Kashmir exercised over the hill chieftains. And, not least, during the reign of powerful rulers, most of these borderlands of the Kashmir formed a part of the Kashmir empire, though ruled indirectly on account of geographical hazards.

* * *

Of all its immediate neighbourhoods, which played an important role in shaping the birth and growth of Kashmir as a cultural realm, those situated on its western and northern borders rank next to none. This is abundantly clear from the striking parallels between Kashmiri culture and the cultures one encounters from Swat to the Punjab and Gilgit to Swat Kohistan. The

DOI: 10.4324/9781003367697-5

fundamental reason for the greater participation of these neighbourhoods in the making of the early culture of Kashmir was not merely the geographical contiguity and easier access; more important in this regard was the far-reaching richness of their technology and culture, owing to their geographical location which connected them with different cultural sites of repute.

In Chapter 2, we have given details showing that the earliest culture of Kashmir was an extension of the pre- and proto-historic cultures of its western, north-western and northern borderlands. While the Palaeolithic culture of Kashmir constitutes an expansion of the Soanian culture, the Neolithic culture of Kashmir is an enlargement of Swat, pre-Harappan and Dardistan cultures. This is evident from the intimate affinities between the Neolithic culture of Kashmir and the Neolithic cultures encountered in these borderlands of Kashmir, be it dwelling houses, bone and stone tools, agricultural and horticultural crops, animal husbandry, pottery, semi-precious stones, ornaments, art, beliefs, language, ethnicity and the like. It is, therefore, no wonder that while, on the one hand, the archaeologists refer to the Neolithic cultural complex of the northern valleys of the subcontinent as an extension of Neolithic of Inner Asia, this culture is also commonly called Northern Neolithic or the Kashmir-Swat Neolithic (see Chapter 2). The linguists extended the area of 'Northern Neolithic' by asserting that the Kashmiri language belongs to the Dardic group of languages which were spoken in the area, comprising the present Gilgit, Chilas, Astor, Gurez, Kashmir Valley, Indus and Swat Kohistan.

Between 1500 and 600 BCE, we see Kashmir passing into a new phase characterised by menhirs, cist graves, iron, rubble structures and spectacular growth in rice cultivation. These cultural aspects also got transmitted to Kashmir from its western, north-western and northern-eastern borderlands. The nearest places where megaliths have been found are Baluchistan, Yasin and Chitral. Cist graves are found in Swat and in many neighbouring valleys—Dir, Chitral etc. collectively called "Gandhara Grave Culture."[4] Rice was cultivated in Swat not later than the mid-third millennium BCE. Millet was also cultivated in Swat around 1500 BCE. Iron objects have been found in Gandhara graves assignable to the opening of the first millennium BCE.[5] It is around the same period that we come to know about iron in Kashmir. Around 1000 BCE we also find a transition from mud or mud brick wall constructions to stone-walled houses at ground level. In the context of Swat, these changes have been explained in the context of immigration events particularly of Indo-Aryan tribes.[6] The same may hold true of Kashmir as well and all evidence points to the immigration of these new people through the territories that bordered Kashmir on its north and west.

In 516 BCE, Darius, the Achaemenian ruler of Iran, extended his empire up to India by annexing Sindh, North-West Frontier and the parts of the Punjab. We learn from Greek sources that at the time of Iranian invasion, Kashmir was a part of Gandhara. This is also corroborated by the Buddhist texts and *Milindapanha*. The Buddhist texts state that in pre-Aśokan days,

Kashmir and Gandhara formed one political unit[7] and *Milindapanha* compounded the two territories as Kashmira and Gandhara.[8] That Kashmir and Gandhara were culturally similar is also substantiated by the prevalence of identical script in both the regions. Kharoshthi was so common in Gandhara that Aśoka had to write some inscription in the north-west in this script. Its prevalence in Kashmir is evidenced by the Aśokan edict at Mansehra (near Abbotabad) situated closely to Kashmir Valley and its continuation as the main script of Kashmir up to the fifth century CE as shown by Harwan tiles. The period from the BCE 180 to the beginning of the sixth century CE is underlined by the successive occupation of the north-west of India by the Indo-Greeks, Śakas, Parthians, Kuṣāṇas, Kidarites and Huns. As Kashmir was also occupied by these Central Asian empire builders, it came to be intimately integrated with its northern and western borderlands, leaving a deep impact on its culture especially when we consider that Gandhara became the hub of a syncretic culture forged of Indian, Greek, Iranian, Central Asian and Chinese cultures.

The art historian, Robert Fisher, reasons out the intimate affinities between the Gandhara and Kashmir art:

> One plausible aspect of the early period that does emerge from the various literary sources, however, is the close connection between Kashmir and the area to the west, Gandhara. Beginning at least with the Achaemenian Persians around 500 BC, and continuing with the Greek and Shaka tribes, the region between Afghanistan and Kashmir was usually viewed as one cultural entity. The name Kashmir was not generally limited to the small Himalayan Valley until times in the early centuries AD. By the time of the Hun invasions, towards the beginning of the sixth century, which also encompassed both regions, Gandhara kings had used Kashmir as a refuge and likewise Kashmiri rulers could find temporary safety in the neighbouring area when needed. Despite invasions and wars, the commercial and cultural exchange between the adjacent regions continued without interruption. Even to later visitors, such as the Chinese monks of the seventh and eighth centuries, the cultures of the two regions, still seemed to be essentially one.[9]

Writing about the impact of Gandhara art and architecture on Kashmir, Stanislaw Czuma says:

> The north-western frontiers of India represent an area that from the earliest times was a meeting point of various cultural influences and was, at the same time, responsible for the dissemination of the Indian culture to the outside world. During the early centuries of the Christian era the territory of Gandhara primarily held this

> distinction . . . since Kashmir was once an integral part of the vast empire it is not surprising that Gandhara tradition to a great extent formed the roots of the Kashmiri style.[10]

John Siudmak, who has extensively written on Kashmir sculpture, also found that the "predominant influence" on Kashmir art "was from the north-west, either from Gandhara or from the post-Gandhara tradition which survived in the region." Siudmak exemplifies his assertion by making a detailed study of Kashmir stone and terracotta sculpture at Bijbehara, Baramulla, Pandrethan and Ushkur.[11]

As in art, so also in Kashmir style of architecture the roots lay in Gandharan inheritance of certain of its aspects. A brief mention of it has been given in Chapter 4. Significantly, the earliest extant temple of Kashmir, Lodu temple, is comparable with the Takht-i-Bahi temple of Swat.[12]

The influence was however a two-way traffic. As Kashmir became a hub of artistic activities, especially from sixth century onwards, the reverse influence becomes marked with it. To quote Pratapaditya Pal:

> Because of the presence as well as the influence of Kashmiri artists in contiguous areas such as Swat in Pakistan, Ladakh in India and Western Tibet, it is often difficult to distinguish between a Kashmiri bronze and one created in these regions.[13]

This is also substantiated by the Kashmiri affinities of the ivory found in Gansu in northwestern China. In a recent study of the Gansu ivory, Diana Rowan concluded that

> [T]he diptych may represent an unusual commission of a late seventh or eighth century Shahi dignitary who lived on the frontiers of Kashmiri influence – a Buddhist frontier familiar with Gandharan diptych forms and narrative cycles, Hindu style and Chinese decorative arts; an area located in the midst of trade routes that carried this portable object of worship to its find spot in northwest China.[14]

In the ancient Buddhist literature Swat (Uddiyana) was famous for being a great centre of Buddhism. This is corroborated by both the archaeological and literary evidence.[15] Subsequently it also became a centre of the doctrine of *mahāsiddha*. It is believed that the doctrine of *mahāsiddha* would have been taught to Abhinavagupta by Budhiraja, a native of Uddiyana.[16] Regarding the exchange of scholars between the two great centres of learning—Kashmir and Uddiyana—Jean Naudou says,

> [I]t is more than probable that the most knowledgeable and zealous of religious belonging to the communities of those districts used to

> come several times in their life to stay in the most illustrious monasteries of the Vitasta Valley, just as Kashmiris, smitten by "tantric" mysteries, used to go for instruction (as did Ratnavajra and Prajnaguhya) close to *yogin* or *dākinī* of Uddiyana.[17]

From the sixth century up to the end of our period, Kashmir not only enjoyed political independence but it also emerged as a great power having sometimes direct and sometimes indirect control over its immediate borderlands. When Mihirakula was expelled from India, he sought shelter in Kashmir and his empire shrunk to a comparatively small area comprising Kashmir, Gandhara and Sind, and it was from Kashmir that he tried to reconquer the last Hun empire.[18] According to Kalhana, Mihirakula preferred Gandhara brahmanas over others and settled them in Kashmir under sate patronage.[19] It was most probably because of the fact that the successors or supporters of Huns ruled in Gandhara and Sind that the Hun ruler of Kashmir, Yudhishthira sought shelter in the court of the Gandharan king, and his grandson and the subsequent ruler of Kashmir, Meghavahana was brought up at the Gandhara court.[20] We will also see in the following pages that there were intimate relations between the ruling families of Kashmir and Sind. The Hun tradition of embarking on military adventures to build vast empires was maintained by many Hun rulers of Kashmir, namely, Narendraditya, Meghavahana, Pravarasena II, Ranaditya, Vikramaditya and Baladitya.[21] It is therefore not surprising that we learn from the Chinese sources that the route from China to Kabul was under the control of Kashmiri rulers[22] and all the adjacent territories on the west and north down to the Takshashila, Hazara and the salt range were ruled by them.[23] The political control of Kashmir over these territories was further tightened under the Karkotas, especially during the period of Lalitaditya and Jayapida, who extended the boundaries of Kashmir beyond its immediate neighbourhood.[24]

It may, however, be mentioned that whenever the position of the central authority weakened in Kashmir, these borderlands of Kashmir did not only throw off the yoke of Kashmir, but they also became a source of great menace to the people of the valley. They used to serve as refuge and base for malcontents and rebels during the time of trouble. They fished in troubled waters and launched murderous attacks on Kashmir to loot and plunder the people. To quote Al-Biruni, "Kashmir suffered much from the inroads of tribes living in and around Gilgit, Askardu and Chilas."[25] This is why, according to Kalhana, Lalitaditya advised his successors not to allow them to become strong:

> Those who dwell there in the [mountains] difficult of access, should be punished, even if they give no offence, because sheltered by their fastnesses, they are difficult to break up if they have [once] accumulated wealth.[26]

It seems that during the later Karkota rulers, Kashmir lost control over most of its borderlands, and it was left to the Utpala ruler, Samkaravarman (883–902) to re-conquer them who, according to Kalhana, occupied the *Takka* land[27] and the territories on the banks of Indus up to Urasa (Hazara).[28] That Kashmir maintained its supremacy over Gandhara is substantiated by the fact that the son and successor of Samkaravarman quelled the rebellious Śahi of Udabhandapura (the capital of Gandhara) and installed a loyalist Toramana on the throne.[29]

The marriage of Kşemagupta (950–958) with Didda inaugurated a new era in cementing the relations of Kashmir with Gandhara and the Punjab. Didda was the daughter of King Simharaja, the ruler of Lohara; and, more importantly, she was the grand-daughter of the Śahi ruler whose rule extended from Kabul to the Punjab. Since Didda was the real power behind the throne of Kşemagupta (which is why he was nicknamed as Diddakśema), and as she actually ruled the country even before she formally assumed power directly in 980 CE, the three kingdoms—Kashmir, Śahi and Lohara—got intimately connected leading to the influx and settlement of the people from the Śahi and Lohara kingdoms in Kashmir. This phenomenon exacerbated after the assumption of the reign of Kashmir by the Loharas in 1003 CE and the fall of Śahi kingdom at the hands of Mahmud of Ghazni around the same time.[30]

After the occupation of north and west of India by the Muslims, Kashmir's relations with these borderlands disrupted for some time.[31] But the compulsions of neighbourliness and interdependence soon prevailed as we find Muslims being recruited in the Kashmir army.[32] It was because of the friendly relations of Kashmir with its Muslim north and west that, among others, we find Shah Mir coming from Swat and given a land grant by the then king of Kashmir, Suhadeva (1301–1320).[33] Significantly, Shah Mir played a leading role in maintaining Kashmir's freedom, which was threatened by a foreign invader—Achhala. This achievement made Shah Mir the peoples' hero[34] and ultimately the ruler of Kashmir in 1339 CE.

Towards the north of Kashmir is Karnaha (modern Karnah), nominally a tributary of Kashmir. The Karnah route gave passage to Śaradi where lies the famous tirtha of ancient Kashmir called Śarda,[35] which was visited not only by the pilgrims of Kashmir but also by the devotees from as distant areas of India as Bengal.[36] Through Śardi leads a route to Dard land comprising Chilas, Hunza, Nagar and Gurez which then connected Kashmir with Central Asia. We have already mentioned that Chilas and its neighbourhood acted as one of the intermediary zones between the neighbouring cultural centres and Kashmir. That Kashmir was a preferred destination for Darads to settle down permanently there is clear not only from such place names as Daradpur, Daradgund, Daradkoot and the like we come across in Kashmir but also from the continuous migrations from the region and their settlements in the valley as is indicated by the coming of a powerful tribe of Chaks under the leadership of Langar Chak during the time of Suhadeva.[37]

According to the contemporary sources, Langar Chak came from Dardistan and the tribe settled at Trehgam and Kupwara.[38] The Chaks were so powerful that they were included in the nobility by Shah Mir, the founder of the Muslim Sultanate and became subsequently kingmakers.[39] It is also worth mentioning that like other hill people, the Challises also launched plundering raids on Kashmir during the times of trouble.[40]

Immediately above Śardi, the valley of the Kishanganga turns into a narrow uninhabited gorge. At the other end of this gorge we reach another territory of Dards. Their settlement on the upper Kishanganga and its tributaries seems to have formed a separate little kingdom, called by a general name Daraddesa in *Rājataraṅgiṇī* of Kalhana.[41] Daradapuri, which was their residence, may have occupied the position of modern Gurez. Like other hill states surrounding Kashmir, Darad land formed a part of the Kashmir kingdom during the powerful rulers; but generally it was an independent principality. Kalhana refers in several passages to the hill fort of Dugdhaghata, which guarded the mountain—route leading into Kashmir territory from inroads of the Darads.[42] During the rule of the later Loharas, we find a frequent mention of Dardas being approached by the claimants to power for support and they are seen fighting side by side with their armies. The '*mleecha*' chiefs who on two occasions during the first half of the 12th century figure as the Darad Rajas' allies against the Kashmiri ruler were perhaps rulers of other Darad tribes further in the Indus who had been converted to Islam.[43]

Indeed, the hilly people were incomparable fighters, which is why it was the policy of every claimant to power to recruit the services of these hill people and establish a network of relations with them including matrimonial relations. On the basis of his personal testimony, Kalhana says that it was only because of some superior war technology that Kashmiri rajas could save their position from the martial groups of the hills surrounding it; otherwise, they were no match to them in physical prowess.

> How could inhabitants of the plains vie with those who live on the mountains? Yet the large quantity of war engines, which achieve un-thought-of results, must be taken into consideration.[44]

* * *

In the north and east of Kashmir are situated the high-level valleys called by the contemporaries as Bhautta land.[45] Bhautta is a generic term used for the people of Tibetan race and language. The Bhautta land is historically divided into two parts carrying distinct appellations, namely, Little Tibet and Great Tibet. The Little Tibet comprised Askardo, Gilgit and Baltistan, and the Great Tibet refers to modern Ladakh province.[46] The two were approached by two different routes. While the Little Tibet was connected by the route passing through Gurez, the Great Tibet was approached through

Zojila route. Like other neighbourhoods, Bhautta land played an important role in shaping the ethnic, cultural and economic history of Kashmir and vice versa. A fairly large number of Kashmiris are of Tibetan race, which is clear from their physiognomy even after the considerable cross-breedings since the occupation of Kashmir by the people of its borderlands around 3100 BCE. This is also substantiated by the place names of Kashmir, such as Bhautta-pur, Bhautta-Gund, Bhautta-Kadaland and the like. The physiognomy of a good number of people of these habitations also corroborates their being originally a Bhautta habitation. Rinchina's coming to Kashmir along with his Bhautta followers during the reign of Suhadeva[47] has, thus, to be seen in the light of this established practice of the settlement of Bhauttas in Kashmir. Apart from contributing to the formation of mosaic ethnic composition of the valley, Kashmir had also close cultural and commercial relations with both Little and Great Tibet and through them with China and Central Asia. While Kashmir exported Buddhism and food to these lands, the latter exported to the former the advanced technology and culture it had borrowed from China and Central Asia, besides giving it access to the Silk Route and through it to the world market as such.

* * *

The history of Kashmir was also closely intertwined with the area stretching between Kishtwar in the south-east and Muzaffarabad in south-west. This hilly belt was fragmented into a medley of petty principalities, namely, Kasthavata (Kishtwar), Bhadravakasa (Bhadarwah), Campa (Camba), Vallapura (Bilawar), about a dozen petty chiefdoms between Bilawar and Rajouri (Rajapuri), Lohara (Lohrin) and Parnnotsa (Punch). During the time when Kashmir was ruled by powerful rulers, these hill states constituted a part of the Kashmir empire; even Trigartta (Kangra) too used to be under the control of Kashmiri kings.[48] As late as 1087–1088, eight kings came to Srinagar to pay their homage to king Kalasa. They were the rulers of Lohara, Urasa, Rajapuri, Vallapura, Kasthavata, Buddhapura (?), Kanda and Campa.[49] However, because of geographical hazards these states could not be kept under control for the most part of our period of study. It was only Lohara, which stayed as a part of Kashmir from 1003, when Kashmir came to be ruled by the ruling dynasty of Lohara. Even though the hill states remained sovereign powers, Kashmir was invariably treated as big brother obviously because of its incomparable might. During the normal circumstances, they constituted the allies of Kashmiri rulers either for extending the boundaries of the Kashmir kingdom or as buffer against the foreign invasions. But these hill fiefdoms were also a source of trouble depending upon the internal conditions of Kashmir. While a successful ruler could mould them into a support structure,[50] the internal political chaos in Kashmir kingdom turned them into breeding grounds of revolts by giving refuge and support to the disgruntled nobles or claimants for power.[51] Invariably the political instability encouraged the hill men to swoop on Kashmir for loot and plunder of the people.[52]

Apart from intimate political and strategic relations, there were close cultural and commercial ties between Kashmir and its south-east and south-west border states. Certainly, a significant number of the population of Kashmir are immigrants from these border states prompted as they were by its comparatively better relief, climate and agricultural productivity. Their settlement was also backed by the rulers who either hired their services for military purposes,[53] or, as in case of the Loharas, encouraged their kiths to settle in Kashmir to form a strong internal support base. They were appointed to high positions. The *thakkuras* (Kmr. *Thakur*), who form a section of the Kashmiri population, originally hailed from these lands and settled in Kashmir in large numbers during the period of Loharas.[54] From the *Rājataraṅgiṇī* of Kalhana, we find *sati* prevalent among only a section of the people. Clearly this was the section of what Kalhana says 'Rajputras' (Rajputs)[55]—the ruling caste of these hill states including the Loharas who ruled Kashmir for more than two centuries making *sati* a reference culture.[56] This is why the orthodox brahmana, Kalhana, castigates those widows of the king who did not become *sati*.[57] Evidently, those queens who voluntarily offered themselves for *sati* were mostly from Rajput families,[58] as we frequently come across the matrimonial relations between the ruling families of Kashmir and the ruling families of the hill states under reference.[59] Ethnically, the people of the borderlands from Kishtwar to Muzaffarabad were *Khasas* who were identical with the later *Khakha* tribes notorious as marauders and turbulent hill men.[60]

Besides participating in the formation of mosaic composition of the Kashmir population, the hill states of the south-west of Kashmir were a lifeline of Kashmir's trade with the Punjab, and through the Punjab with other parts of the Indian subcontinent. After all, the Bhimbar route was the shortest route connecting Kashmir with the Punjab; and Thana was the traditional *mandi* (trade entrepot) between Kashmir and the Punjab. According to Abul Fazl, the linguistic landscape of Kashmiri begins from Thana.[61] And MA Stein's personal observation of the presence of "the large percentage of Kashmiri element in the population of *Prunts* (Punch) attests to the closeness and remote antiquity of its relation to Kashmir."[62]

Beyond these immediate high valleys, Kashmir had also close relations with Trigarta (Kangra), Kuluta (Kulu), Jalamdhara (Jalandhar) and Sindhu (Sind). Apart from forming tributary states of the Kashmir empire during the reign of powerful rulers, there were close relations between Kashmir and these territories based on cultural, matrimonial and diplomatic relations. We find a brahmana, Keśava from Trigarta [Kangra] as one of the ministers of Ananta.[63] And the chief queen of Ananta, Suryamati, was the daughter of the prince of Jalandhara.[64]

There were also intimate contacts between Kashmir and neighbouring Sindh and Multan. The rulers of Sindh frequently sought help from Kashmiri rajas against their internal adversaries and external aggressors. When Chach invaded Multan, its ruler Bachhara sent letters to the raja of Kashmir for help, which the latter politely refused citing the reason of its own political instability.[65] And when Bachhara was defeated, he "with his followers and dependents proceeded to the mountains of Kashmir."[66] It is evident that Kashmir was one of the safe heavens for the defeated rajas of the neighbouring territories. The close relations were further cemented by the matrimonial relations between the royal families of Sind and Kashmir. The daughter of Chach was married to the king of Kashmir.[67] It was on account of these intimate relations between the rajas of Sind and Kashmir that the fugitive Arab commander (in the service of raja Dahir and his son Jasiah) sought refuge from the ruler of Kashmir and he was received with open arms and bestowed the patronage he deserved as a faithful general of the raja of Sind.[68]

The close relationship between Kashmir and Sind is also demonstrated in the circulation of the forms and patterns of art and architecture between Kashmir and the Indus Valley. According to Flood, some of the details of the ivory found in Mansura or Multan

> suggest affinities with the sculpture of Kashmir, known to have been the centre of ivory carving during the eighth and ninth centuries. . . . These include the triple projectionson the diadems worn by the horsemen, the typical "Kashmiri crown" (the fillet with crescent and disk). . . . If, as I believe, the ivory was worked in Mansura and Multan, its strong Himalayan affinities might reflect contemporary contacts between Kashmir, the Indus Valley and Gujarat, elsewhere reflected in imports of Kashmiri sculpture and the adoption of characteristic Kashmiri forms (including trefoil arches and pyramidal roofs) in some of the Hindu temples of the Salt Range.[69]

The intimacy between Kashmir and Sind was so deep that neither the Arab conquest of Sind nor the establishment of the Muslim sultanate (six hundred years after the Muslim conquest of Sind) could disturb their age-old relations. This is evident from the fact that the matrimonial relations between the Indigenous royal family of Sind and the ruling family of Kashmir continued up to the Sultans as we find Sultan Shihab al-Din having his two queens from Sind. They were Lakṣmi and Laśa.[70]

Notes

1 Allchin and Allchin (1981), 116.
2 Grierson (1919), 8(2): 253.
3 Pal (1989a), vi.
4 For details about "Gandhara Grave Culture," see Antonini and Stacul (1972); Dani *et al.* (1967).
5 Antonini and Stacul (1972); Dani *et al.* (1967).

6 Stacul (1989), 268.
7 Dutt (1985), 5.
8 *Milindapanho*, 331.
9 Fisher (1989a), 29–30.
10 Czuma (1989), 61–62.
11 Siudmak (1989), 41–48.
12 Fisher (1989a), 30.
13 Pal (1989a), V.
14 Rowan (1985), 282.
15 Naudou (1980), 34, fn. 70, 71.
16 Ibid, 35–36.
17 Ibid, 37.
18 Kalhana, I: 289sqq.
19 Ibid, I, 307.
20 Ibid, II, 144–46; III: 2.
21 Ibid, Book III.
22 See Ray (1969), 44.
23 See Hiuen Tsiang, I: 136, 143, 147, 163.
24 Kalhana, IV: 131 sqq, 519sqq.
25 Al-Biruni, I: 207.
26 Kalhana, IV: 346
27 Ibid, V, 150.
28 Ibid, V, 216–17.
29 Ibid, V, 232–33.
30 See Chapter IV.
31 Al-Biruni, I: 206.
32 Kalhana, VII: 1149; VIII: 885–87, 919–923, 2264.
33 Jonarāja, 15; *Bahāristān-i Shāhī*, f. 46.
34 Ibid, 26.
35 For details, see Stein (1979), II: 279–289.
36 Kalhana, IV: 324–25.
37 *Bahāristān-i Shāhī*, f. 46.
38 Ibid.
39 Hassan (2005), 46, 110sqq
40 Al-Biruni, I: 207.
41 Kalhana, II: 435.
42 Ibid, II, 406.
43 Ibid, VIII, 2762–64, 2766.
44 Ibid, VIII, 2558.
45 Stein (1979), II: 435.
46 Ibid.
47 Jonarāja, 18.
48 Kalhana, III: 285; V: 144; VIII: 1531.
49 Ibid, VII, 588–590.
50 Ibid, V, 140.
51 Ibid, VIII, 538–40.
52 Al-Biruni, I: 207.
53 Kalhana, VIII: 323, 1083–1086.
54 Ibid, VII, 706, 738–39, 775, 780, 784, 835; VIII: 1942, 2278.
55 Ibid, VIII, 2334.
56 See Mohan (1981), 230–35.
57 Kalhana, VIII: 2334.

58 Mohan (1981), 232–35.
59 Kalhana, VIII: 218.
60 Stein (1979), II: 392.
61 Abul Fazl (1939), III: 822
62 Stein (1979), II: 433.
63 Kalhana, VII: 204–205
64 Ibid, VII, 150–52
65 Kūfī, 28–29.
66 Ibid, 29.
67 Ibid, 40.
68 Ibid, 160.
69 Flood (2009), 55.
70 Jonarāja, 42–43.

6

CONCLUSION

> Ancient History is like an inheritance shared by many.[1]
> —(Partha Chatterjee)

The present insistence on a borderless world to ensure free flow of goods, services and ideas, as well as to unite the divided humankind and to resolve the conflicts by making the national boundaries soft and more permeable, is not entirely an innovative idea. It is inspiring to recall the Ancient and Middle Ages when the political regions were inextricably bound up with one another and the free movement of people and goods was a normal feature. It is precisely this fascinating story which this book is all about by making a case study of Kashmir—Kashmir which, because of unfortunate reasons arguably owing to the subversion of its geographical centrality and history of connectivity, has been much in news for a considerable time now. Indeed, today's Kashmir is entirely different from what it had been for about 5,000 years since the human settlements began in it. Unlike its present geographical siege, it was an unbounded region having intimate relations with its immediate and distant neighbourhoods. Clearly, no aspect of Kashmir history can become intelligible to us if we ignore the region as a site of connectivity, linkage and flow.

Arguing against the notion of spatially bound regional identity in the present-day world, Ash Amin writes:

> The salient point is that cultural globalization has become the *everyday* filter through which regional attachment or sense of place is developed and expressed. The result is not necessarily a weakened sense of place, but a *heterotopic sense of place* that is no longer reducible to regional moorings or to a territorially confined public sphere, but is made up of influences that fold together the culturally plural and the geographically proximate and distant.[2]

DOI: 10.4324/9781003367697-6

Exactly the same situation obtained during the premodern times except for the fact that there existed many imitable models simultaneously, they spread slowly in the then poor communication technologies, the influences radiating from outside were often reworked in the local crucible and "purifying impulses of modernity"[3] were an aberration rather than a rule. Hence, one important dimension of the history of Kashmir unfolded by this book is that the early Kashmir is the product of two processes—circulation and translation. There emerged many great cosmopolitan ecumenes in the neighbouring world of Kashmir, which provided a larger organising framework for the cultural life of its (Kashmir's) proximate neighbourhoods. The latter translated the borrowed historical processes and cultural goods on their own terms giving birth to many hybrid cultural centres in the immediate borderlands of Kashmir. And it is these proximate and distant cultural geographies which became the "everyday filter" through which Kashmir developed and expressed its sense of place. Though the evidence in this regard has not come down to us fully, whatever scanty information has survived to us reflecting technology, science, agriculture, crafts, trade, religion, philosophy, social structure, art, architecture, coinage, script, language, literature, amusements, recreations, costume, coiffure, food, drinks, place names, personal names, administrative organisation, governance and so on, it becomes quite clear that culturally Kashmir and the neighbouring world belonged to the same cosmopolitan complex; and in certain respects Kashmir proved considerably productive in forging this cosmopolitanism by virtue of its role as a nexus between different cultural networks, and also because of the favourable courtly milieus.

As many cultural sites appeared on the remote and immediate borders of Kashmir from time to time with varying time spans but each of long periods and with powerful compositional/unifying forces, they became the mirrors for the ruling elite of Kashmir through which they saw their faces and reached at self-appraisals. The result was that culturally the region was neither immobile nor any longer reducible to regional moorings. The imitation of *reference models* did not only satisfy the quest for respectability and prestige, but it also simultaneously possessed tangible potentialities for material and cultural development. All in all, the royal courts became the sponsors of trans-regional cultural flows in their quest to cast their dominions in the mould of *reference cultural sites*. No wonder, then, Kashmir witnessed continuous influx of experts in different fields throughout the period of our study. Participation of the court cultures in cosmopolitan ecumene had downward filtration effect. Unable to resist the temptations of "prestigious imitation,"[4] the ruling elite became the *reference group* for the subjects to imitate their life styles in search of finding a respectable position in the society. During the times when Kashmir formed a part of the great empires that arose on its borders or when it itself emerged as an empire, more factors weighed in favour of making Kashmir and its neighbourhood a cosmopolitan world. Consolidation of conquests necessitated cultural integration with the core of the empire as well as building of a strong support structure. Both these demands encouraged migrations and facilitated various processes of territorial perforation, connectivity and geographical transfer of cultures and the cultural agents.

It may, however, be admitted that the state, though the most important instrument of consequential cultural transfer and transformation, was only one of the many such channels which knit Kashmir and the surrounding world together. Of the other influential modes, mention may be made of trade, education, religion and the "individuals possessed of sufficient cognitive skills to circulate and translate between different verbal and social languages,"[5] for example, the peripatetic Pandit Bilhana of Kashmir who travelled to Mathura, Kanyakubja, Vārānasi, Dāhala, Dhāra, Somanātha and finally to South India;[6] or the itinerant craftsmen from the "Turuśka country" who offered his services to king Kalasa of Kashmir to put a gilt parasol over the Śiva temple.[7]

The unending inflows and contacts from the neighbouring world made Kashmir a place of complex ethnic mosaic of population and changing ethnic identities over time. More importantly, Kashmir became a mini-global culture as the cultural centres, which were the immediate fountainheads of the local cosmopolitanism, were themselves largely the products of circulation and contact. To quote Sheldon Pollock, "there exist no cultural agents who are not always – already transcultured"; consequently, "the cultural materials being transferred are *always hybrid themselves*."[8]

With constant waves of immigrations and persistent cultural interaction and exchange, Kashmir society continued to be in flux—in the process of making/never completely formed. In this respect, Kashmir is not different from any other society which experienced repeated encounters with different cultural systems making it a fascinating story of "*métissages*," negotiation, accommodation and hybridity layer upon layer without having completely erased even the layers of remote past (though they were given different forms and imbued with new meanings) and without having any end to its openness. Being essentially a place of cross-cultural interactions, it is easy to understand Kashmir's fame as a space for toleration, accommodation and unorthodoxy. That even *cārvākas* and many other categories of non-conformists had a free play in the society,[9] and the Jews, Christians and Muslims[10] were liberally patronised, and a "*domba*" could find a place in the cosmopolitan courtly milieus[11] amply substantiate the fact that premodern societies were marked by a "cosmopolitan cultivation of fragmentation" and "openness to alterities."[12]

Indeed, the early history of Kashmir represented in a variety of sources is "incommensurate with sectarian historiographies and inconceivable to purveyors of orthodoxies and purities of every sought"[13]—the conclusion which Finbarr Flood arrived at on the basis of material evidence and textual sources including the evidence from Kashmir.[14] The same conclusion can be derived from the change of religions/sects along with the change of rulers and their hybrid modes of self-representation, the two important phenomena we have noticed throughout the period of this study, suggesting that the social and religious identities were "not immutable but socially constructed" and subject to change according to an "orientation to power" best captured by a Kashmiri proverb: *yukun wāv tokun nāv* (to set sail in the wind's direction). While unorthodoxy runs like a thread in almost the whole history of early Kashmir and is adequately documented in this book, an interesting thing not highlighted so far though being of supplementary importance to the narrative is that the texts and oral tradition generally prefer ethnic, regional, occupational and other secular appellations to religious categories, for example, Bhotta, Darda, Turuśka, Yavana, Khasa, Tukhara, Rajaputra, Thakkura, Takka, Khokha and Bomba.[15] The ethnicity was also constructed on the basis of tribal background, occupations or some contingencies. For instance, the brahamanas were divided into 103 *gotras* (tribal divisions), and each *gotra* was divided into distinctive families famous after family appellation called *kram*. *Kram* is often the relic of a nickname applied to the ancestor of the subdivision. And when during the rule of Muslims some of them held different positions in the state apparatus, they came to be called after those offices such as Razdan, Fotadar, Ambardar, Ganju, Karawani, Diwani, Qazi, Muhatasib, Naqib, Amin and Waguzari, which became their permanent surnames.[16]

What is more, the perforated borders and global connectivity, in conjunction with favourably courtly milieus, made the valley an advanced centre of learning, a place of innovations and a meeting ground of transborder traders cumulatively making Kashmir such a prosperous *mandala* that the poet-chronicler, Kalhana could not imagine it "even in heaven."[17]

While arguing that the early culture of Kashmir is transborder in its constitution, we acknowledge the occurrence of many simultaneous developments which gave the region a special identity characterised by an ethno-cultural mix sourced from its immediate borderlands and distant neighbourhoods. As the variegated ethnicities and variety of cultural goods drawn from exogenous sources underwent an amazing metamorphosis from diversity into hybridisation within the geographical boundaries of Kashmir, it became the culture of the place—the culture of Kashmir or Kashmiri culture. The paramount role of endogenous processes in remoulding the exogenous influences can be gleaned from every aspect of Kashmiri society. Evidently the process of translation and negotiation emanated from geography, mentality, cultural values, power, patronage, the choices made by elites, pragmatism and the demands of congruence and compatibility substantiating the claim that "in circulating, things, men and notions often transform themselves."[18] Thus like any other region, Kashmir was both within the world around it and out of it.

The significant role of the process of mediation, negotiation and translation in shaping regional/local cultures is seen even in such a sensitive aspect as religion. We have seen that from the sixth century CE to the beginning of the fourteenth century CE, Kashmir was a part of the Sanskritic cosmopolis. Yet, it constructed its own distinctive world view by appropriating, rehistoricising and reading new signs and meanings of the "cosmopolitan Sanskritic sphere" to borrow the language of Sheldon Pollock. This is best captured by the *Nīlamata Purāna* (NP) written in the seventh–eighth century CE to effect ritual–ideological transition from non-brahmanic to brahmanic hegemony and dominance. It provides the Puranic Kashmir its own cosmos, which runs parallel to the subcontinental cosmos though the reconstruction of the sacred geography of Kashmir was done within the wider context of the subcontinental sacred geography "by adopting textual manipulations and semantic strategies."[19] Whether the creation of parallel sacred geography was done to map 'political vision' "for a Kashmiri kingship that desired to rule over the entire earth, a nuanced way of devising hegemony over seventh to the tenth century north India?"[20] or was the appropriation of the sacred geography of India a creative response to meet the challenge posed by the geographical hazards which made it difficult for the ordinary people to visit the original sacred places in the subcontinent?[21] In any case, however, the construction of a parallel sacred geography reinforced the popular imagination which for geographical reasons considered Kashmir a world in itself, especially when the NP conceives Kashmir as the place of gods and goddesses; where there was "not a space as large as a grain of seasmum without a tirtha," according to Kalhana;[22] and where the NP, for example, claimed that "the Ganga [Indian Ganga] does not excel Vitasta,"[23] but even supersedes the former as the Ganga only leads to heaven while the Vitasta paves the path to salvation.[24] Walter Slaje also arrives at the same conclusion when he says that "on hearing 'Ganga' any member of the Kashmir society would have thought of the Ganga *in their country* in the first place, but only secondly of the Ganga in the Indian plains."[25] Thus the NP is not only a typical example of translation but even emblematic of a fundamental reconceptualisation of Kashmir and its identity.

Clearly, the geographical conditions of Kashmir together with the deeply embedded local practices conspired in the making of what may be called Kashmiri Brahmanism which, in many respects, was at variance with the belief system of the brahmanas of the plains. For example, the Kashmiri sources mention the permission to eat meat and fish as a *deśaguna*, a virtue of the country.[26] Also, the Kashmiri brahmanas had their own red-letter days, not observing, for example *Dussehra*, *Holi* and *Diwali*, the most important festivals observed in the Indic mainland.[27] Perhaps they considered themselves superior to the brahmanas of India. That is why, according to Lawrence, "the Kashmiri Brahmans did not intermarry with the Brahmans of India."[28]

The repeated diasporas and contacts from many directions no doubt resulted in the formation of religious, ethnic and occupational categories at micro levels; but the porous religious and social borders and, much more, the language of the masses—*Koshur* and the collective concern of protecting the country from internal revolts and foreign invasions (though a large number of inhabitants were themselves invaders turned Kashmiris) created a broader unity in diversity facilitated by the trough-like geography of the Kashmir Valley.[29]

This book has also sufficiently demonstrated that Kashmir did not become merely an extension or appendage of the prominent cultural centres that emerged on its borders; instead, it itself came up as an important centre and significantly participated in trans-regional cultural sphere, though the initial inspirations had radiated from beyond its borders. In this regard, Kashmir's contribution to Sanskrit learning—grammar, poetics, literary theory, logic, philosophy, Buddhism, Śaivism and Vaiṣṇavism—with far-reaching influences on the neighbouring world is well known to the students of early history.[30] Also, for a long time Kashmir retained the position of a powerful empire with its frontiers beyond its natural ramparts; and for a couple of decades the Kashmiri king claimed to be the King of Kings. It was during this period that the NP described Kashmir as the 'middle country' (*madhyadeśa*) of India.[31] Designating Kashmir as *madhyadeśa* and endowing it with all auspicious signs was obviously inspired by the will to build Kashmir's own individual and independent position with all the symbols of divine and auspicious landscapes and attributes as are encountered in the *madhyadeśa* within India itself. Therefore this textual practice was as much an ideological tool to effect cultural transition as was it a political instrument to legitimise Kashmir's suzerainty over India even though it did not fall within the Middle Region of India.[32] Closely implicated in this process were the *Visnudharmamottara Purāna* and *Rājataraṅgiṇī* of Kalhana. Debunking, on the grounds of factuality, Kashmiris' projections of their rulers as universal conquerors, Al-Biruni writes in reference to Lalitaditya,

> According to their account he ruled over the whole world. But this is exactly what they say of most of their kings. However, they are incautious enough to assign him a time not much anterior to our own time, which leads to their lie being found out.

To be sure, the conception of imperial sovereignty is ubiquitous across the world of Sanskrit text production. Unlike most of the modern readers who dismiss the representation of the 'political trans-regionality' of the inscriptions and texts of the 'Sanskrit cosmopolitan period,' Pollock finds a meaning in this "political fiction."

> Here we grasp that fictions can themselves be social facts, that ideals are actually existing values, that imagination is information – and

> that, accordingly, the epic geomorphology of political aspirations may have exerted existential force not just on medieval thinkers and writers but on rulers, too.[33]

To sum up, Kashmir and its neighbouring world had entangled histories, mutually influencing and constituting one another. There is no doubt that like its proximate borderlands, Kashmir was deeply influenced by the successive cosmopolitan ecumenes that emerged in its neighbourhood; but without getting dissolved in them it forged its own shape. Nevertheless, as the material was translocal and the time-tested "local," it gave the structure a cosmopolitan and majestic form, thanks to circulation and courtly milieus characterised by openness, accommodation and ambition to make Kashmir an empire, a paradise with all enviable features—tranquillity,[34] learning, material prosperity, "spiritual merits" and natural beauty[35]—which even the heaven would envy, according to Kalhana, the representative Sanskrit poet-historian of eleventh- to twelfth-century Kashmir. This was the Kashmiri identity during early Kashmir, not the attempts to confine it within the regional/national or ethno-religious incarceration. After all, all history of early Kashmir is the history of inflows, connectivity, change, multiple pasts, changing identities, continuous cultural mixing and translation of translations.

Notes

1 Chatterjee (2021).
2 Amin (2004), 37.
3 Pollock, Bhabha, Breckenridge and Chakrabarty (2002), 12.
4 Mauss (1973), 2: 73. "Prestigious imitation was a reflection of localised endeavours to enhance status and authority by adopting more 'Universal' norms of self-representation. They say much about the porosity of elite cultures and little about distinctions in religious belief or practice." Flood, 74.
5 Flood, 264.
6 Witzel (2008), 84, n. 208.
7 Kalhana, VII: 528–531.
8 Pollock (1996), 246.
9 *Āgamadambara*, Act. III; *Nītikalpataru* 130.1–11; Kalhana, IV: 345; Jonarāja, 14; Bronkhorst (2008), 281–299.
10 Kūfī, 160; Kalhana, IV: 55sqq; VII: 188, 1149; VIII: 885–87, 919–23, 2.2.6.4. For more details, see Wani (2004), Chapter II; Massignon, 178–180.
11 Kalhana, V: 354sqq.
12 Stone (1996), 156, 160.
13 Flood, 261.
14 Ibid, 3, 4, 68, 69.
15 Kalhana, I: 90, 312, 317; IV: 168, 211; V: 152, 199; VII: 51, 56, 70, 118–19, 200, 217, 414, 520, 528, 1001, 1064, 1149; VIII: 1091, 2264, 2487, 3412.
16 For details, see Koul (1991).
17 Kalhana, I: 42.
18 Markovits, Pouchepadass and Subrahmanyam (2003a), 2–3.

19 Sharma (2008), 139.
20 Ibid.
21 Slaje (2012), 9–32.
22 Kalhana, I: 38.
23 *Nīlamata Purāna*, 428.
24 Ibid, 322.
25 Slaje (2012), 25.
26 Witzel (2008), 79.
27 For details, see Walter Lawrence (2004), 264–66.
28 Lawrence, 304–05.
29 That Kashmiri was the language of the common people, see Kalhana, V: 397–98. And that protection of the independence and integrity of the country was the collective will of the people, see *Nīlamata Purāna*, 868–869; Kalhana, IV: 845.
30 The famous eleventh-century peripatetic pandit and *kavi* (poet) of Kashmir, Bilhana wrote with pride, "There is no village or country (*janapada*), no capital city or forest region, no pleasure garden or school where learned and ignorant young and old, male and female alike do not read my poems and shake with pleasure." Sheldon Pollock rightly says that Bilhana "may have been exaggerating the accessibility of his work across social orders, but he was describing not just a possible world but the actual world for which Sanskrit poets and intellectuals had been writing for the preceding thousand years." Pollock (2006), 356.
31 Inden (2008), 524.
32 Ibid, 524 sqq.
33 Pollock (2006), 249.
34 *Nīlamata Purāna*, 869; Kalhana, IV: 345.
35 Kalhana, I: 39, 42.

BIBLIOGRAPHY

Primary Sources

Abhinavagupta, *Tantraloka*, edited by Mukand Ram Shastri (Vol. 1), and Pandit Madhusudan Kaul Shastri (Vols. 2–12), (Allahabad and Bombay, 1921–38).

Abul Fazl, *Ā'īn-i-Akbarī*, 3 Vols., (Lucknow, 1869).

Abul Fazl, *Ā'īn-i-Akbarī*, Vol. III, Eng. tr. Jarrett, (Calcutta, 1927), reprint, (Delhi, 1989).

Abul Fazl, *Akbar Nama*, Eng. tr. H. Beveridge, 3 Vols., (Calcutta, 1897–1921), reprint, (Calcutta, 1979).

Al-Biruni, *Kitab fi Tahqiq ma li'l-Hind*, edited and translated into English by Eduard C Sachau, under the title *Alberuni's India*, (London, 1888), reprint, 2 Vols., (New Delhi, 1993).

Allchin, BR, "Earliest Traces of Man in Potwar Plateau, Pakistan – A Report of British Archaeological Mission," *South Asian Studies*, Vol. 2, (1986).

Allchin, FR and R Knox, "A Preliminary Report on the Excavation at Lewan, 1977–78," In: H Hartel (ed.), *South Asian Archaeology*, (Berlin, 1979).

Al-Mas'udi, Abu'l-Hasan 'Ali, *Muruj al-dhahab wa mada'adin al-jawhar*, 9 vols., edited and translated by C Barbier de Meynard and Pavet de Courteille, (Paris, 1861–1877).

Al-Mas'udi, *Les prairies d'or*, translated by C Barbier de Meynard and Pavet de Courteille, and Charles Pellat, (Paris, 1962).

Al-Muqaddasi, Mohammad ibn Ahmad, *Kitab Ahsan al-Taqasim fi marifat al aqalim*, edited by MJ de Geoje, Bibliotheca Geographorum Arabicorum, Vol. 3, (Leiden, 1967).

Amarakośa, edited by HG Śastri, (Varanasi, 1970).

Anandavardhana, *Dhvanyaloka*, Critical edition with English translation and notes by Krishnamoorthy, (Dharwar, 1974).

Anon, *Ḥudūd al-'Alam*, edited by Manuchihr Sutudeh, (Tehran: Intisarat-i Danishgah-i Tehran, 1962).

Anonymous, *Bahāristān-i Shāhī*, RPD, 491.

Antonini, C Silvi and G Stacul, *The Protohistoric Graveyards of Swat*, 2 Vols., (Rome, 1972).

Aśokavadana (The Legends of Emperor Aśoka in Indian and Chinese Texts), translated by DK Biswas, (Calcutta, 1967).

Balādhuri, *Futūh al-Buldān*, (ed. MJ De Geoje) Vol. III, (Leiden, 1866).

Basu, A and A Pal, *Human Remains from Burzahom*, (Calcutta, 1980).
Bayhaqi, Abu'l-Fazl Mohammad b. Hosayn, *Tarikh-i Bayhaqi*, edited by Ali Akbar Fayyaz, (Mashad, 1971).
Beal, S, *The life of Hiuen Tsang* by Shaman Hwui Li, (London, 1911).
Bernier, F, *Travels in the Mughal Empire – 1656–1668*, edited by A Constable and VA Smith, reprint, (Delhi, 1983).
Bilhana, *Vikramānkadevacaritam*, translated by SC Banerji and AK Gupta, (Calcutta, 1965).
Bleazby, GB, *List of Coins and Medals belonging to the Pratap Singh Museum, Srinagar* (Srinagar, 1900).
Bryusov, A, "Neolithic-dwellings in the Forest Zone of the European Part of the USSR," In: *Proceedings of the Prehistoric Society*, New Series, Vol. 21, (Cambridge, 1952).
Bühler, G, *Detailed Report of a Tour in Search of Sanskrit Mss. Made in Kásmîr, Rajputana, and Central India* (Bombay & London, 1877).
Buth, GM and RN Kaw, "Plant Husbandry in Neolithic Burzahom, Kashmir," In: DP Agarwal, Sheela Kusumgar and RV Krishnamurthy (eds.), *Current Trends in Geology*, Vol. VI, Climate and Geology of Kashmir and Central Asia: The Last 4 million years, (Delhi, 1985).
Buth, GM, RS Bisht and GS Gaur, "Investigation of Paleobotanical Remains from Semthan, Kashmir," *Man and Environment*, Vol. VI (1982).
Collins, BA and MH al-Tai, *Al-Muqaddasi, The Best Divisions for Knowledge of the Regions*, (Reading, 1994).
Costantini, Lorenzo, "The Beginning of Agriculture in the Kachhi Plains: The Evidence of Mehrgarh." In: B Allchin (ed.), *South Asian Archaeology*, (1981), (Cambridge: Cambridge University Press, 1984), 29–33.
Cribb, Joe, "Early Medieval Kashmir Coinage – A New Hoard, and an Anomaly." *Numismatic Digest*, Vol. 40 (2016).
Cunningham, Alexander, *An Essay on the Arian Order of Architecture, as Exhibited in the Temples of Kashmir*, (Calcutta, 1848a).
Cunningham, Alexander, *Coins of Medieval India*, (London, 1894).
Czuma, Stanislaw, "Ivory Sculpture." In: Pal, Pratapaditya (ed.), *Art and Architecture of Ancient Kashmir*, (Bombay, 1989).
Dāmodaragupta, *Kuṭṭanī-mata Kāvya*, edited by M Kaul, *RASB*, (Calcutta, 1944).
Dani, AH, "Excavations in the Gomal Valley." In: *Ancient Pakistan*, Vol. 5, (Pakistan, 1970–71).
De Cardi, B, "Excavations and Reconnaissance in Kalat, West Pakistan: The Prehistoric Sequence in the Surab Region," In: *Pakistan Archaeology*, Vol. 2, (Karachi: Department of Archaeology, Ministry of Education, Government of Pakistan, 1965), 86–182.
de Terra and Paterson, *Studies in the Ice Age of India and Associated Human Cultures*, (Washington, 1939)
Dhar, Somnath, *Kautilya and the Arthasastra*, (New Delhi, 1981).
Diddamari, Khwaja Muhammad A'zam, *Waqi'at-i Kashmir*, (Urdu translation by Iqbal Akadami Pakistan), reprinted by J&K Islamic Research Centre, (Srinagar, 1998).

Dodia, Rekha *et al.*, "New Pollen Data from the Kashmir Bogs: A Summary," In: DP Agarwal, Sheela Kusumgar and RV Krishnamurthy (eds.), *Current Trends in Geology*, Vol. VI, Climate and Geology of Kashmir and Central Asia: The Last 4 million years, (Delhi, 1984).

Dowson, J, "Route from Kashmir, via Ladakh, to Yarkand, by Ahmad Shah Nakshahbandi (sic)," *Journal of the Royal Asiatic Society of Great Britain and Ireland*, Vol. 12 (1850), 372–385.

Drabu, VN, *Saivagmas*, (New Delhi, 1990).

Fairservis, WA, *Excavations in the Quetta Valley, Western Pakistan*, Anthropological Papers of the American Museum of Natural History, Vol. 45, Part 2 (New York, 1956).

Gardizi, Abd al Hai Dhuhaq, *Zain al Akhbar*, ed. Mohammad Nazim, (Berlin, 1928).

Gaur, GS, "Semthan Excavations – A Step towards Bridging the Gap between the Neolithic and Kushanas." In: BM Pande and BD Chattopadhyaya (eds.), *Essays in Archaeology and History in Memory of Shri A. Ghosh*, Vol. I, (New Delhi, 1987).

Gupta, PL, *Coins* (New Delhi, 1969).

Halim, MA, *Excavations at Sarai Khola*, Part I & II, AP (Karachi, 1970–72), Nos. 7 & 8.

Hanley, Asha, "Kists in Kashmir", *Times of India Magazine* (December 2, 1979).

Harlon, JR and D Zohary, "Distribution of Wild Wheat and Barley," *Science*, Vol. 153, No. 3740 (1966), 1074–80.

Hiuen Tsang, *Ta T'ang-Si-Yu-Ki*, [629 AD]. Eng. tr. by Sameul Beal under the title *Si-Yu-Ki: Buddhist Records of the Western World*, Vol. I, (London, 1911).

Hole, F and KV Flannery, "Excavations at Ali Kosh Iran 1961," *Iranica Antiqua*, Vol. 2 (Leiden, 1962), 97–148.

Hunt, HV et al, "Genetic Diversity and Paleogeography of Broomcorn Millet (*panicum miliaceum L.*) across Eurasia," *Molecular Ecology*, Vol. 20, No. 22 (2012).

Ibn Hawqal, Abu'l-Qasim, *Kitāb ṣurat al-arḍ*, edited by JH Kramers, Bibliotheca Geographorum Arabicorum, Vol. 3, (Leiden, 1967).

Ibn Khaldun, *Muqaddimah*, tr. Franz Rosenrhal, (London, 1967).

Ibn Khaldun, *Muqaddimah*, tr. Franz Rosenthal; abridged and edited by NJ Dawood, (London, 1978).

Indian Archaeology – A Review (1960–61 to 1973–74 & 1978–79 to 1984–85).

Jarrige, JF and M Lechevallier, "Excavations at Mehrgarh – Baluchistan: Their Significance in the Prehistorical Context of the Indo-Pakistan Borderland." In: M Taddei (ed.), *South Asian Archaeology 1977*, (Naples, 1979), 463–535.

Jayanta Bhatta, *Āgamadambara*, (ed. by Dr Raghvan), Mithali Vidyapītha (Samvat, 2020).

Jettmar, Karl, "Bronze Axes from the Karakorum: Results of the 1958 Expedition in Azad Kashmir," *Proceedings of the American Philosophical Society*, Vol. 105, No. 1 (1961), 98–104.

Jonarāja, *Divtīya Rājataraṅgiṇī*, English translation by JC Dutt, (Calcutta, 1898).

Joshi, JP and Madhu Bala, "Manda: A Harappan Site in Jammu and Kashmir." In: GL Possehl (ed.), *Harappan Civilization*, (New Delhi, 1982).

Joshi, RV, SN Rajaguru, RS Pappu and BP Bopardikar, "Quaternary Glaciations and Palaeolithic Sites in the Liddar Valley (Jammu and Kashmir)," *World Archaeology*, Vol. 5, No. 3 (1976).

Kak, RC, *Ancient Monuments of Kashmir*, (London, 1933).

Kak, RC, *Handbook of the Archaeological and Numismatic Sections of the Sri Pratap Singh Museum, Srinagar* (Calcutta, 1923)

Kalhana, *Rājataraṅgiṇī*, (Eng. tr. MA Stein), 2 vols. Reprint (Delhi: Motilal Banarsidass, 1979).

Kangle, RP (ed.), *The Kutilya Arthaśāstra*, (Eng. Translation), Book. II, (Bombay, 1972), (Delhi, 1986), part II.

Kautilya, *Arthśāstra*, (Eng. tr. R Shamasastry), Book II, Chapter I, (Bangalore, 1915).

Khan, FA, "Excavations at Kot Diji," *Pakistan Archaeology*, No. 2, (1965).

Khazanchi, TN and KN Dikshit, "The Grey Ware Culture of Northern Pakistan, Jammu and Kashmir and Punjab," *Puratattva*, No. 9, (New Delhi, 1979–80).

Khazanchi, TN, "North-Western Neolithic Cultures of India". In: *Newsletter*, Nos. 7 and 8, Indian Institute of Advanced Study (Shimla, 1977).

Khazanchi, TN, "Pit Dwellers of Burzahom," *The Illustrated Weekly of India*, Vol. 97, No. 36, (September, 1976), 25–27.

Khuihami, Pir Ghulam Hassan Shah, *Tarikh'i Hassan*, Vol. 1, *Kashmir ka Geographia*, edited and translated by Sharief Hussain Qasmi (Srinagar, 2013).

Konow, S, *Kharoshthi Inscriptions with the Exception of those of Asoka, being Corpus Inscriptionum Indicarum*, Vol. II, (Calcutta, 1929); reprint, (New Delhi, 1991).

Ksemendra, Lokaprakaśa, translated by A Weber, *Indische Studies*, Vol. XVII, (1898).

Kṣemendra, *Narmamālā*, edited by Pt. Madhusudan Kaul Shastri, (Poona, 1923).

Kṣemendra, *Nītikalpataru*, edited by VP Mahajan, (Poona, 1956).

Kṣemandra, *Samayamātrikā*, edited by Pt. Durga Prasad and KB Parab, (Bombay, 1925).

Kūfī, 'Ali bin Hamīd, *Chāch-nāma*, translated by Mirza Kalichbeg Fredunbeg, Reprint (Delhi, 1979).

Lal, BB, "Palaeoliths from the Beas and Banganga Valley, Punjab," *Ancient India*, Vol. 12 (1956).

Legge, J, *Fa-Hien – A Record of the Buddhist Kingdoms*, (London, 1877).

Levi, Sylvan and Chavannes, *L'Itinéraire d' Ou-kong (751–790)* traduit et annote, extrait du *Journal Asiatique*, (Paris, 1895).

Lone, Farooq A; Maqsooda Khan and GM Buth, *Palaeoethnobotany, Plants and Ancient Man in Kashmir*, (Delhi, 1993).

Luders, H, *Mathura Inscriptions*, (Gottingen, 1961).

MacDonnell, G and RAI Conningham, "The Metal Objects and Metal – Working Residues." In: Robin Conningham and Ihsan Ali (eds.), *Charsadda: The British – Pakistani Excavations at the Bala Hisar*; BAR International Series 1709, (London, 2007), 151–59.

MacNeish, Richard S and Jane Libby (eds.), *Origin of Rice Agriculture: Preliminary (1994) Report of the Sino-American Jiangxi (PRC) Project*, *SAJOR* (Publication in Anthropology, No. 13), (El Paso, 1995).

Mahāvamsa, translated by Wilhelm Geiger, (London, 1912).

Malik, Haidar, *Tārikh-i Kashmir*, RPD, 29, Srinagar.
Mani, BR, "Excavations at Kanispur: 1998–99 (District Baramulla, Kashmir)," *Pragdhara*, Vol. 10, (2000), 1–28.
Mani, BR, "Further Evidence on Kashmir Neolithic in the Light of Recent Excavations at Kaniṣkapura," *Jisha*, Vol. I, No. 1, (2004), 137–43.
Mankha, *Śrikanthacarita*, edited by Pt. Durga Prasad and KP Parab, (Bombay, 1900).
Meadow, RH, "Faunal Exploitation in Eastern Iran and Baluchistan: A Review of Recent Investigations." In: G Gnoli and L Lanciotti (eds.), *Orientalia Iosephi Tucci Memoriae Dicata* II, ISMEO, (Rome, 1987), 881–916.
Meldagard, J; P Morten and H Thrane, "Excavations at Tepe Guran Luristan," *Acta Archaeologica*, Vol. 34, (1963), 97–133.
Mellaart, J, *Excavations at Hacliar*, 2. Vols. Vide Shashi Asthana, *Pre-Harappan Cultures of India and the Borderlands*, (New Delhi, 1985).
Milindapanho, edited by V Trenckner, (London: Royal Asiatic Society, 1928).
Miller et al., "Millet Cultivation across Eurasia: Origins, Spread, and the Influence of Seasonal Climate," *The Holocene*, Vol. 26, No. 10 (2016), 1566–75.
Minorsky, V, *Ḥudūd al-'Alam, "The Regions of the World: A Persian Geography, 372 A.H.–982 A.D.*, [1937], (Karachi, 1980).
Mishkāti, Bābā Dā'ūd, *Asrār al- Abrār*, RPD, 56.
Mughal, MR, "Introduction to the Pottery of Periods I and II of Sarai Khola." In: *Pakistan Archaeology*, No. 8, (1972), 117–124.
Nīlamata Purāna, edited and translated by Vaid Kumari Ghai, 2 Vols., (Srinagar, [1968] 1988).
Ou-k'ong, *L'Itinerarie d'Ou-k'ong*, *Journal Asiatic Society of Bengal*, Vol. VI, (1895).
Pande, BM, "A Neolithic Tectiform from Burzahom, District Srinagar, Kashmir," *Journal of the Indian Anthropological Society*, Vol. 7/2, (1972).
Pande, BM, "Neolithic Hunting Scene on a Stone Slab from Burzahom, Kashmir." In: *Asian Perspective*, Vol. XIV, (1971), 194–98.
Pande, BM, "The Neolithic of Kashmir – New Discoveries," *The Anthropologist*, Vol. XVII, No. 1 and 2, (1970), 25–41.
Pandit, RS (tr.), *Kalhana's Rājataraṅgiṇī*, (New Delhi, 1968).
Paterson, TT and H Drummond, *Soan the Palaeolithic of Pakistan*, (Karachi, 1962).
Piggot, Stuart, "Notes on Certain Metal Pins and a Mace Head in the Harappan Culture," *Ancient India: The Bulletin of Archaeological Survey of India*, No. 4, (1948).
Ramhurmuzi, Buzurg ibn Shahriyar, *Kitāb 'ajā'ib al-Hind (Livre des merveilles de l'Inde)*, edited by PA van der Lith and L Marcel Devic, (Leiden, 1883–86).
Remusat, A, *Nouveaux Melanges Asiatiques*, Vol. I, (Paris, 1829).
Rendell, H and RW Dennell, "Dated Lower Palaeolithic Artefacts from Northern Pakistan," *Current Anthropology*, Vol. 26, No. 5, (1985).
Ross, EJ, "A Chalcolithic Site in Northern Baluchistan," *Journal of Near Eastern Studies*, Vol. 5, No. 4, (1946).
Saar, SS, *Archaeology: Ancestors of Kashmir*, (New Delhi, 1992).
Sahni, Daya Ram, "Pre-Mohammedan Monuments of Kashmir," *Annual Report, Archaeological Survey of India*, (Calcutta, 1915–16).

Salim, M, "The Palaeolithic Culture of Potwar," *Journal of Central Asia*, Vol. 20, No. 2, (Islamabad, 1997).
Sankalia, HD, "New Evidence for Early Man in Kashmir," *Current Anthropology*, 2nd edition, (Pakistan Poona, 1974a).
Sarangadeva, *Saṅgītaratnakāra*, edited by Subrahmanaya Sastri, (Madras, 1953), II. 1.
Saraswat, KS and AK Pokharia, "Plant Resources in the Neolithic Economy at Kanispur, Kashmir," paper presented at the Joint Annual Conference of the Indian Archaeological Society, Indian Society of Prehistoric and Quaternary Studies, *Indian History and Culture Society*, (Lucknow, 2004).
Sayyid Ali, *Tarikh-i Kashmir* (MS), J&K Research Library, Srinagar.
Sen, S, *Old Persian Inscriptions*, (Calcutta, 1920).
Sharma, AK, "Animal Burials from Burzahom – A Neolithic Settlement in Kashmir," *Journal of Oriental Institute of Baroda*, No. 1 and 2, (1968a).
Sharma, AK, "Early iron users of Gufkral". In: BC Nayak and NC Ghosh (eds.), *New Trends in Indian Art and Archaeology*, Vol. I, (1992), 63–68.
Sharma, AK, "Excavations at Gufkral – 1981," *Puratattva*, Vol. 1979–80, No. 11, (1982a).
Sharma, AK, "Excavations at Gufkral," paper presented at XII Annual Congress at ISPQS Waltair, 29–31 December, (Allahabad, 1981).
Sharma, AK, "Excavations at Gufkral," paper presented at XIII Annual Congress at ISPQS, 25–27 October, (New Delhi, 1982b).
Sharma, AK, "Neolithic Human Burials from Burzahom, Kashmir," *Journal of Oriental Institute of Baroda*, Vol. XVI, No. 3, (1967).
Sims-Williams, N and J Cribbs, "A New Bactrian Inscription of Kaniṣka the Great," *Journal of the Institute of Silk Road*, Art and Archeology 4, (1996), 75–142.
Sircar, DC, *Select Inscriptions*, [Calcutta, 1942], 2nd edition, (Calcutta, 1965).
Skjaervo, PO and US Williams, *Khotanese Manuscripts from Chinese Turkistan in the British Library: A complete catalogue with texts and translations*, (London, 2002).
Smith, VA, *Coins of Ancient India: Catalogue of Coins in Indian Museum, Calcutta*, (Delhi, 1972).
Sohini, SV, "The Chavillakara Fragments in Kalhana's Rājataraṅgiṇī," *Journal of the Bihar Research Society* (JBRS), Vol. 36, No. 1/2, (1950).
Solecki, K and L Rose, "Two Bone Hafts from Northern Iraq," *Antiquity*, Vol. 37, (1961).
Spate, M, G Zhang, MA Yatoo and A Betts, "New Evidence for Early 4th Millennium BP Agriculture in the Western Himalayas: Qasim Bagh, Kashmir," *Journal of Archeological Science: Reports*, Vol. 11 (2017), 568–577.
Śrivara, *Jaina-Rājataraṅgiṇī*, Eng. tr. by JC Dutt, (Calcutta, 1898).
Stacul, G, "Dwelling and Storage Pits at Loebanr III (Swat, Pakistan) 1976 Excavation Report," *East and West*, Vol. 27 (1977), 227–53.
Stacul, G, "Excavations in rock-shelter near Ghaligai (Swat west Pakistan)." *East and West*, Vol. 17, No. 3 and 4, (1967).
Stacul, G, "Further Evidence for the Inner Asia complex from Swat." In: G Possehl (ed.), *South Asian Archaeology Studies*, (1992), 111–21.

Stacul, G, "Kalako-deray, Swat; 1992–93 Excavation Report," *East and West*, Vol. 45 (1995).
Stacul, G, "Swat, Pirak and Connected Problems (Mid-2nd Millennium BCE)," In: Catherine Jarrige (ed.), *South Asian Archaeology*, Vol. 1 (Wisconsin, 1989), 267–70.
Stacul, G, C Bruno and L Costantini, "Prehistoric and Protohistoric Swat, Pakistan (CE 3000–1400BC)," In: *IsMeo*, (Rome, 1987).
Stacul, G, "Neolithic Inner Asian Traditions in Northern Indo-Pakistani Valleys," In: A. Parpola and P. Koskikallio (eds.), *South Asian Archaeology 1993*, Vol. II (Helsinki: Suomalainen Tiedeakatemia, 1994), 707–14.
Stein, MA, *Ancient Khotan*, (Oxford, 1907).
Strabo, *Geographica*, edited and translated by HC Hamilton and W Falconer, London, 1903), Book XV. Chapter 1.
The Milindapanho: Being Dialogues Between King Milinda and the Buddhist Sage Nagasena. The Pali Text, edited by V Trenckner, (London, 1880).
Todd, IA, "Asikli Huyuk a Protoneolithic site in Central Anatolia," *Anatolian Studies*, Vol. 16, (1966), 139–63.
Vats, MS, *Excavations at Harappa*, 2 Vols., (Delhi, 1940).
Vohra, Rohit, "Arabic inscriptions of the Late First Millinium AD from Tangtse in Ladakh," In: Osmaston, Henry and Denwood, Philip (eds.), *Recent Research on Ladakh*, Vols. 4 and 5, (London, 1995), 419–429.
Walter, HB, *Catalogue of the Greek and Etruscan Vases in the British Museum*, (London, 1896).
Wanpo, H, Ciochon, R, Yumin, G, Larick, R, Qiren, F, Schwarcz, H, Yonge, C, Vos, John De and Rink, W, "Early Homo and Associated Artifacts from Asia," *Nature*, Vol. 378, (1995), 275–78.
Watters, Thomas, *On Yuan Chwang's Travels in India, 629–645 AD*, ed. by TW Rhys Davids and SW Bushell, Vol. 1, [London, 1905], reprint, (New Delhi, 1988).
Yule, H, *Travels of Marco Polo*, 2 Vols., (London, 1903).

Secondary Sources

Agrawal, DP, Sheela Kusumgar and RV Krishnamurthy (eds.), *Current Trends in Geology*, Vol. VI, *Climate and Geology of Kashmir and Central Asia: The Last 4 million years*, (Delhi, 1984).
Agrawal, DP, *The Archaeology of India*, (London, 1982).
Agrawal, RC, *Kashmir and its Monumental Glory*, (New Delhi, 1998).
Ahmad, Iqbal, *Kashmir Coins*, (Delhi, 2013).
Ahmad, Khwaja Nazir, *Jesus in Heaven on Earth*, [Lahore, 1952], reprint, (Lahore, 1999).
Akhtar Mohi-ud-Din, *A Fresh Approach to the History of Kashmir*, (Srinagar, 1998).
Akhtar Mohiud-Din, "Antiquity of Kashmiri Language," *Journal of Centre of Central Asian Studies* Vol. II, (1991).
Allchin, Bridget and Raymond Allchin, *The Rise of Civilization in India and Pakistan*, (Cambridge, London and New Delhi, 1981).
Allchin, FR and B Allchin (eds.), *South Asian Archaeology*, 2. Vols., (Delhi, 1997).

Allchin, FR and N Hammond (eds.), *The Archaeology of Afghanistan: From Earliest Times to Timurid Period*, (London, 1978).

Altaf, Shafqat, *Foreign Influences on Kashmiri Vocabulary*, (Srinagar, 2014).

Amin, Ash, "Regions Unbound: Towards a New Politics of Place," *Geografiska Annaler*, Vol. 86B, No. 1 (2004).

Arberry, AJ (ed.), *The Legacy of Persia* (Oxford, 1953).

Art Treasures of Jammu and Kashmir – A brochure, (Srinagar: Directorate of Archives, Archaeology & Museums, 1988).

Asher, Katherine B and Thomas R Metcalf (eds.), *Perceptions of South Asia's Visual Past*, (New Delhi and Oxford, 1994b), 161–77.

Ashplant, TG and Gerry Smyth, "Schools, Methods, Disciplines, Influences," In: TG Ashplant and G Smyth (eds.), *Explorations in Cultural History*, (London and Sterling: Pluto Press, 2001).

Asthana, Shashi, *History and Archaeology of India's Contacts with Other Countries: From Earliest Times to 300 BC*, (Delhi, 1976).

Asthana, Shashi, *Pre-Harappan Cultures of India and the Borderlands*, (New Delhi, 1985).

Aymard, Maurice and Harbans Mukhia (eds.), *French Studies in History: The Inheritance*, Vol. I, (Delhi, 1988).

Bagchi, PC, *India and China*, (Calcutta, 1950).

Bandey, Aijaz A, *Early Terracotta Art of Kashmir: 1st-3rd century AD* (Srinagar, 1992).

Bandey, Aijaz A, *Prehistoric Kashmir*, (Delhi, 2009).

Basham, AL, "The Kashmir Chronicle," In: CH Philips (ed.), *Historians of India, Pakistan and Ceylon*, (London, 1961).

Bausani, A, "Religion in the Saljuq Period," In: JA Boyle (ed.), *The Cambridge History of Iran*, Vol. V, (Cambridge, 1968)

Bayly, CA, Sven Beckert, Mathew Connelly, Isabel Hofmeyr, Wendy Kozol and Patricia Seed, "AHR Conversation: On Transnational History," *American Historical Review*, 111 (2006), 1441–64.

Beazley, JD, *Attic Black-Figure Vase-painters*, No. 8, (Oxford: Clarendon Press, 1956).

Benerjee, NR, *The Iron Age in India*, (Delhi, 1965).

Bennett, T, "Texts, Readers, Reading Formations," *Literature and History*, Vol. 9, No. 2, (1983), 214–27.

Bentley, Jerry, "Cross-Cultural Interaction and Periodization in World History," *AHR*, Vol. 101 (1996).

Bentley, JH, (ed.), *The Oxford Handbook of World History* (Oxford, 2011).

Berk, P, *Varieties of Cultural History*, (Cambridge, 1997).

Bhan, JL, "Iconographic Interaction between Kashmir and Central Asia." In: BK Kaul Deambi (ed.), *Kashmir and Central Asia*, (Srinagar, 1987).

Bhan, JL, *Kashmir Sculptures*, Vol. 1, (New Delhi: Readworthy Publications, 2010).

Bhan, JL, "Tile – A Vital Link between Kashmir and Central Asia," In: GM Buth (ed.), *Central Asia and Western Himalayas – A Forgotten Link*, (Jodhpur: Scientific Publishers, 1986).

Bhushan, J Brij, *Indian Jewellery, Ornaments and Decorative Designs*, (Mumbai: Taraporevala, 1964).

Biddulph, J, *Tribes of the Hindoo-Koosh*, (Kolkata, 1980).

Biersack, A, "Local Knowledge, Local History; Geertz and Beyond," In: L Hunt (ed.), *The New Cultural History*, (Berkely, CA, 1989).

Bisht, RS, "Reflection on Burzahom and Semthan Excavation and Later Mythology Periods in Kashmir Valley." In: GM Buth, (ed.), *Central Asia and Western Himalayas- A Forgotten Link*, (Jodhpur, 1986).

Biswas, A, *The Political History of Huns in India*, (Delhi, 1973).

Bivar, ADH, "The History of Eastern Iran," In: Yarshater (ed.), *The Cambridge History of Iran*, Vol. 3, (Cambridge, 1983).

Bopearachchi, O and AU Rahman, *Pre- Coins in Pakistan*, (Islamabad, 1995).

Bopearachchi, Osmund, "Contribution of Greeks to the Art and Culture of Bactria and India: New Archaeological Evidence." In: *The Indian Historical Review*, Vol. XXXII. No. I, (2005).

Borovka, G, *Scythian Art* (New York, 1967).

Bosworth, C Edmund, "Notes on the Pre-Ghaznavid History of Eastern Afghanistan," *Islamic Culture*, Vol. 9, (1965), 12–24.

Bosworth, C Edmund, "The Coming of Islam to Afghanistan," In: Yohanan Friedman (ed.), *Islam in Asia*, Vol. 1, *South Asia*, (Boulder, CO, 1984), 1–22.

Bosworth, C Edmund, *The History of the Saffarids of Sistan and the Maliks of Nimruz (247/861 to 949/1542–3)*, (New York, 1994).

Bosworth, C Edmund, Ubaidallah b. abi Bakra and the Army of Destruction in Zabulistan (79/698), *Der Islam*, Vol. 50, (1973), 268–83.

Bosworth, C, "The Early Ghaznavids," In: RN Frye (ed.), *The Cambridge History of Iran*, Vol. IV, (Cambridge, 1975).

Braidwood, Robert J and Bruce Howe, *Prehistoric Investigations in Iraqi Kurdistan* (Chicago, 1960).

Braidwood, Robert J and Linda Braidwood, "Jarmo – A Village of Early Farmers in Iraq," *Antiquity*, Vol. 24 (1950).

Breckenridge-Appadurai, Carol A (ed.), *Cosmopolitanism*, (Durham and London, 2002).

Brentjes, Burchard, *Arms of the Sakas* (Varanasi, 1996).

Bronkhorst, Johannes, "Udbhaṭa, a Grammarian and a Cārvāka." In: Mrinal Kaul and Ashok Aklujkar (eds.), *Linguistic Traditions of Kashmir: Essays in Memory of Pandit Dinanath Yaksha* (New Delhi, 2008).

Bronner, Y *et al* (eds.), *South Asian Texts in History: Critical Engagements with Sheldon Pollock*, [2011], reprint (Delhi, 2016).

Bronner, Yigal, "From Conqueror to Connoisseur: Kalhana's Account of Jayapida and the Fashioning of Kashmir as a Kingdom of Learning," *The Indian Economic and Social History Review*, Vol. L, No. 2, (2013).

Brown, Percy, *Indian Architecture: Buddhist and Hindu Periods* (Bombay, 1959).

Buth, GM (ed.), *Central Asia and Western Himalayas – A Forgotten Link*, (Jodhpur, 1986).

Carr, KE, "Chicken History – Where are Chickens from? India and China," *Study Guides*, (2017), https://quatr.us/china/history-chickens.htm.

Cavalli-Saforza, L Luca, Paolo Menozzi, and Alberto Piazza, *The History and Geography of Human Genes*, (Princeton, 1994).

Chandra, Moti, *Costumes, Textiles, Cosmetics and Coiffure in Ancient and Medieval India*, (Delhi, 1973).

Chandra, Moti, *Prācīna Bhāratīya Veśa Bhūsā*, Archaeological Survey of India, Central Archaeological Library, New Delhi, Book No. 7702, (New Delhi, 1979).
Chandra, Moti, *The World of Courtesans*, (New Delhi: Vikas Publishing, 1973a).
Chang, K, *The Archaeology of Ancient China*, (New Haven, 1963).
Chang, TK, *Archeology in China*, Vol. I, (Cambridge, 1959). Chapter 2, ref. 91
Chatterjee, Partha, *The Truths and Lies of Nationalism: As Narrated by Charvak*, (New Delhi, 2021).
Chatterji, JC, *Kashmir Shaivaism*, (The Kashmir Series of Texts and Studies, Vol. II.), [1914], 8 Vols., (Srinagar, 1962).
Chatterji, Sunita Kumar, *Languages and Literatures of India*, (Calcutta, 1963).
Chattopadhyay, BD, "Historical Context of the Early Medieval Temples of North India." In: BD Chattopadhyaya (eds.), *Studying Early India*, (Delhi 2003).
Chattopadhyay, BD, *The Age of the Kuṣāṇas – A Numismatic Study*, (Calcutta, 1967).
Chattopadhyaya, KC, *Proceedings of the All India Oriental Conference*, (1937).
Cheng, T, *Prehistoric China*, Vol. I, (Cambridge, 1959).
Clark, HR, "Muslims and Hindus in the Culture and Morphology of Quanzhou from the Tenth to the Thirteenth Centuries," *Journal of World History*, Vol. 6, No. 1, (1995), 49–74.
Clifford, James, *Routes: Travel and Translation in the Late Twentieth Century*, (Cambridge MA: Harvard University Press, 1997).
Colledge, MAR, *Parthian Art*, (Ithica, 1977).
Colpe, Cartsten, "Development of Religious Thought," In: Yarshater (ed.), *The Cambridge History of Iran*, Vol. 3, (Cambridge, 1983).
Conningham, Robin and Ihsan Ali (eds.), *Charsadda: The British – Pakistani Excavations at the Bala Hisar*; BAR International Series 1709, (2007).
Coomaraswamy, AK, *History of Indian and Indonesian Art*, Dover edition, (New York, 1965).
Costantini, L, *Vegetal Remains in Prehistoric and Protohistoric Swat* (Rome, 1987).
Cox, Whitney, "Saffron in the Rassam," In: Y Bronner *et al.* (eds.), *South Asian Texts in History: Critical Engagements with Sheldon Pollock* (Delhi, [2011], 2016).
Cunningham, Alexander, "An Essay on the Arian Order of Architecture, as Exhibited in the Temples of Kashmir," *Journal of Asiatic Society of Bengal*, Vol. XVII, Part II, (1848), 241–327.
Cunningham, Alexander, *Later Indo-Scythians* (Varanasi, 1962).
Cunningham, Alexander, *The Stupa of Bhahrut – A Buddhist Monument* (London, 1879).
Cunningham, *Ancient Geography of India*, (London, 1871).
Cutler, Anthony, "Gifts and Gift Exchange as Aspects of the Byzantine, Arab and Related Economies," *Dumbarton Oaks Papers*, Vol. 250, (2001).
Dani, AH, (ed.), *Indus Civilization: New Perspective*, (Islamabad, 1981).
Dani, AH, "Kidarites in Gandhara and Kashmir," In: BA Litvisky et al (eds.), *History of Civilizations of Central Asia, Vol. III: The Crossroads of Civilizations: AD 250–750*, (UNESCO, 1994).
Dani, AH, *Chilas: The City of Nanga Parvat*, (Islamabad, 1983).
Dani, AH, *History of the Northern Areas of Pakistan*, (Islamabad, 1989).

Dani, AH, "Timargarha and the Gandhara Grave Culture: Introduction," *Ancient Pakistan*, No. 3 (1967), 1–55.

Dar, Saifur Rahman, *Taxila and the Western World*, (Lahore, 1984).

Dasgupta, Shashibushan, *Obscure Religious Cults*, [Calcutta, 1946], reprint, (Calcutta, 1976).

Davis, RH, "Indian Art objects as Loot," *Journal of Asian Studies*, Vol. 52, No. 1, (1993), 22–48.

Davis, RH, *Lives of Indian Images*, (Princeton, 1997).

Davis, RH, "Three Styles in Looting India," *History and Anthropology Great Britain*, Vol. 6, No. 4, (1994a), 293–317.

Davis, RH, "Trophies of War: The Case of the Chalukya Intruder," In: Katherine B Asher and Thomas R Metcalf (eds.), *Perceptions of South Asia's Visual Past*, (New Delhi and Oxford, 1994b), 161–77.

De Laet, SJ (ed.), *History of Humanity*, Vol. I, *Prehistory and the Beginnings of Civilization*, (Paris and London, 1994).

de Terra, Hellmut and TT Paterson, *Studies in the Ice Age of India and Associated Human Cultures*, (Washington, 1939).

Deambi, BK Kaul (ed.), *Kashmir and Central Asia*, (Srinagar, 1987).

Deambi, BK Koul, *History and Culture of Ancient Gandhara and Western Himalayas*, (Delhi, 1985).

Dean, Carolyn and Dana Leibsohn, "Hybridity and its Discontents: Considering Visual Culture in Colonial Spanish America," *Colonial Latin American Review*, Vol. 12, No. 1, (2003), 5–35.

Dennell, RW, "The Early Stone Age of Pakistan: A Methodological Review," *Man and Environment*, Vol. XX, No. 1, (Pune, 1995).

Devahuti, D, *Harsha: A Political Study*, (Delhi, 1983).

Diksht, KN, "The Neolithic Cultural Frontiers of Kashmir." In: *Man and Environment*, Vol. VI, (1982).

Dirks, Nicholas B, "The Pasts of a Palaiyakarar: The Ethnohistory of a South Indian Little King," *Journal of Asian Studies*, Vol. 41, No. 4, (1982), 655–83.

Dirlik, Arif, "Confounding Metaphors, Inventions of the World: What Is World History For?" In: Benedikt Stuchtey and Eckhardt Fuchs (eds.), *Writing World History, 1800–2000* (Oxford, 2003), 91–133.

Drabu, VN, *Kashmir Polity*, (New Delhi, 1986).

Durrani, FA, "Indus Civilization: Evidence West of Indus." In: AH Dani, (ed.), *Indus Civilization: New Perspective*, (Islamabad, 1981).

Durrant and Durrant, *The Story of Civilization IX*, *The Age of Voltaire*, (New York, 1965).

Durrant, Will, *The Story of Civilization II: The Life of Greece* (New York, n.d.).

Dutt, Nalinaksha, *Buddhism in Kashmir*, (Delhi, 1985).

Dyezkowski, Mark, *The Doctrine of Vibration: An Analysis of the Doctrines and Practices of Kashmir Shavism*, State University of New York Series in the Shaiva Traditions of Kashmir, (Albany, 1987).

Elliot, HM and John Dowson, *The History of India as Told by Its Own Historians*, [1867–77], reprint, Vol. 2, (Delhi, 1990).

Fabian, Johannes, *Language and Colonial Power: The Appropriation of Swahili in the Former Belgian Congo, 1880–1939*, (Cambridge, 1986).

Fairservis, WA, *The Roots of Ancient India*, (New York, 1971).
Febvre, Lucien, "Une question mal posée: Les origins de la Réforme française et le problem general des causes de la Réforme," *La revue Historique*, Vol. 159, (1929).
Fergusson, James, *History of Indian and Eastern Architecture*, (Cambridge, 1876).
Fisher, Robert E, "Stone Temples." In: Pratapaditya Pal (ed.), *Art and Architecture of Ancient Kashmir*, (Bombay, 1989a).
Fisher, Robert E, "The Enigma of Harwan." In: Pratapaditya Pal (ed.), *Art and Architecture of Ancient Kashmir*, (Bombay, 1989b), 1–16.
Flood, Finbarr B., *Objects of Translation: Material Culture and Medieval "Hindu-Muslim" Encounter* (Princeton and Oxford, 2009).
Fuller, DQ, "Agricultural Origins and Frontiers in South Asia: A Working Synthesis". In: *Journal of World Prehistory*, Vol. 20, No. 1 (2006), 1–86.
Fyfe, Theodore, *Hellenistic Architecture*, (Cambridge, 1934).
Gabunia, L and A Vekua, "A Plio-Pleistocene Hominid from Dmanisi, East Georgia, Caucasus." In: *Nature*, Vol. 375 (1995).
Ganguly, OC, *Rāgas and Rāginīs*, (Bombay, 1948).
Ganhar, JN and PN Ganhar, *Buddhism in Kashmir and Ladakh*, (New Delhi, 1956).
Geertz, C, "Deep Play: Notes on the Balinese Cockfight." In: C Geertz (ed.), *The Interpretation of Cultures; Selected Essays by Clifford Geertz*, (Hutchinson, 1975), 412–53.
Geertz, C, *The Interpretation of Cultures; Selected Essays by Clifford Geertz*, (Hutchinson, 1975a).
Ghirshman, R, *Iran: Parthians and Sassanians*, (London, 1962).
Ghosh, A (ed.), *Indian Archaeology 1964–65: A Review*, (Faridabad: Archaeological Survey of India, 1969).
Ghosh, Suchandra, "Blurring the Boundaries: Movement and Migration at the Cross Roads of Asia (c. 5th century BCE – c. 3rd century CE)," *Journal of Ancient Indian History*, XXVI, (2011).
Ghosh, TT and DK Chakrabarti, *Man and Environment*, Vol. IV (1980).
Gnoli, G and L Lanciotti (eds.), *Orientalia Iosephi Tucci Memoriae Dicata* II, ISMEO, (Rome, 1987).
Goepper, Roger, "Clues for the Dating of the Three-Storeyed Temple (Sumtsek) in Alchi, Ladakh," *Asiatische Studien*, Vol. 2, (1990), 159–69.
Goodall, Dominic, Shaman Hatley, Harunaga Isaacson and Srilata Raman (eds.), *Śaivism and the Tantric Traditions: Essays in Honour of Alexis G.J.S. Sanderson*, Gonda Indological Studies, No. 22, (Leiden: Brill, 2020), 283–320.
Gould, EH, "Entangled Histories, Entangled Worlds: The English Speaking Atlantic as a Spanish Periphery," *American Historical Review*, 112 (2007), 764–86.
Granoff, P, "Saraswati's Sons: Biographies of Poets in Medieval India," *Asiatic Studies/Etudes Asiatiques*, Vol. 49, No. 2, (1995).
Greenblatt, SJ, *Learning to Curse: Essays in Early Modern Culture*, (New York and London, 1990).
Grierson, George A, *Linguistic Survey of India*, Vol. VIII, part II, (Calcutta, 1919). rep. Delhi
Groote, GJ, *The Prehistory of Japan* (New York, 1951).
Guha, Amalendu (ed.), *Central Asia: Movement of People and Ideas from Times Prehistoric to Modern*, (New Delhi, 1970).

Guha, BS, *Racial Elements in the Population*, (Oxford, 1944).

Gulshan Majid, "Harwan Ruins: A study of Iranian Influences," In: SM Afzal Qadri (ed.), *Cultural Heritage of Kashmir*, (Srinagar, 1997).

Gulshan Majid, "The Frove: A Connecting Link between Zoroastrianism and Kashmir." In: *The Journal of Central Asian Studies*, Vol. 7, (1996).

Gupta, SP, *Archaeology of Soviet Central Asia and Indian Borderlands*, (Delhi, 1979).

Gupta, SP, *Archaeology of Soviet Central Asia and Indian Borderlands*. Vide Shashi Asthana, *Pre-Harappan Cultures of India and the Borderlands*, (New Delhi, 1985).

Gupta, SP, *Disposal of the Dead and Physical Types in Ancient India* (Delhi, 1972).

Habib, Irfan (ed.), *The Shared Heritage: The Growth of Civilization in India and Iran* (Delhi 2002).

Habib, Irfan and Faiz Habib, *Atlas of the Ancient Indian History* (Oxford and Delhi, 2012).

Habibi, Abdul Hai, "The Oldest Muslim Inscription in Middle Asia," *Museums Journal*, Vol. 6, No. 1 and 2, (1954), 70–75.

Habibi, Abdul Hai, "The Temple of Sunagir, Zoon or Zoor in Ancient Afghanistan," In: *Yadname-ye Jan Rypka, Collection of Articles on Persian and Tajik Literature*, (Prague: Academia Publishing House, 1967).

Haddon, AC, *The Races of Man and Their Distribution* (New York, 1925).

Hajni, Muhi-ud-Din, *Discourses of Mohi-Ud-Din Hajini*, compiled by Ameen Fayaz, (Halqae-e-Adab Sonawari Hajin: Kashmir, 2013).

Hallade, M, "The Ornamental Veil or Scarf," *East and West*, Vol. 15, No. 1/2, (1964–1965), 36–49.

Hamdani, Agha Hussain, *The Frontier Policy of the Delhi Sultans*, (Islamabad: National Institute of History and Cultural Research, 1986).

Hans, Luuk, *The History of Cock-fighting*, (Netherlands: Aviculture-Europe Foundation, 2014).

Harmatta, J (ed.), *Hecataeus to Al Huwàrizmī*, Series 1, Vol. III (Budapest, 1984).

Harmatta, J, "Kidara and the Kidarite Huns in Kashmir." In: J Harmatta (ed.), *Hecataeus ti Al Huwàrizmī*, Series 1, Vol. III (Budapest, 1984a).

Harmatta, J et al. (eds.), *History of Civilizations of Central Asia, Vol. II, The Development of Sedentary and Nomadic Civilizations: 700 BC to AD 250* (Paris, 1994).

Harmatta, J, et al., "Religions in the Empire," In: J Harmatta, et al. (eds.), *History of Civilizations of Central Asia, Vol. II, The Development of Sedentary and Nomadic Civilizations: 700 BC to AD 250*, (Paris, 1994a).

Hartel, H (ed.), *South Asian Archaeology*, (Berlin, 1979).

Hassan, Mohib-ul, *Kashmir under the Sultans*, [1959], (New Delhi, 2005).

Hay, Jonathan, "Toward a theory of intercultural," *RES*, 35, (New York, 1999).

Hegde, KTM, "Analysis of Ancient Indian Deluxe wares," *Archaeo – Physika*, 10 (1978), 141–55.

Hellback, H, "Commentary on the Phytogensis of Triticum and Hordeum," *Economic Botany*, Vol. 20, (1966).

Herzfeld, E, *Memoirs of the Archeological Survey of India, No. 38: O-Sasanian Coins*, (Calcutta, 1930).

Hobsbawm, Eric, *On History*, [reprint] (Abacus, 2008).

Holt, Frank L, *Alexander the Great and Bactria* (Leiden, 1993).
Houben, Jan EM (ed.), *Ideology and Status of Sanskrit: Contributions to the History of the Sanskrit Language*, (Leiden, 1996).
Hunt, L (ed.), *The New Cultural History*, (Berkely, CA, 1989).
Huntington, Susan, *The Art of Ancient India; Hindu, Buddhist, Jain* (New York and Tokyo, 1985).
Hutton, JH, "Prehistory of Assam," *Man in India*, Vol. VII (1928), 228–32.
Ibrahim, Asma, "Greek Rulers in the land of Sind," *Yavanika*, No. 3 (1993).
Iliffe, JH, "Persian and the Ancient World," In: AJ Arberry (ed.), *The Legacy of Persia* (Oxford, 1953).
Inden, Ronald, "Imperial Puranas: Kashmir as a Vaiṣṇava Centre of the World," In: Ronald Inden, Jonathan Walters and Daud Ali (eds.), *Querying the Medieval Texts and History of Practices in South Asia*, (Oxford and New York, 2000).
Inden, Ronald, "Kashmir as Paradise on Earth." In: Aparna Rao (ed.), *The Valley of Kashmir: The Making and Unmaking of a Composite Culture?* (Delhi, 2008).
Inden, Ronald, Jonathan Walters and Daud Ali (eds.), *Querying the Medieval Texts and the History of Practices in South Asia*, (Oxford and New York, 2000a).
Ingholt, *Gandhara Art in Pakistan*, (New York, 1957).
Iyer, LA, *Travancore Tribes and Castes* (Trivandrum, 1969).
Jan, Shazia Shafiq, *A Study of Kushan Rule in Kashmir*, PhD thesis, (Srinagar, 2006).
Jarrige, JF and Meadow Richard, *Scientific America*, Vol. 243, No. 2 (1980), 122–32.
Jenkins, K (ed.), *The Postmodern History Reader*, (London, 1997).
Jones, S, R Martin and D Pilbean (eds.), *The Cambridge Encyclopedia of Human Evolution* (Cambridge, 1992).
Joshi, Jagat Pati, "Religious and Burial Practices of Harappans: Indian Evidence." In: GC Pande (ed.), *History of Science, Philosophy and Culture in Indian Civilization*, Vol. I, part I, *The Dawn of Indian Civilization upto 600 BC*, (New Delhi, 1999).
Joyeux-Prunel, Beatrice *et al*, *Circulations in the Global History of Art* (London, 2015).
Kaelas, Lili, "Megalithic Monuments of Europe," In: SJ Late De, AH Dani, JL Lorenzo and RB Nunoo (eds.), *History of Humanity: Prehistory and the Beginning of Civilization*, (Paris, 1994).
Kafadar, Cemal, *Between Two Worlds: The Construction of Ottoman State*, (Oakland, California: University of California Press, 1995).
Kane, PV, *History of Dharmaśāstras*, Vol. II, (Poona, 1941).
Kashmiri, Aziz, *Christ in Kashmir*; (Srinagar, 1988)
Kaufmann, Thomas Dacosta et al., "Reintroducing Circulations: Historiography and the Project of Global Art History," In: Beatrice Joyeux-Prunel et al., (eds.), *Circulations in the Global History of Art* (London, 2015).
Kaul, Advaitavadini, *Buddhist Savants of Kashmir: Their Contribution Abroad*, (Srinagar, 1987).
Kaul, Jayalal, *Lal Ded*, (New Delhi: Sahitya Akademi, 1973),
Kaul, Mrinal and Ashok Aklujkar (eds.), *Linguistic Traditions of Kashmir: Essays in Memory of Pandit Dinanath Yaksha* (New Delhi: DK Printworld, 2008).
Kaul, Shonaleeka, *The Making of Early Kashmir: Landscape and Identity in the Rajatarangini*, (Delhi and Oxford, 2018).

Knutson, Jesse, "Poetic Justice: On Kalhana's Historical Aesthetics." In: *Comparative Studies of South Asia, Africa and the Middle East*, Vol. 35, No. 2, (2015), 281–93.

Koshelenko, GA and VN Pilipko "Parthia," In: *History of Civilizations in Central Asia, Vol. II. The Development of Sedentary and Nomadic Civilizations: 700 B.C to A.D. 250*, (Paris, 1994).

Koul, Anand, *The Kashmiri Pandit*, [1924], reprint (Delhi, 1991).

Kramers, JH and G Wiet, *Configuration de la terre (Kitāb ṣurat al-arḍ)*, Vol. 2, (Paris, 1964).

Kurz, Otto, "Cultural Relations between Parthia and Rome," In: Yarshater (ed.), *The Cambridge History of Iran*, Vol. 3, No. 1, (Cambridge, 1983).

Kuwayama, Shoshin, "Historical Notes on Kapisi and Kabul in the Sixth-Eighth Centuries," *Zinbun*, Vol. 34, No. 1, (1999), 25–77.

LaCapra, D, *History and Criticism* (Ithica, NY, 1985).

Lahiri, N, *The Archaeology of Indian Trade Routes upto c. 200 BC* (Oxford and Delhi, 1992).

Larick, R and RL Ciochon, "The African Emergence and Early Asian Dispersals of the Genus Homo." In: *American Scientist* (North Carolina, United States: Sigma Xi, 1996).

Late De, SJ (ed.) and AH Dani, JL Lorenzo, RB Nunoo (co. eds.), *History of Humanity: Prehistory and the Beginning of Civilization*, (Paris, 1994).

Law, BC, *India in Early Texts of Buddhism and Jainism*, (London, 1940).

Lawrence, Walter, *The Valley of Kashmiri*, [1895], Reprint, (Srinagar, 2004).

Leeuw, JE van Lohuizen-De, *The "Scythian" Period: An Approach to the History, Art, Epigraphy and Palaeography of North India from the 1st Century B.C. to the 3rd Century A.D.*, (Leiden, 1949).

Lepenies (ed.), *Entangled Histories and Negotiated Universals: Centers and Peripheries in a Changing World*, (Frankfort, 2003).

Leskov, AM, "Mobilier Funeraire: Treasures from the Scythian Barrows," *The Journal of Central Asian Studies*, Vol. 7, No. 1 (1996).

Litvinsky, BA *et al* (eds.), *History of Civilizations of Central Asia, Vol. III: The Crossroads of Civilizations: AD 250–750*, (Paris, 1994).

Litvinsky, BA, "The Hephthalite Empire," In: BA Litvinsky et al. (eds.), *History of Civilizations of Central Asia, Vol. III: The Crossroads of Civilizations*: AD 250–750, (Paris, 1994).

Loewe, M and EL Shaughnessy (eds.), *The Cambridge History of Ancient China*, (Cambridge, 1999).

Lommel, Andreas, *Prehistoric and Primitive Man*, (New York, 1966).

Luczanits, Christian, "The Early Buddhist Heritage of Ladakh Reconsidered." In: John Bry (ed.), *Ladakhi Histories: Local and Regional Perspectives*, (Boston, 2005), 65–96.

Ludden, David, "History outside civilization and the mobility of South Asia," *South Asia: The Journal of South Asian Studies*, Vol. 17, No. 1 (1994), 1–23.

Maclean, Derryl N, *Religion and Society in Arab Sind*, (Leiden, 1989).

Madan, TN, "Kashmir, Kashmiris, Kashmiriyat: An Introductory Essay". In: Aparna Rao (ed.), *The Valley of Kashmir: The Making and Unmaking of a Composite Culture?* (New Delhi, 2008).

Maisey, FC, *Sanchi and its Remains*, (London, 1892).

Mani, BR, "Kashmir Neolithic and Early Harappan: A linkage". In: *Pragdhara*, Vol. 18, (2008), 229–47.

Mani, BR, *The Civilization*, (Delhi, 1987).

Markovits, Claude, Jacques Pouchepadass and Sanjay Subrahmanyam, "Introduction – Circulation and Society under Colonial Rule." In: Markovits, Pouchepadass and Subrahmanyam (eds.), *Society and Circulation: Mobile People and Itinerant Cultures in South Asia*, 1750–1950, (Delhi: Permanent Black, 2003a).

Markovits, Claude, Jacques Pouchepadass and Sanjay Subrahmanyam (eds.), *Society and Circulation: Mobile People and Itinerant Cultures in South Asia*, 1750–1950, (Delhi: Permanent Black, 2003).

Marquart, J and JJM de Groot, "Das Reich Zābul und der Gott Žūn vom 6.-9. Jahrhundert," In: Gotthold Weil (ed.), *Festschrift Eduard Sachau zum Siebzigsten Geburtstage*, (Berlin, 1915), 248–92.

Marshal, John and Dr. Vogel, "Excavations at Charsada, the Ancient Capital of Gandhara," *ASI*, (New Delhi, 1902–03), 141–84.

Marshall, John H, *Taxila: An Illustrated Account of Archaeological Excavations*, Vol. II, (Cambridge, 1951).

Marshall, John H, *The Buddhist Art of Gandhara: the Story of the Early School, Its Birth, Growth and Decline*, (Cambridge, 1960).

Massignon, Louis, *The Passion of al-Hallaj – Mystic and Martyr of Islam*, Eng. tr. from the French by Herbert Masson, Vol. I entitled, *The Life of al-Hallaj*, Bolligen Series, 98, (Princeton, 1982).

Masson, VM and VI Sarianidi, *Central Asia: Turkmenia before the Achaeminids*, (New York, 1972).

Mauss, Marcel, "Techniques of the Body," *Economy and Society*, Vol. 2, (1973).

Mc Crindle, *The Invasion of India by Alexander the Great*, (Michigan, 1896).

Mc Govern, *Early Empires of Central Asia*, (Charlotte, NC, 1939), 17.1.

Meenakshi, K, "The Siddhas of Tamil Nadu." In: R Champakalakshmi and S Gopal (eds.), *Tradition, Dissent and Ideology: Essays in Honour of Romila Thapar*, (Delhi, 1996).

Mellaart, J, *The Neolithic of the Near East*, (London, 1975).

Mitra, Debala, *Pandrethan, Avantipur and Martand*, (New Delhi, 1977).

Mittre, Vishnu and R Savithri, "Food Economy of Harappans." In: GL Posshel (ed.), *Harappan Civilization: A Contemporary Perspective*, (New Delhi, 1982), 205–21.

Mohan, Krishna, *Early Medieval History of Kashmir*, (New Delhi, 1981).

Mohapatra, GC, "Acheulian Distribution in the Siwalik of Punjab." In: RK Sharma (ed.), *Indian Archaeology: New Perspectives*, (Delhi, 1982).

Mohibbul Hasan (ed.), *Historians of Medieval India*, (Meerut, 1968).

Mongait, A, *Archaeology in the USSR*, (London, 1961).

Mukherjee, BN, "Central Asia and the Indian Subcontinent: The Migratory links of the Sakas," *The Journal of Central Asian Studies*, Vol. I, No. 1, (1990).

Mukherjee, BN, *Mathura and its Society: The Saka-Pahlava Phase*, (Calcutta, 1981).

Mukherjee, BN, *The Rise and Fall of Empire*, (Calcutta, 1988).

Mukhopadhyay, Bahatha Ansumali, "Ancestor Dravidian Languages in Indus Civilization: Ultra Conserved Dravidian Tooth-word Reveals Deep Linguistic Ancestry and Supports Genetics," *Humanities and Social Sciences Communications*, Vol. 8, Article No. 193 (2021).

Munawar, Naji and Shafi Shouq, *Kashri Adbuk Tawarikh*, (Srinagar, 1992),

Narain, AK, *The Indo-Greeks*, (Oxford: London, 1957).

Naseem, Mohammad, *The Neolithic Cultures of North Western Indo-Pakistan*, (Delhi, 1982).

Naudou, Jean, *Buddhists of Kashmir*, (Delhi, 1980).

Nayak, BC and NC Ghosh (eds.), *New Trends in Indian Art and Archaeology*, Vol. I, (1992).

Nazki, AR, "Sharda: History and Importance." In: K Warikoo (ed.), *The Other Kashmir: Society, Culture and Politics in the Karokoram Himalayas*, (Delhi, 2014).

Nemec, John, "Innovation and Social Change in the Vale of Kashmir, Circa 900–1250 CE." In: Dominic Goodall et al. (eds.), *Śaivism and the Tantric Traditions: Essays in Honour of Alexis G.J.S. Sanderson*, Gonda Indological Studies, No. 22, (Leiden, 2020), 283–320.

Obrock, Luther, "Landscape in its Place: The Imagination of Kashmir in Sanskrit and Beyond," *History and Theory*, Vol. 59, No. 1, (2020), 156–164.

Obrock, Luther (ed.), *Marc Aurel Stein, Illustrated Rajatarangini*, (Hale, 2013).

Obrock, Luther James, "Transition and History: The Development of a Kashmiri Textual Tradition from ca 1000–1500," PhD dissertation, (Berkeley, CA, 2015).

Osterhammel, J, "World History," In: A Schneider and D Woolf (eds.), *The Oxford History of Historical Writing, Vol. 5: Historical Writing since 1945*, (Oxford, 2011), 93–112.

Pal, Pratapaditya (ed.), *Art and Architecture of Ancient Kashmir*, (Bombay, 1989).

Pal, Pratipaditya, "Introduction." In: Pratipaditya Pal, (ed.), *Art & Architecture of Ancient Kashmir*, (Bombay, 1989a), v–viii.

Pal, Pratipaditya, "Kashmir and the Tibetan Tradition." In: Pratipaditya Pal, (ed.), *Art & Architecture of Ancient Kashmir*, (Bombay, 1989b), 117–35.

Pal, Pratipaditya, "Metal Sculpture." In: Pratipaditya Pal, (ed.), *Art & Architecture of Ancient Kashmir*, (Bombay, 1989c), 77–94.

Pande, GC (ed.), *History of Science, Philosophy and Culture in Indian Civilization, Vol. I, part I, The Dawn of Indian Civilization upto 600 BC* (New Delhi, 1999).

Pande, KC, *Abhinagupta: An Historical and Philosophical Study*, [1935], reprint, (Banaras, 2018).

Pandit, BN, *Aspects of Kashmir Śaivism*, (Srinagar, 1977).

Pandit, BN, *Specific Principles of Kashmiri Śaivism*, (New Delhi, 1997)

Pant, RK, "Kashmir Neolithic – A Reappraisal," paper presented at XII Annual Congress of IAS and VII Conference of ISPQS, jointly held at Allahabad, (1981).

Papastergiadis, Nikos, "Tracing Hybridity in Theory," In: Pnina Werbner and Tariq Madood, (eds.), *Debating Cultural Hybridity: Multicultural Identities and the Politics of Anti-racism*, (London, 1997), 257–81.

Parpola, A and P Koskikallio (eds.), *South Asian Archaeology*, (Finland, 1994).

Parpola, A, *Deciphering the Indus Script*, (Cambridge, 1994).

Patel, Kiran Klaus, "Transnational History," *European History Online (EGO)*, (Institute of European History (IEG): Mainz, 2010). www.ieg-ego.eu/patelk-2010-en URN

Pati, Biswamoy *et al* (eds.), *Negotiating India's Past: Essays in Memory of Partha Sarathi Gupta*, (Delhi, 2003).

Penlebury, JD, *The Archaeology of Crete – An Introduction*, (London, 1939).

Philips, CH (ed.), *Historians of India, Pakistan and Ceylon*, (London, 1961).

Pollock, Sheldon, "The Death of Sanskrit," *Comparative Studies in Society and History*, Vol. 43, No. 2, (2001), 392–426.

Pollock, Sheldon, *The Language of the Gods in the World of Men*, (Barkley, CA, 2006).

Pollock, Sheldon, "The Sanskrit Cosmopolis, 300–1300: Transculturation, Vernaculturation, and the Question of Ideology," In: Jan EM Houben (ed.), *Ideology and Status of Sanskrit: Contributions to the History of the Sanskrit Language*, (Leiden, 1996).

Pollock, Sheldon, Homi K Bhabha, Carol A Breckenridge, and Dipesh Chakrabarty, "Cosmopolitanism," In: Carol A Breckenridge-Appadurai (ed.), *Cosmopolitanism*, (Durham and London, 2002).

Porter, Barbara Nevling, *Images, Power, and Politics: Figurative Aspects of Esarhaddon's Babylonian Policy*, (Philadelphia, 1993).

Possehl, G (ed.), *South Asian Archaeology Studies*, (New Delhi: Oxford & IBH, 1992).

Possehl, G (ed.), *Harappan Civilization: A Contemporary Perspective*, (New Delhi, 1982).

Prakash, Buddha, *India and the World*, (Hoshiarpur, 1964a).

Prakash, Buddha, *Political and Social Movements in Ancient Punjab* (Delhi, 1964b).

"Proceedings of the Seminar on OCP and NBP." *Bulletin* of the *Indian Archaeological Society*, Vol. 5, (1971–72).

Puri, BN, *India under the Kuṣāṇas*, (Bombay, 1965).

Puri, BN, "The Sakas and Indo-Parthians." In: *History of Civilizations in Central Asia, Vol. II. The Development of Nomadic Civilizations. 700 BC to AD 250*, (Paris, 1994).

Qadri, SM Afzal (ed.), *Cultural Heritage of Kashmir*, (Srinagar, 1997).

Qureshi, Ishtiyaq Hussain, *The Muslim Community of Indo-Pakistan Sub-continent (1610–1947)*, First Indian edition Delhi, (Delhi, 1984).

Rao, Aparna (ed.), *The Valley of Kashmir: The Making and Unmaking of a Composite Culture?* (New Delhi, 2008).

Rawanbakhsh, Mohammad Husain, "Khari ki khud ra ba zangir-I 'adl Anu Shirwam mālīd ba āindagan chi guft", *Roznama Mardam-i-Salari*, (2007). www.mardomsalari.com

Rawlinson, G, *Five Great Monarchies of Ancient Eastern World*, Vol. IV, (London, 1867).

Ray, HC, "History of Sanskrit Literature of Kashmira," *Indian Historical Quarterly* (IHQ), Vol. 31, No. 3, (1955), 232–56.

Ray, S, *Dynastic History of Northern India (Early Medieval Period)*, 2 Vols., (Calcutta, 1936).

Ray, SC, *Early History and Culture of Kashmir*, (New Delhi, 1969).

Rendell, H, "The Pleistocene sequence in the Soan Valley, Northern Pakistan," *South Asian Archaeology*, (1981).

Renfrew, JM, *Palaeoethnobotany: The Pre-historic Food Habits of Near East and Europe*, (London, 1973).

Rosenfield, JM, *Dynastic Arts of the Kuṣāṇas*, (Los Angeles, CA and Barkley, 1967).

Rostovtzeff, MI, "Dura and the Problem of Parthian Art," *Yale Classical Studies*, Vol. 5, (1935), 155–304.

Rowan, Diana P, "Reconsideration of an Unusual Ivory Diptych," *Artibus Asiae*, Vol. 46/4, (1985), 251–304.

Roy, Kumkum, "The Making of a Mandala: Fuzzy Frontiers of Kalhana's Kashmir." In: Biswamoy Pati et al. (eds.), *Negotiating India's Past: Essays in Memory of Partha Sarathi Gupta*, (Delhi, 2003).

Roy, Kumkum, *The Power of Gender and Gender of Power: Exploration in Early Indian History*, (New Delhi, 2010).

Sachsenmaier, Dominic, "World History as Ecumenical History?" *Journal of World History*, Vol. 18, No. 4, (2007).

Sahu, Bhairabi Prasad (ed.), *The Changing Gaze: Regions and the Construction of Early India*, (New Delhi, 2013).

Sahu, Bhairabi Prasad, "Legitimation, Ideology, and State in Early India." In: Bhairabi Prasad Sahu (ed.), *The Changing Gaze: Regions and the Construction of Early India*, (New Delhi, 2013a), 179–215.

Saifur Rahman Dar, *Taxila and the Western World*, (Lahore, 1984).

Sanderson, Alexis, "Religious Change in Kashmir," *Keynote Lecture, Kyoto University, Centre for Eurasian Cultural Studies*, (2015), 1–17, https://www.academia.edu/16364102.

Sankalia, HD, *Indian Archaeology Today*, (Bombay, 1952).

Sankalia, HD, "Iranian Influences on Early Indo-Pakistan Cultures." In: Amlendu Guha, (ed.), *Central Asia*, (Delhi, 1969).

Sankalia, HD, "Prehistoric Colonization in India: Archaeological and literary Evidence," *Puratattva*, No. 8, (Delhi, 1975–76).

Sankalia, HD, *Prehistory and Protohistory of India and Pakistan*, (Poona, 1974b).

Sankalia, HD, *Prehistory of India*, (New Delhi, 1977).

Sankhyan, RA and G Weber, "Evidence of Surgery in Ancient India: Trepanation at Burzahom (Kashmir) over 4000 years ago," *International Journal of Osteoarchaeology*, Vol. II, Issue 5, (2001), 375–80.

Sarkar, H, "Some Aspects of Megalithic Culture in India." In: *Puratattva*, No. 11, (1982), 49–55.

Sarkar, H, *Studies in Early Buddhist Architecture of India*, (New Delhi, 1966).

Saxena, KS, *Political History of Kashmir: B.C. 300 – A.D. 1200*, (Lucknow, 1974).

Schlumberger, Daniel, "Parthian Art," In: Ehsan Yarshater (ed.), *The Cambridge History of Iran*, Vol. 3, (Cambridge, 1983).

Seigel, M, "World History's Narrative Problem," *Hispanic American Historical Review*, Vol. 84, (2004), 431–46.

Sen, Mohit and MB Rao (eds.), *Das Kapital Centenary Volume – A Symposium*, (New Delhi, 1968).

Shaffer, JG, "The Later Prehistoric Periods," In: FR Allchin and N Hammond (eds.), *The Archaeology of Afghanistan: From Earliest Times to Timurid Period*, (London, 1978).

Shali, SL, *Kashmir History and Archaeology Through the Ages*, (Delhi, 1993).

Shali, SL, *Settlement Pattern in Relation to Climatic Changes in Kashmir*, (Delhi, 2001).

Sharma, AK, "Neolithic Gufkral." In: GM Buth, (ed.), *Central Asia and Western Himalayas – A Forgotten Link*, (Jodhpur, 1986).

Sharma, GR, "India and Central Asia from 6th century BC to 6th century AD." In: Amalendu Guha (ed.), *Central Asia: Movement of People and Ideas from Times Prehistoric to Modern*, (New Delhi: Vikas Publications, 1970).

Sharma, Mahesh, "Puranic Texts from Kashmir: Vitasta and River Ceremonial in the *Nilamata Purāna*," *South Asia Research*, Vol. 28, No. 2, (2008), 123–45.

Sharma, RK (ed.), *Indian Archaeology: New Perspectives*, (Delhi, 1982).

Sharma, RS, *Advent of the Aryans in India*, (Delhi, 2003).

Sharma, RS, "Iron and Urbanization in the Ganga Basin," *Indian Historical Review*, Vol. 1, (1974).

Sharma, RS, "Material Background of the Origin of Buddhism." In: Mohit Sen and MB Rao (eds.), *Das Kapital Centenary Volume – A Symposium*, (New Delhi, 1968b).

Sharma, RS, *Material Culture and Social Formations in Ancient India*, (Delhi, 1983).

Shrava, Satya, *Kuṣāṇa Numasmatics*, (New Delhi, 1985).

Singer, C, EJ Holmyard and AR Hall, *A History of Technology, Vol. I, From Early Times to Fall of Ancient Empires*, (Oxford, 1954).

Singh, P, *The Neolithic Culture of Western Asia*, (London, 1974).

Sinha, BP (ed.), *Potteries of the Ancient India*, (Patna, n.d.).

Siudmak, John, "Early Stone and Terracotta Sculpture." In: Pal (ed.), *Art and Architecture of Ancient Kashmir*, (1989).

Siudmak, John, *The Hindu-Buddhist Sculpture of Ancient Kashmir and its Influences*. (Leiden, 2013).

Slaje, Walter, "Kashmir Minimundus: India's Sacred Geography en miniature," In: Roland Steiner (ed.), *Highland Philology*, (Wittenberg, 2012).

Slaje, Walter, "The Last Buddhist of Kashmir as Recorded by Jonaraja." In: Wagish Shukla (ed.), *Sanskrit Studies*, Vol. II, Samvat 2062–63 [CE 2006–07], (Delhi, 2007).

Spiegel, Gabrielle M, "Genealogy: Form and Function in Medieval Historical Narrative *History and Theory*, Vol. 22, (1983), 43–53.

Spiegel, GM, "History, Historicism and the Social logic of the Text in the Middle Ages." In: K Jenkins (ed.), *The Postmodern History Reader*, (Routledge, 1997).

Steiner, Roland (ed.), *Highland Philology*, (Universitat-Verlag Halle-Wittenberg, 2012).

Stern, Fritz, *Verities of History*, (New York, [1956], 1972).

Stern, Philip Van Doren, *Prehistoric Europe, Great Britain*, (Great Britain, 1970).

Stewart, Tony, "In Search of Equivalence: Conceiving Hindu-Muslim Encounter through Translation Theory," *History of Religions*, Vol. 40, No. 3, (2001).

Stone, Gregory B, "Review Article: The Age of Others," *Medieval Encounters*, 2/3, (1996).

Stuchtey, Benedikt and Eckhardt Fuchs (ed.), *Writing World History, 1800–2000* (Oxford, 2003).

Subrahmanyam, Sanjay, "Connected Histories: Notes towards a Reconfiguration of Early Modern Eurasia," *Modern Asian Studies*, 31 (1997), 735–62.

Subrahmanyam, Sanjay, "Golden Age Hallucinations," *Outlook India Magazine*, (August 20, 2001), www.outlookindia.com

Swisher III, CC, GH Curtis and Widiasmoro, "Age of the Earliest known Hominids in Java, Indonesia," *Science*, Vol. 263, (1994).

Sykes, P, *History of Persia*, Vol. I, (London, 1930).

Taddei, M (ed.), *South Asian Archaeology 1977* (Naples: 1979), 463–535.

Taran, WW, *The Greeks in Bactria and India*, [Cambridge, 1938], reprint, (New Delhi, 1980).

Taranatha, *History of Buddhism in India*, edited by Debiprasad Chattopadhya, (Simla, 1970)

Teng, Muhammad Yūsuf, *Shinakht*, (Srinagar: J&K Cultural Academy, 1988).

Thakur, Upendera, *The Huns in India*, (Varanasi, 1967).

Thapar, Romila, *Asoka and the Decline of the Mauryas*, (Oxford, [1961], 2012)

Thapar, Romila, 'Kalhana', In: Mohibbul Hasan (ed.), *Historians of Medieval India*, [1968], reprint, (New Delhi: Meenakshi Prakashan, 1983).

Thapliyal, Uma Prasad, *Foreign Elements in Ancient Indian Society*, (New Delhi, 1979).

Tignor, R, Jeremy Adelman, Stephen Aron, Stephen Kotkin, Suzanne Marchand, Gyan Prakash, Michael Tsin, *Worlds Together: Worlds Apart: A History of the World from the Beginnings of Humankind to the Present*, 3rd edition, (New York, 2011).

Vavilov, NI, "The Origin, Variation, Immunity and Breeding of Cultivating Plants," *Chronica Botanica*, 13, (1951), 1–66.

Waheed, Abdul, *Traditional Agricultural Technology of Kashmir*, M Phil dissertation, (Srinagar: History Department, University of Kashmir, 2000).

Wani, Aman Ashraf, *Exogenous Influences in Kashmir from the Neolithic Times to the Advent of the Christian Era,* M Phil dissertation, (Srinagar, 2002).

Wani, Aman Ashraf, *Kashmir and the Neighbouring World: A Study in Contacts and Influences (From the Mid First Century A D to the Beginning of the Fourteenth Century)*, PhD thesis, (Srinagar, 2013).

Wani, Mohammad Ashraf, *History Beyond Borders: Contacts with the Neighbouring World and the Evolution and Growth of Culture in Ancient Kashmir*. (Patiala, 2015).

Wani, Muhammad Ashraf and Aman Ashraf Wani, *Prehistory of Kashmir*, (Srinagar, 2018).

Wani, Muhammad Ashraf, *Islam in Kashmir*, (Srinagar, 2004).

Warikoo, K (ed.), *The Other Kashmir: Society, Culture and Politics in the Karakoram Himalayas*, (Delhi, 2014).

Warikoo, K, "Trade Relations between Central Asia and Kashmir Himalayas during the Dogra Period (1846–1947)," *Cahiers d'Asie centrale*, (1996), 113–124.

Werbner, Pnina and Tariq Madood, (eds.), *Debating Cultural Hybridity: Multicultural Identities and the Politics of Anti-racism*, (London, 1997).

Werner, Michael and Benedict Zimmermann, "Beyond Comparison: Historie Croisee and the Challenge of Reflexivity," *History and Theory*, 45, (2006), 30–50.

Werner, Michael and Benedict Zimmermann (eds.), "Histoire Croisée: Between the Empirical and Reflexivity," *Annals Histoire, Sciences Sociales*, Vol. 58, No. 1, (2003), 7–36, (tr. from French by JPD Systems).

Wilson, HH, *Hindu History of Kashmir*, (Calcutta, 1960).

Winetrout, Kenneth, *Arnold Toynbee*, (Boston, MA, 1975).

Wink, Andre, *Al-Hind: The Making of the Indo Islamic World*, Vol. I: *Early Medieval India and the Expansion of Islam, 7th – 11th Centuries*, (New Delhi, 1996).

Witzel, Micheal, "The Kashmiri Pandits: Their Early History." In: Aparna Rao (ed.), *The Valley of Kashmir: The Making and Unmaking of a Composite Culture?* (New Delhi, 2008).

Witzel, Micheal, *The Veda in Kashmir – History and Present State of Vedic Tradition in the Western Himalayas*, 2 Volumes, (Harvard, 2021).

Yarshater, Ehsan, "Introduction," In: Yarshater (ed.), *The Cambridge History of Iran*, Vol. 3 (1), (Cambridge, 1983a), Xvii–Lxxvi.

Yarshater, Ehsan, "Iranian Common Beliefs and World-View," In: Yarshater (ed.), *The Cambridge History of Iran*, Vol. 3, (Cambridge, 1983b).

Yarshater, Ehsan (ed.), *The Cambridge History of Iran, Vol. 3, No. 1/2, The Seleucid, Parthian and Sasanid Periods*, (Cambridge, 1983).

Yatoo, Mumtaz A, *Characterising Material Culture to Determine Settlement Patterns in North West Kashmir*. Unpublished PhD thesis (Leicester, 2012.

Yatoo, Mumtaz A, and Aijaz A Bandey, "Relations of Neolithic Kashmir with South and Central Asia – A Comparative Analysis of Material Culture from New Sites in Kashmir," *The Journal of Central Asian Studies*, Vol. XXI, (2014), 37–44.

Yazdani, G, *Ajanta – The Colour and Monochrome Reproductions of the Ajanta Frescoes Based on Photography*, (London, 1930).

Young, Robert, *Colonial Desire: Hybridity, in Theory, Culture, and Race*, (London, 1995).

Zeimal, EV, "The Kidarite Kingdom in Central Asia," In: BA Litvisky et al (eds.), *History of Civilizations of Central Asia, Vol. III: The crossroads of civilizations AD 250 to 750*, (Paris, 1994).

INDEX

Note: Page numbers in *italics* indicate figures, **bold** indicate tables and n denote notes.

Beidha (Levant) 39
belles letters 206
betel leaves 218
Bhavabhūti 199
Bhima Śhahi 223
bi-metallic coinage 94
Bilhana 202
blasphemous 235
Bleazby, GB 94, 106
Bloch, Marc 6
block-on-block methods 28
boat bridges 220
Bodhisattva statues 113, 189, 209
bone tools 39–40
Bopearachchi, Osmund 97–99
bounded spaces and identities, world of 3
Brahmadeya 160
brāhmanas 235
Brahmanism 197, 221
Brahmi 73
brain drain (*vidvaddurbhiksa*) 199
Brhadbuddha 250
Bronner, Yigal 198
broomcorn millet 45
Brown, Percy 14
Buddha Matreya, concept of 125
Buddhajiva **141**
Buddhavarman **141**
Buddhayaśas **140**
Buddhism 122, 197, 208, 220; and its expansion 136–137; Fourth Buddhist Council 137–143, **140–142**; impact on 112–113; in Tibet 209; introduction of 77; religious syncretism 125; revival of 154–155
Buddhist learning 207
Bulbul Langar 248
Bulbul Shah 248
Bull type coins 106
Burzahom site 30–32; Aceramic Neolithic 30; Ceramic Neolithic-A 30; Ceramic Neolithic-B 31–32; rice cultivation 45–46

Caelian Philae 97
caitya 250
Camel type coins 106
ćandālās 235
Caṅkuṇa, Tuhkhara 191, 217
Caṅkunavihāra 217
carnelian beads 43, 48
catuhśālā 250
cavalry 214
Centre of Learning, Kashmir as 196–210
Ceramic Neolithic-A: Burzahom 30; Gufkral 33
Ceramic Neolithic-B: Burzahom 31–32; Gufkral 33
Chach Nama 190, 221
chaityas 127–128
Chalcolithic period, beginning of 62–63
Chandrapida (*Tchen-tolo-pi-li*) 193
Chandrapida Vajraditya 187
China silk (cinanasuka) 213, 220
Chinese Turkistan 217, 241
chip style 126
chiton 99
Circle of Mothers 155
circulation, mechanisms of 70–78
cist graves 66–67
citta 238
civilization, western categories 1
coiffure 132
coiling method 42
coinage 16, *161–162*; Hun ruler 150–151; Huvishka's 124; iconography of 16; in Indian subcontinent 94–96; of Kujula Kadphises 122
collyrium 226
confederacy 195
connected histories 5
copper coins 63, 94
copper punch-marked coins 74–75, 79
corvée 195
Cosmas Indicopleustes 145
cosmopolitan ecumenes and transculturation: art and architecture 96–101; Buddhism and its expansion 136–143; costume and coiffure 128–133; encounters with 89; food and drinks 133–135; Greeks in Kashmir and Hellenistic influences 89–96; Hun conquest of Kashmir 145–160; Huns and the Indic turn 143–145; immigrations and settlements 117–128; impact 136; Kidarites and Kashmir 135–136; Kusāna Kashmir 115–118, **118**; language 128; Śaka–Parthian presence 101–114
Costantini, Swat 46

Cox, Whitney 21, 206
Cribb 151–152
cross-cultural networks: Buddhist architecture 240; centre of learning, Kashmir as 196–210; commercial contacts 210–219; cosmopolitan Kashmir, making of 231–239; empire, making of an 185–196; inflows and connectivity 219–231; interaction 16; sculpture 240–256; stone temples 239–240
crucibles 47
cultural artefacts 12–13
cultural circulation 13, 196
cultural comingling 57–59
cultural exchange 212
cultural foundations of Kashmir: Burzahom 30–32; Gufkral 32–33; inflows, contacts 27–29; Kanispur 34–35; Neolithic revolution 29–30; Palaeolithic and Neolithic Cultures, making of 27–29; Qasim Bagh 35
cultural hybridity 6
cultural paranoia 1
cultural translation 4
culture: circulatory character of 3; in regional context 12
Cunningham, Alexander 15, 94
Czuma, Stanislaw 240

Dakṣinā ācāra 226, 233
Dakṣināpatha 191
damaras 119, 235
Damodara II 91, 91
Damodaragupta 204
Daradapuri 275
Dardas 232
Dardic 21–22; group of languages 55
Darius 270
Davis, Richard 189, 192
Demetrius 90
deśaguna 236
Deva Shahi Khingila 148
Dhamorai 90
Dharmamitra **141**
dharmaraja (stupa) 208
Dharmaśāstra 206
Dharmayaśas **140**
Dharmottara 199
dhyana (Buddhist form of yoga) 139
diaper masonry 108
diaper pebble style 126, 165
diaper rubble style 126, 165
Didda 202
die-striking technique 94
digvijaya 149
dīnārra 95
Diodotus, Silver coin of *161*
Dirks, Nicholas 192
dog, taming of 43
dombās 235
Dravidas 227
Dravidian Vernaculars 206
Du Xingman (Tu Hsing-man) 208
Dukhang 209
du'ong 44
Durlabhavardhana 121, 186, 219
dwelling pits: Neolithic cultures 38–39, 42

Early Neolithic of Kashmir: immigrations, connections and making of 36–37; and Neolithic cultures of neighbouring world 38–41
early settlers: language and identity of 52–54; surnames on identity of 54–55
earth houses 39
ecumenical history 5
Ekangas 195
emmer wheat 40–41
entangled histories 5
ethnographic evidence 56
Eucratides, Copper coin of *161*
Euthydemus 90; silver coin of *161*

Falsehood 105
Fateh Allāh Kashmiri 247
Fazl, Abul 8
feudal barons 195
fine globular red-ware pot 48
fine grey ware 42
Firdawsi 249
Fisher, Robert 104, 127, 234, 239
flat-topped plateau 30
flexed burial 32
Flood, Finbarr 3, 13, 210, 245
Fourth Buddhist Council 19, 137–143, **140–142**
fowl, taming of 43
fractional burials 32
fravardin 111
free-standing monuments 63

free thrashing wheat 45
Frove 111
fuzzy frontiers 186

gajemeh 113
Gandhara art 14, 96, 113, 239, 241
Gandhara Grave Culture 63, 66, 270
Gauda 193
Gautama Sanghdeva **140**
gene sequencing 45
Ghaznavid Sultans 230, 211, 255
Glan Dar-ma 209
global history 5
Gnosticism 104
gods on earth 152
Gondophares 108
Gondophares I 102
Gopa hill (Gopadri) 153
Gopalavarman (902–904) 195
Graeco-Buddhist art 96
Graeco-Indian cultural synthesis 239
Graeco-Roman arts 100
Graeco–Iranian World, impact of 101–102
grandiose *digvijayas* 190
Greek 73; religious cults 119
Grierson, George 242
gritty dull ware 42
Guddasetu 91–92
Gufkral site 32–33; Aceramic Neolithic 32–33; Ceramic Neolithic-A 33; Ceramic Neolithic-B 33; millet cultivation 45; rice cultivation 45–46
guluband 132
Gunavarman **141**
Gupagrahara 153
Gupta art 240
Gurez-Baltistan route 9

Habban 108
Hallaj, Mansur al 230, 254
handmade pottery and types 42
Hari Parbat 105
Harmatta, J. 123–124, 135
harpoon 40
Harśagupta 149
Harśa's reign 202, 245
Harut 105
Harwan chaitya 127
Harwan site 14, 104
Harwan tiles 97, 109
Hebrew language 242
Hecataeus of Miletus 67
himation 99
Hinayāna Buddhism **142**
hindiyah 243, 255
Hindu learning 204
Hiranyakula 145
Hirpura–Bimbar route 218
history beyond borders 2
Hoinar tiles 15
holy practice 59
Homo erectus 28; chopper type tools of 28
Homo habilis 27; Palaeolithic tools of 28
hora shastra 99
Hordeum vulgare Linn Varhexastrichum 41
Horseman type coins 106
horticulture 46
Hoynar 105
human burials 49
human figures, facial characteristics of 14
human motifs 120
Hun rulers: Buddhism, revival of 154–155; coinage 150–151; conquest of Kashmir 145–160; Cribb on two series of Kashmir gold coins 151–152; dominance of Śaivism 153–154; Kashmir's emergence as an empire 148–150; new villages and towns, emergence of 157–160; religion 152–153; Śaivism, revival of 155; successive 148; and the Indic turn 143–145; Vaiṣṇavism 155–157
Huṣka 116
Hutmara 105
Huvishka coinage 117, 124

Ibn Khaldun 191
imitable model 196
imperial kingdom 188
imperial organisation 76–77
Inden, Ronald 18, 58, 185
Indian contacts 67–78; Achaemenian influences 67–68; circulation, mechanisms of 70–78; Mauryan influences 68–70
Indic mainland 11
Indic *Weltanschauung* 17
Indic world 219
Indigenous symbols, in coins 95

Indo-Afghan race 56
Indo-Greek model 106
Indo-Greeks/Indus-Greeks 90
Indo-Parthians 106
Indo-Scythian empire 102
internal dissensions 196
international history 5
Intertwined Lions, Stone *23*
Iranian contacts 67–78; Achaemenian influences 67–68; circulation, mechanisms of 70–78; Mauryan influences 68–70; religious cults 119
iron: intensive use of 71; working, beginning of 63

Jagadānanda 234
Jaluka 70
Jami Mosque 248
janghatrana 114
japastutih syādadhamā homapūjādhamādhamā 233
Jayadatta 193
Jayaka 218
Jayapida 193
Juṣka 116

Kabul Valley 208
Kailaśa mountain 221
Kalasa 227
Kālodaka 185
Kalpa tree 200
Kalpadruma 245
Kamalavati 217
Kamarajya (Kamraz) 217
Kamboja 213
kancuka 114, 129
Kaniṣka 116; Copper coin of *168*; Council 138; Gold dinar of *168*
Kaniṣkapur 116
Kanispur 34–35, 40
Kapatesvara (modern Kothar) 228
karewas 72
Karkotas 212; dynasty 188; Naga 188; rulers 250
Karna-Chilas route 9
Kashgar 9
Kashmira (goddess Uma) 186
Kashmiri calendar 205
Kasmirajam 113
Kaul, Shonaleeka 9, 189
Kaula ācāra 233
Khaldun, Ibn 6, 92
khānaqāh 248
Kharoshthi script 73–74
Khasas 232
Khazanchi, TN 35
Kidara coin type 135
Kidarites: impact 136; and Kashmir 135–136
King Durlabhaka–Pratapaditya II 213
King Kalaśa 203
King Menander (155–130 CE) 92
king on horse back 103
Kitāb fi tahqiq-i-mal'l-Hind 230
Kitāb-ul-Hind 17
Knutson, Jesse 249
Koshur 21
kram 284
kśatriyas 235
Kşemagupta's reign (950–958) 222–223
Kṣemendra 214, 247
Kṣīra 198, 199
Kujala Kasasa Yavugasa dhramathidasa 122
Kujula Kadphises 115
Kula-Kaula 238
kulah 130
Kumarajiva (344–413 CE) 139
kundalini by yoga 236
Kusāna Kashmir 115–118
Kuṣāṇa 'Sahi (king of Kuṣāṇas) 136
Kuṣāṇas site 14; cosmopolitan ecumene 117–118; expert preparing wine 134; male dress of 129–130; music, dance and drama 134–135; ornaments at 133; women's costumes 130–132

Lakhana-Narendraditya 156
Lal Bazar (the market of jewels) 215
L'li'Badakhshan (jewel of Badakhshan) 215
Lalitaditya 212
land revenue grantees 193
language: and identity of early settlers 52–54; cosmopolitan ecumenes and transculturation 128; Dardic group of 55
lapis lazuli 43
law codes 198
learning, great centre of 197
lehanga 226
Lens culinaris 41
Lens esculenta 41
Levallois–Mousterian tools 28

Lewan site 39
linga 215
Lingam worship 236
Lo-Stupa 155
loan-oriented language 21–22
local history 5
Loebanr site 39
logico-epistemological works 208
Lokaprakasa 214
longue durée 255
lord of Mathra 193
Ludden, David 3

The Madam's School of Thought (*Kuttanimata*) 199
Madhyadeśa 231
Magas 120
mahābhandāgāra 191
Mahābhārata 185
Mahābhāsya (ca. 150 BCE) 72
mahāmati 238
mahāpratīharapīda 191, 193, 220
maharaja rajatiraja 103
Mahārthamanjarī 207
mahāsādhanabhāga 191
mahāsamdhivigraha 191
mahaśvasala 191
Mahavamsa 77–78
Mahāyāna Buddhism **142**
Maheshwarananda 234
Mahesvarānanda 207
Majeed, Gulshan 105, 112
makārās 233–234
Mālinīvijayottara 238
Mālinīvijayottaratantra 237
Manao-Bago 124
manāqib khawāns 247
mandala 195
Mankha 227
Mansur Al-Hallaj 210
Marshall, John 100
Martand temple 191
Marut 105
masonry style 14
Massignon, Louis 199–200
mat impression 31
Mata ācāra 233
material culture 13–17
Matha 224
māthas 201
Mature Neolithic of Kashmir: aboveground houses 44; animal burials 49; ethnographic evidence 56; horticulture 46; human burials 49; language and identity of early settlers 52–54; Naga cult 50–52; and Neolithic cultures of neighbouring world (*see* Neolithic cultures of neighbouring world); new crops, introduction of 45–46; new stone tools 47–48; pig 46; place names as source 55–56; pottery types 48; rock art 49–50; summing up 56–57; surnames on identity of early settlers 54–55
Maues 102
Maurya, Chandragupta 68–70
Mauryan influences 68–70
meat (*mamsa*) 247
medium of contact 5
megaliths 63–66; cist graves 66–67; Iranian and Indian Contacts 67–78
Megarian bowls 97
Meghamatha 155
melancholy verse 206
menhir alignments *see* free-standing monuments
Mesopotamian tradition 15
metadoxy 251
metonymic 189
Middle Neolithic cultures: cattle 43–44; handmade pottery and types 42; inflows, contacts and making of 41–42; pea 43
middle province 186
Mihirakula 145–146; as ruler of Kashmir 146–147
Milindapanha 98
millet cultivation 45
Mir, Shah 255
mleccha gayānah 247
mlecchakanda 134
Mlecchas 69–70, 147, 211
M'Lefaat (Iraq) 39
Moga 102
money currency 95
Mongol invasion 231
monistic Śaivism 234
monolithic 232
Morāka 159
Muhammad, Kile Gul 38
mukhta māl 132
Muktapida Lalitaditya (*Mu-to-pi*) 187, 194

multi-cropping agriculture system 46
Muslim singers 247
mystic of Islam 255

Naga cult 50–52
nagarakhanda 218
Nagarjuna 138
Nāgas 58, 17, 188
Nagasena, Buddhist philosopher 92
naked philosophers 104
nandi pada symbol 123
narus 40
nation, western categories 1
nationalism 3
Naushirwān-I'Adil 246
Neanderthal man 28
Neish, Richard S Mac 46
Nemec, John 206, 237
Neolithic culture of Kashmir: modern scholars, views of 35–36; plural sources 36
Neolithic cultures of neighbouring world 38; Aceramic Neolithic 38; agriculture 40–41; bone and stone tools 39–40; dwelling pits 38–39; red-ochreous painted floors 39; stock raising 41
Neolithic revolution 29–30
new crops, introduction of 45–46; millet cultivation 45; rice 45–46
new stone tools 47–48; beads of precious stones, terracotta bangles and shells 48; copper objects 47; shouldered celt 47; spindle whorls and crucibles 47; stone harvesters 47
Nike type coins 106
Nīlamata Purāna (NP) 17, 58, 121, 143, 186, 221, 237, 251, 285
Nilambra 235
Nīlmata Purāna 226
Nitikalapatru 214
non-Vedic Śaivites 233
Nona 213
Nonamatha 213
Northern black polished ware (NBPW) 72–73
Nyayamanjari 234

Obrock, Luther 11
observatory 198
199 *gotras* 121
orthodoxy 251
oryza sativa 45
Oslango. Laroaspo 124
Ou-k'ong 208, 251

Padataditaka 152
Padmaraja 218
Pahlavika 101
Paiśācas 58
Paisaci 55
Pal, Pratapaditya 15
Palas 224
pañcamahāśabda 193, 220
Pancaratra Brahmans 187, 226
Pancharatra order 18, 192
panchayat 236
Pandit Sothala 228
Pandita Jayapida 198
Panicum miliaceum 45
Panicummillaceum see broomcorn millet
Panj Nihayat 194, 229
pantheon 232
paradhvajah 149
Parama-bhattaraka Maharajadhiraja Shri Shahi Khingala Odya (tya) na-Shahi 148
Paramaśiva 233
Parihaspora 190, 239
Parthian coins 106
Parthian shot 107
Passion of al-Hallaj 200
Patanjali's *Mahabhasya* 198
pattikam (Kmr. *patka*) 114
pea 43
pebble style 126
pedigree coins 94
penge 45
People of the Rock Art 49
Persianate-Islamic culture 230
Pharro 124
Philip II, coins of 94
philosophico-linguistic theories 205
physiognomy 94, 120
pig 46
pīr-murīd 248
Piśācas 17
Pisum arvense Linn 43
Pisum sativum 43
pitakas 137
place names as source 55–56
polished stone axes 40
Pollock, Sheldon 3, 128, 189, 197

Polo, Marco 230, 247
Polybius 6
Poonzu 93
porridge (*karambhaka*) 216
pottery types 48
Potwar plateau 39
Prakāsha 233
Pratapaditya Pal 209
pratimāsu alpabuddhīnam 233
Pravarapura, modern Srinagar 186
Pravarasena II (c. 570 CE) 149
Prayaga 187, 193
pre-NBPW 58; increase in rice cultivation 60–61
precious stones 43–44; beads of 48
prehistoric world 4
preliterate world 14
present-national sentiments 3
principal tool types 29
professional historians 1
proliferation of cults 232
punch-marked coins 74–75, 79
Punyatrata **140**
Purāna 219
Puranadhisthana 75
Purānas 221
Puranic process 237
pure animal style 110
Pushkalavati 98

Qadi 211
Qasim Bagh 35; millet cultivation 45
Qateh-Yazgrad 15, 103
Qur'ān 247

Rabatak inscription 115
radiocarbon dates 45
ragas 134
Rājataraṅgiṇī 11, 191, 195; Kashmir was subjected to Indo-Greek 91; *damaras* in 119; successors of Pravarasena II 149; in Context of Persianate Islamic Historiography 249; celebration of achievements 197; of Kalhana 19–20
Rājavihāra 250
Ramad (Levant) 39
ramshackle rule 231
Rashtrakutas 211
Rāwanchandra 249
Ray, SC 235
red-ochreous painted floors 39
reference culture 70–71, 92
regional history 5
religious tolerance 98
rice 45–46; culture, promotion of 71–72
Rinchana (1320–1323) 256
ritual subordination 189
Rock Art people 29, 49–50
rock engraving 29
Rockefeller collection 209
roohan posh (flowers of souls) 112
roohan tsuchi (breads in memory of souls) 112
Roy, Kumkum 20, 189, 190
rubble stone style 14, 126

sacred law 147
sacrificial fire (hōma) 233
saffron 219; cultivation in Kashmir 113; in Rasam 207
Śahis 221; of Udabhāndapura 195
Śaiva Āgamas 233
Śaiva religion 206
Śaivas 185
Śaivism 8, 17, 226, 232, 238; dominance of 153–154; revival of 155
Śaka–Parthian culture: agricultural technology 113; architecture and art 107–108; art 108–109; Buddhism, impact on 112–113; coinage 106–107; dress and ornaments 113–114; evidence of 103–106; Graeco–Iranian World, impact of 101–102; military technology and strategy 107; nature of 102–103; religion 109–112; site 14; sun worship 113
Śakastan 101
Salt Route (*Lavanasarāni*) 218
Samaya ācāra 233
Śambhu Nātha of Jalandhara 234
Samgramaditya 221, 234
Samkaravarman 195
Sanghabhuti **140**
Sangram 71
sangrāmās 251
Sankalia, HD 35
Sanskrit Buddhism 128, 138
Sanskrit Indo-Aryan languages 242

Sanskritic cosmopolis 21
Sanskritic culture 199
Sanskritic garb 242
Saoshyant 113
saracenes [Muslims] 247
Śarada (goddess of learning) 198; script 207
Sarai Khola bone tool 40
Saraswati (goddess of knowledge) 203
Śardadeśa (land of the goddesses of learning) 203
Sassanian kings 244
Satcitananda 233
satrapies 90, 119
Saussala (1112–1120 CE) 214
Scythia 101
Scythian coins 106
Scythio-Parthian-Kuṣāṇa costumes 99
Scytho-Kuṣāṇa style 134
Second Urbanisation, period of 76
semi-ashlar masonry 126
semi-Vedic Śaivites 233
Semthan (700–500 BCE) 58; archaeological site 13
seraglio 244
Setaria italica 45
Seven Ṛṣis (Great Bear) 203
Shah Mir 249
Shah, Sayyid Sharaf al-Din Bulbul 255
Śhahi kingdom 223
Shahr'i Khas (historic Srinagar) 215
shared history 5; between 1500 and 600 BCE 270; Achaemenian ruler of Iran 270–271; area stretching 276–277; Buddhist literature Swat (Uddiyana) 272–273; contemporaries as Bhautta land 275–276; Gandhara art and architecture, impact of 271–272; Hun tradition on military adventures 273–274; immediate neighbourhood 269–270; intimate affinities 271; Karnah route 274–275; marriage of Kşemagupta (950–958) with Didda 274; political and strategic relations 277; and Sindh and Multan 277–278; trade with Punjab 277
Sharika 105
Sharma, Mahesh 187
shouldered celt 47
Si-Yu-Ki 19
Siddhamatrika 205
Silk Route 212
silver bowls [resembling skulls] 216
Sindhu 193
Sino-Tibetan language 36
Siudmak, John 90–91, 241, 272
Slaje, Walter 7, 208
Sogdian 101
Songtsen Gampo 209
Sopore-Bandipora route 115
spindle whorls 47
SPS Museum 16, 124
squat caps 114
Śrikanthacarita 227
stable Sanskritic identity 11
standing Poseidon 103
standing victory 103
state exchequer 214
steatite 43
Stein, MA 223, 226, 245
stock raising 41
stone architecture 73
stone chambers (so-called tombs) 63
stone hammer methods 28
stone harvesters 47
stone temples 239
stone tools 40
stucco figures 15
stupas 69, 127
subterranean houses 32, 39
śudra 235
Sūfism 248
Suhadeva 248, 249, 255
Suhrawardi saint 248
Sui dynasty 208
sun worship 113
surapratistha 192
Surkh Kotal (Bactria) 14, 108
Suryamati 215
Sus cristatus see pig
Sutrapatika 137
Suyya 194
Śvantā Armati 110
Swat 272–273
Syed Sharf–Ud-Din Bulbul Shah 231
syncretic culture 15

Taing, Mohammad Yusuf 242, 247
Taittiriyesvara 226
Takkas 215

Tang China 241
tanka 226
Tantras 233
Tantrians 195
Tantric Śaivites 233
Tantricism 247, 235
Tape Asiab (Iran) 39
Tape Sarab (Iran) 39
Tarim Basin 208
tattva 238
Taxila copper plate of Patika 110
technological and cultural revolution 59–62, **60**
temple Hinduism 18
terracotta bangles and shells 48
textual sources 17–21
thakkuras (Kmr. *Thakur*) 277
thalis (pans) 97
Thapar, Romila 70
theistic 236
thick coarse grey ware 42
Third Buddhist Council Moggaliputta Tissa 78
Thonmi Sambhota 209
Tibetan language 209
Tilak 254
tirtha of Śarada 228
tirthas 218
Tiruvalleswarar temple 8
toilet trays 97
Toramana coins 146
Tou-kiue (Turks) 208, 221
tout court 206
town planning: Greek 96; Śaka–Parthian culture 107–108
Toynbee, Arnold 6
trans-regional culture 219
translocal history 5
Trayambaka School 221, 234
trepanning marks 32
Tribhuvanasvāmin 253
Trika ācāra 233
Trilochanpala 223
Tripitaka 138
Triticum aestivum 41
Triticum dicoccum 34, 40
Triticum sphaerococcum 41
Triticumaestivum see free thrashing wheat
Tsang, Hiuen 19, 116, 120, 188, 196–197, 208, 212, 251
Tukharian Buddhist 208, 221
Tukharistan 213
Tunga 223
Turkish dynasty 208
Turkish warfare 223
turquoise Jasper 43
twice born 17

Uccala's (1101–1111 CE) 218
universal conqueror 195
universal history 5
Upadeśa-śāstra 138
upper Palaeolithic culture 37
Urasa (Hazara) 195
urbanism, beginning of 75–76
Ushkar 109
Ushkur 239
Utpala dynasty 194, 200, 222, 254
Utpalas 222
uttariya 129

Vairochana Vihāra 143
Vaişņava kingdom 187
Vaişņava Saraswats 226
Vaiṣṇavas 185
Vaiṣṇavism 8, 17, 223, 226, 232
vaiśya 235
Vajheṣka 116
Vajraditya 252
Vajrayana 209
Vākpatirāja 199
Vama ācāra 233
Varāhaparvata 185
Varnaśramadharma 232, 235
vase 31
Vasiṣka 116
Vasukra 204
Vasukula 145
Veda 204
Vedavedangaparaga 205
Vedic gods 236
Vedic Śaivism cult 236
Vedic Vaiśnavism cult 236
Vedic–Puranic gods 251
vertical fallacy 3
Vibāsā-śāstra 138
vihāras (*sangramas*) 128
Vijnānabhairava 234
Vikramaditya Tribhuvanamalla 202, 227
Vikramāṅkadevacarita 206, 227
Vima Kadphises 115, 123

Vimalāksa **141**
Vinaya Pitaka 137
viṣaya 238
Vishnudharmottara Purāna (VDhP) 17, 186, 221
Viṣṇu *Muktākeśaca* 216
Vitasta 193
Vonones 102
votive terracotta plaques 127
vyākaraṇa 206

wadurs 72
Walīd, Caliph 229
war, cause of 2
war horses 107
water wheels 198
Weijie (Wei-tsie) 208
Wenming, Yan 46
wheel-thrown red ware pot 31
Witzel, Michael 226
wood Maitrya 209

Xenophobia 1
Xiajiadian culture 49

Yarkand 9, 213
Yaśaśkara 201, 222
Yaśovarman of Kanauj (Kanyakubja) 189
Yatoo, Mumtaz 35
Yueh-chis' (Kuṣāṇas) 101

Zain ud-Dīn Rishi 112
Zamorin of Calicut 211
Z'ana Shah Sa'bun zool 111, 112
Zoroastrianism 77, 92, 98, 111, 120
Zulju's invasion 231

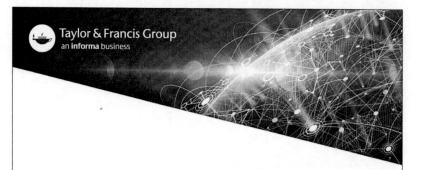